BEYOND FREUD
A Study of Modern Psychoanalytic Theorists

Edited by

JOSEPH REPPEN, Ph.D.

 THE ANALYTIC PRESS
1985

Distributed by
LAWRENCE ERLBAUM ASSOCIATES, PUBLISHERS
Hillsdale, New Jersey   London

Distributed solely by

Lawrence Erlbaum Associates, Inc., Publishers
365 Broadway
Hillsdale, New Jersey 07642

Library of Congress Cataloging in Publication Data

   Main entry under title:

   Beyond Freud.

         Includes bibliographies and index
         1. Psychoanalysis--Addresses, essays, lectures.
   1. Reppen, Joseph.   II. Freud, Sigmund, 1856-1939.
   [DNLM: 1. Psychoanalytic Theory. WM 460 B573]
   BF173.B479 1985   150.19'5   84-28225
   ISBN 0-88163-009-8

Printed in the United States of America
10 9 8 7 6 5 4 3 2 1

To Kyra, Eve, and Alexander

Contents

Preface

The wellspring of ideas that originated with Sigmund Freud are today being expanded by the intellectual vitality and energy of a host of creative psychoanalytic thinkers. This volume presents the work of 14 modern analytic theorists. The clear influence of Freud's ideas is deeply reflected in various ways throughout this book and, although many of the theorists presented are at varying degrees of agreement with each other and Freud, they are all basically informed by the original genius of Sigmund Freud. Indeed, the title of this volume, *Beyond Freud*, intends in no way to disparage the originality of psychoanalysis. Instead, it intends to demonstrate how Freud's thinking and how the Freudian text have been used to expand ideas beyond Freud. That the work of two philosophers who have been attracted to Freud is included is a living testament to that profound genius and vision.

Beyond Freud grew out of my interest in the evolution of psychoanalytic theory, the history of ideas, and in my study of comparative psychoanalysis. This interest was expanded by my editorship of the *Review of Psychoanalytic Books*. As editor of the *Review* I have witnessed an even greater expansion of Freudian thought as well as an enormity of work in applied psychoanalysis informed by a Freudian perspective.

The inclusion of these 14 theorists is not intended to diminish the contributions of others. Erik Erikson, Melanie Klein, Anna Freud, the interpersonal school, many mainstream Freudians, the major ego psychologists, Winnicott and other object relations theorists are not included in this volume because their writing is either not recent or there is already a considerable body of literature on their work. Not every scholar/theorist included in this book is a practicing psychoanalyst, but all are modern, vital, and informed; and, most importantly, their work continues to enlighten, enrich, and influence younger analysts and students. In fact, these 14 theorists are of such considerable intellectual influence, an influence beyond clinical analysis, that my choice was made quite easily. Each theorist provides a unique vision of contemporary psychoanalysis that should endure for some time.

In most instances, the author of the chapter on the psychoanalytic theorist has known the theorist about whom they write or has been deeply involved in their work as a part of their own professional life. In one case, the author is a co-worker, in another a former analysand, and so on, so that there is an intimate and deep connection.

While this book was in its planning stages, an Epilogue was to be included to show where the future of psychoanalytic theory might be headed. However, in thinking about this over a long time I decided to exclude an Epilogue and to leave speculations about future directions up to the reader. I felt that it would be presumptuous to speculate as to where psychoanalysis is heading. This book is thus an introduction to modern psychoanalytic theorists who have gone beyond Freud and an opportunity for the reader to draw conclusions of their own. I hope that the reader will read this book in an open-minded way, not as advocacy but as information.

Certainly, there is a clash of ideas and theories in this volume, and the welter of schisms, schools, and factions in psychoanalysis are well presented. The natural science/hermeneutic debate can be clearly viewed in this work. The Epilogue might have expressed a hope for a more pluralistic, integrative psychoanalysis. Psychoanalysis is a new science compared to the older natural and physical sciences, and, as an infant science, it is still evolving. Psychoanalytic theory fifty years from now may be quite different than it is today, informed perhaps by computer models and othe discoveries as yet unknown in science and philosophy.

Finally, I would like to gratefully thank each of the authors who has written a chapter in this book. They have done so with enthusiasm and intelligence, and represent the highest levels of psychoanalytic scholarship. They are scholars writing about scholars. That there are so many independent lines of thought within psychoanalysis is proof, perhaps, of all the possible ways in which man may be viewed and to the incredible richness of the Freudian endeavor which inspires in so many ways. Perhaps the seeming confusion we see may one day develop into a more integrative, informed, sophisticated, pluralistic psychoanalysis that might return us more deeply to the original *power* of Freud within a truly modern context. In the meantime, I hope *Beyond Freud* will be informative of the present provocative clash of ideas and of the dialogue and dialectic of Freudian inspired thought.

Joseph Reppen, Ph.D.

1 John Bowlby: An Ethological Basis for Psychoanalysis

Victoria Hamilton

The work of an original thinker often calls to mind a key idea: Darwin's "survival of the fittest," Einstein's "relativity," or Freud and "sexuality." We associate John Bowlby with his lifelong study of the crucial role played by attachment and its corollary, loss, in human development. He has assembled his major work in three volumes entitled *Attachment* (1969), *Separation* (1973), and *Loss* (1980). Bowlby's 'Attachment Theory,' together with the view of separation and mourning that it incorporates, is as novel to the study of human relationships as Darwin's theory was to the study of evolution. Yet Bowlby's (1979a) work is based upon and reflects the most obvious features of everyday life.

> Family doctors, priests, and perceptive laymen have long been aware that there are few blows to the human spirit so great as the loss of someone near and dear. Traditional wisdom knows that we can be crushed by grief and die of a broken heart, and also that a jilted lover is apt to do things that are foolish or dangerous to himself and others. It knows too that neither love nor grief is felt for just any other human being, but only for one, or a few, particular and individual human beings. The core of what I term an "affectional bond" is the attraction that one individual has for another individual. (p. 67)

Few would disagree with this statement. And yet, as with many new and simple ideas, we encounter considerable resistance to its implications. Bowlby is a psychoanalyst and psychiatrist who was trained in the Freudian tradition of psychoanalysis. Since 1946, when he assumed responsibility for the Children's Department at the Tavistock Clinic,

1

London (swiftly renaming it the Department for Children and Parents), Bowlby has focused his research and therapeutic skills on the study and treatment of young children and their families. This experience has provided him with the basis for both his theory of normal infant and child development and a new view of pathology and its treatment. Although his work is enriched by fields such as ethology, cognitive psychology and systems theory, Bowlby's preoccupation with the joys and sorrows, the hope and despair, incurred in the making, sustaining and breaking of affectional bonds, places his contribution squarely within the arena of psychoanalysis. More than any other branch of medicine and psychology, psychoanalysis claims to investigate the emotional life of man. Nevertheless, despite over thirty years of research and teaching, Bowlby's conception of attachment has not yet been integrated into the discipline and still remains foreign to the thinking of most psychoanalysts.

In this chapter, I shall attempt to supply reasons for the resistance of psychoanalysts to Bowlby's thesis. Indeed, by reference to some of his most basic assumptions about human psychology, Bowlby himself offers various solutions. Throughout his work, he stresses the over-riding importance of the parameter "familiar/strange" in the development of human beings from the cradle to the grave. From infancy on, we tend to orientate towards the familiar and away from the strange, a trait that has survival value for human beings and other species. We change our beliefs with reluctance and would rather stick with the familiar model. Ironically, psychoanalysts do not recognize that this "cognitive bias" (Bowlby, 1980) is functional and tend to regard the preference for the familiar as regressive.

The painful nature of the material that Bowlby presses upon us also elicits resistance. The reading of *Separation* and *Loss* is a test of endurance since both volumes spell out the grief to which an analyst must bear witness if he is to meet the pathologies of despair and detachment. To support his view of attachment and the repercussions of a disruption of affectional bonds, Bowlby draws on personal accounts of bereavement, on observations of children who have lost their parents either temporarily or permanently, and on works of literature. It is Bowlby's (1980) belief and experience that "He oft finds med'cine who his grief imparts" (p. 172) and that, in psychotherapy, "the deep vase of chilling tears that grief hath shaken into frost" (p. 320) must break. The therapist, like the poet, must have a capacity to endure and express the suffering that antecedes its cure.

The crux of Bowlby's thesis is that the pains and joys of attachment cannot be reduced to something more primary such as the sexual or death instincts. Just as a child's love for his mother does not result from the gratification of his oral desires, so the heart-rending expressions of grief quoted by Bowlby do not denote destructive or guilty wishes that have been repressed. They may simply describe the painful process of healthy mourning.

> It is impossible to think that I shall never sit with you again and hear you laugh. That everyday for the rest of my life you will be away. No one to talk to about my pleasure. No one to call me for walks, to go "to the terrace." I write in an empty book. I cry in an empty room. And there can never be any comfort again. (Carrington, in Bowlby, 1980, p. 229).

Although many analysts fail to comprehend the relevance of Bowlby to the consulting room, his ideas are rooted in the Freudian context. Although he departs radically from parts of the Freudian tradition, he develops many ideas that Freud held to be important (particularly in his later life). Throughout his work, Bowlby acknowledges this debt and quotes passages from Freud's later work to support the theory of attachment. In 1938, Freud describes the relationship of the child to his mother as "unique, without parallel, laid down unalterably for a whole lifetime, as the first and strongest love-object and as the prototype of all later love relations—for both sexes" (p. 188). In the 1940s and early 1950s, when Bowlby first published his observations on disturbances in children and young people who had been separated from their parents, Freud's theories provided a stepping-stone away from the then popular stress on constitutional and inherited factors and gave him a framework with which to emphasize the importance of mother–child relations. Moreover, the effects of World War II upon both bereaved adults and young children in care spelt out, to all, the stark realities of separation and loss. Dorothy Burlingham and Anna Freud (1942) had reported on the suffering of the children in their care at the Hampstead Nurseries, London, and James Robertson, a psychiatric social worker familiar with their work, had begun a series of studies of children separated from their parents who were living in residential nurseries and hospitals. The plight of these children was unmistakable and terrible. The World Health Organization was interested in the many thousands of post-war refugees and approached Bowlby to write a report on the mental health of homeless children. This report, entitled *Maternal Care and Mental Health*, was published in 1951. It was later popularized and reissued under the title, *Child Care and the Growth of Love*.

Child Care and the Growth of Love is a refreshing and readable book, full of observations, anecdotes and practical advice. Since all the heavy, statistical material is omitted in the popular version, the hypotheses advanced seem almost naive when viewed from the context of the sophisticated and well-documented model of attachment we have before us today. In this early work, Bowlby's basic insight into the origins of pathology stands out loud and clear: maternal care in infancy and early childhood is essential for mental health. The importance of this discovery, Bowlby (1953) felt,

> may be compared to that of the role of vitamins in physical health (p. 69) . . . The outstanding disability of persons suffering from mental illness, it is now realized, is their inability to make and sustain confident, friendly, and cooperative relations with others. The power to do this is as basic to man's nature as are the abilities to digest or to see, and, just as we regard indigestion or failing vision as signs of ill-health, so have we now come to regard the inability to make reasonably cooperative human relations (p. 109).

In the intervening 40 years, psychoanalysts of varying orientations—Freudian, Anna Freudian, Jungian, and Kleinian—have responded to many of Bowlby's ideas in a piecemeal fashion. All would acknowledge the importance of his work and, with few exceptions, would claim that the nature of the mother-child relationship together with the vicissitudes of separation and loss, have significant implications for therapeutic intervention. Nevertheless, the proportion of practicing psychoanalysts who have been able to grasp the larger picture of human relationships and development outlined by the theory of attachment remains small.

In addition to the painful nature and unfamiliarity of Bowlby's point of view, the alienation felt by many psychoanalysts may proceed from an ambivalent and even negative attitude towards research in the behavioral sciences. Bowlby's theory depends more upon direct observation of attachment and separation behavior than upon inferences drawn from the analysis of adults. Freud himself waged a comparable battle with the behavioral sciences of his day in his search for knowledge of man's mental life. But now that psychoanalysis has been established for almost 100 years, this posture amounts to little more than prejudice and exacerbates the isolation of psychoanalysis from related branches of human psychology and biology. Psychoanalysts often argue that research, based upon the observation of "external reality," is irrelevant to analytic work, the domain of which is the exploration of "inner" or "psychic reality." Some psychoanalysts even argue that the study of normal infant and cognitive development would impede their "intuition" into the unconscious phantasy life of the patient.

In my view, neglect of research findings has led to a fixation in the psychoanalytic theory of development. The Victorian picture of children, implicit in Freud's theory, has changed very little in the century since psychoanalysis began. A dominant feature of this picture is of a withdrawn, asocial, narcissistic and egotistical creature. Young children must be socialized into affectionate relationships with others and induced to learn about the outside world through the frustration of their wishes and the civilization of their instincts. As Freud (1905) said, "All through the period of latency children learn to feel for other people who help them in their helplessness and satisfy their needs, a love which is on the model of, and a continuation of, their relation as sucklings to their nursing mother" (pp. 222–223). Through her care and affection, the mother "teaches" her child to love. One of the leading child psychoanalysts of today, Margaret Mahler (Mahler, Pine, & Bergman, 1975), describes the newborn as little more than a vegetable. Only "by way of mothering . . . the young infant is gradually brought out of an inborn tendency toward vegetative, splanchnic regression and into increased sensory awareness of, and contact with, the environment" (p. 42).

This statement, based upon direct observation, is totally inconsistent with the body of infant research that has been assembled by the disciplines of ethology, developmental psychology, anthropology and pediatrics. The contrasting picture of the infant, to which Bowlby has made a large contribution, is of an alert and curious creature who becomes intensely attached and most sensitively attuned to his or her mother. The full impact of human attachment seems almost as unpalatable to psychoanalysis today as was Freud's discovery of childhood sexuality. Bowlby's insight into the conflict between the methods of traditional psychoanalysis and conventional scientific research is that, like workers in many other disciplines, the psychoanalyst must be capable of assuming two roles that require two very different mental outlooks. Whereas the scientific attitude discourages personal involvement and advises emotional detachment as a requisite for rigor and objectivity, the art of psychotherapy requires a capacity for immersion and imagination.

In order to delineate some of the major theoretical implications of Bowlby's research for the discipline of psychoanalysis, I will focus on four aspects of his theory of attachment. These are (1) instinct theory, control theory, and evolution; (2) the nature and function of attachment behavior from infancy to old age; (3) normal and pathological processes of mourning in response to separation and loss; and (4) psychoanalysis as art and science.

INSTINCT THEORY, CONTROL THEORY AND EVOLUTION

All studies of human behavior, except those based upon the most extreme theories of learning and conditioning, posit certain basic behavioral patterns, which have traditionally been termed instincts. Although there is disagreement about the nature of these basic patterns, all agree that the term "instinctive" denotes those behaviors that are common to the members of a species and that are more or less resistant to environmental influences. Bowlby's model of attachment is built upon a theory of instinct that is widely accepted by biologists and physiologists but differs radically from that of traditional psychoanalysis. There is disagreement not only over the kind of instincts deemed common to man – for example, instincts for sex or self-preservation – but also over the meaning of the term "instinct" itself.

The psychoanalytic concept of instinct derives from Strachey's translation of Freud's *trieb*. Some psychoanalysts now consider that the translation of *trieb* as "drive" is a more precise rendering of Freud's thinking. Ornston (1982) has pointed out that Strachey "clustered and clumped" Freud's wording into single Latin and Greek terms, thereby losing the subtleties of Freud's distinctions. Freud himself used the term *instinkt* quite selectively. *Instinkt* was more of a technical term and referred to a precisely determined activity. *Trieb,* on the other hand, was used to refer to a "surging and rather undifferentiated need" (Ornston, 1982, p. 416). Thus, problems of translation have compounded the confusions arising out of the psychoanalytic view of the instincts and of the behaviors and emotions to which they supposedly give rise.

Like Freud, Bowlby defines the concept of instinct precisely. The contemporary concept, proposed by biologists and ethologists, offers an alternative account of human motivation that has not yet been incorporated into psychoanalytic theory. Even critics of the traditional view seem unaware that a coherent alternative exists. In accordance with the scientific framework of his day, Freud used the term to denote an inner motivating force or drive that operates as a causal agent. An instinct is activated from within by an accumulation of stimuli and is terminated when the energy aroused flows away. For example, the oral instinct is aroused by hunger and, when a mother nurses her baby, she reduces the amount of pent-up libido (energy) to a tolerable level.

Bowlby substitutes the phrase "instinctive behavior" for the more common noun "instinct." The adjective "instinctive" is intended to be descriptive and leaves open the question of motivation. Human behavior varies in a systematic way, and yet, as Bowlby (1969) notes, there are so many regularities of behavior and certain of these regularities are so striking and play so important a part in the survival of individual and species that they have earned the named 'instinctive' " (p. 38). Bowlby (1969) describes four main characteristics of behavior that traditionally have been termed instinctive:

 a. It follows a recognizably similar and predictable pattern in almost all members of a species (or all members of one sex);

b. It is not a simple response to a single stimulus but a sequence of behavior that usually runs a predictable course;

c. Certain of its usual consequences are of obvious value in contributing to the preservation of an individual or the continuity of a species;

d. Many examples of it develop even when all the ordinary opportunities for learning it are exiguous or absent (p. 38).

This account shows that the ethological view of instinctual responses is based upon a very different dynamic to the Freudian view. First, the term "instinctive" always refers to an observable pattern of behavior, which is activated by specific conditions and terminated by other specific consummatory stimuli. For instance, attachment behavior in a child is readily elicited under certain environmental conditions such as cold, bright light, sudden darkness, loud noise, the appearance of strange or unexpected objects and under certain internal conditions such as fatigue, hunger, ill health, and pain. Nearly all the behaviors elicited by these conditions are terminated by contact with and responsiveness from the mother. Second, instinctive patterns are usually linked together and do not occur in isolation. This means that a particular behavioral pattern is not linked causally to one motivating system, but results from the coordination – or the lack – of a number of instinctual responses. Integration is often achieved through the avoidance of various hazards, such as cold weather, sharp objects, loud and sudden noises, and so forth. Here, the care and protection afforded by mother plays a unique integrating function.

Third, many attachment behaviors are reciprocal and only function effectively within a social system. For instance, an infant's proximity-seeking behaviors are matched by the mother's retrieving behaviors. The latter resemble the child's attachment behaviors in their biological function – namely, protection from danger and survival. Indeed, in Bowlby's estimation, the feedback system involved in watching and visual orientation is more important than the oral instinctual behaviors emphasized by psychoanalysis. Many attachment behaviors only make sense within a social context and have been suitably termed *social releasers* and *social suppressors*. Babbling, for instance, is most readily released and increased by human faces and voices, particularly by the sight and sound of the mother. In general, friendly responses such as smiling and babbling are easily elicited and reinforced by human stimuli. The situation is usually reversed with respect to crying. Here, social stimuli are the main terminators or suppressors. For instance, picking up and holding the infant is the most rapid terminator of crying from nakedness. Rocking and rapid walking is the most effective suppressor of crying from loneliness, although not of crying from pain, cold or hunger.

A more thorough exposition of the new concept of instinctive behavior requires a review of changes that have occurred since Freud's day in two other disciplines: one, the new field of cybernetics (also referred to as systems theory, information theory or control theory), and the theory of evolution. Most psychoanalysts have not followed these developments and thereby compound their misconception of Bowlby's work.

Since most analysts are unfamiliar with control theory, they are unable to grasp that Bowlby offers an alternative theory of motivation. According to cybernetic theory, behavior is organized homeostatically into systems that are activated by certain signals and terminated by others. This model's characterization of causation calls into question methods used by psychoanalysts in determining the source of a patient's pathology. The analyst attempts to reconstruct past events that overdetermine current behavior in the life of his patient. Cybernetic explanation, on the other hand, is always negative. In cybernetic explanation, we do not look for the cause of an event. Instead, we first consider alternative possibilities and then ask what knocked these other alternatives out of the running. The negative nature of cybernetic explanation is conceptualized by the term restraints. When we look at a particular behavior pattern, we ask, What were the restraints that excluded alternatives from the system? An excellent example of this distinction between restraints that are negative and clues that are positive has been given by the anthropologist Gregory Bateson (1967):

> For example, the selection of a piece for a given position in a jigsaw puzzle is "restrained" by many factors. Its shape must conform to that of its several neighbors and possibly that of the boundary of the puzzle; its colour must conform to the color pattern of its region; the orientation of its edges must obey the topological regularities set by the cutting machine in which the puzzle was made; and so on. From the point of view of the man who is trying to solve the puzzle, these are all clues, i.e., sources of information which will guide him in his selection. From the point of view of the cybernetic observer, they are restraints (p. 400).

Zoologists and ethologists working in the field have used this restraint model of explanation for a long time. The ethologist Niko Tinbergen (1972) has described the life of animals observed in their natural habitat as "a multi-dimensional tightrope act" (p. 200). The fittest are those life forms that are not eliminated by environmental pressures. Animals survive, reproduce and evolve within the restraints of many variables. Success depends upon their capacity to cope with a bewildering variety of obstacles. However, the healthy and happy man balks at such a suggestion. He does not feel that negatives have governed his success. But the cybernetic model does not imply a tragic outlook. It does not seek to explain why people behave as they do but why, at any one time, an individual behaves one way rather than another.

In accordance with the cybernetic model, Bowlby (1969) suggests that we call the successful outcome of an activated behavioral system *goal corrected* rather than *goal directed*. Human beings constantly revise, extend, and check their working models of the environment and adjust their behavior accordingly. As with the system of *negative feedback* in cybernetics, goal corrected systems are designed to control behavior so as to adjust any discrepancies between initial instruction and performance. This approach further implies "that no single adaptation is viewed as ideal; it is always the compromise result of many different, and often conflicting, demands. When we analyze human behaviour, we usually study one behavioral characteristic and one environmental pressure at a time" (Hamilton, 1982, p. 11). We lose sight of the broader context. We may not see the competition between conflicting activities or that different environmental pressures are dictating incompatible responses. An event is not the outcome of a number of causes but the end product of a process of elimination of many factors, none of which may be causally related to the final outcome.

Psychoanalysts are particularly interested in emotional ambivalence and conflict behavior, such as that between approach and withdrawal. Bowlby points out that the activation of such conflicts often will result in so-called compromise behavior. The individual plays out fragments of two different systems. Within this class of compromise behavior I would include tics or stereotyped and inappropriate gestures. An action may be dissociated from its context or cut across by a contrary action. A person may signal his attraction to another only to negate his own initiative by rejecting the other's response. This compromise behavior represents an exchange between two people. Originally the two incompatible sequences of behavior were enacted by two separate people – for instance a mother and her child. Behavioral systems may also be "redirected" to another goal in the way that has been traditionally described as *displacement*. Actions or feelings are, in Bowlby's terms, *redirected* from one person on to another person or object. We should not equate compromise behavior with neurosis, however. Even a curious, securely attached child may exhibit both clinging and exploratory behavior in a novel environment. Tinbergen (1972) discusses the compromises that birds must negotiate between safety and nourishment. Camouflage protects the birds while they are motionless. However, they must eat. As Tinbergen (1972) said: "While they could feed more efficiently if they never had to freeze, and would be better protected against predators if they never had to move, they can do neither, and selection, rewarding overall success rather than any isolated characteristics, has produced compromises" (p. 154–155).

Both cybernetics and psychoanalysis concern themselves with the **information** carried by events and objects rather than with the event or objects themselves. They do not investigate forces, drives, impacts, or energy exchanges except as they confer meaning to concrete events. There is no information or communication without context. A word acquires meaning in the larger context of the utterance, which again has meaning only in a relationship. For instance, the schizophrenics' "word salad" becomes intelligible through study of the communicational patterns and relationships within his family. Communication between psychoanalyst and client acquires meaning in the context of the *transference relationship.*

In addition to goal correction, systems theory discovers another restraint governing behavior. "Nothing"–that which is not–can exert a powerful influence. Information theory refers to this as a zero message. Zero messages, such as absence or unresponsiveness, may cause extremely strong emotions. Bateson (1970) gives as an illustration of a zero cause "the letter which you do not write" (p. 452). This letter "can get an angry reply." Increasingly, psychoanalysts now look at the negative trauma, which is not an event such as incest, the birth of a sibling, or an aggressive attack, but rather is a lack of psychological connection. This focus emerges from the many studies of the narcissistic personality disorder over the past decade. A prolonged absence of connectedness and responsiveness often lies at the root of the despair, apathy, and detachment that characterize attachment pathologies.

An evolutionary perspective is necessary to make sense of the last two characteristics of instinctive responses listed by Bowlby (see p. 7): first, that the consequences of a sequence of instinctive responses may contribute to the preservation of an individual or the **continuity** of a species, second, an instinctual response may develop in an individual "even when the ordinary opportunities for learning it are exiguous or absent" (Bowlby, 1969, p. 38). Clinicians usually do not consider the evolutionary context. Frequently, their background is in medicine and they have not been trained to interpret the behavior of individuals within the context of species survival. Moreover, clinical practice does not provide much opportunity to acquire this perspective.

Consideration of the evolutionary perspective should affect psychoanalytic theory and practice. What sort of inferences do clinicians make when they are unable to explain behavior in terms of the individual, including his or her particular history and present environment? The practitioner usually concludes that such behavior is caused by "constitutional" factors or that it is a bizarre externalization of the patient's phantasy life. Melanie Klein's concept of persecutory anxiety, a state that gives rise to all sorts of destructive phantasies and is itself consequent upon the workings of the death instinct, exemplifies this sort of explanation. Bowlby's interpretations of children's fears and phobias spring from the evolutionary view of attachment and entail a very different theory of explanation to that of the death drive.

The new concept of instinctive behavior, familiar to ethologists for many years, makes the traditional antithesis between innate and acquired characteristics unnecessary. Every class of behavior is a product of the interaction of genetic endowment and a specific environment. Although the human species has a tremendous capacity for versatility and innovation, many behavioral systems only operate in their environment of evolutionary adaptedness. Moreover, this adaptedness is a property not only of the individual but of the population.

THE NATURE AND FUNCTION OF ATTACHMENT BEHAVIOR FROM INFANCY TO OLD AGE

In 1958, Bowlby published "The Nature of the Child's Tie to His Mother." This paper marked the second major juncture in Bowlby's intellectual development and was pivotal to many of the ideas that he pursued later. In this work, the somewhat anecdotal comments and observations of "Child Care and the Growth of Love" (1953) coalesce into a coherent theory. He no longer underpins his argument with references to Freud but rather to ethology and the new evolutionary point of view. Bowlby had not yet incorporated the systemic approach, but his terms now belonged to that framework.

This paper confronted the various psychoanalytic schools with a direct challenge. Despite subsequent developments in Bowlby's attachment theory, this critique remains a valuable summary of many of the major differences between the attachment and psychoanalytic viewpoints. Much of the paper is devoted to an informative and incisive account of four traditional theories of the child's tie to the mother:

1. *The theory of secondary drive.* According to the view, the baby becomes interested in and attached to his mother as a result of her meeting the baby's physiological needs. In due course, the infant learns that she is also the source of gratification.

2. *The theory of primary object sucking.* The infant has an inbuilt need to relate to a human breast, to suck it, and to possess it orally. In due course, the infant learns that attached to the breast is a mother with whom he or she must develop a relationship.

3. *The theory of primary object clinging.* There exists an inbuilt need to touch and cling to a human being, and this need is on a par with the need for food and warmth.

4. *The theory of primary return-to-womb craving.* Infants resent their extrusion from the womb and seek to return there.

In this early account of attachment, Bowlby includes the theory of primary object clinging. This view had been proposed by Imre Herman in Budapest and adopted by Alice Balint and Michael Balint. Together with W. R. D. Fairbairn and Donald Winnicott, they were to become prominent members of the British Middle Group. This school of psychoanalysis, to which Bowlby belongs, shares with him an emphasis on bonding and object relating over gratification or the avoidance of pain. Bowlby (1958) lists five instinctual responses – sucking, clinging, following, crying and smiling. These five instinctual responses "serve the function of binding the child to the mother and contribute to the reciprocal dynamic of binding the mother to the child. . . . Unless there are powerful in-built responses which ensure that the infant evokes maternal care and remains in close promixity to his mother throughout the years of childhood, he will die" (p. 369).

Bowlby remarks upon the vast discrepancy between formulations springing from empirical observation and those made in abstract discussions. He points out that leading child analysts with first hand experience of infancy, such as Anna Freud, Dorothy Burlingham, Melanie Klein, Therese Benedek, and René Spitz, are apt to describe such interactions in terms suggesting a primary social bond. In their theorizing, however, they persist in describing social interaction as secondary.

Bowlby's paper also challenges the traditional psychoanalytic view of orality. First, he downplays both sucking and the primary orientation towards the mother's breast. He argues that psychoanalytic theory is fixated on this response and that clinging and following play a more central role in later disturbance. Both Bowlby and Margaret Mahler emphasize the importance in the ontogenesis of pathology of disturbances arising during the second half of the second year. In Mahler's view, the rapprochement phase of the separation-individuation process is particularly stormy because the child's growing independence conflicts with the continuing need for mother's care and control. Bowlby focuses more upon the mother's rejection of the child's clinging and following. He also points out than an infant's oral behavior has two functions: attachment as well as feeding. Western culture has overlooked the fact that the infant spends more time in nonnutritional sucking than in feeding. Whereas traditional psychoanalysis views oral symptoms as regressive to an earlier, more infantile stage of development, Bowlby interprets such disturbances as displacements. Within the context of attachment, oral symptoms designate the substitution of a part for a whole. They chronicle the splitting off of feeding from the rest of a relationship. Compulsive thumb sucking might express a frustrated attachment or even a displacement of the nonnutritional aspect of feeding itself, rather than regression to some autoerotic stage.

In similar fashion, Bowlby distinguishes sexuality from attachment in loving (traditionally called libidinal) relationships. Although these two systems are closely related and share some of the same patterns of behavior, they are distinct. Their activation varies independently of one another. Each directs itself towards a different class of objects and is sensitized at a different age.

As already noted, Bowlby holds attachment behavior to be instinctual and on a par with the pursuit of sex and food. He expresses his fundamental difference with traditional psychoanalysis most clearly in his interpretation of the complex repertoire of behaviors with which the infant maintains proximity to his or her caretaker. For Bowlby, the primary function of this behavioral system is to insure the child's survival and protection from predators. Most psychoanalysts do not think in such terms. Although they do enumerate various primitive mechanisms of defense, none of these concern the survival of the individual in his or her environment. The term "defense" is used to refer to psychological processes, such as projection, projective identification, idealization, denial, splitting, repression, and regression. Bowlby follows traditional usage by reserving the word "defense" for psychological defenses and using the word "protection" when talking about the function of attachment behavior. Since this distinction does not exist in traditional theory, the child's tenacious efforts to keep close to his mother are not usually seen as related to a social system in which they elicit reciprocal responses of retrieval and picking up. Rather, the child's demands for closeness are interpreted onesidedly as a denial of separateness or as an attempt to omnipotently control the "object" for the fulfillment of narcissistic wishes. The infant is seen as using crying and clinging as weapons of control. Some analysts even believe that the infant's clinging and grasping and enjoyment of being held indicate a wish for return to the womb.

In general, the evolutionary viewpoint leads us to interpret a great deal of human behavior, whether of children or mature adults, as cooperative rather than self-seeking. Since the unit of biological adaptation is the social group and not the individual, survival depends upon cooperation. Psychoanalysis has concentrated on those behavioral systems that are limited by particular events, such as orgasm, eating, or elimination, and has ignored systems such as attachment whose goal is a constant state. Attachment theorists believe that only an indirect relationship exists between such interactions as feeding, weaning and toilet training, and a healthy attachment. Attachment is neither a developmental stage nor a system limited by an event. Its continuing set-goal is a certain sort of relationship to another specific individual. Attachment is regarded as the product of a control system that maintains homeostasis by means of behavioral rather than physiological processes. The maintenance of proximity between child and mother is a kind of environmental homeostasis. As Bowlby points out, there are many alternative ways of maintaining this homeostasis. However, the organization that controls these behaviors is conceived as permanent and central to a child's personality. This organization is never idle. As Bowlby (1969) says: "In order for a control system to perform its function effectively it must be equipped with sensors to keep it informed of relevant events, and these events it must continuously monitor and appraise." In the case of an attachment control system, the events being monitored fall into two classes: one, potential danger or stress (external or internal), and two, the whereabouts and accessibility of the attachment figure.

The distinction between behavioral systems that are limited and those that are ongoing affects the conception of development. As one would expect, current views of human biology and control theory differ greatly from those of psychoanalysis. The traditional model implies that there is one developmental line. Personality disorders derive their form from stages that were normal at some earlier phase of life. In normal development, the individual is thought to progress through the oral, anal, phallic and genital stages. If fixations occur, the person "regresses" back down the ladder. Thus, the various disorders of later life repeat phases of healthy childhood. The diagnostician considers the resolutions and fixations appropriate to each stage in order to decide whether the adult before him or her suffers from a pregenital, anal-sadistic, narcissistic, borderline, oedipal or neurotic disturbance.

Bowlby's model, drawn from control theory and ethology, proposes that at birth, there exists a large array of potential pathways. Development progressively diminishes these alternatives. We should look not for the cause of a fixation but at the restraints that lead an individual to choose one alternative over another. Returning to Tinbergen's analogy, healthy development resembles the adjustments that a tightrope walker must make continuously in order to maintain his or her balance. Either excessive sensitivity or insensitivity to environmental changes will cause the tightrope walker's downfall. In human development, sensitivity from birth allows for maximum adaptability to the social environment. This biological perspective, which stresses the cooperative nature of human behavior, is opposite to and contradicts Freud's view that avoidance and withdrawal precede approach behavior. According to Attachment Theory, avoidance and withdrawal are most readily activated when the infant is able to discriminate the familiar from the strange.

Questions about the ontogenesis of mental disorder raise the problem of how to measure attachment. Initially, theorists sought to measure normal or abnormal behavior by reference to the strength of the attachment between the individual and his or her childhood attachment figures. However, these reseachers soon noted that intense attachment did not necessarily indicate a good or harmonious mother-child relationship. Paradoxically, attachment behavior can be most intense when a mother discourages or threatens her child's need for proximity. The traditional viewpoint might diagnose such a child as perverse or masochistic. But the child's stubborness makes systemic sense if his or her instinctual apparatus is geared toward proximity as the means of survival. The threat of withdrawal would redouble the child's efforts. Fear stimulates attachment behavior. A victim will often develop a strong attachment to the person who causes his or her suffering, especially if, as in the case of a young child, there is nowhere else to turn. Loss of an attachment figure is the child's foremost fear.

Research on attachment shows that the two most most important variables in the creation and maintenance of a secure attachment are the sensitivity of a mother's responsiveness to her baby's signals and the amount and nature of interaction between the two. Degrees of security or insecurity provide the yardstick by which we measure a healthy attachment. Consequently, Bowlby (1973) has substituted the term "anxiously attached" for the traditional description of an insecure child as overdependent. Clinging behavior, illustrative of anxious attachment, has often been described as jealous, possessive, greedy, immature, overdependent, or intensely attached. Bowlby's concept of anxious attachment respects the natural desire for a close relationship without pejorative connotations.

In addition to a child's protest and upset over his mother's departure, researchers now regard various other correlations as indicative of the security of an attachment. Foremost among these are the child's behavior upon reunion with the mother, and comparison of his behavior at home with his or her behavior in a strange (often experimental) setting. Anxiously attached children often fail to greet their mothers upon return. Furthermore, they are less exploratory than their secure counterparts, not only in a strange situation but also at home in their mothers' presence. Ainsworth and Bell (1970a) have correlated children's ambivalence in a strange situation with general ambivalence in the home environment. Ambivalent children tend to resist contact when picked up and to ask to be picked up when they are set down. They do this whether at home or in a strange environment. Logically, one might expect proximity-seeking behavior to be incompatible with exploration. However, Ainsworth, together with other attachment researchers, have noted that most children do not explore constructively when **avoiding** contact. Avoidant children tend to move around hyperactively or to alternate uncomfortably between avoiding and seeking contact. In addition, children who resist contact, are often more angry, aggressive and disobedient than children for whom contact is pleasurable.

Bowlby correlates the development of "puzzling phobias" (see Freud, 1962, p. 168) with anxious attachment. When a child is unable to communicate directly his fears about separation, he may try to redirect or displace onto animals or other puzzling objects the anxieties he feels in relation to his parents. He may be furious and terrified that the parent will desert him, but he dares not express such feelings lest by so doing he provokes that which he most fears. Instead, he complains about something else, or he may have temper tantrums that express both rage and fear. Bowlby reinterprets Freud's case of Little Hans in this light.

In volume one of *Attachment*, Bowlby suggests that five main classes of behavior should be considered in any attempt to assess the attachments of a child. These are:

1. Behavior that initiates interactions, such as greeting, approaching, touching, embracing, calling, reaching, and smiling.
2. Behavior in response to the mother's interactional initiatives that maintains interaction (all the initiating behaviors plus watching).
3. Behavior to avoid separations, such as following, clinging, and crying.
4. Exploratory behavior, as it is oriented toward the mother.
5. Withdrawal or fear behavior, especially as it is oriented toward the mother.

None of these considerations fit the Freudian picture of the infant or young child, which describes the infant as being enclosed in a state of primary narcissism, "shut off from the stimuli of the external world like a bird in an egg" (Freud, 1911, p. 220). The child's object relations are seen as minimal. The contrasting view of attachment theorists points to the quality of mother-infant interaction, which is built up out of communication 'games' as well as proximity-maintaining behaviors. The success or failure of this mutual endeavor is crucial to the arousal of a baby's interest in the first weeks of life. Indeed, Ainsworth and Bell (1970b) have correlated the attachment behavior of 1-year-old children placed in a strange situation with the extent to which they had been permitted to be an active partner in the feeding situation as 3-month-old infants. Such findings suggest that the mother's ability to conceive of the relationship as a partnership affects the development of both attachment and exploration.

One fascinating detail of this research, which again contradicts the primary narcissism hypothesis, pertains to fluctuations in the responsiveness of each partner to the initiatives of the other. The infants responded on every occasion when the mother initiated interaction. However, whereas some mothers were encouraged by their baby's social advances, others evaded them; where some mothers were made more solicitous by their child's crying, others became more impatient. By the time the children's first birthday was reached, the magnitude of the differences between one pair and another could hardly be exaggerated.

Two other researchers, David and Appell (1969), describe, at one extreme, a pair who interacted almost continuously throughout the baby's waking hours, and, at the opposite extreme, a pair who were hardly ever together, mother occupying herself with housework and largely ignoring her daughter. In a third pair, mother and son spent much time silently watching each other while each was engaged in some private activity. Such findings suggest that mothers play a much larger part in determining interaction than do infants. For instance, although initially there is little correlation between a baby's crying and a mother's responsiveness, by the end of the first year, a baby cared for by a sensitive, responsive mother cried much less than one cared for by an insensitive or unresponsive mother.

One of the strengths of attachment theory, initiated by Ainsworth (1982) and Bowlby (1982) is that it has stimulated a very able group of developmental psychologists to make such empirical studies of socioemotional development. These studies would be extremely useful to psychoanalysts, particularly those working with children and young people.

As is only too obvious to the layman, a child's pattern of attachment usually correlates with the way his mother treats him. By preschool age, this matrix will have become a function of the child himself or herself. This internalization or, in Bowlby's terms, "cognitive map" of attachment may also correlate with the child's participation in the regulation of his or her care and mothering. Bowlby likens the regulation of mothering to the regulation of food. Both mothers and professional people often ask whether or not a mother should meet her child's demands for her presence and attention. If she gives in on mothering, will this encourage the child to demand that she give in on everything else? Will the child ever become independent? Bowlby (1969) responds with an answer which he tells us is "now well known":

> From the earliest months forward it is best to follow a child's lead. When he wants more food, it will probably benefit him; when he refuses, he will probably come to no harm. Provided his metabolism is not deranged, a

child is so made that, if left to décide, he can regulate his own food-intake in regard to both quantity and quality. With few exceptions, therefore, a mother can safely leave the initiative to him. . . . Thus, in regard to mothering—as to food—a child seems to be so made that, if from the first permitted to decide, he can satisfactorily regulate his own "intake." Only after he reaches school years may there be occasion for gentle discouragement. (p. 356)

By 4 to 5 years of age, the child's capacity to consider another person's point of view provides additional clues to the status of the child's goal-corrected partnership. Another variable by which we can measure the security of an attachment is a child's resilience. A child whose background state is one of anxious attachment will have few resources to draw on when faced with untoward and stressful circumstances. In conclusion then, the organization of attachment, which is initially labile, becomes progressively more stable. This development may be cause for optimism or concern.

Let us now consider what the attachment model implies for the growth of self-reliance. Psychoanalysts have looked at development as a linear progression from a state of dependence to one of independence. This has distorted our understanding not only of dependence in childhood but also of independence in adulthood. For Bowlby, self-reliance goes hand in hand with reliance upon others. Confidence in the attachment figure and in the self are built up together. Indeed, the capacity to rely on others when occasion demands and to know upon whom it is appropriate to rely is essential for true self-reliance. Many people have confused self-reliance with the kind of independence that Bowlby characterizes as compulsive caregiving and compulsive self-sufficiency. The compulsive caregiver and the fiercely self-sufficient person will experience their own needs for love and care through, respectively, administering to others or apparently needing nothing. Bowlby believes that a person's success in finding appropriate people to help him or her through hard times depends upon childhood experiences. This ability holds a special importance for dealing with a serious loss. A major determinant of reaction to loss is the way the bereaved's attachment behavior was evaluated and responded to by the bereaved's parents—whether they could share his or her fears, unhappiness, and grief or whether he or she had to bear sorrows alone. The solitary child has a hard time finding a comforting shoulder in later life. Such people shun the thought and disavow the need for solace. What children learn to expect in the nature of comfort from their parents determines in large part whether, as adults, bereavement will make them sad or whether it will overwhelm them with despair and depression.

NORMAL AND PATHOLOGICAL PROCESSES OF MOURNING IN RESPONSE TO SEPARATION AND LOSS

"The great source of terror in infancy is solitude" (James, 1890). A similar sentiment was expressed indirectly in a poem quoted by Bowlby that was written by an 11-year-old girl whose parents were abroad for some years:

> The beauty of love has not found me
> Its hands have not gripped me so tight
> For the darkness of hate is upon me
> I see day, not as day, but as night.
>
> I yearn for the dear love to find me
> With my heart and my soul and my might
> For darkness has closed in upon me
> I see day, not as day, but as night.
>
> The children are playing and laughing
> But I cannot find love in delight
> There is an iron fence around me
> I see day, not as day, but as night.

Bowlby could not study attachment without encountering the suffering that ensues from the breaking or disruption of affectional ties. In the years between the publication of "The Nature of the Child's Tie to His Mother" in 1958 and *Attachment* in 1969, Bowlby published five papers on separation anxiety, grief and mourning in infancy and early childhood, processes of mourning, and pathological mourning. The publication of *Attachment* was followed in a similar fashion by the second and third volumes in the series, *Separation* (1973) and *Loss* (1980). The latter two volumes, based on the attachment model, again provide a very different picture of human responses to separation and loss than that of traditional psychoanalysis. Their central and simple thesis is that, just as attachment is the primary source of well-being in human beings, so loss is the major source of suffering.

Bowlby looks at human loss and distress on two levels: first, the inevitable grief, anger, and despair that result when ties are broken, and second, the ways we organize ourselves to deal with these painful and often conflictual feelings. Just as in his study of affectional ties Bowlby first searched for regularities in the attachment behaviors common to human beings, so Bowlby detects prototypical responses to loss and separation. The uniformity of these responses makes sense in the context of the theory of attachment and the evolutionary framework.

By the time Bowlby wrote *Separation* and *Loss* the most common successive responses to loss – protest, despair, detachment – had been well documented by other authors, foremost among whom were James and Joyce Robertson. Although many psychoanalysts had recognized that separation from loved ones is a principal source of anxiety, there was still considerable reluctance to assimilate this simple formula into clinical practice. In addition, Freud's influence had led to the belief that the processes of both adult and childhood mourning and normal and pathological mourning differed considerably. Bowlby pointed out, however, that, as in the case of attachment, there is considerable similarity between the mourning of children and of adults and that many of the responses to loss that had hitherto been regarded as neurotic were quite natural. Attachment, unlike dependence, remains as an organizational system throughout life; so grief, even in its normal course, has a long duration. A bereaved person may experience for a long time an insatiable yearning for, and an "irrational" but natural striving to recover, the lost person. These feelings may return intermittently for the rest of the individual's life.

Although most attachment theorists would now characterize the three phases of protest, despair and detachment as typical of normal mourning in both children and adults, in fact an additional initial phase is usually described as well as – depending on whether the loss is final or temporary – a fifth and final phase. Prior to the protest and angry attempts to recover the lost object, most people experience a sense of numbness and disbelief. During this period, bereaved individuals must adjust all their expectations and beliefs. Whereas psychoanalysis uses the term "denial" to describe the state of disbelief, Bowlby renames it "selective exclusion." The fifth stage, experienced only when loss is temporary, is characterized by extremely ambivalent behavior upon reunion with the lost person. This can be demonstrated by a lack of recognition and absence of all emotional affect at one extreme and, at the other, by clinging, acute fear of being left, and bursts of anger lest the person desert again.

Bowlby links the three most common reactions to loss – protest, despair, and detachment – with three processes, all of which contain considerable potential for future disturbance. These are separation anxiety, grief and mourning, and defense. Separation anxiety is a reaction to the danger or threat of loss; mourning is a reaction to actual loss; and defense is a mode of dealing with anxiety and pain. As with attachment, the outcome of these responses depends largely on the ways other people respond to the feelings of the bereaved person.

Following Freud, most psychoanalysts have concentrated exclusively upon the last of the three phases – detachment and defense. Although Freud and Melanie Klein accorded a central place to anxiety in everyday life, neither recognized that separation anxiety was as primary as, for instance, castration or persecutory anxiety. W. R. D. Fairbairn and Ian Suttie were the first psychoanalysts to assign a primary status to separation anxiety. Not until Freud's seventieth year, in *Inhibitions, Symptoms and Anxiety* (1926), did he perceive that separation and loss were principal sources of psychopathology. Hitherto, Freud had linked anxiety to fears of castration, to the harshness of the superego, to aggression, and to the death instinct. Even analysts such as Anna Freud and Melanie Klein who remarked on the universal distress shown by infants and young children when their mothers were absent continued to ask, Why are they anxious? What are they afraid of? Many ingenious explanations have been proposed to answer these questions: the birth trauma, signal anxiety, anxiety consequent on repression of libido, persecutory and depressive anxiety, and guilt about aggressive impulses.

Bowlby has made various suggestions as to why psychoanalysts have found it so very difficult to conceptualize in theory that which they so clearly observe. First, Bowlby makes the common observation that the psychoanalytic theory of normal development is almost entirely based upon work with adult patients. Obviously, in clinical practice, the psychoanalyst is constantly preoccupied with the understanding of defenses that, although once useful for survival, are now obsolete. When these findings are projected back onto the theory of infant and child development, we find an imbalance towards a study of the mechanisms of defense, and an ignorance of the normal child's expressions of loss, grief, and anxiety.

Second, traditional psychoanalysis assumes that a child does not seek out other people for their own sake but only as containers or modulators of tension, anxiety, aggression and so forth, or as sources of gratification. This tenet discourages the idea that a child might react directly to the absence of a loved one.

Third, Bowlby believes that the lack of distinction between cause and function has not only harmed psychoanalytic theory in general but also that this confusion particularly impedes its understanding of the anger that so often follows a loss. This anger is caused not just by the separation. Bowlby believes that its function is to recover the lost person. Not only do anger and reproach ensure the person's return, they also threaten him so that he or she dare not desert again. In a responsive mother-child relationship, the child's anger is often very effective. The aggressive wishes not only express the simple desire to hurt the person who has inflicted pain and suffering, but they are also intended to punish the person for desertion and to reinstate proximity.

Fourth, Bowlby makes another distinction between guilt and grief in response to loss. Freudian and Kleinian theory lose track of the difference between these two responses. Grief and mourning are expressions of depressive guilt. Guilt is a "natural" reaction to loss. For Bowlby, grief covers an amalgam of emotions–anger, anxiety, and despair. Guilt, on the other hand, may often signify displacement and may result from an angry reproach against the self instead of the lost person. When the expression of natural feelings, such as yearning, anger, and reproach, are discouraged (which is very often the case, particularly when the bereaved are young children), these feelings can be redirected either to third parties or on to the self. When reinforced socially, these displacements can generate various pathological behaviors, such as denial of permanent loss with sustained secret beliefs in reunion or vicarious caregiving and sympathy for other bereaved persons. Repressed yearning can lead to compulsive wandering, depression, and suicide. Depressed people often tend to idealize their attachment figures. In traditional theory, idealizations are often thought to mask aggressive and destructive phantasies. According to Bowlby, however, such depressed people, particularly children, may be entertaining two completely incompatible models of relationship–their own and that of their caretakers. When circumstances are favorable, however, anger, reproach, and yearning fade following their expression to the appropriate person. The mourner finally accepts that his loss is permanent and that his or her feelings are nonfunctional. These responses are then succeeded by a period of disorganization and almost unbearable grief. However, if this grief is expressed to and understood by others, it can lead to reconnection with the world and "a relieving sweet sadness may break through" (Bowlby, 1963, p. 7).

Fifth, Bowlby makes a crucial distinction, ignored in traditional theory, between "natural" and "reasonable" fear. This distinction affects our understanding of separation anxiety and of the responses to actual or threatened loss. Following Freud, psychoanalysts have concluded that when anxiety is not related to real danger, it signifies a neurosis. Absence per se does not seem to threaten life or limb. However, as we noted earlier, the zero message exerts just as much influence as its positive counterpart. Even among mature adults, mourning often is mixed with acute and "irrational" terror. Nearly all bereaved persons report symptoms such as insomnia and fear of being alone or of going to strange places. All these feelings are natural to separated children. The loss of a secure base threatens both children and adults as much as physical assault. This phenomenon, Bowlby (1973) notes, prompts the psychoanalyst to engage in "a prolonged hunt for some primal danger situation" (p. 169). The analyst concludes that the expressed fear is not the real fear. So many of the fear stimuli that affect us seem inappropriate in the modern context. We don't see too many saber-toothed tigers these days! Nevertheless, it is perfectly natural for a young and vulnerable child to fear the existence of dangerous creatures. All children exhibit some fear of the dark, of being alone, of loud or sudden noises, of bright lights and of looming objects, particularly when these appear in combination. Bowlby points out that these same phenomena frighten the same child much less if they occur when the child is with an older, trusted person. All these fears are viewed by Bowlby and other ethologists as natural. They contribute to survival in the environment of evolutionary adaptedness. As Bowlby notes, these fears still hold their survival value. Although in the city we need not worry too much about wild animals, we still need to remain alert to danger. City children are vulnerable to traffic accidents, for example, and many city parents worry about the risk of criminal assault. Besides, the fear of wild and dangerous animals is still reasonable in many parts of the world. Even in Los Angeles, a young child growing up in certain hillside areas must treat his environment with some caution. Chances are they are sharing the hill with a family of coyotes and the odd rattlesnake. Fears are often ordered hierarchically. For instance, children will follow their mothers in the face of dangerous traffic rather than risk separating from her. When we investigate a fear that has become unmanageable, we would consider its evolutionary context before making our interpretation. Otherwise, we risk taking up arms against a mechanism of survival.

Sixth, Bowlby's concept of defense—renamed selective exclusion—also reflects the systemic approach. In the normal course of events, we exclude a vast proportion of information from consciousness. This protects our attention from distraction and overload. The selective exclusion of information is as necessary and adaptive as the reduction of flexibility that follows from specialization. Both contain the potential for maladaptation, however. Persistent exclusion is usually maladaptive; nor does automatic attachment and attachment behavior necessarily contribute to survival. Change can be economical, but it is difficult; and correction requires skilled attention. Bowlby (1980) also stresses the diversionary role of defensive activity, "for the more completely a person's attention, time and energy are concentrated on one activity and on the information concerning it, the more completely can information concerning another activity be excluded" (p. 66). Any activity—work or play—can be undertaken as a diversion. The only psychological requirement is absorption. Much defensive exclusion is related to suffering. A response is disconnected from its context in an interpersonal situation and relocated upon the self. This gives rise to symptoms such as hypochondria, guilt and morbid introspection. For

Bowlby, no system is more vulnerable to defensive exclusion than attachment. For instance, pathology may develop if defensive exclusion continues beyond the initial stages of bereavement.

The evolutionary context makes Bowlby's theory of attachment and mourning seem simple, even blindingly obvious. Human beings come into the world genetically biased to develop certain behaviors that, in an appropriate environment, result in their keeping close to whoever cares for them. This desire for proximity to loved ones persists throughout life. Only when children feel secure in their primary attachments can they go out with confidence to explore and make the most of their world.

PSYCHOANALYSIS AS ART AND SCIENCE

If we consider the development of psychoanalysis over the past nine decades, we find that new discoveries have rarely led to consolidation, let alone to critical discussion. Indeed, the extreme subjectivism of many psychoanalysts generates one quarrel after another. Psychoanalysts avoid rational methods of discrimination between rival hypotheses. It seems that any interpretation can be supported from within the terms of any one theory. Relationships between analysts are not usually built on the pursuit of a common, though tricky, endeavor, but on loyalty to a particular faith. Does such and such an analyst believe in Freud, Jung, or Klein? Does this analyst practice "real" analysis?

And yet, the whole edifice of psychoanalysis – its theory of development and its theory of cure – depends upon the assumption that adult pathology stems from problems, real or phantasied, in infancy. An outsider might then assume that psychoanalysts would keep up with the findings of those disciplines to which their field is most closely related – in particular, cognitive and developmental psychology and human biology. Surely, analytic research would benefit from the study of infants and children in natural settings. Instead, psychoanalysts tend to fall back on so-called veridical reconstructions of infancy gathered from the clinical material of adults. The paucity of observational studies diminishes the number of independent variables with which to correlate analytic reconstructions. Inevitably, the psychoanalytic theory of normal personality development has remained weak and open to criticism.

By contrast, a minority of psychoanalysts, such as John Bowlby, James Robertson and Christoph Heinicke, are attuned to the methodological limitations of retrospective research. As a result, they have undertaken various *pro*spective studies that follow the behavior of children about to undergo experiences of separation from their mothers. Since analysts of all orientations seem to agree that separation in childhood plays an undeniable role in adult pathology, one might expect that the observation of separation behavior in a variety of settings could offer a fertile ground for intergroup study. In my opinion, those analysts who have undertaken such studies manifest greater agreement over their findings, show less of a propensity for schisms, and have found it easier to maintain a more open and scientific attitude towards the work of their colleagues. An analyst's views of infancy crucially affects his interpretations of unconscious material. It makes a great deal of difference to the patient whether the analyst sees him or her as a bundle of id impulses, a raging orally fixated infant, a frustrated narcissistic self, a thinking and curious creature, or a victim of a broken attachment.

In a recent article, "Psychoanalysis as Art and Science," Bowlby (1979b) draws attention to two very different aspects of the discipline of psychoanalysis: the art of psychoanalytic therapy and the science of psychoanalytic psychology. In so doing, he emphasizes on the one hand, the distinctive value of each and, on the other, the gulf that divides them "in regard both to the contrasting criteria by which each should be judged and the very different mental outlook that each demands" (p. 3). As Bowlby observes, this distinction is not confined to psychoanalysis. "It applies to every field in which the practice of a profession or a craft gives birth to a body of scientific knowledge – the blacksmith to metallurgy, the civil engineer to soil mechanics, the farmer to plant physiology, and the physician to the medical sciences. In each of these fields the roles differentiate. On the one hand are the practitioners, on the other the scientists, with a limited number of individuals attempting to combine both roles. As history shows, this process of differentiation often proves painful and misunderstandings are frequent" (p. 3). Bowlby attributes much of the confusion in psychoanalysis to the lack of differentiation of these two roles. He contrasts the roles of practitioner and research scientist under three headings and uses the case of medicine as an example:

1. *Focus of study.* The practitioner aims to take into account as many aspects as possible of each and every clinical problem with which he must deal. This requires him to draw on any scientific principle that may appear relevant and also to draw on his own personal experience of the condition in question. The research scientist must have a very different outlook. He aims to discern the general patterns underlying individual variety and, therefore, ignores the particular and strives for simplification. He also tends to concentrate on a limited aspect of a limited problem.

2. *Modes of acquiring information.* In his role of giving help, the practitioner is permitted access to information of certain kinds that are closed to the scientist. He is permitted to intervene and privileged to ob-

serve the consequences of such interventions. The research scientist, however, has the advantage of enlisting new methods to cross-check on observations made and on hypotheses born of older methods.

3. *Mental attitudes—scepticism and faith.* If he is to be effective, a practitioner must have faith. He must be prepared to act as though certain principles and certain theories were valid. He is likely to choose between various theories on the basis of his own experience. As Bowlby points out, such faith is not a bad thing in clinical practice. A great majority of patients are helped by the practitioner's faith and hope. The very lack of these qualities may make many excellent research workers ill suited to be therapists. The scientist, on the other hand, must exercise a high degree of criticism and self-criticism. In his world, neither the data nor the theories of a leader, however much personally admired, may be exempt from challenge and criticism.

Bowlby (1979b) believes that it is only by recognizing these differences that the strengths of each role can be used to fullest advantage "or that any person can occupy both of them with any hope of success" (p. 5). The repercussions of Bowlby's view are serious because it calls for a reversal of the set adopted by a great number of psychoanalysts—namely, unquestioning faith in a theory and scepticism in their practice. Bowlby's cross-checking of the reports of adult patients with observations of young children should reduce the analyst's scepticism of his patient's memory. For example, Bowlby takes very seriously the reported threats of separation made by parents to their children. Not only should the analyst cross-check his findings with those of neighboring disciplines, but he must be able to review his work critically outside his consulting room, either by taking notes or by detailed discussion of case notes or tape recordings with his colleagues. Bowlby proposes that analysts might keep a detailed record of the responses of their patients before and after each weekend, each vacation, and each unexpected interruption of the sessions, with an equally detailed record of how the analyst dealt with them. This would enable the analyst to check the repertoire of responses a given patient presents on these occasions, and also the changes in response the patient presents over time.

In my view, the medical bias in psychoanalysis has led not only to neglect of the two roles required of the research psychoanalyst, but also to an underestimation of the art of psychoanalysis. Fearful of his emotional responses to the patient and of his imaginative powers, the analyst, aiming to maintain a "scientific" attitude, may remain aloof, neutral and dissociated from the interactions with his patient. The art of psychotherapy, according to Bowlby (1979b) requires "all the intuition, imagination and empathy of which we are capable. But it also requires a firm grasp of what the patient's problems are and what we are trying to do" (p. 12). For instance, analysts who are not prepared to meet the heavy burdens of dependence should be careful about their choice of patients. In order to have such a firm grasp of the patient's problems, questions of etiology and psychopathology should be clarified and the practitioner should be informed of the whole range of family experiences that evidence shows affect the development of the child. Although medical science is competent to deal with this area of psychopathology, it eschews the use of imagination, and psychoanalysis has suffered accordingly. In addition, analysts have followed Freud in his equation of imagination with phantasy and the creative process with sublimation. Like Freud, many analysts continue to regard art as an anarchic process motivated by sublimation. They continue to ignore the skills and rules that are involved in every creative process.

Bowlby's work is a testimony to the skills of imagination, immersion and objectivity. Not only does his trilogy present a simple point of view based on the distillation of a vast array of research, it also portrays the extraordinary depth of feeling of a unique individual. Few psychoanalytic books evoke the utter grief, despair and loneliness that bereaved persons, particularly children, have suffered. Most psychoanalytic texts prefer to discuss the stereotyped defenses against feeling – aggression, projection, denial, and so forth. One might conclude that few psychoanalysts are themselves capable of suffering the depths of anxiety and sadness that are only too painfully obvious to all those who have worked with young children.

> ... Dick ... told him about his own father's death, which had happened when Dick was a child at Dublin, not quite five years of age. "That was the first sensation of grief," Dick said, "I ever knew. . . . I remember I went into the room where his body lay, and my mother sat weeping beside it. I had my battledore in my hand, and fell a-beating the coffin, and calling papa; on which my mother caught me in her arms, and told me in a flood of tears papa could not hear me, and would play with me no more...And this," said Dick kindly, "has made me pity all children ever since and caused me to love thee, my poor fatherless, motherless lad." (Thackeray, H. E., in Bowlby, 1980, p. 265)

REFERENCES

Ainsworth, M. D. S. (1982). Attachment: Retrospect and prospect. In C. M. Parkes & Joan Stevenson-Hinde (Eds.), *The place of attachment in human behavior* (pp. 3–31). New York: Basic Books.

Ainsworth, M. D. S., & Bell, S. M. (1970a). Attachment, exploration and separation:

Illustrated by the behavior of one-year-olds in a strange situation. *Child Development, 41*, 49–67.

Ainsworth, M. D. S., & Bell, S. M. (1970b). Some contemporary patterns of mother-infant interaction in the feeding situation. In A. Ambrose (Ed.), *Stimulation in early infancy* (pp. 133–171). London: Academic Press.

Bateson, G. (1967). Redundancy and coding. In *Steps to an ecology of mind* (pp. 399–410). New York: Ballantine Books, 1972.

Bateson, G. (1970). Form, substance and difference. In *Steps to an ecology of mind*. New York: Ballantine Books.

Bowlby, J. (1951). *Maternal Care and Mental Health*. Geneva: World Health Organization.

Bowlby, J. (1953). *Child Care and the Growth of Love*. Harmondsworth, England: Penguin Books.

Bowlby, J. (1958). The nature of the child's tie to his mother. *International Journal of Psycho-Analysis, 39*, 350–73.

Bowlby, J. (1963). Pathological mourning and childhood mourning. *Journal of the American Psychoanalytic Association, 11*, 500–41.

Bowlby, J. (1969). *Attachment and Loss: Vol. 1. Attachment*. London: Hogarth Press.

Bowlby, J. (1973). *Attachment and Loss: Vol. 2. Separation*. New York: Basic Books.

Bowlby, J. (1979a). *The making and breaking of affectional bonds*. London: Tavistock.

Bowlby, J. (1979b). Psychoanalysis as art and science. *International Review of Psychoanalysis, 6*, 3–14.

Bowlby, J. (1980). *Loss: Sadness and depression*. London: Hogarth Press.

Bowlby, J. (1982). *Attachment* (rev. ed.). London: Hogarth Press.

Burlingham, D., & Freud, A. (1942). *Young children in wartime*. London: Allen & Unwin.

Burlingham, D., & Freud, A. (1944). *Infants without families*. London: Allen & Unwin.

David, M., & Appell, G. (1969). Mother-child relation. In J. G. Howells (Ed.), *Modern perspectives in international child psychiatry* (pp. 98–120). Edinburgh, England: Oliver & Boyd.

Freud, S. (1905). Three essays on the theory of sexuality. *Standard Edition, 7*, 135–243.

Freud, S. (1911). Formulations on the two principles of mental functioning. *Standard Edition, 12*, 215–226.

Freud, S. (1926). Inhibitions, symptoms and anxiety. *Standard Edition, 20*, 77–175.

Freud, S. (1938). An outline of psychoanalysis. *Standard Edition, 23*, 144–207.

Hamilton, V. (1982). Narcissus and Oedipus: The children of psychoanalysis (p. 11). London: Routledge & Kegan Paul.

James, W. (1980). Principles of human psychology. New York: Holt, Rinehart & Winston.

Mahler, M., Pine, F., & Bergman, A. (1975). The psychological birth of the human infant (p. 42). New York: Basic Books.

Ornston, D. (1982). Strachey's influence: A preliminary report. *International Journal of Psycho-Analysis, 63*, 409–426.

Robertson, J. (1953). *Some responses of young children to loss of maternal care. Nursing Times, 49*, 382–386.

Tinbergen, N. (1969). Ethology. In *The Animal in its world – Explorations of an ethologist, 1932–1972* (Vol. 2) (pp. 130–160). London: Allen & Unwin.

Tinbergen, N. (1972). Early childhood autism – An ethological approach. In *The animal in its world – Explorations of an ethologist, 1932–1972* (Vol. 2) (pp. 175–199). London: Allen & Unwin, 1973.

2 George S. Klein: Psychoanalytic Empiricist

Frederic J. Levine, Ph.D.
Joseph W. Slap, M.D.

INTRODUCTION AND BIOGRAPHY

By the time of his sudden death in 1971 at age 53, George S. Klein had already made many compelling contributions to psychology and psychoanalysis. He was then working on what was probably his most important contribution, a reexamination and attempt at restatement of basic psychoanalytic theory which was published posthumously as *Psychoanalytic Theory: An Exploration of Essentials* (1976) under the editorship of Merton M. Gill and Leo Goldberger. Although this book was in a still incomplete form, many consider that its daring sweep and powerful insights will have an enduring impact on psychoanalysis.

That Klein was a man of great personal magnetism, energy, and leadership ability, as well as a scientist and theoretician, is given ample testimony by the numerous activities his friends, students, and colleagues have dedicated to his personal and professional memory. Preceding each meeting of the American Psychoanalytic Association is a meeting of the George S. Klein Research Forum, dedicated to the advancement of research in psychoanalysis; the main lecture at the annual meeting of Psychologists Interested in the Study of Psychoanalysis (a group of American Psychological Association members) is the George S. Klein Memorial Lecture; and annually in his beloved Stockbridge, Massachusetts, researchers and psychoanalysts meet in the George S. Klein–David Rapaport Study Group. In addition, there have been a number of panels, symposia, and memorial publications dedicated to the advancement of Klein's work (Gill and Holzman, 1976; Mayman, 1982; Reppen, 1980).

George Klein was born in Brooklyn, New York, in 1919. He was educated at the City College of New York and Columbia University, where he developed what was to be a lifelong interest in the study of perception. After receiving his doctorate, Klein served during World War II in the United States Army Air Force, where he performed statistical studies and co-authored several reports on selection, diagnosis, and prediction of outcome in patients.

In 1946, Klein joined the staff of the Menninger Clinic in Topeka, Kansas, under the supervision and instruction of David Rapaport. The few years he spent there were to have a profound impact on the rest of his intellectual life. At that time, the Menninger Foundation provided the best available clinical psychological training to nonphysicians and was alive with the clinical and theoretical ferment stimulated by Rapaport and his colleagues. To this exciting atmosphere were attracted a number of people, including Philip Holzman, Herbert Schlesinger, Lester Luborsky, and many others who have continued to be among the foremost leaders in psychoanalytically oriented clinical psychology, as well as a number of outstanding medical psychoanalysts. Klein quickly became an important figure and guiding spirit in this group. He studied Rapaport's diagnostic psychological testing procedures and took some patients in psychotherapy, but his main contributions at the Menninger Foundation were in the area of research. In this first major phase of his career, as a result of the joining of his experimental background with his exposure to psychoanalysis, Klein and his colleagues produced a series of studies of individual consistencies in perceptual and cognitive behavior that added the terms "cognitive control" and "cognitive style" to the technical lexicon. The fact that Klein was the leader in this research was obscured by the alphabetical listing of the authors of the major comprehensive publication on the subject (Gardner, Holzman, Klein, Linton, & Spence, 1959; see also Holzman, 1982).

In 1949, Klein began a personal psychoanalysis while still at the Menninger Foundation. In 1950, he went to Harvard as a visiting professor and continued analysis there. While at Harvard, Klein became interested in an organismic view of psychology in which neurological mechanisms would be included along with the psychological. He later came to explicitly reject this position and made significant theoretical contributions in his attempt to disentangle the quasi-neurological speculations of metapsychology from the clinical theory of psychoanalysis.

In 1952, with Robert R. Holt, a former colleague at the Menninger Foundation, Klein founded the Research Center for Mental Health at New York University, where he remained for the rest of his career.

This center became the heart of an outstanding graduate program in clinical psychology and clinical research laboratory, producing research on the interface between psychoanalytic and experimental issues. Klein also started his own clinical practice at this time and began to turn to more purely psychoanalytic theoretical concerns in his writings. He wrote his paper on consciousness (Klein, 1959a), which developed yet another perspective on the ways in which ego processing of perceptual and cognitive data can vary independently of drives and needs, and began to develop his theoretical critique of the psychoanalytic drive theory. His clinical experience broadened as he became affiliated with the Austen Riggs Center in Stockbridge, Massachusetts, and his efforts to distinguish the psychological from the metapsychological within psychoanalytic theory increased.

During this time, Klein founded the *Psychological Issues* monograph series, which continues to be the major publication vehicle aimed at fulfilling the goals that Klein (1959b) enunciated in his first issue: "To develop its theoretical potentialities psychoanalysis must scrutinize data from all fields of psychological and psychiatric inquiry" (pp. iii–iv). Klein also continued his experimental investigations of such varied fields as dream content and the effects of drugs and cultural deprivation. He undertook a formal psychoanalytic education and was graduated from the New York Psychoanalytic Institute. There he was a leader in obtaining the right of nonmedical graduates to have full privileges to conduct a psychoanalytic practice. During this final period of his life, Klein's primary scholarly interests moved more fully in the direction of clinical psychoanalytic theory, and he produced the papers (and papers in progress) that were published in the posthumous volume on *Psychoanalytic Theory* (1976).

In reviewing Klein's odyssey from research to psychoanalytic theorist, certain themes consistently appear. First is Klein's energy, innovative talent, and leadership ability. A second theme is the persisting influence of his academic psychological studies of perception. These became the vehicle through which he first expressed his interest in the ego's autonomous role in directing behavior, in contrast to theories stressing needs or drives as the main controlling forces. This view, heavily influenced by David Rapaport, ultimately evolved into Klein's criticism of the drive theory of psychoanalysis. Somewhat surprisingly, perhaps, along with this criticism Klein also produced a telling critique of the tenets of ego psychology, many of which had been formulated by his mentor, Rapaport. It may be said that as Klein absorbed the insights of ego psychology, he at first found them liberating, but later began to find them constricting and limiting as his appreciation of clinical data and theory grew. Even in his final works, however, Klein's emphasis as a psychoanalytic theorist was always on the broad group of phenomena that make up what had been called the ego – those autonomous processes, structures, and motives that he believed were important contributors to personality functioning independent of the driving power of sensual needs. In this respect, he was trying to broaden the scope of psychoanalytic inquiry beyond the limited data base provided by the patient on the couch.

A third major theme in Klein's work is his consistent emphasis on theoretical rigor and precision, which led him ultimately to see many flaws in the classical drive and structural theories of psychoanalytic metapsychology. As part of his lifelong effort to integrate various branches of psychology, Klein proposed substituting for parts of metapsychology several concepts from the work of Piaget and cognitive psychologists, which he felt would simplify psychoanalytic theory and make it closer and more responsive to the data of observation.

A further, minor trend was Klein's enduring interest in creativity and the artistic process. His wife, Bessie Boris Klein, is a painter and Klein, too, enjoyed painting at times. He periodically returned to a consideration of the interrelationship of needs and ego processes in the "reparative" work of the creative act.

COGNITIVE CONTROLS: PSYCHOANALYTIC EGO PSYCHOLOGY IN THE RESEARCH LABORATORY

When Klein went to the Menninger Foundation following World War II, a prominent trend in research on perception was the "New Look" (Postman, Bruner, & McGinnies, 1948), a group of studies demonstrating that motives or needs could influence and significantly alter the registration and judgment of perceptual data. Prior to that time, experimental psychologists had investigated the formal details of perceptual and thought processes, but had assumed that these functions operated stably, regardless of the individual's purposes and need states. In contrast, this new group of investigators found that in some situations, drives would "sensitize" the individual to perceive stimuli related to the drive state; in others, suppressive effects were observed as a result of "perceptual defense." Data in these studies were notoriously inconsistent, and individual differences in these effects were conspicuous but had not been explained. In Klein's (1958) view, these findings were having an exaggerated impact:

> There was at the back of our minds a feeling that while motivation-in-perception studies were rectifying older sins of omission, they were also

assuming that if only a drive is intense enough it can bend any or all cognitive structures to its aim. While no one committed himself blatantly to such a statement, the drift of empirical work seemed to be moving steadily toward it. Some way had to be found in theory of providing for effective processing without renouncing the possible pervasiveness of motivational influence upon thought [pp. 87–88].

Klein's response, through his research, was to demonstrate that while it is true that needs and motives influence perception, these influences vary from individual to individual, as a result of differences in the preexisting structural characteristics of style or pattern of thinking. He and his group identified a number of what they believed to be intra-individually consistent patterns of perceiving and thinking, which could be detected in the laboratory, and showed that these patterns shaped ways in which motives or needs influenced or distorted perception. These cognitive structures – first called cognitive attitudes and later cognitive controls – were thought of "as ways of contacting reality, whereby one's intentions are coordinated with the properties, relations, and limitations of events and objects" (Klein 1958, p. 88). In an early influential study, Klein (1954) examined the effects of thirst on perception of objects that had to do with thirstiness and drinking, comparing the performance of thirsty and nonthirsty subjects on the same tests. He divided both groups according to their performance on a cognitive test intended to detect contrasting ways in which people typically deal with distracting, intrusive feelings, such as thirstiness. Klein found that the different cognitive attitudes identified by that test did cause characteristically different kinds of distortions in thirsty subjects.[1]

Although the "New Look" studies constituted one of the first areas in which psychoanalytic ideas (i.e., the importance of needs and motives) had an impact on research in perception, Klein showed that impact to be one-sided – considering only the influence of drives (like the early psychoanalytic id psychology) and not the role of the coordinating and controlling structures of the ego. His research, which was conceptualized according to the ego psychology of Heinz Hartmann, Erik Erikson, and particularly his teacher, David Rapaport, was intended to correct this imbalance.

With his collaborators, Klein investigated various aspects of the cognitive controls to flesh out the understanding of their roles in ego

---

[1]These studies were, of course, not close experimental analogues of psychoanalytic propositions. There is no reason to expect thirst to have similar motivational properties to those of the "drives" with which psychoanalysis concerns itself because, unlike libido and aggression, thirst is not ordinarily a focus of conflict and defense.

functioning. Underlying the specific perceptual attitudes that were initially identified, Klein (1958) believed, were ego structures of broad generality and significance for personality functioning, which seemed "to reflect highly generalized forms of control as likely to appear in a person's perceptual behavior as in his manner of recall and recollection" (p. 89). Studies of these control principles explored their possible relationships to other ego processes, particularly the classical defense mechanisms, patterns of personality organization as identified in projective testing, modes of handling stress, and learning and intellectual ability (Gardner, Holzman, Klein, Linton, & Spence, 1959; Gardner, Jackson, & Messick, 1960; Holzman, 1962; Holzman & Klein, 1956; Klein and Schlesinger, 1951). Klein and his coworkers (Holzman & Klein, 1956) tended to assume that while each cognitive control might undergo an epigenetic development, these structures probably had their roots in constitutional givens—what Hartmann (1939) called apparatuses of primary ego autonomy. Thus, they speculated, cognitive control patterns might form an important part of the constitutional matrix that determines the individual's character structure, reliance on particular defense mechanisms, and choice of particular symptoms and psychopathological patterns (see, for example, Shapiro, 1965, pp. 13–14). Although Klein (1958) stated that "cognitive attitudes seemed to resemble what psychoanalysts have called character defenses" (p. 88), he believed they were not actually defenses, resulting from conflicts, but precursors or predisposing conditions, which contributed to the choice of defenses. In any individual, the patterning or arrangement of cognitive controls would constitute a superordinate structure, "cognitive style."

The following cognitive control principles were studied by Klein and his group:

1. *Leveling-sharpening*. Consistent individual differences were found between people (known as sharpeners) who tend to clearly distinguish newly perceived stimuli from their previous experiences, and "levelers" who tend to show a high degree of assimilation between new percepts and old ones, resulting in judgments of current stimuli as being similar to previously perceived ones. Some data suggested that levelers might have generally hysteroid personalities and favor the use of the defense mechanism of repression (Gardner, Holzman, Klein, Linton, & Spence, 1959; Holzman, 1962). Klein and his co-workers reasoned that a tendency to assimilate new events to existing schemata was similar to Freud's (1915) definition of secondary repression as "the attraction exercised by what was primally repressed upon everything [in consciousness] with which it can establish a connection" (p. 148).

2. *Scanning.* Individuals high on scanning were thought to "deploy attention to relatively many aspects of stimulus fields . . . [they are] constantly scanning the field" (Gardner, Holzman, Klein, Linton, & Spence, 1959, p. 47) and were also said to "narrow awareness and keep experiences discreet; and . . . to separate affect from idea" (p. 46). These characteristics were considered cognitive analogues to the defense mechanism of isolation, which was found to be correlated to scanning in some people, as rated in the Rorschach test (Gardner, Holzman, Klein, Linton, & Spence, 1959).

3. *Equivalence range.* Equivalence range denoted a dimension of individual differences in preference for using broad and inclusive versus narrow and precise categories in classifying objects and events. No connection was suggested between this control principle and defenses.

4. *Tolerance for unrealistic experiences.* People were found to differ in the flexibility and efficiency with which they accepted and dealt with ambiguous situations, with situations that "controvert conventional reality," and perhaps also with affects (Gardner, Holzman, Klein, Linton, and Spence, 1959).

5. *Constricted-flexible control.* Flexible controllers were considered to be individuals who function efficiently on tasks even when experiencing strong drives, feelings, or other distractions; constricted controllers' adaptive functioning was impaired by these things. Constricted controllers were thought to tightly suppress feelings and impulses, whereas flexible controllers were freer and less compulsive. Here too, a theoretical connection was made to the use of the defense of isolation of affect.

6. *Field articulation.* This is the field dependence–independence variable extensively studied by Witkin (Witkin, Dyk, Faterson, Goodenough, and Karp, 1962). It is a thoroughly explored dimension of individual differences in the tendency to focus on background versus "figure" cues in many situations. Field articulation is connected to numerous aspects of personality and cognitive functioning.

Klein conceptualized cognitive controls as quasi-motivational – he believed they direct behavior, but, unlike drives, they do not lead to discharge or consummation. Like defenses, they shape the expression of drives and control drives, but he saw them as more general than defenses – as basic, conflict-free, "positive" causes of behavior. In his research on cognitive controls, Klein attempted to broaden knowledge of primarily and secondarily autonomous ego functions. He also began to elaborate what was to become a continuing theme of his work – his view that psychoanalytic drive theory, with its basis in physiological need states, was an inaccurate and inelegant way to formulate human motivation. As he put it (Klein, 1958):

It seems more parsimonious to follow Woodworth's (1918), Woodworth and Schlosberg's (1954), and Hebb's (1949) lead and think of drive as a construct which refers, on the one hand, to "relating" processes – the meanings – around which selective behavior and memories are organized; and in terms of which goal sets, anticipations, and expectations develop, and, on the other hand, to those processes which accommodate this relational activity to reality [p. 92].

CONTRIBUTIONS TO PSYCHOANALYTIC THEORY

A. States of Consciousness

Klein expanded his research into the mechanics of thought and perception as "tools" of adaptation after leaving the Menninger Foundation. Having first studied individual differences in apparently enduring, relatively autonomous cognitive structures, his attention now turned to another conflict-free area of the determination of perception and cognition: studies of the effect on thinking of variations in states of consciousness – subliminal stimulation, dream research, and the influence of drugs.

Very early in the development of psychoanalysis, Freud (1900) had pointed out that incidental experiences perceived on the periphery of awareness are processed differently by the organism than events of greater importance, which are dealt with in the focus of consciousness. Incidental experiences tend not be be remembered consciously but to contribute heavily to the day residue of dreams. Unlike the contents of focal consciousness, they are more subject to the primary process than to secondary process modes of thinking. Studies of sublimal registration (by Poetzl, 1917 and Fisher, 1954 as well as by Klein, 1959a) produced findings that confirmed and elaborated Freud's early observations. Subliminal stimuli activated a range of conscious and unconscious meanings, which could be discerned in dreams, imaginative products, and various indirect aspects of verbal and nonverbal behavior but were not available to conscious recall. Thus, the state of consciousness of the individual – as affected by attention, chemicals, and the sleep state – has significant effects on the extent to which primary process, assimilatory cognition – as opposed to secondary process, accommodative cognition – is active. This bridge between psychoanalysis and academic psychology was significant to the latter as well. Laws of perception that were developed in the laboratory were now seen as specific only to particular states of awareness. Since perception is a cognitive event, under conditions in which reality content is not prominent registrations are recruited to very different, more primitive conceptual schemata than those that are ordinarily dominant in focal attention (Klein, 1959a; 1966).

B. Critique of Metapsychology

Having spent a lifetime doing both academic research and clinical psychoanalytic work, Klein found many flaws in the ways in which existing theories from both vantage points had attempted to account for the meanings of human behavior. He believed that academic psychology, in its efforts to encompass the findings of psychoanalysis, had actually found ways to omit and ignore the most salient features of Freud's insights. By directing attention to generalized conceptions of the determining influence of infantile experience on adult behavior, academicians had focused attention away from the specific issue of infantile sexuality. Phenomenological and humanistic psychological theories, which stress the present moment and conscious experience, have little place for the unconscious. This, of course, is also true of behaviorism. Social psychiatry stresses environmental rather than intrapsychic causation. But Klein saw classical psychoanalysis as also burdened by a mechanistic theory—metapsychology—which is not only unnecessary but is actually harmful to the understanding of meanings and the practice of psychoanalysis. Other authors as well (see particularly Gill, 1976; Guntrip, 1969; Holt, 1976; Schafer, 1968; Waelder, 1962), some of them earlier than Klein, have pointed out that Freud produced both a clinical theory and a metatheory, at different levels of logical analysis, and that the existence of these two theories has created many serious problems. Although Klein was therefore not the first to espouse this point of view, his was a most compelling voice.

Klein's first step toward rectifying this situation was to search for the "essential theoretical understructure that constitutes 'clinical psychoanalysis' " (1976, p. 1). Clinical theory, he specified, attempts to organize and explain psychoanalytic data from the viewpoint of the patient's experiences and motivations, both conscious and unconscious. This approach contrasts to the body of theory that attempts, as Klein (1976) put it, "to place psychoanalysis in the realm of natural science by providing an impersonal, nonteleological view of the organism as a natural object subject ultimately to the laws of physics, chemistry, and physiology. Teleological considerations—the patient's standpoint—are irrelevant to this level of explanation" (p. 2).[2] For Klein (1976), purposive considerations were at the very heart of clinical theory, which does not "distinguish sharply between description and explanation; to describe a per-

---

[2]Klein used the word "teleology" at times as though it were synonomous with "purposiveness" or "intention." Although this usage is incorrect and, as will be seen, some of Klein's motivational constructs may be open to criticism as truly teleological, it will be retained here in an effort to accurately represent Klein's statement of his own ideas.

son's intention or aim is to say that what a person is doing is also why he is doing it" (p. 2). In view of these convictions, Klein attempted to carefully disengage the clinical theory from the mechanistic metapsychological theory.

Like his predecessors, Klein attributed the existence of the two psychoanalytic theories to Freud's philosophy of science, which, in turn, was determined to a significant degree by the intellectual climate of the late nineteenth century. As Klein understood this philosophy, it rejected concepts of intention and meaning, considering them unacceptable terms of scientific explanation. Freud struggled to construct a neuroanatomical-physiological model, the *Project for Scientific Psychology* (1895). Although he was forced to abandon the Project, his search for neurophysiological levels of explanation continued to manifest itself, for example, in the optical apparatus model in Chapter 7 of *The Interpretation of Dreams* (1900) and in the instinctual drive theory of motivation, with its concepts of energic excitations, cathexes, and reservoirs of energy.

Klein considered the concepts of drive and energy to be the central flaw of metapsychology, a flaw attributable to Freud's reliance upon the Brucke-Meynert value system. These concepts, he believed, are not only inherently implausible but also irrelevant to the clinical psychoanalytic enterprise. Freud's drive-reduction model, Klein (1976) stated, "is more appropriate to a rat than to a human being, and is as congenial to violently antipsychoanalytical theories as to Freud's metapsychological ones" (p. 47). Metapsychological concepts are not verifiable by the clinical method and are based on the reification of such hypothethical constructs as drives and the psychic structures of id, ego, and superego. They do not deal with the basic intent of psychoanalysis—unlocking meanings—and cannot substitute for terms that are descriptive of human experience and object relations. Nonetheless, as a consequence of these dual theories, psychoanalysts have tended to assume that they actually work on the basis of clinical concepts, which they take for granted as observable or inferable phenomena, and to think of metapsychology as the underlying basic theory that explains those concepts. In contrast, Klein considered that the concepts of the clinical theory, if correctly understood, were at an appropriate level of abstraction to replace metapsychology. They are explanations in psychological terms, are personal and purposive, and are not translatable into physical or neuroanatomical models.

For Klein (1976), "the phenomenological concepts, the logic of the analyst's inferences, and the extraphenomenological concepts of function, purpose, and meaning of experience and behavior make up psychoanalytic theory" (p. 51). Within this realm he made a distinction between experiential and functional concepts. Experiential concepts are the mental contents that the analyst attributes to the patient, including both the patient's conscious experiences and unconscious fantasies. These are verifiable in the psychoanalytic situation. Functional concepts, such as projection, introjection, and repression, are inferred processes connecting the accessible and inaccessible levels of experience, and cannot be verified in the clinical setting. They "almost always have to do with purpose, function and accomplishment" (Klein, 1976, p. 50). Using these conceptual tools, analysts are able to observe regularities in behavior that are not recognized by other students of the mind.

Psychoanalysis, for Klein, deals with the histories of meanings throughout a person's life. He understood personality as formed through syntheses that evolve out of conflicts – that is, points of crisis in the individual's life. Since there are commonalities in these crises, it is possible to specify critical developmental periods. These phenomena are not reducible to physiological and neurological processes and it would be fallacious to think that such processes are more real or valid as scientific data, than observations of people's intentions and meanings. As Klein (1976) said: "Statements of purpose or meaning and principles of physiological regulation are two mutually exclusive ways of being aware of our bodily activities" (p. 62).

1. Sexuality and Sensuality. Klein began his task of teasing apart the two psychoanalytic theories by examining Freud's two theories of sexuality. Freud was led by his clinical observations to expand the meaning of sexuality from its ordinary use, referring to adult procreative ability, to a wide variety of behaviors beginning in infancy and developing throughout life. The invariant factor in all sexuality (i.e., in all those experiences which Freud referred to as libidinal) Klein (1976) felt, is "a capacity for a *primary, distinctively poignant, enveloping experience of pleasure*" (p. 77). These experiences, which Klein felt are best termed "sensual," do not depend simply on the removal of "unpleasure," but are positive excitatory processes. Sensual pleasure has a number of special characteristics that cause it to be a highly significant motivational force and that create a unique potential for conflict surrounding it. It can serve various functions that are not originally primarily sexual; it can be experienced in organs and activities that are usually nonsexual, and, conversely, sexual organs can lack erotic sensation at times.

Recognition of the distinction between sensuality and sexual behavior was a fundamental difference between Freud and other theorists. Sensuality has a characteristic development, which interlocks with all other developmental areas. This made it possible for Freud to understand how sexual development affected, and is affected by, a person's symbolized cognitive record of interpersonal encounters. In Klein's view, sexual needs do not exert a driving force upon behavior; instead, the experience of sensual pleasure acquires important developmental meanings, and these lead to a craving for repetition of the experience. It is in this way, rather than because of biological drive, that sexuality attains its great motivational force. Since these experiences occur originally in relationships with parents and other early objects, the sensual cravings take the form of specific object-related desires. They also are highly subject to the inevitable contradictions and conflicts arising between the plasticity of sensual arousal and the constraints of social guidance and expectations. It is this plasticity and these unavoidable contradictions that create a potential for intrapsychic conflict surrounding sexuality.

Sexuality *feels* as though it is a drive – in Klein's (1976) words, "as if an alien pressure were developing from within" (p. 96) – but it is neither necessary nor logical to assume that this feeling of impulsion reflects the presence of an actual, concrete drive quantity or mechanism. In this respect, the concept of libidinal drives is a theoretical reification of an experience – a "hybrid concept" (Slap and Levine, 1978). The strength of a sexual motive is not based on some drive force, but on the functional significance of the sexual appetite in cognitive terms – the meaning of the activated schema of sensuality. In drive theory, said Klein (1976) the essence of sexuality "is not an experience, but a contentless physiological event" (p. 110), and the clinical and drive concepts of sexuality imply different biological formulations. In one it is a pleasurable experience that is sought repetitively in order to reexperience the pleasure, and in the other it is a need to relieve pressure and tension. In the clinical theory the focus is on sensuality as a higher mental function; in the metapsychological theory, sensuality is a peripheral function. As Klein (1976) phrased it: "The critical difference of emphasis between the two viewpoints . . . [is] that in the drive theory pleasure is derived not from the pursuit of drive, but from the getting rid of it" (p. 119). Klein believed that the theoretical preeminence of the drive model led to a failure to fully test the implications of the clinical theory and impeded efforts to enlarge clinical understanding.

2. Ego Psychology. Klein traced the problems of the two psychoanalytic theories in his analysis of the theory of the ego (1976), which he considered "a concept in search of an identity" (p. 121). Freud had formulated the ego unsystematically as the representative of reality, essentially a set of functions and processes standing for survival and self-preservation. As is still the case for many clinicians, Klein (1976) noted,

Freud was "inclined to regard the ego mainly in the light of its participation in conflict and in its partnership with instinctual drives pressing for discharge. [He paid] scant attention to the adaptive functions of the ego as a system" (p. 130). This was satisfactory, in Klein's view, within the framework of the early psychoanalytic conception of drives as blind motivational forces controlled by some structure. With the expansion of motivational theory initiated by the conception of the active role of signal anxiety as a motivating, directive factor, however, Freud assigned an enlarged and elaborated role to the ego, but left crucial issues unsettled. These included the questions of what energy is employed by the ego in its activities; the energic basis of signal anxiety; and whether primary process functions such as condensation and displacement are within the scope of the ego. In addition, Klein believed that Freud had hinted at the possibility of autonomous structures and motivations in the ego, and thus, Klein was convinced that this required further development. Freud fell short in that he did not see the ego as "positive creator" of behavior, and did not confront "the crucial issue of the independence of the ego processes from libidinal control" (Klein, 1976, p. 131).

Following Freud, ego psychological theorists, especially Hartmann, Erikson, and Rapaport, proposed solutions for these problems. These solutions often involved a broadened focus of psychoanalytic interest from psychopathology to general psychological questions, and to "all psychological 'disequilibria,' whether specifically psychopathological or not" (Klein, 1976, pp. 145–146). They placed greater emphasis on the adaptive point of view and on independent, conflict-free motivations and structures within the ego. Klein characterized the changes in psychoanalysis as: (1) from a narrow concern with conflict to concern with dilemma and crisis; (2) from concern with defense to an interest in adaptational controls; (3) from concern with sexual and aggressive drives to general motives such as mastery and the synthetic principle; and (4) from giving priority to the unconscious to greater priority for conscious phenomena such as affects.

Klein saw these as salutary new emphases for psychoanalytic theory. However, he believed that they were not done justice by the metapsychology of Hartmann and Rapaport, which is essentially an expanded theory of ego controls, established to compensate for the deficiencies of the drive theory of motivation. Ego psychology tended to see the ego either as a reified entity or simply as an unsystematic grouping of functions. (Klein considered this a throwback to faculty psychology.) The ego's relationship to drives remained ambiguous. Drive was spoken of as both independent of the ego and involved with ego development. Drives develop and have structure, but it is not clear whether they are part of the ego. Finally and centrally, like all metapsychological explanations and like academic psychology as well, these theories suffer from a focus on process rather than motivation. According to Klein (1976), "To the extent that we pursue the process explanation, we are distracted from the need to improve upon psychoanalytic propositions regarding the aims, motives and goals of behavior" (p. 158).

> Ego psychology is torn between two objectives of *explanation*: It offers a half-hearted and half-annotated commitment to explanation in terms of purpose on the one hand and to mechanism on the other. It faces the choice either of trying to sophisticate a conception of a regulatory mechanism, building into it ever more detailed assumptions of processes to implement its heretofore implied reifications, or of frankly restricting the scope and the terms of ego theory to the level of motivational explanation that brought psychoanalysis into being in the first place – an endeavor exclusively concerned with understanding behavior in relation to psychological dilemma, conflict, task, and life history, an enterprise that explores, in Waelder's (1936) terms, the "multiple functions" of action. This is the shoemaker's last of the psychoanalyst. Sticking to it and pointing his theorizing in this direction, the psychoanalyst would shed all pretense of offering a nonteleological, mechanistic picture of ego processes, such as is implied by such impersonal terms as homeostasis, equilibrium, cathexis, energy and its modifications, and the like [pp. 159–160].

REFORMULATION OF PSYCHOANALYTIC THEORY

A. The Emergence of Structure from Experienced Incompatibility: The Self Schema

Klein's critical analysis of metapsychology was virtually complete at the time of his death, but his attempts to reformulate psychoanalytic theory at a clinically relevant level were in a preliminary stage. In this reformulation, he took as a central tenet of Freud's genetic and structural theories the idea that structural residues of past conflicts persist as organizing principles of behavior and thought. He noted (1976): "The concept that intrapsychic order and the motives governing action arise from *experienced* disorder is basic to psychoanalytic theory" (p. 165). Crisis and conflict, then, are not only pathogenic, but also play a constructive role in personality development; and Klein felt that psychoanalysis should be broadened to encompass "normal" as well as pathological development.

Klein proposed a number of modifications and elaborations of psychoanalytic theory. First, although he recognized that intrapsychic conflicts over unacceptable wishes (those that conflict with social constraints and expectations) have a uniquely important role, he believed that there are other "incompatible experiences" (for example, the contradiction between old behavioral modes or attitudes and new ones that occur at a point of conflict-free developmental change) that are of similar developmental significance and should be dealt with by theory. All such incompatibilities present "threats to the integration" of the self and are felt as painful experiences, such as "estrangement from self." Their resolution takes the form of a cognitive-emotional schema that frames later perceptions and actions.

A key aspect of Klein's thinking in this area is his introduction of the concept of the self, or self-schema, which is certainly among the more elusive and controversial concepts of psychoanalytic theory.[3] Klein (1976) pointed out that, as had been recognized by psychoanalytic structural theory, "conflict occurs only in relation to an integrating organization that is capable of *self*-observation, *self*-criticism, and choice, and that can regulate emotional needs and their expression" (p. 171). However, since classical theory at times sees the ego as the locus and resolver of conflict and at other times as a *party* to conflict (e.g., between an "ego aim" and a drive), some organization *beyond* or supraordinate to the ego must be conceptualized to provide for integration of aims and adjudication of contradictions. Thus, in Klein's words, "the notion of *self* . . . now seems indispensable" (p. 172). Klein cited Hartmann's (1950) concept of the self as a further "grade" of personality organization and H. Lichtenstein's (1964) formulation that the self is the source of the experience of successful and failed integration.

Klein conceived of the self as active in regard to the problems it confronts—both in resolving the demands made on it and in initiating purposes of its own. He cited as an early exposition of this position Waelder's view that the ego is not simply a passive, mechanistic switchboard, but has "its own peculiar activity" (Klein, 1976, p. 47), that is, "an active trend toward the instinctual life, a disposition to dominate or, more correctly, to incorporate it into its organization" (Waelder, 1936, pp. 47–48). For Klein, the synthetic function has the purpose of helping the individual to maintain integrity among conscious aims, motives, and values; and the self is the source of this feeling of integrity. The sense of the self has two aspects in dynamic equilibrium. One is individ-

---

[3]Klein's work preceded the publication of Heinz Kohut's self psychology and apparently was developed completely independent of it. Eagle (1982) believes that Klein's thinking on this score did not share the problems and weaknesses of Kohut's. Perhaps because of the preliminary nature of Klein's formulations, however, the two conceptions of self do, at times, appear similar, and they may therefore be susceptible to many of the same criticisms.

uality – "an autonomous unit, distinct from others as a locus of action and decision" (Klein 1976, p. 178); the other is "'we-ness" – "one's self construed as a necessary part of a unit transcending one's autonomous actions" (p. 178). An example of "'we-ness" is oneself as part of a family, community, or profession. Klein follows closely upon Erikson's (1963) ideas here, particularly Erikson's concept of the sense of identity, which implies an overall continuity extending from the past into the future and from a particular place in the community's past into anticipated work accomplishment and role satisfaction. Thus, the parameters of the sense of self involve conscious feelings of continuity, coherence, and integrity of thought in respect to both autonomy and "we-identity."

Having laid this groundwork, Klein proposed a redefinition of the concept of intrapsychic conflict in the broader context of "synthesizing efforts" necessitated by crises that threaten the coherence, continuity, and integrity of the self. These crises are of several kinds: wishes that are incompatible with the self-concept (intrapsychic conflict proper); traumatic experiences in which the person is passively overwhelmed; experiences inducing feelings of finiteness or loss of important roles or objects; and developmental crises "when the adaptational modes of one stage no longer suit the requirements of a new stage" (Klein, 1976, p. 190). Concomitantly, Klein (1976) reconceptualized anxiety as a signal of threat to self-identity, a feeling of discontinuity in selfhood akin to helplessness or meaninglessness:

> From such experiences of cleavage, whether of the nature of conflict, trauma, or developmental crises, arise efforts at solution in the form of a realignment of aims and goals. The more relevant a motivation is in bringing about a solution to a crisis of selfhood, the more lasting, generalized, and thereafter relied upon it is in the economy of personality. Thus the resolution of experienced incompatibility is the major basis of motivational structure. Motivations, rather than being regarded as arising from a "parallelogram of impersonal forces" defined in terms of intensity, are regarded as arising as resolutions of issues of self-integration and self-perpetuation [p. 208].

These experiences of incompatibility, conflict, or cleavage in the self, and their resolutions, are organized as cognitive structures with motivational effects. These structures, which Klein called "schemata" (a term borrowed from cognitive psychology [Bartlett, 1932]), encompass the relevant wishes, object representations, affects, and defenses – all of which together form the representation of conflict. As Klein wrote:

> "The component tendencies of a conflict are embodied as an unconsciously sustained structure (unconscious fantasy) which may be repetitively enacted throughout life . . . [p. 185].

... The terms of incompatibility and the solutions adopted to reduce the incompatibility are internal structures which state themselves as themes, affective positions, and styles of action and thought. The structured residues of incompatibilities are dynamisms, which organize the aims of behavior. Structurally, they are meaning schemata ... [p. 193].

... Such internalized representations of conflict and their defensive aspect are features of that created *inner environment* which serves as the person's notions of and dispositions toward the "real world," providing the means of encoding it and making it meaningful" [p. 199].

Klein saw the efforts to preserve self-identity as falling into two main categories. One is repression, which he defined as a dissociation of the threatening conflict from the mainstream of the self-identity structure. The other is active reversal of passive experience, that is, repetition of events experienced passively, yielding a sense of active mastery.

B. A Motivational System Based on Pleasure-seeking

In order to replace the quasi-physiological concept of drives that originate in the soma and "push" the psyche, and the tension-reduction model of the pleasure principle, Klein conceptualized motivations as active strivings for *experienced* pleasures. He considered pleasure as an experience within the province of the ego, just as anxiety is an experience and activity of the ego, and in his formulations he relied heavily on parallels with Freud's development of the concept of anxiety. In Freud's early model, anxiety was understood as a direct consequence of the disturbance in psychic economy caused by failure of adequate discharge of libidinal energy; later, as signal anxiety, it was conceived as an anticipatory reaction of the ego to danger. As a complementary concept to signal anxiety, Klein proposed the existence of actively created, anticipatory "signal pleasures;" and just as there are basic prototypical anxiety experiences (fear of separation, fear of castration, etc.), Klein postulated six prototypical pleasure experiences. He saw these "vital pleasures" as innately given and not reducible or analyzable to simpler components. Each pleasure was seen as having its greatest impact on development at a particular phase of the life cycle; and Klein diagramed their probable epigenetic development and interrelationships in an Erikson-like table. The six "vital pleasures" were as follows:

1. *Pleasure in reduction of unpleasant tension.* Although Klein believed that Freud had overestimated the significance of tension reduction as a motivational aim, he did nonetheless agree that it was highly important. In addition to release of drive tension and reduction of anxi-

ety, Klein also included here numerous other experiences of relief from unpleasant feelings, such as experiences of unfamiliarity or strangeness, lack of recognition of people or situations, and task incompleteness. In all these situations, tension reduction yields positively pleasurable feelings and not just an absence of unpleasure. Consequently the experience is actively and repeatedly sought.

2. *Sensual pleasure.* This is the broad group of pleasurable psychosexual experiences, ranging from genital sexuality to tickling and "contact comfort" that Freud recognized as interrelated and as having a characteristic development. Here, too, Klein stressed active pleasure seeking, and not merely the removal of unpleasure. Sensuality is characterized by plasticity – i.e., displaceability in terms of zone, mode, and object choice.

3. *Pleasure in functioning.* Klein (1976) asserted that there is inherent pleasure in the exercise of many conflict-free apparatuses and functions, which is sought for its own sake. "The gratification of bodily needs does not account for activities that an infant engages in spontaneously: . . . there are times when he seems to grasp, suck, babble, squeeze, and pull for no reason other than the pleasure of their repetition" (p. 223). More broadly, this is a "pleasure [in] . . . efficient use of the central nervous system for the performance of well-integrated ego functions" (p. 224).

4. *Effectance pleasure.* Klein (1976) said: "The component that distinguishes effectance from pleasure in functioning is the pleasure in observing the successful correspondence of *intention* and effect" (p. 225). This is pleasure in accomplishment and mastery, not merely in the exercise of capacities.

5. *Pleasure in pleasing.* Klein was impressed by the infant's early ability to know how to act pleasing to the mother, and he believed that doing so was inherently pleasurable for the infant. As he noted (1976): "Generating pleasure in another is . . . an occasion . . . for being affirmed in one's being" (p. 228). This form of pleasure is the basis for the need for affiliation with other people, the need to belong, which Klein considered a universal purpose, actively pursued: "The fact that pleasure arises from such a source [pleasing others] tells us too that the affiliative requirement has roots just as deep as those pleasure potentials that are more directly localized and originate in the 'body ego' " (p. 229).

6. *Pleasure in synthesis – aesthetic pleasure.* In infant observation, animal research, and observations of adult life, Klein (1976) saw many examples of the pleasurable effect of the "delighted contemplation of *restored* or *discovered order*" (p. 229). He saw this as an important motive for play and creative artistic activity. Klein (1976) also viewed this pleasure as closely connected to the principle of active reversal of passive ex-

perience and the "necessity in man . . . of having to create a self-identity" (p. 230)–two of the main conceptual pillars of his formulations.

Although Klein (1976) saw these "vital pleasures" ordinarily as fundamental motivational givens, he also recognized that there could, at times, be other unconscious motives for pursuing these aims, noting that "inherently pleasurable activity can be extrinsicallly motivated as well" (p. 234). Thus, pleasures can serve defensive functions; and behavior can at times be motivated toward excessive pleasure seeking and at other times toward excessive avoidance of pleasure.

C. The Maintenance of Self-Integrity

1. Repression. Klein delineated two broad categories of activity by which the coherence, identity, continuity, and integrity of the self can be maintained in the fact of threat due to conflict, developmental incompatibility, or trauma: *repression,* and *active reversal of passive experience.* As is the case with other psychoanalytic concepts that have evolved over many years, repression is ordinarily used with both clinical and metapsychological meanings and is consequently subject to some confusion and lack of precision. Psychoanalysis did not begin with a drive theory. Rather, in his early formulations Freud attributed psychopathhology to the preemptive power of unconscious memories and ideas; that is, to mental contents dissociated from consciousness but nonetheless active. Because the power of the repressed ideas appeared to derive from their sexual content, Freud eventually altered his emphasis from the ideas themselves to the drives that he presumed to underlie them as the sources of intrapsychic conflict. It is consistent with the *clinical* theory of psychoanalysis, however, to understand intrapsychic conflict as occurring between opposing sets of ideas (with their associated affects, object representations, and aims), or between the self-schema (the nonconflictual "main mass of ideas," feelings, attitudes, and aims) and a meaning schema that is contrary to the self, and hence threatens its maintenance, integrity, and continuity. The understanding that conflict derives from a clash between the ego and a drive is consistent only with the mechanistic concept of metapsychology. Klein saw repression, then, as one mode of coping with conflicting meaning schemata. He evolved a unique understanding of this phenomenon based largely on his orientation, derived from academic psychology, of seeing the mind as an apparatus for learning and adaptation.

Klein (1976) pointed out that repression does not necessarily operate by prohibiting the individual from having any awareness of conflicts.

Rather, it leaves a gap in comprehension of the warded-off material, without impeding its behavioral expression. In fact, its function is to permit the expression of the conflicted wish, while at the same time protecting the integrity of the self-schema by denying it "the attributes of self-relatedness . . . [excluding it] from the self as *agent*, self as *object*, and self as *locus*" (p. 242).

In repression, the threatening meaning schema is dissociated from the self and continues to have a motivating influence on behavior and thought. It functions in the mode that Piaget designated as *assimilation;* that is, it provides a code for understanding, reacting to, and internalizing new experiences, while its own existence and effects are uncomprehended and unchangeable because no feedback is possible about them. Repression can impede adaptation, growth, learning, accurate perception, and cognition. Undoing of repression is not only recovering the memory of traumatic event or conflictual idea, but also understanding its meaning, bringing about "comprehension in terms of a previously uncomprehended relationship, the perception of a causal link to which the person had been impervious" (Klein, 1976, p. 248).

Klein considered it more accurate to think of repression in terms of its mode of operation—the splitting off of an organization of ideas that are threatening to the self and that then function in a purely assimilative fashion—rather than in terms of the unconscious, whether conceived of as a system or as a quality of experience.

2. Reversal of Voice. The second major strategy available for resolution of threats to self-coherence, according to Klein, is the principle of reversal of voice, or active reversal of passive experience. This concept has a long history in psychoanalysis. Its clearest statement occurs in *Beyond the Pleasure Principle* (Freud, 1920) in Freud's description of a game played by his grandson. The same concept is at the heart of the defense mechanism of identification with the aggressor. In Klein's view, it is also the essence of Freud's description of signal anxiety—an instant, miniature act of reversal, an active repetition of a trauma. Although the concept of active reversal has long been available and allusions to it occur in various contexts, however, it is fair to say that it has not before been accorded a central and important role and has not been well integrated into the main body of psychoanalytic theory. Klein proposed that it is a principle of major importance, not a defense mechanism, coordinate with and "equally vital" to repression.

In its basic form, active reversal is observed most clearly in children who respond to traumata of various kinds by actively repeating the painful experience (usually in play or fantasy), or by doing to another person what was done to them, so that they make it seem to occur under their control. In this way, the painful experience is mastered and internalized, modifying and differentiating some aspect of the self-schema by accommodation, to restore its harmony and integration. *Accommodation* is Piaget's term for a process complementary to assimilation, in which new data is recognized as different from past experiences, and the schema is changed to encompass it. As Klein (1976) explained it: "The heart of the principle [of reversal of voice] is that when a passively endured encounter or relationship is affectively coded, a search for information is stimulated, towards two ends: a) to make the experience understandable in relation to the self; b) to position the internalized relationship within the self-schema as usable information related to the self-as-agent" (p. 285). In contrast to repression, which is a regressive solution to incompatibility that restricts the personality, Klein (1976) saw active reversal as a progressive mode, a "positive" mechanism, leading to "growth through reconstruction, innovation and integration" (p. 196) and requiring advanced development. This concept, he wrote,

captures the essential distinction between activity and passivity which Rapaport (1953) intuitively felt to be one of the fundamental foci of psycho-analytic theory generally and of a dynamic conception of ego organization in particular. I believe it is the essential dynamic aspect of what is usually encompassed by the term "will." The principle encompasses such diverse phenomena as play, novelty, curiosity, repetitive working through of traumatic experiences, interruption phenomena, and certain aspects of art-making. From a developmental standpoint it encompasses . . . competence motivation; perhaps most important of all, it provides a dynamic basis for identification. In psychoanalytic therapy the positive or adaptive aspects of transference, as Loewald (1960) has emphasized, are explainable in its terms [Klein, 1976, p. 261].

In passing, Klein (1976) suggested that the principle of active reversal might also account for aggression: "Activities of reversal of voice could be considered synonymous with the 'aggressive drive'—not in the sense of a specific aggressive *motive* to destroy but as manifestations of an instinctual aggressive potential" (p. 264). This idea has much in common with the concept of nonhostile aggression as employed by Marcovitz (1973). He conceived of aggression as consisting of a spectrum of interpersonal behaviors ranging from simple activity at one extreme, through such phenomena as self-assertion, dominance, and self-defense, to hatred at the other pole. This broad, dynamic view of aggression is easily reconciled with the principle of active reversal of passive experience.

D. Developmental and Structural Consequences of Repression and Active Reversal

Klein conceived of the two mechanisms for maintaining self-integrity as a duality with widespread consequences—sometimes interacting, sometimes contrasting—throughout psychological life. He specifically called attention to the following:

1. *The repetition compulsion.* The motive to repeat phenomena can reflect *either* the continuing activity of repressed meaning schemas *or* the active reversal and repetition of passively experienced events. In one case, the repetition is assimilative and in the other, accommodative.

2. *Internalization processes—fractionation and identification.* Repression "fractionates" the self by splitting off unacceptable mental contents. Often these contents consist of the schemata of interpersonal relationships, including an image of the object, an image of the self in interaction with the object, and an affect image.[4] According to Klein (1976), these split-off interpersonal schemata, called introjects, preserve the threatening relationship within the personality, in dissociated form: "From the subjective phenomenological (not necessarily conscious) point of view the introject is experienced as an alien presence. . . . It is felt as part of the body, or one's thought, but not as part of the self" (p. 295). The internalization process involving reversal of voice, on the other hand, is identification. Through accommodation, the self-schema is modified, differentiated, and enlarged to bring into it "the values, manners, and interpersonal modes of others" (p. 292). Experientially, when a successful identification occurs, there is no felt separation between the newly internalized mental contents and the self as a whole. In fact, ego identity is largely composed of identifications formed by means of active reversal of voice. Similarly, the superego is the result of active incorporation of prohibitions that were originally passively experienced. Introjection is a defense mechanism and identification a nondefensive structuring process.

3. *Pathology.* At times, repression and active reversal operate simultaneously in regard to the same objects, with pathological consequences. For example, a man may identify with certain aspects of his father and repressively introject other, opposite aspects. The result may be ambivalence and symptomatology.

4. *Creativity and art.* Klein (1976) considered the art-making impulse as an effort to remedy a sense of "fracturing of selfhood and anxieties that herald . . . such a threat" (p. 206), primarily through the opera-

---

[4]This is similar to Kernberg's (1980) concept of self-object-affect "units" in the ego.

tion of active reversal of voice. Here, in response to some painful failure or rejection, the artist uses his talent to convert previously repressed, fractionated fantasies into creative products. In this process, the artist is actively mastering (through repetition) both the early conflicts that had been dissociated and the current traumata.

E. Psychotherapy

Klein considered classical psychoanalysis both inefficient and perhaps less effective than other, modified forms of treatment. He believed its main value was as a method of training and research; however, he felt its true potential as a naturalistic setting for data gathering was not being achieved, in part because of a lack of systematic research approaches to analysis and in part because of the stultifying effect of metapsychology on creative clinical thinking.

The theoretical formulations he proposed were partly intended as a remedy for this problem. However, Klein said relatively little about the direct clinical application of his ideas—perhaps because of their incompletely developed state.

Characteristically, Klein's few direct comments about treatment concerned active, growth-inducing aspects of psychotherapy, which he felt had received too little consideration in the past. He suggested that the principle of reversal of voice contributes a new dimension to understanding transference repetition. In addition to transference being a regressive expression of split-off conflicts, Klein postulated that through active reversal in transference (or perhaps the "treatment alliance"), direct, positive personality change is brought about. In effect, this appears to refer primarily to growth through identification with adaptive functions of the therapist and the treatment process itself.

DISCUSSION: KLEIN'S CONTRIBUTIONS TO PSYCHOANALYTIC THEORY

George Klein turned his creative, inquiring intelligence to a remarkable scope of problems and tasks. He was at the forefront of his field almost from the first. He was an innovator of research methodology and had an ability to challenge theory and to see problems in new ways, both in the laboratory and in his theoretical formulations. It is probably correct to view him, as Goldberger (1982) has said, as primarily a psychologist and only secondarily a psychoanalyst. His work was always at the interface of the two fields, beginning with explorations in the use of experimental methods to enhance psychoanalysts' knowledge of ego functioning, and culminating in the seeming paradox of his proposals to use concepts from general psychology to create a clinically relevant theory for psychoanalysis, free of what he saw as the counterproductive burden of metapsychology. As Goldberger (1982) points out, Klein was unusually talented at synthesizing concepts from many fields–for example, making Piaget meaningful to psychoanalysts. He notes: "The gift that George Klein evidenced was being able to cross conceptual and theoretical boundaries, a brand of creativity that bespeaks a mature thinker."

The manifest form of Klein's work changed radically over time, not only in his shift of emphasis from laboratory research to theoretical formulation, but also in his sudden change from leadership in the expansion of Rapaport's ego psychology to a diametrically opposite, clinical and phenomenological point of view. Throughout his career, however, certain basic themes can be clearly discerned. From the beginning, in perceptual research and then in psychoanalysis, he was dissatisfied with explanations based, as he saw it, too heavily on drive causality and too little on structure. He was persistently and articulately critical of the drive concept itself, considering it both inaccurate and logically unsound, and he ultimately developed these ideas into his sweeping indictment of metapsychology. Finally, he always advocated an enhanced role in psychoanalysis for "positive" growth potentials, conflict-free motives, and autonomous structural characteristics. In all these areas he was constantly interested in broadening the scope of psychoanalysis to encompass normal, conscious, and nonconflictual phenomena as well as pathology, while at the same time he strove to maintain its fidelity to clinical experience.

Klein's impact as a leader, teacher, and pioneer in the study of unexplored territory was unquestionably significant. Similarly, although Klein was not alone as a critic of metapsychology, his careful dissection of the inconsistencies and logical defects of the two psychoanalytic theories had considerable value, not only for theory building, but also in helping the psychoanalytic clinician cope with the complex, layered conceptual heritage handed down by Freud and his followers. Previously, analysts who were resistant to metapsychology were vulnerable to the charge of being "atheoretical." Klein, however, contended that the focus of attention should be on *meaning*, not mechanism; and that clinical concepts, correctly framed, are sufficient to stand as the basic theory. They have the advantage of being closer to the clinical material, more responsive to pressures of the data.

These assertions had a stirring effect on those analysts who were defensive about their aversion to metapsychology, and led one (Slap, 1980) to write:

Klein liberates such analysts. He confers upon us theories much as the Wizard of Oz dispensed courage, heart and intelligence to creatures who already had them. More than that, Klein congratulates us for our scientific integrity, our willingness (we knew not what else to do) to stick with the observational data rather than to fudge. Suddenly we are the purists and the emperor has no clothes [p. 170].

In the words of another commentator (Gedo, 1977), Klein's book on *Psychoanalytic Theory* (1976) "lives up to its promise to explore the essentials of psychoanalytic theory with so much authority that no future work in the field will qualify to be taken seriously which does not come to grips with Klein's arguments" (p. 320).

On the other hand, the usefulness and validity of many of Klein's new formulations, created to replace metapsychology, have been the subject of much disagreement. One reviewer (Loeb, 1977) concludes that Klein "clearly separates data-related, clinical psychoanalytic theory from data-unrelated metapsychological psychoanalytic theory"; he feels that Klein's new model was derived from clinical theory and "should be highly useful and relevant to both therapists and researchers" (p. 215). In contrast, another critic (Chessick, 1980) expressed concern about the "radical nature" of Klein's proposed theoretical revisions; and Frank (1979) saw Klein's entire enterprise as flawed: "It is difficult to see where Klein's basic principles would be useful in application to either the clinical or theoretical psychoanalytic situation" (p. 193).

In his suggested revisions of clinical theory, Klein often struggled with major problems and dilemmas of psychoanalysis, areas with which many were dissatisfied. Although many of his solutions did not succeed in forming a model that is free of internal contradictions and logical flaws as well as consistent with clinical data, in our view his deliberations do have heuristic value. Included here are such matters as whether psychoanalysis requires (or whether it can encompass) conceptions of "active, positive" forces for growth and mastery; the related issue of the autonomy and conflict-free status of various motives and structures; the nature and role of the "self"; repetitive "mastery"; activity-passivity; and the role of conscious experience in psychoanalysis.

We see much merit in Klein's delineation of a cognitive model of repression and in his invocation of the Piagetian constructs of assimilation and accommodation to describe the different modes of processing data used by dissociated (repressed) mental contents and those that are not split off. Indeed, one of us has co-authored a paper that sought to bring this model to the attention of a wider audience (Slap & Saykin, 1983). We see this model as embodying the advantages of Freud's early concept of repression as dissociation of a set of mental contents from "the main mass of ideas," which then remain active as an unconscious fantasy shaping behavior (by assimilation). This model of repression is close to clinical experience, accounts in a superior fashion for the impact of current life experiences on the mind, and absorbs and explains in an internally consistent way numerous phenomena, including transference, repetition, and symptom formation (all of which reflect assimilation). As Klein himself said: "Psychoanalytic understanding lies precisely in the recognition of themes 'which we have never lived down nor successfully outlived' " (p. 185). We find this model of repression helpful in this clinical task.

However, Klein's complementary principle of "reversal of voice"—although based on often-noted clinical observations of undeniably real phenomena—stands on much shakier ground, as is the case for many of the factors that he construes as "positive," "growth-inducing," and the like. We do not consider it justifiable either on theoretical or clinical grounds to dichotomize behavior and experience as Klein does so often into regressive-progressive, positive-negative, defensive-nonconflictual, and sensual-autonomous. It is as much a misunderstanding of repression to view it as totally maladaptive, regressive, and so forth as it is to view active, identificatory turning passive-to-active as entirely nondefensive. After all, the ego expansion of latency is founded on repression of infantile sexuality; and in identification with the aggressor and many other instances, reversal of voice is used as a *defense* to create for oneself the illusion of being aggressive and to deny passivity. Of course, in each of these instances, the other side of the coin is also present—identification with the aggressor can be adaptively useful.

Klein's concept of the self-schema is more difficult to evaluate, because his use of it varied. At times his "self" is a clinical concept—an active self-identity and a *sense* of self—which contrasts with the abstract concept of the ego as a structure. It seems consistent with clinical experience to conceptualize intrapsychic conflict as an internal struggle between repressed fantasy and the main, integrated system of self-representations, ideals, values, and wishes.

At other times, however Klein's self-schema is a superordinate structure, with its own inherent need for self-consistency that has the status of an autonomous motive. Further, the conception of conflict is broadened and redefined in cognitive terms as a problem of resolution of "incompatible tendencies"; and conscious experiences such as anxiety or feelings of estrangement are considered to be direct reflections of intrapsychic realities—that is, of deficiences in self-integrity. In these formulations, Klein replaced the old metapsychology with a new and, if anything, more abstract one. It is subject to the same criticism of inappropriateness in level of discourse and unresponsiveness to clinical data that Klein leveled at the old metapsychology. In addition, it shares many of the difficulties we have elsewhere found in Kohut's self psychology (Levine, 1978, 1979; Slap & Levine, 1978), such as the reliance on hybrid concepts in which levels of data and theory are inappropriately mixed. Among these is the concept that internal structural psychic conditions are directly reflected in conscious experience.

Klein's postulated series of vital pleasures, too, has both features that we find valuable and problematic ones. The concept that pleasure is to be seen as within the scope of the ego and as a positive experience of gratification and consummation rather than merely a tension release contributes to the internal consistency of psychoanalytic theory. Klein did not claim priority for this idea, which, he pointed out, is similar to suggestions made by Ludwig Eidelberg, Mark Kanzer, and Thomas Szasz. We have serious disagreements, however, with his list of vital pleasures because—as he himself pointed out—just these conscious experiences and motives regularly occur as disguised, derivative representations of unconscious conflict. In addition, his treatment of sensual pleasure leaves one with the impression that such matters as gender identity, sexual appetite, and the procreation of the species are essentially accidental. In his discussion of these motivational constructs, we believe Klein fell prey to a number of fundamental fallacies that appear repeatedly in his work: the need to dichotomize conflictual and nonconflictual forces; the enumeration of presumably autonomous motives, without supporting data, resulting in a fragmented conception of human beings as extensively "preprogrammed" (analogous to the instinctual patternings in lower animals), which is inconsistent with the flexible nature of human adaptation; and the predilection to accept conscious mental contents as basic, unanalyzable data. These problems, of course, might have been eliminated if Klein had been able to subject his work to further revision.

Klein focused part of his critique of metapsychology on its persumably inappropriate avoidance of "teleological" explanation. As defined by *Webster's New Twentieth Century Dictionary* (25th edition, 1950), teleology is "the doctrine which asserts that all things which exist were produced for the end which they fulfill." Many of Klein's own explanatory rubrics, in fact, fit this definition of teleology, with its attendant implication of arbitrariness and untestability by any independent data source. Freud's clinical theory was *not* teleological in the same way. It is true that it did not have recourse to extrapsychological realms of data, such as neurophysiology; however, it does involve a systematic method of forming and testing hypotheses about a *psychological* realm (the unconscious) that is not directly observable but that can be inferred from future behavioral observations. When Klein's conceptions of self and dissociated schema are used in a clinical sense – as referring to *conflict related* psychic organizations with conscious and unconscious features – they are useful aids in organizing data and inferences. If they are conceived of in reified, structurelike terms, they have the same stultifying, counterproductive effect Klein saw in classical metapsychology.

In summary, we see Klein's theoretical work as a valuable but not fully successful contribution to the effort that has been undertaken by many theorists to remedy the often-noted difficulties of metapsychology. We find Klein's analysis of these difficulties particularly cogent and valuable. His proposed solutions contain many heuristically valuable elements, but also very significant weaknesses.

Klein's earlier work on cognitive controls, through which he attempted to enrich psychoanalytic ego psychology by research methods, similarly does not appear, at this point, to have fully achieved its objectives. Although there was a great deal of interest in the study of cognitive controls and styles for some time, it has not yet fulfilled its promise as a bridge between academic psychology and psychoanalysis, or as providing a means of determining "constitutional givens" that contribute to the formation of defenses and other personality structures. Further research did not always demonstrate the postulated unitary character of the cognitive controls or the anticipated direct connections between these structures and defenses. However, research has suggested that similar cognitive control behaviors may reflect *different* personality determinants in different individuals; that controls may differ in degree of relative autonomy; and that many other factors such as sex differences, developmental variations and fine distinctions in measurement of these cognitive processes remain to be understood (see, for example, Levine, 1966, 1968; E. Lichtenstein, 1961; Spivack, Levine, and Sprigle, 1959).

REFERENCES

Bartlett, F. C. (1932). *Remembering: A study in experimental and social psychology.* Cambridge: Cambridge University Press.

Chessick, R. D. (1980). Critique: Psychoanalytic metapsychology. *American Journal of Psychotherapy, 34,* 127–130.

Eagle, M. N. (1982, August 24). Contribution to M. Mayman (Chair), *George Klein: A seminal figure in psychoanalysis.* Scientific program presented at the annual meeting of Psychologists Interested in the Study of Psychoanalysis, Washington, D.C.

Erikson, E. H. (1963). *Childhood and society* (2nd ed.). New York: Norton.

Fisher, C. (1954). Dreams and perception: The role of preconscious and primary modes of perception in dream formation. *Journal of the American Psychoanalytic Association, 2,* 389–445.

Frank, A. (1979). Two theories or one? Or none? *Journal of the American Psychoanalytic Association, 27,* 169-202.

Freud, S. (1895). Project for a scientific psychology. *Standard Edition, 1,* 295-397.

Freud, S. (1900). The interpretation of dreams. *Standard Edition, 4-5.*

Freud, S. (1915). Repression. *Standard Edition, 14,* 141-158.

Freud, S. (1920). Beyond the pleasure principle. *Standard Edition, 18,* 7-64.

Gardner, R. W., Holzman, P. S., Klein, G. S., Linton, H. B., & Spence, D. P. (1959). Cognitive control: A study of individual consistencies in cognitive behavior. *Psychological Issues, 1* (4, Monograph 4).

Gardner, R. W., Jackson, D. N., & Messick, S. (1960). Personality organization in cognitive attitudes and intellectual abilities. *Psychological Issues, 2* (4, Monograph 8).

Gedo, J. E. (1977). [Review of *Psychoanalytic theory: An exploration of essentials,* by George S. Klein, and *Psychology versus metapsychology: Psychoanalytic essays in memory of George S. Klein,* edited by M. M. Gill and P. S. Holzman.] *Psychoanalytic Quarterly, 46,* 319-324.

Gill, M. M. (1976). Metapsychology is not psychology. In M. M. Gill & P. S. Holzman (Eds.), Psychology versus metapsychology: Psychoanalytic essays in memory of George S. Klein. *Psychological Issues, 9* (4, Monograph 36, pp. 71-105).

Gill, M. M., & Holzman, P. S. (Eds.) (1976). Psychology versus metapsychology: Psychoanalytic essays in memory of George S. Klein. *Psychological Issues, 9* (4, Monograph 36).

Goldberger, L. (1982, August 24). *George Klein's contribution to psychology—A tribute.* Paper presented at the annual meeting of Psychologists Interested in the Study of Psychoanalysis, Washington, D.C.

Guntrip, H. (1969). *Schizoid phenomena, object relations and the self.* New York: International Universities Press.

Hartmann, H. (1939). *Ego psychology and the problem of adaptation.* New York: International Universities Press, 1958.

Hartmann, H. (1950). Comments on the psychoanalytic theory of the ego. In *Essays on Ego Psychology* (pp. 113-141). New York: International Universities Press, 1964.

Hebb, D. O. (1949). *The Organization of Behavior.* New York: Wiley.

Holt, R. R. (1976). Drive or wish? A reconsideration of the psychoanalytic theory of motivation. In M. M. Gill & P. S. Holzman (Eds.), Psychology versus metapsychology: Psychoanalytic Essays in memory of George S. Klein. *Psychological Issues, 9* (4, Monograph 36, pp. 158-197).

Holzman, P. S. (1962). Repression and cognitive style. *Bulletin of the Menninger Clinic, 26,* 273-282.

Holzman, P. S. (1982, August 24). *The contributions from George Klein's Menninger years.* Paper presented at the annual meeting of Psychologists Interested in the Study of Psychoanalysis, Washington, D.C.

Holzman, P. S., & Klein, G. S. (1956). Motive and style in reality contact. *Bulletin of the Menninger Clinic, 20,* 181-191.

Kernberg, O. (1980). *Internal World and External Reality.* New York: Jason Aronson.

Klein, G. S. (1954). Need and regulation. In M. R. Jones (Ed.), *Nebraska Symposium on Motivation.* Lincoln: University of Nebraska Press, pp. 224-274.

Klein, G. S. (1958). Cognitive control and motivation. In Gardner Lindzey (Ed.), *Assessment of Human Motives* (pp. 87-118). New York: Grove Press.

Klein, G. S. (1959a). Consciousness in psychoanalytic theory: Some implications for current research in perception. *Journal of the American Psychoanalytic Association, 7,* 5-34.

Klein, G. S. (1959b). Editorial statement. In E. H. Erikson, Identity and the life cycle: Selected papers. *Psychological Issues, 1* (1, Monograph 1). pp. iii–v.

Klein, G. S. (1966). The several grades of memory. In R. M. Loewenstein, L. M. Newman, M. Schur and A. J. Solnit (Eds.), *Psychoanalysis – A general psychology: Essays in honor of Heinz Hartmann* (p. 377–389). New York: International Universities Press.

Klein, G. S. (1976). *Psychoanalytic theory: An exploration of essentials.* New York: International Universities Press.

Klein, G. S., & Schlesinger, H. J. (1951). Perceptual attitudes toward instability: Prediction of apparent movement experiences from Rorschach responses. *Journal of Personality, 19,* 289–302.

Levine, F. J. (1966). *The relationship of constricted-flexible control to cognitive handling of impulses in three vocational groups.* Unpublished doctoral dissertation, University of Michigan.

Levine, F. J. (1968). Color-word test performance and drive regulation in three vocational groups. *Journal of Consulting and Clinical Psychology, 32,* 642–647.

Levine, F. J. (1978). [Review of *The restoration of the self,* by Heinz Kohut.] *Journal of the Philadelphia Association for Psychoanalysis, 4,* 238–246.

Levine, F. J. (1979). On the clinical application of Heinz Kohut's psychology of the self: Comments on some recently published case studies. *Journal of the Philadelphia Association for Psychoanalysis, 6,* 1–19.

Lichtenstein, E. (1961). *The relation of three cognitive controls to some selected perceptual and personality variables.* Unpublished doctoral dissertation. University of Michigan.

Lichtenstein, H. (1964). The role of narcissism in the emergence and maintenance of a primary identity, *International Journal of Psycho-Analysis, 45,* 49–56.

Loeb, F. F. (1977). [Review of: *Psychoanalytic theory: An exploration of essentials,* by George S. Klein.] *American Journal of Psychiatry, 134,* 215.

Loewald, H. (1960). On the therapeutic action of psycho-analysis. *International Journal of Psycho-Analysis, 41,* 16–33.

Marcovitz, E. (1973). Aggression in human adaptation. *Psychoanaytic Quarterly, 42,* 226–233.

Mayman, M. (Chair). (1982, August 24). *George Klein: A seminal figure in psychoanalysis.* Scientific program. Presented at the annual meeting of Psychologists Interested in the Study of Psychoanalysis, Washington, D.C.

Poetzl, O. (1917). The relationship between experimentally induced dream images and indirect vision. *Psychological Issues, 2,* Monograph 7, 1960, pp. 41–120.

Postman, L., Bruner, J. S., and McGinnies, E. (1948). Personal values as selective factors in perception. *Journal of Abnormal and Social Psychology, 43,* 142–154.

Rapaport, D. (1953). Some metapsychological considerations concerning activity and passivity. In M. M. Gill (Ed.), *The collected papers of David Rapaport* (pp. 530–568). New York: Basic Books, 1967.

Reppen, J. (Ed.). (1980). Symposium on G. S. Klein's *Psychoanalytic theory: An exploration of essentials. Psychoanalytic Review, 67,* 161–216.

Schafer, R. (1968). *Aspects of internalization.* New York: International Universities Press.

Shapiro, D. (1965). *Neurotic styles.* New York: Basic Books.

Slap, J. W. (1980). Part 2. In J. Reppen (Ed.), Symposium on G. S. Klein's *Psychoanalytic theory: An exploration of essentials. Psychoanalytic Review, 67,* 168–172.

Slap, J. W., & Levine, F. J. (1978). On hybrid concepts in psychoanalysis. *Psychoanalytic Quarterly, 47,* 499–523.

Slap, J. W., & Saykin, A. (1983). The schema: Basic concept in a nonmetapsychological model of the mind. *Psychoanalysis and Contemporary Thought, 6,* 305–325.

Spivack, G., Levine, M., & Sprigle, H. (1959). Intelligence test performance and the delay function of the ego. *Journal of Consulting Psychology, 23,* 428–431.

Waelder, R. (1936). The principle of multiple function: Observations on over-determination. *Psychoanalytic Quarterly, 5,* 45–62.

Waelder, R. (1962). [Review of *Psychoanalysis, Scientific Method, and Philosophy,* by S. Hook.] *Journal of the American Psychoanalytic Association, 10,* 617–637.

Witkin, H. A., Dyk, R. B., Faterson, H. F., Goodenough, D. R., & Karp, S. A. (1962). *Psychological Differentiation.* New York: Wiley.

Woodworth, R. S. (1918). *Dynamic Psychology.* New York: Columbia University Press.

Woodworth, R. S., & Schlosberg, H. (1954). *Experimental Psychology.* New York: Holt.

3 Roy Schafer: Searching for the Native Tongue

Donald P. Spence, Ph.D.

In taking a long look at the work of Roy Schafer and the major themes he has explored and discussed, it is tempting to try to find a single thread that leads from his initial publications on diagnostic tests to his more recent work on action language and narrative appeal. To search for such a thread is, of course, to put into practice one of Schafer's better-known claims. He has argued for the central place of the narrative in the way we view someone's life and works, and if I am able to make the pieces of his own career fit together in a persuasive fashion, I can make his point even as I am describing it. To find such a thread will, furthermore, help to uncover some of the similarities beneath what seem like differences in his approach to psychoanalytic phenomena and also to show how each phase of his career is, in a certain sense, a reaction to what had gone before. Such an attempt, it should be noted, may also take advantage of hindsight, and as a result, what seems to be a smoothly flowing progression of ideas may be, in fact, quite different from the way they were originally conceived. Nevertheless, this newly discovered sequence may also reveal its own kind of truth, even though it may not match the experience of the author.

But first I must back off and look at the central problem facing any follower of Freud. When Freud was alive and writing psychoanalytic theory, it was assumed that science was the *only* path to the truth and that the mission of science was to discover the whole truth about the natural world. The human observer was something apart from the thing observed, and any piece of reality was as much an object of study as an apple or a raindrop. To *see* the world clearly (with an emphasis on the visual metaphor) became the goal of science. Troublemakers such as Heisenberg, Heidegger, and Wittgenstein were still over the horizon.

The visual metaphor and the clear separation between observer and observed are emphasized in Freud's conception of the process of free association and in his well-known metaphor of the patient as passenger on the train, reporting the scene outside the window to a listening seatmate (the analyst). Tangible reality was assumed to be either outside or inside the head (as in *reality* testing" and "psychic *reality*"); and in the metaphor of psychoanalysis as a kind of archaeology which uncovers (reconstructs) the past, Freud called attention to the tangible nature of what had been – memory is laid down in "mnemonic residues," waiting to be uncovered and brought to light. The analyst, listening with evenly hovering attention, was assumed to be the near-perfect observer who, because detached from the subject, was in an ideal position to see and hear with maximum fidelity and minimum error. The patient as observer of his or her inner life was the complement of the analyst as observer of the patient. The symmetry of the two roles is brought out clearly in Freud's (1912) statement that "the rule of giving equal notice to everything is the necessary counterpart to the demand made on the patient that he should communicate everything that occurs to him." (p. 112).

The naive realism contained in this model always hovered in the background, despite the gradual accumulation of findings to the contrary. Discovery of the transference was the most obvious embarrassment to this point of view, because what is transference but the realization that reality is not simply "out there," waiting to be described, that what the patient "sees" is often a product of his or her own experience, and that the subject matter of psychoanalysis largely consists in disentangling the different faces of what is apparently observed (i.e., in finding flaws with the positivistic model)? But the larger world view was not significantly changed because transference was assumed to be a transient disturbance (a treatment-activated "neurosis") that ran its course from symptom to cure. Even the discovery of countertransference did not significantly affect the world view, because motes in the eye of the analyst were assumed to be subject to repair by way of the training analysis and occasional consultations as the need arose. The perfectly analyzed analyst, listening with "evenly hovering" attention, was the model of the neutral, detached (scientific) observer who was in the perfect position to see the (physical) field clearly. It was not recognized that even this model of neutrality was perhaps listening with a bias toward coherence and continuity, not fully aware that the "story" being heard was only one of many possible ways to understand the patient and his or her associations. Nor was it fully realized that the meaning in the patient's associations was not always "out there" but many times was influenced by the immediate context of the hour and that a comparison of patient's and analyst's views of the treatment might reveal significant differences that were not necessarily the workings of transference or countertransference. Similar questions could be raised about the status of the past, to what extent it could be reconstructed in some reliable manner, and to what extent the content of memories was influenced by the context of the session and by the immediate hopes and fears of the patient.

The continuous tension between naive realism and the Freudian model led to various kinds of compensatory strategies. Conceptual terms tended to become more and more ossified, as if the shifting nature of the subject matter could be held in place by sheer repetition of the explanatory concepts. Despite Freud's concession that the metapsychology was to be seen as only a set of temporary conventions that would be replaced by more appropriate terms as the phenomena became better understood (Freud, 1915, p. 117), the metapsychology seemed to take on a life of its own. It could even be argued that philosophical realism played an important role in the choice of such concrete terms as "structure," "mechanism," "splitting," and "barrier" and that the hoped-for reality which could not be seen in practice could be found in descriptions *about* practice. Whatever the reasons, there grew up a tradition of rewriting the clinical event in the largely mechanistic terms of the theory, giving the literature a solidity and a tangibility that had been assumed in practice but never found.

A similar compensation can be found in Freud's tendency to posit real events in the past as causes of the patient's current symptoms (see Jacobsen & Steele, 1979). It is well known that Freud first assumed that real seduction was the cause of a later neurosis; but even after he recognized that the memory was probably false, he continued to introduce real events in his explanatory accounts. Witnessing his parents' intercourse was the central event in the Wolf Man's neurosis; viewing a monograph in a store window was a significant cause of the Botanical Monograph dream—the hard stuff of reality was at the root of many symptoms. By always moving the hard facts backward in time, they could be maintained as explanatory devices even if never actually discovered in the treatment (see Jacobsen and Steele, 1979, for a fuller discussion of this tendency). Thus, the link to reality was always assumed, and the patient's associations were listened to as *derivatives* or *transformations* of significant pieces of the past.

In similar fashion, the unconscious was conceived to be a potentially knowable structure that had form and content and that impinged on the patient's behavior in a reliable and accountable manner. The task of psychoanalysis was to discover its contents and make them available to the patient; the assumption of a knowable reality applied as much to within as to without. The transference was equally analyzable, and once significant distortions had been accounted for, the patient would "see" the analyst as the analyst "really was." It was never admitted that probably no amount of analysis could ever accomplish this task.

Overlaying the growing tension between an outmoded realism and the nonneutral analyst was the conflict between public and private. Freud never felt it necessary to disclose all the facts in reporting his cases, either because telling too much might risk his authority, because it would jeopardize the doctor-patient relationship, or because it would not add significantly to his power of persuasion (see Freud, 1912, p. 114). Within this tradition of privileged withholding, it became respectable to write *about* the data instead of making it available; and as this tradition persisted, the clinical details of the case were overlaid by abstract concepts. No such taboos applied to the metalanguage – it could be used with impunity – and so it happened that the specific observations of the clinical hour were translated into more general (and in many cases, meaningless) categories. In the process, the postulates of naive realism could be reaffirmed, and because no one else was present when patient talked to doctor, no one could say whether or not what was described was really "out there."

We can now call on Wittgenstein to make clear what happened next. As the language of metapsychology became the normal language of psychoanalysis, it became second nature to see the clinical happenings in terms of the theory. All observations became theory laden and yet were reported as though they were the pure stuff of observation. Fit between observation and theory was not always perfect, but because the raw data were never available, the match or mismatch could never be checked. In this way the metalanguage and its naive realism could be perpetuated indefinitely. In some ways, the followers of Freud, because they were wearing his blinders, were somewhat worse off than the founder himself. Language was slowly poisoning observation, and because of the private nature of the data, no one else could participate in the debate.

We now return to Roy Schafer and to his place within this zeitgeist. Because of circumstances of training and experience, he was at odds with the tradition on several counts. He trained at the City College of New York with Gardner Murphy, a well-known personality theorist, and graduated in 1943; he then entered a long association with David Rapaport, first at the Menninger Foundation in Topeka, Kansas, and then at the Austen Riggs Center. He received his Ph.D. in clinical psychology from Clark University in 1950 and completed formal training in psychoanalysis at the Western New England Institute for Psychoanalysis in 1959. He has been president of the Western New England Society and clinical professor of psychiatry at Yale University; and is currently adjunct professor of psychology in psychiatry at the Cornell University Medical College and training analyst at the Columbia University Center for Psychoanalytic Training and Research. In 1975 he was appointed the first Sigmund Freud Memorial Professor at University College in London, and in 1983, he received the American Psychological Association's Award for Distinguished Professional Contribution to Knowledge.

Early signs of Schafer's impatience with the tradition of privileged withholding appear in his books on diagnostic testing, which are notable for their verbatim excerpts from patient protocols (Rapaport, Gill, & Schafer, 1945–46, Schafer 1948, 1954). In these works we have not only diagnostic impressions of a series of patients but a verbatim record of their responses to the Rorschach test, TAT, Wechsler-Bellevue Scale, and other diagnostic instruments. Schafer explicitly connects the diagnostic summary with parts of the protocol, so that the referents for such diagnostic impressions as hysterical or obsessive character could be found directly in the data. By giving the complete record, Schafer and his collaborators also make it possible for the reader to develop alternative formulations. Standard procedure and standard format, one might think, but consider how rarely we discuss alternative formulations in the clinical literature (Kohut, 1979, is a notable exception) and how we *never* have access to the complete data from a complete case.

Concern for the clinical data and for the problems of observation and terminology appear in the early pages of *Aspects of Internalization* (Schafer, 1968). The reader of the psychoanalytic literature may well ask, says Schafer in his introduction, "What does this mean?" He sees the need to introduce order into the discussion by first sorting out the terms, adopting clear definitions of the critical phenomena, and, when possible, attempting to talk about these phenomena in plain language accessible to the professional reader. In efforts that anticipate one of the main themes of his later work, Schafer takes pains to demystify the standard psychoanalytic formulation and get rid of the implicit anthropomorphism and demonology of the traditional metapsychology. By trying to bring the clinical phenomena out of the shadows and into the field of observation, Schafer is once again showing the respect for the data that characterized his earlier books on diagnostic testing and that would appear in his attention to observable behavior in his later book on action language (Schafer, 1976). Traditional metapsychology is seen to be the enemy of observation, not only because it structured the questions to be asked but also because it shifted the discussion away from the concrete "lurking presences" (in the case of internalization) to the abstract "cathected object representation." Some of this shift might be attributed to a fashionable distrust of Melanie Klein and her too vivid (and hence dubious) demonology; some might be due to a belief that a proper science should use Latin whenever possible, so that "cathected object" sounds more respectable than "lurking presence." Schafer is one of the first psychoanalytic writers since Freud to take the chance of being clear rather than sounding learned, one of the first to show a concern for language and a willingness to be open and forthright about experience. Theory is important, but not at the expense of the phenomena, and if these cannot be reliably described, defined, and contrasted with one another in a systematic manner, the theory will be a wasted enterprise, superficially impressive but at bottom meaningless.

Aspects of Internalization can be read on two, quite different levels. It is, first, an attempt to identify the phenomena of internalization, identification, introjection, and incorporation and to compare and contrast these clinical events. From the clinical descriptions a number of definitions are generated that lead, in turn, to a clarified theory. The examples are often strikingly specific and explicitly linked to theory; thus each section of the chapter on identification amplifies one part of the lengthy definition that is printed at the beginning of the chapter. Even the definitions are arresting, as in the following example:

> An introject is an inner presence with which one feels in a continuous or intermittent dynamic relationship. The subject conceives of this presence as a person, a physical or psychological part of a person (e.g., a breast, a voice, a look, an affect), or a person-like thing or creature. He experiences it as existing within the confines of his body or mind or both, but not as an aspect or expression of his subjective self. . . . The introject is experienced as capable of exerting a particular influence on the subject's state and behavior, and of doing so more or less independently of his conscious efforts to control it [Schafer, 1968, p. 72].

In order to explain what are often fleeting phenomena, rarely seen for any length of time, Schafer tries to place them in a more familiar context by beginning with experiences that are relatively commonplace. The daydream is one such starting point; from here, Schafer goes on to show how it may often imply a significant shift in reality testing, with the result that the subjective experience is taken as more real than otherwise. Under these conditions, the introject may come into existence as a piece of psychic reality. The role of introject is further broadened by using the model of projection. In this mode, the internalized object is not felt directly, but its influence is mediated by the significant people in one's life. As this projected role is amplified, the person "out there" disappears and his or her place is taken by the projected object (as in a paranoid system).

The main argument of *Aspects of Internalization* is to show how identification, introjection, and incorporation can each be understood as specific forms of internalization, with each form using a set number of mechanisms and appearing under certain specified conditions. To carry out this task, Schafer must necessarily rely more on subjective experience than theory, because the latter tends to be used inconsistently and often introduces more ambiguity than clarification. In his revised formulation, Schafer makes clear how the subtypes of internalization can be ordered along a primary-secondary process continuum, with incorporation being the most primitive, followed by introjection and then identification. Incorporation refers to the concrete representation of the longed-for object, often in an oral mode; at times it may take the form of a transitional object inside the head. Introjection is a more socialized and less regressive form of internalization – an introject, as noted in the definition earlier, refers to an inner presence that one feels and is influenced by. And finally, identification is the least regressive of the subtypes and the most abstract. One may identify with one's teacher even when not being aware of a conscious presence, and the source of the identification may not be discovered without a good deal of introspection. Not all incorporations are assembled into introjects and not all introjects are turned into identifications; nor is the sequence necessarily developmental or phase specific. There seems to be no need to first compose an introject before going on to form a stable identification, and many times an introject may appear only when identification begins to break down. Thus, the theory of internalization lacks the kind of tidiness and order that would lead to specific developmental or behavioral predictions, and the data are probably more interesting, in their various manifestations, than any kind of theoretical underpinning. Certainly, the more descriptive parts of *Aspects of Internalization* are more arresting than the theoretical conclusions and (at least to my ear) written with more excitement and urgency.

At a second level, *Aspects of Internalization* can be read as an outstanding demonstration of clear clinical description – a sample of exposition that, if successful, would encourage others to follow suit and think twice before using archaic terms or outdated concepts. By bringing the phenomena out of the shadows of metapsychology and by fashioning a set of contrasting definitions, Schafer is able to find many overlaps between the unusual and the commonplace. In so doing, he is able to sensitize his readers to aspects of internalization that they may experience all the time but are probably not able to label as such. In this branch of psychoanalysis particularly, the data of observation are difficult to identify because they tend to lie on the edges of awareness and are highly dependent on partially regressed stages of consciousness. It follows that to ask a patient directly about the presence of an internalized object is to often cause it to disappear, because the very fact of asking encourages and reinforces secondary-process modes of function. In contrast to the transitional object of the nursery, which we see the infant fondle, talk to, and take to bed, the felt presence of a dead father is never seen, rarely hallucinated, and only referred to indirectly and by implication. It thus becomes doubly significant, in mapping out this shadowy terrain, that the language of observation be used precisely and consistently, and it is in this regard that *Aspects of Internalization* stands head and shoulders above most of its competitors.

Despite its clear clinical examples and careful use of language, however, *Aspects of Internalization* failed to bring about a much-needed revision in the style and terms of psychoanalytic exposition. The attempt failed in part because the critique of metapsychology was relatively polite and low-key; more specific criticisms were needed, and they would not appear until Schafer's next book, *A New Language for Psychoanalysis* (1976). In addition, the needed stylistic changes were easily overlooked. Good exposition becomes transparent precisely because it offers no problem for comprehension; therefore, the lesson being learned, although doubtless appreciated at some level, may not be part of the reader's conscious experience and is thus quickly forgotten. Three years after Schafer had called attention to the demonology of traditional theory, we were again offered such phrases as: "the phase-appropriate internalization of those aspects of the oedipal objects that were cathected with object libido" (Kohut, 1971, p. 41), and "the internalization of the narcissistically invested aspects of the oedipal and pre-oedipal object takes place according to the same principle" (p. 48). Where is the patient in these descriptions? Where are the data? What country is being described and who are its inhabitants? Metalanguage had so screened off the data of interest from the reader that once again it had taken on a reality in its own right. Far from being the temporary scaffolding of Freud, ready to be dismantled when better models came along, it had acquired permanent status and seemed bent on edging out the clinical phenomena.

As language became less precise and more abstract, it more than ever began to corrupt observation and diminish the significance of the data. If we are on the lookout for "narcissistically invested aspects of the oedipal object," we will be seeing and understanding much less of the clinical encounter than if we are on the lookout for lurking presences of the absent father or other concrete manifestations of the different aspects of internalization. Given the fleeting nature of the data in the first place, their recognition is just about doomed by fuzzy language and pretentious concepts. The more rarefied the language, the greater room for argument and controversy.

It may be impossible to speak knowingly of cause and effect, but I suggest that the writings of Kohut and the advent of Kohutian forms of discourse prompted Schafer to be even more specific about the data of observation and to shift his focus from inside to outside the head. If the subtleties of the internalized object were lost in the new language of object relations, then the time seemed ripe to shift the argument to what could be seen—namely, actions—and to recast psychoanalytic theory in terms of what could be *looked at* and *pointed to*—namely, action language. If the outlines of the introject are always shifting and its location debatable, then we can bring it outside the head by calling thinking an instance of action (Schafer, 1976, p. 13). With action language firmly in charge, in Schafer's (1976) words, we "shall neither engage in speculation about what is ultimately unutterable in any form nor build elaborate theories on the basis of unfalsifiable propositions" (p. 10). (Schafer is talking about theories of mental activity at the beginning of infancy, but the same argument could be applied to a wide range of elusive phenomena, including the majority of the examples discussed in *Aspects of Internalization*.) Actions have the virtue of being more clearly visible and more clearly "out there" than feelings or thoughts, and there is a certain appeal to bringing all psychoanalytic phenomena out of the person and into the clear light of day. If we cannot speak with certainty about "where" we feel angry or know exactly what is meant by such expressions as "I am angry up to here," then there is a temptation to redefine emotion as action and simply say "he acted angrily." But a close reading of *Aspects of Internalization* makes it clear that the pieces of clinical reporting that ring so true and that carry so much clinical appeal in Schafer's earlier books are the very pieces that will be dismantled by a systematic translation into action language. In return for consensus and agreement, we seem to be in danger of trading away the very stuff of psychoanalysis. If psychic reality must be recast into action language to make it knowable, then we may have given away the very stuff of greatest interest to the practicing analyst. Gone forever—or at least radically transformed—would be the lurking presences, the vague demonic feelings, fleeting déjà vus, the sense of enthrallment to the past, and the awareness of the uncanny—the full range of subjective reports we have been hearing from patients over the past 100 years.

A positivistic bargain is being struck. If the vague sense of a lurking presence or a sadistic mother cannot be reliably defined and accounted for in terms of metapsychology—and the failure of metapsychology on this score seems obvious—and if attempts at clinical description that do justice to the data are more poetry than science, out of reach of all but the few, then it might still be possible to improve communication by *calling* the phenomena something else. If our terms are better chosen, perhaps some of our descriptive problems might be solved. What we lose with respect to the nuance and subtlety of observation may be more than offset by an increase in consensus and reliability. This approach seems laudable; but it betrays a concern for description and control that poses serious obstacles to its being accomplished, and its positivistic position may represent a fatal flaw. We have seen how asking questions of certain kinds of fleeting phenomena will cause them to disappear; it would seem to follow that the traditional subject-object separation cannot be applied to certain kinds of data and that other methods of study must be devised.

The problem is that the object to be described—for example, the longed-for absent father, the memory of an early girl friend, or the sense of the analyst as secretly sadistic and vengeful—is not the traditional object of study that can be set apart from the observer and studied in isolation. It is not an action that can be pointed at, not a thing that can be photographed; rather, it must necessarily be studied in context when and where we find it. It is this sensitivity to context and to the stream of experience that Schafer illustrated so well in *Aspects of Internalization*, and to which he returns in his most recent work on the concept of narrative (Schafer, 1983). But for a variety of reasons, he preferred to set it aside in *A New Language* and shift his focus to observable behavior.

The central theme is sounded in the first chapter (Schafer, 1976). After stating that "it is high time we stopped using this mixed physiocochemical and evolutionary biological language" (p. 3) of metapsychology, Schafer proposes the alternative of action language:

> We shall regard each psychological process, event, experience, or behavior as some kind of activity, henceforth to be called action, and shall designate each action by an active verb stating its nature and by an adverb (or adverbial locution), when applicable, stating the mode of this action. Adopting this rule entails that . . . we shall not use nouns and adjectives to refer to psychological processes, events, etc. . . .
>
> . . . We must understand the word action to include all private psychological activity that can be made public through gesture and speech, such as dreaming and the unspoken thinking of everyday life, as well as all initially public activity, such as ordinary speech and motoric behavior, that has some goal-directed or symbolic properties. . . . When speaking of any aspect of psychological activity or action, we shall no longer refer to location, movement, direction, sheer quantity, and the like, for these terms are suitable only for things and thinglike entities. . . . In order to state ob-

servations in a form suitable for systematic general propositions . . . we shall use only the active voice and constructions that clarify activity and modes of activity [pp. 9–11].

Here are some of Schafer's (1976) examples: Rather than say "What comes to mind?" the analyst using action language might say, "What do you think of in this connection?" (p. 148). Rather than say, "His repression of this dangerous impulse was too weak to prevent it from gaining consciousness," the action analyst might say, "By failing to be sufficiently on guard about not doing so, he thought consciously of the action he wished to perform and would have performed had he not deemed it too dangerous to do so" (p. 206). Instead of saying, "He can't control his sexual drive," the action analyst might say, "He continues to act sexually even though he also wishes he did not do so (or rebukes himself for doing so)" (pp. 207–208).

Speaking somewhat later in the book in a more general vein, Schafer (1976) argues that his aim is to eliminate the

unsuitable, confusing, unnecessary and meaningless metaphors and metaphorical preconceptions that are inherent in Freud's eclectic metapsychological language. In this endeavor I shall be building a technical language using plain English locutions. It is one that should make it possible to specify in a relatively unambiguous, consistent, parsimonious, and enlightening way the psychological facts and relations that are of special interest to psychoanalysts and their analysands" [p. 123].

A New Language for Psychoanalysis is divided into three main sections. In the first, "Preparatory Studies," Schafer presents some of the philosophical difficulties with traditional metapsychology and Freud's unsatisfactory solutions to what Ryle has called the "ghost in the machine." Schafer focuses in particular on the problem of the disappearing person and on the fact that metapsychology has no place for the "I" or agent. A brief discussion of some alternatives (Hartmann's adaptive ego, Erikson's concept of identity, and Kohut's narcissistic self) finds them each unsuccessful to some degree; what Schafer calls the "mover of the mental apparatus" remains clouded behind a screen of theory. Action language is presented as a possible solution to a long-standing theoretical gap. By using what Schafer calls the "native tongue of psychoanalysis," we should be able to catch sight of the disappearing person.

The second section describes action language, illustrating how it might be applied to a number of clinical situations and how it clarifies such problems as internalization and resistance and the understanding of such disclaimed actions as slips of the tongue, motivated forgetting, and so forth. The third section applies action language to emotion by translating noun into verb or adverb. (Instead of saying, "I am happy about my recent promotion" I might better say, "I view my recent promotion happily".) This section presents many examples of how common language is heavily dependent on metaphor and how metaphor can be misleading and lead to bad theory. Schafer makes clear how it has invaded metapsychology.

One problem is apparent from the outset. In an effort to divorce himself from the traditional Freudian metaphor, Schafer must also cut himself off from popular speech and from the way we have grown up thinking about our body and our feelings. For example, the use of location to express altered states (as in, "I must have been out of my mind") is a tradition beginning long before Freud. In an effort to speak unambiguously about important issues, action language may do quite the opposite and make them seem strange and foreign because they are being described in unfamiliar language. This dislocation becomes most apparent when dealing with the lurking presences and other vague experiences so well described in *Aspects of Internalization,* because these represent actions only in the weakest sense of the word; to describe them in action language risks turning them into unfamiliar specimens.

As Meissner (1979) has argued in his recent critique, metaphor is meant to be taken metaphorically: "I would have to wonder whether Schafer's approach to such language is entirely too literal and fails to take into account the significance of figures of speech. ... I am not arguing here that such propositions cannot be interpreted in the sense that Schafer gives to them.... The issue that I am addressing ... is that such expressions do not necessarily connote that [literal] meaning" (p. 293). Metaphor can be misleading if taken literally; on the other hand, if taken poetically it can capture an important truth about ways of thinking and feeling that we all share and on which theory must build. Metaphor may be particularly useful in at least two contexts: in the generation of new theory where we need tentative formulation (Freud's comments on temporary conventions come to mind), and in the dialogue with the patient, where we are attempting to capture a vague experience for the first time. To insist on action language when the patient is fumbling for the best expression may often inhibit the discovery process that psychoanalysis tries so hard to foster. To insist on action language while building theory may unnecessarily restrict the scope of the enterprise by limiting our attention to phenomena that can be clearly described.

Schafer was particularly impressed by the way in which language in general and the passive voice in particular can be used in the service of resistance, and one of the most original chapters in *A New Language for Psychoanalysis* is titled "Claimed and Disclaimed Action." Language is easily used to project ideas of helplessness and disclaimed responsibility, as in "the impulse seized me," "my conscience torments me," "this hour just rushed by," and "doubts creep into my mind." In each of these cases, metaphor becomes defense because the patient is acting *as if* things just happened to him or her rather than the patient causing them to happen. But the metaphor can be heard on two levels. To hear it as a metaphor is to give the patient credit for using it in a figurative sense, saying something like, "my conscience torments me – so to speak," which opens the way to analyzing the defense. To hear it as a literal statement of the patient's view of life, on the other hand, is to run the risk of challenging the patient who is following the basic rule and saying what comes to mind. Thus, to treat speech in the literal way that Schafer suggests is to seriously complicate the analytic relationship by saying to the patient, in effect, "You must say whatever comes to mind but you will be held responsible for each and every word." As I have written elsewhere (Spence, 1982): "To call attention to instances of disclaimed action would seem to imply to the patient that he is really not free to say whatever comes to mind but that, in a subtle and all-embracing way, he is being held responsible for his thoughts and – what is more – being held responsible by the analyst. Thus one could argue that the adoption of action language may seriously jeopardize the analytic contract" (p. 171).

Now, it is certainly basic to psychoanalysis to assume as Schafer (1976) does, that the patient "actively brings about that from which he or she neurotically suffers" (p. 145), and some of Schafer's most telling anecdotes describe ways in which passive victims are led to see that they have been all the while secretly arranging their misfortune. But should these accounts of disclaimed responsibility be analyzed in the traditional manner of gradual interpretation and working through, or by a specific focus on the patient's words guided by the belief that each psychological event, process, experience, or behavior is some kind of action? The emphasis on the right and wrong way of saying things (what Anscombe, 1981, calls "linguistic legislation") would seem to raise serious questions as to whether associations can truly be free, whether tentative formulations are open to dispassionate study, and whether the patient and analyst are collaborating in a mutual enterprise of trust and discovery or one in which the patient is always put in an adversary position. Even though Schafer has intended his new language to be a replacement for metapsychology and not a recipe for how to practice psychoanalysis, it is inevitable that sensitivity to issues of avoiding and claiming responsibility would necessarily have an effect on treatment (see Spence, 1982).

By focusing on action and activity, on visible over invisible, and on clearly stated rather than roughly approximated, Schafer inevitably turns from id to ego and, in so doing, raises serious questions about the central standing of the unconscious. And yet, here is where psychoanalysis begins its quest and acquires its distinctive character. As Meissner (1979) writes:

> If the patient comes to the analysis bearing a burden of unconscious conflicts and resistances, hidden motives and significances embedded in his current and past life experience, it is that with which the analyst must work. If these aspects of the patient's experience are experienced somehow passively – granted that they may involve the disclaiming action that Schafer describes – the analyst must begin by accepting that passivity and that condition of disclaimed action and engage the patient in a process which draws him towards a lessening of resistance, an increasing availability to conscious exploration of unconscious motives, meanings, and conflicts, and thus gradually lead the analysand in the direction of a more action-based orientation. In other words, psychoanalytic theory needs to be *a theory of non-action*. [p. 306; italics added].

If we follow Meissner and claim that psychoanalysis is a theory (and even more, a practice) of nonaction, we begin to see why Schafer's proposals seem to generate such controversy. And it may also offer a clue to one of the troubling characteristics of metapsychology – the fact that the person disappears in a field of force and a network of hypothetical structures. We have seen that one of the main goals of *A New Language for Psychoanalysis* was to make the patient visible again, and it was this concern that led to the stress on action and responsibility and the concept of human agency. But it may be that only by making the person inactive and not responsible (as in the classic treatment situation) can we ever discover the deeper reasons for that individual's hopes and fears. And it may be that only by creating a theory which is explicitly *not* about the person as conscious agent can we begin to generate a suitable context of explanation.

By putting the stress on the patient as agent, Schafer has necessarily weakened our sense of psychic reality and its fleeting phenomena. One sense of the loss comes out in comparing *Aspects of Internalization* with the chapter on internalization in a *A New Language for Psychoanalysis*. In the former, psychic reality was described with a dramatic richness of language that seems almost poetic; in the latter, the descriptions are more prosaic and less familiar. "It is our custom," writes Schafer in *A New Language for Psychoanalysis* (1976), "to speak of introjects as though they were angels and demons with minds and powers of their own. We speak of them not as an analysand's construction and description of experience but as unqualified facts. . . . We forget . . . that the introject can have no powers or motives of its own, and no perceptual and judgmental functions, except as, like a dream figure, it has these properties archaically ascribed to it by the imagining subject" (p. 163). In other words, the ascribing should be taken as a form of action, and its products become the responsibility of the patient. But this renaming tends to decrease the extent to which the analyst can empathize with the patient's experience, making the analyst less sensitive to just how haunting the presence may feel. And to say that the patient is only ascribing these properties does not lessen their impact, just as calling transference reaction unreal does not make it disappear. Here is an instance in which the sense of an introject as angel or demon captures an important part of the experience; it represents a piece of clinical data that we lose by turning to action language. And to the extent that the translation does not match the patient's experience, we run the risk of increased misunderstanding and losing touch with the data.

Schafer hoped that action language would replace metapsychology; we now begin to see reasons why this will not happen. Not only does it fail to capture the richness of the clinical data; it also fails as an explanation. Although, as we have seen, it is not close enough to inner experience to give a sense of familiarity and recognition, it is ironically too close to provide a suitable explanation. This failure comes about because the person as agent represents only the conscious part of the psychoanalytic domain. To use action terms to generate a general theory is something like trying to explain what happens inside the atom by studying the psychology of the nuclear freeze movement. The failure of Schafer's alternative makes us realize the need for some kind of abstract system that describes experience but is not cast in the terms of experience, much as the theory of color vision describes a common happening but is framed in terms of frequencies rather than perceived hues.[1]

What needs to be kept in mind is Freud's observation that the explanatory system is only temporary and will undoubtedly be revised as new facts are discovered. As a provisional model, it is clearly not meant to be taken literally; it is only the metaphor for the moment and useful only as it seems to provide explanation. But it must also preserve a certain distance from the phenomena to be explained, and we now begin to see that the problem of the disappearing patient may have been a sign that Freud was on the right track. Although terms like "force" and "direction" may seem too crudely mechanistic, they have the advantage of being psychologically neutral — a key requirement for any general theory. To frame the model in terms of subjective impressions (as in self psy-

---

[1]The problems of focusing on the person as agent are further demonstrated by a look at the object school of Kohut and his associates. Depending on subjective reports to generate the units of our theory puts us at the mercy of unreliable witnesses and invisible data; once we move inside the head, we have given up any hope of consensus or external validation.

chology) is to rule out the possibility of making any kind of meaningful discovery about the mind, because it rules out any investigation in the unconscious.

How then can we summarize the impact of Schafer's revisionary program? Beginning with the distaste for metapsychology and its crude physics of force and mechanism, *A New Language for Psychoanalysis* held out the hope of returning to the data of behavior and to the "native tongue of psychoanalysis"–action language. Although at times cumbersome to apply and not suited to everyone's tastes, in other contexts it helped us think more carefully about clinical facts, sensitizing us to certain locutions and letting us see farther into the everyday language of the analytic hour. Certain kinds of expressions (in particular, the references to disclaimed action) were being heard for almost the first time and in a rather new way. By showing us what new meanings could be uncovered that were not anticipated by Freud, Schafer paved the way for new ways of reading the text of the hour and opened the door to new ways of listening.

But there were difficulties with the new language as well, and in many ways, it did not behave like a long-lost native tongue (see Schafer, 1976, p. 362). To translate anger into "acting angrily" or resistance into "engaging in actions contrary to analysis while also engaging in analysis itself" (p. 224) is to complicate rather than clarify, and some would argue that the meaning lost in going to action language is every bit as great as the meaning lost in going to metapsychology. And the translations are not always transparent. *A New Language for Psychoanalysis* tends to read as if observations were there for the making; we now realize that all observation is theory laden and that Schafer's native tongue is no exception. Action language, because it deemphasizes unconscious and passive experience and emphasizes responsibility and conscious choice, carries significant implications for the process of treatment. Many of these implications are not explicit, and some of the criticisms of Schafer may stem from private readings of the words "active" and "passive," readings that he never intended but that his program must accommodate.

In certain respects, the most significant impact of *A New Language for Psychoanalysis* has been to whet our appetite for a general theory. The difficulties in dealing with the unconscious and with affect in action language would seem to suggest that some kind of abstract metatheory is a necessary next step. It is also clear that this metatheory cannot be written in the units of everyday experience. Since action belongs to a relatively restricted domain of behavior, a good part of our emotional and unconscious life simply cannot be expressed properly in these terms (the chapters on emotions are the least convincing of the book). The ground where we choose to build our theory must be equidistant from both ego and id, from conscious and preconscious, from past and present; and the units of this theory must lend themselves to translation into clinical concepts (and vice versa) with no significant loss of meaning.

Even though action language has been found wanting, the discussions around it have opened up central issues that are basic to the future of psychoanalysis. By identifying certain kinds of expressions that appear in the patient's language and by showing how they may carry certain implications for the treatment, *A New Language for Psychoanalysis* has significantly increased what might be called our sensitivity to surfaces. By calling attention to the way in which patients use and hide behind language and by hearing literally (and often for the first time) certain stock expressions of the trade, action language has increased our ability to listen carefully. In this respect, it belongs to a well-founded analytic tradition. Schafer's attention to the data of the consulting room is consistent with his earlier books on testing and their emphasis on verbatim protocols. The emphasis on language and the text of the analytic hour puts the focus on units that can be studied, measured, and stored. Even though they are clearly not the whole story (see Spence, 1981), they are clearly data that cannot be ignored.

What, finally, is the status of Schafer's "linguistic legislation"? The current interest in how patients and analysts really speak may have produced a significant and humbling change in our attitude toward the actual data. Schafer took the position that sloppy language leads to sloppy thinking (a direct outgrowth of the Wittgenstein school) and that by cleaning up the way we (patients and analysts) speak about ourselves and our feelings, we can gain greater precision and build better theory. But it is now becoming apparent that the language contains its own wisdom and that careful attention to the native tongue of metaphor and common speech may teach us important things about the clinical encounter, things we can learn in no other way. The close look taken by Dahl and his colleagues (Dahl, Teller, Moss, & Trujillo, 1978) at the way analysts really speak and the coding scheme developed by Gill and Hoffman (1982) to analyze the appearance and intepretation of pieces of the transference are efforts in this direction. As computer procedures come into play and allow us to store and retrieve vast files of patients' speech, we may discover regularities that we never knew existed. Thus, metaphor may not only be used in the service of resistance, as Schafer has pointed out, but subtle shifts in wording may signal subtle shifts in defense. If analysts are educated about such shifts, they will be able to deepen their awareness of the meaning of the hour and improve the timing of their interpretations.

In Schafer's most recent book, *The Analytic Attitude* (1983), he has turned back to more classical times. Although there are occasional pieces on action language, the overall tone seems more conservative and closer to Freud. Even the chapters on narration and the discussion of the patient as a teller of stories seem to be making manifest what was latent in Freud's approach. In one section, for example, Schafer tells us that "Freud used two primary narrative structures, and he often urged that they be taken as provisional rather than as final truths" (p. 213).

The analytic attitude as seen by Schafer can be characterized as one of empathy and trust, which generates an atmosphere of safety. There are many technical ways of achieving this atmosphere, some of which Schafer discusses at length, but the theoretical advantages are also emphasized and clarified. Only by fostering an atmosphere of safety (see Schafer, 1983, chapter 2) can the analyst create the conditions for both the identification of resistance and its dissolution; for understanding the patient's story in all of its complexity; and for seeing clearly the transference and how it changes over time. Safety permits the patient to show himself or herself in all aspects—naked and clothed, present and past, angry and happy. Safety is central because discovery is seen as the key to treatment: "The appropriate analytic attitude is one of *finding out* . . . what the analysis itself will be or be concerned with; where the principal work will be done; . . . how this work will best be done; . . . and how to establish a termination of the analysis" (Schafer, 1983, p. 21).

Neutrality becomes a central part of the atmosphere of safety. The ideal analyst should be curious and open to surprise. Schafer (1983) says the analyst should take "nothing for granted (without being cynical about it) and [remain] ready to revise conjectures or conclusions already arrived at [and] tolerate ambiguity or incomplete closure over extended periods of time . . ." (p. 7). The avoidance of either-or thinking is another aspect of this neutrality and has an obvious relation to the construction of multiple histories (Schafer, 1983, chapter 13) and to the tolerance of different schools of treatment (see chapter 17, "On Becoming a Psychoanalyst of One Persuasion or Another").

What is less emphasized in this picture is the influence of what might be called the analyst's world view. Analysts come to their task from a special background of training and experience; as a result, they hear the material from within a certain context. Many descriptive terms have already acquired specific meanings, and as a result, the analyst will inevitably form images of the significant figures in the patient's life— images determined by a turn of phrase that the analyst finds familiar or influenced by reference to a particular piece of history with which the analyst has personal associations. Once formed, these images tend to persist, and though they may be sensed as incomplete, they are less often sensed as wrong, waiting to be corrected. Moreover, correction can never be fully realized because one of the more effective corrections—a face-to-face meeting with the person in question—will probably never happen. Although it is certainly true that analysts should remain always ready to revise their conclusions, Schafer seems to underestimate the difficulties of this task. No one would disagree with the importance of neutrality and empathy and open-mindedness, but more attention could be paid to the technical and philosophical problems entailed in this quest.

Schafer's picture of the neutral analyst tends to overlook the fact that all observations are theory laden and that certain kinds of material can *only* be understood by first forming a provisional model. There seems to be a contradiction between neutrality and forming a provisional hypothesis. True enough, as Schafer says (1983) the "simplistic, partisan analyst, working in terms of saints and sinners, victims and victimizers, or good and bad ways to live" (p. 5) is clearly shortchanging the patient; on the other hand, provisional models are always needed to provide a context for isolated impressions and to suggest areas that still wait to be discovered. The determining role of the primal scene is one such model; the possibility of such exposure and its impact on the patient, both immediate and delayed, is a constant concern of many analysts. In similar fashion, when working with a patient who is the oldest child they will be sensitized to such events as the birth of the second child and be constantly on the alert for its derivatives.

The use of provisional models can be witting or unwitting. If it is too much of the second we may speak of countertransference; If too much of the first, of failure of empathy (as in the cool, detached analyst who is always forming hypotheses and "testing" them against the "data"). What is less well understood is that much of psychoanalytic theory is still provisional; that assumptions about primal scene exposure or sibling rivalry represent one class of hypotheses that may not be confirmed and need to be replaced by others. Thus, one of the common violations of neutrality stems from an overcommitment to theory and an emphasis on certain parts of the received wisdom.

The issue of alternative explanations is taken up at length in *The Analytic Attitude* chapter on multiple histories, and a number of different models are developed and discussed in the subsequent chapters on "Narration in the Psychoanalytic Dialogue," "Action and Narration in Psychoanalysis," and "The Imprisoned Analysand." Analysis as journey is one example, as Schafer (1983) makes clear (with references to the *Odyssey*, the *Divine Comedy, Huckleberry Finn,* and *Ulysses*): "The journey is one of the world's great storylines. . . . We know that in the dreams of analysands all journeys are, among other things, trips through transference country" (p. 259). Using this model helps the analyst to decode certain kinds of dream material and to understand the emergence of certain kinds of childhood memories—travel *then* may be related in subtle ways to travel *now*. Another model, developed at length in Chapter 16, is the model of analysis as prison. Schafer develops with great sensitivity the positive and negative aspects of this storyline. The happy prison and the safety of closed places may be seen as an ironic extension of Schafer's earlier emphasis on the importance of safety in the analytic attitude; under certain circumstances, the analysis becomes too safe and threatens to become interminable. The prison model has obvious links with the use of passivity as defense and resistance, two of the major themes in *A New Language for Psychoanalysis*. And from another point of view, the model of the happy prison (safe, but going nowhere) is the complement of the journey of discovery in which each day brings new adventure and a new outlook.[2]

Where does the narrative come from? In the last part of the chapter on "The Imprisoned Analysand," Schafer (1983) begins to explore this question with the provisional suggestion that the story is developed jointly by both parties: "By this I do not mean that they have developed it in a happy collaboration; I mean rather that each has made a contribution, often of different sorts, at different times, and with different degrees of awareness, reflectiveness, and conflictedness" (p. 278). How does this mesh with neutrality? It is becoming clear, as Schafer goes on to point out, that the story is not simply being uncovered. This follows from the fact that multiple narratives can be constructed and that several different models can account for the same pieces of clinical material. Good analysts seem to work within the hermeneutic circle, using a provisional model (what the European philosopher Hans–Georg Gadamer would call "fore-understanding") to build a scaffolding to support the early data, taking subsequent data to reframe and extend (or dismantle) the scaffolding, and using the revised framework to see further into the patient's story and to discover new pieces of information.

Thus, neutrality would seem to consist in the ability to be sensitive to new narratives (new scaffoldings) as they emerge in the material and as they suggest themselves during the analysis, *not* in the absence of models. The analytic attitude becomes a deepened awareness of possible storylines. We can no longer go back to the myth of the analyst as blank screen who evenly registers all information by giving equal weight to each new item; if this is neutrality, it is as outmoded as the Monroe Doctrine. At the same time, as the analyst appears less neutral than we once assumed, it becomess increasingly urgent that we develop a neutral

---

[2]Not to be overlooked is the model that assumes that the narrative lies in the clinical material, waiting only to be "discovered." Freud took some pains to emphasize this model of analyst as archaeologist in order to counter charges of suggestion and influence, and it has come down to us as part of the received wisdom. One of the implicit themes of *The Analytic Attitude* is that this model is probably wrong.

metatheory – a theory that can handle all possible narratives and provide a framework for all clinical observations. Thus, the focus shifts from the neutral analyst (an impossibility) to a neutral theory, and it is in this domain that we may look for Schafer's contributions in the years to come.

In coming back to the complexities of the analytic attitude and in trying to go beneath the surface of the experience, Schafer has returned to the poetic strains of *Aspects of Internalization* and its respect for the clinical phenomena. His tone seems more mellow and less didactic. Gone are the legislative turns of phrase that marred many portions of *A New Language for Psychoanalysis*, and the reader feels a greater familiarity with the people and the landscape being described. Ambiguity seems less an obstacle to understanding (recall the criticism of metaphor in *A New Language for Psychoanalysis*) and more a potential source of wisdom (as in the idea of multiple histories). Schafer seems more willing to take the patient's story at its own words and to treat it with the same kind of respect we show a text. The impatience with bad usage or faulty observation that ran through much of *A New Language for Psychoanalysis* has been replaced by the respect for the clinical happening that came out so clearly in *Aspects of Internalization*.

In developing the importance of psychoanalysis as narrative, Schafer (1983) underlines the importance of the tale and of how it is told; the importance of context and structure over isolated fact; and the variety of ways in which a life can be presented and understood. "The truth of a psychoanalytic fact," he writes, "resides ultimately in the way it fits into the system of interpretation within which it and its significance have been defined" (p. 277). To emphasize the relational nature of truth is to push back the Ice Age of Positivism and to argue against the traditional subject-object separation of Big Science. The patient's history is no longer an object of study like a bluebird or a molecule, but a constantly changing story that the patient is writing and rewriting, together with the analyst, inside and outside the analytic hour. We are just beginning to listen.

REFERENCES

Anscombe, R. (1981). Referring to the unconscious: A philosophical critique of Schafer's action language. *International Journal of Psycho-Analysis, 62,* 225–241.

Dahl, H., Teller, V., Moss, D., & Trujillo, M. (1978). Countertransference examples of the syntactic expression of warded-off contents. *Psychoanalytic Quarterly, 47,* 339–363.

Freud, S. (1912). Recommendations to physicians practicing psychoanalysis. *Standard Edition, 12,* 111–120.

Freud, S. (1915). Instincts and their vicissitudes. *Standard Edition, 14,* 117–140.

Gill, M. M., & Hoffman, I. Z. (1982). A method for studying the analysis of aspects of the patient's experience of the relationship in psychoanalysis and psychotherapy. *Journal of the American Psychoanalytic Association, 30,* 137–167.

Jacobsen, P. E., & Steele, R. S. (1979). From present to past: Freudian archeology. *International Review of Psychoanalysis, 6,* 349–362.

Kohut, H. (1971). *The analysis of the self.* New York: International Universities Press.

Kohut, H. (1979). The two analyses of Mr. Z. *International Journal of Psycho-Analysis, 60,* 3–27.

Meissner, W. W. (1979). Critique of concepts and therapy in the action language approach to psychoanalysis. *International Journal of Psycho-Analysis, 60,* 291–310.

Rapaport, D., Gill, M. M., & Schafer, R. (1945–46). *Diagnostic psychological testing* (2 vols.). Chicago: Year Book Publishers.

Schafer, R. (1948). *The clinical application of psychological tests.* New York: International Universities Press.

Schafer, R. (1954). *Psychoanalytic interpretation in Rorschach testing.* New York: Grune & Stratton.

Schafer, R. (1968). *Aspects of internalization.* New York: International Universities Press.

Schafer, R. (1976). *A new language for psychoanalysis.* New Haven: Yale University Press.

Schafer, R. (1983). *The analytic attitude.* New York: Basic Books.

Spence, D. P. (1981). Psychoanalytic competence. *International Journal of Psycho-Analysis, 62,* 113–124.

Spence, D. P. (1982). On some clinical implications of action language. *Journal of the American Psychoanalytic Association, 30,* 169–184.

Benjamin B. Rubinstein: Contributions to the Structure of Psychoanalytic Theory

4

Morris N. Eagle, Ph.D.

Most of the analysts and theorists included in this volume have attempted to add to psychoanalytic theory by developing their own clinical and theoretical formulations. This sort of endeavor is visible and often even produces adherents and disciples. A few theorists contribute by attempting to clarify the basic structure of psychoanalytic theory. Because they work quietly and do not often generate the kind of stir that creates followers, it is all too easy to overlook their contributions. A strength of this volume is that it recognizes the important contributions of one such theorist, Benjamin B. Rubinstein.

In his writings, Rubinstein is essentially a philosopher of psychoanalysis. But this simple statement does not really capture the nature and quality of his work. Rubinstein is an analyst with many years of clinical experience, and his work on the conceptual status of psychoanalysis is written, so to speak, from the inside. The basic questions he poses are questions that arise in the course of clinical work (and that most of us slough over and ignore). But what he brings to this probing is a remarkable and sophisticated philosophical knowledge and style of thinking. After coming to the United States from Finland, through the efforts of David Rapaport, Rubinstein, as Holt (1967) notes, "made himself into one of the few persons who know as well as Rapaport did the divergent literatures of psychoanalysis and the philosophy of science" (p. 18). He also brings to his task an intellectual honesty and conceptual clarity that is unsurpassed by any work in this area. In this paper I will discuss both Rubinstein's specific ideas and some general issues which these ideas generate, beginning with a brief attempt to place Rubinstein's work in a wider historical and intellectual context.

Broadly speaking, modern efforts to explain human behavior and distinctively human features (such as consciousness and mentation) have taken one of two philosophical directions. One approach is to view human beings as nothing but mechanism, as essentially sophisticated machines. A clear and classical expression of this position is La Mettrie's (1912) *Man a Machine*. A more sophisticated and biological version of this view is Huxley's epiphenomenalistic view of consciousness, as expressed in the title of his 1874 paper, "On the Hypothesis that Animals are Automata." According to this conception, states of consciousness and presumably other psychological phenomena are no more than effects of bodily processes. As Huxley stated it: "The mind stands related to the body as the bell of the clock to the works..." (see Edwards, p. 103). What follows from La Mettrie's and Huxley's general philosophical position is that explanations of human behavior are, in principle, not essentially different from explanations of physical and chemical phenomena.

An alternative approach is that accounts of human behavior require special explanatory methods and principles. The neo-Kantian distinction between *Geissteswissenschaften* and *Naturwissenschaften* and the emphasis associated with Dilthey (1961) on *Verstehen* as the appropriate method for the study of human phenomena are the prime historical examples of this approach. Recent emphasis on empathy as the distinctive data-gathering method for psychoanalysis (e.g., Kohut, 1959, 1977) and on the so-called clinical theory of psychoanalysis (e.g., Klein, 1976) as well as recent attempts to conceptualize psychoanalysis as a hermeneutic discipline (e.g., Habermas, 1971, 1979; Ricoeur, 1970, 1977; Schafer, 1976; see also Grünbaum, 1983, for a superb critique of this point of view) can be seen as contemporary expressions of Dilthey's neo-Kantian program.[1]

In contrast to the above views in which human beings are seen as *either* nothing but mechanism *or* immune from laws of nature is recognition that we are from one perspective persons and from another, organisms. This ontological insight permits Rubinstein to reject a dichotomous either-or approach to explanations of human behavior. Instead, it leads him to accept the complementarity of explanation by way of meanings and causes (which parallels the basic complementarity of person and organism) and to recognize the complex inter dependence between the so-called clinical theory and metaphyschology of psycho-

---

[1]Within philosophy, certain formulations concerning the nature of human action and its claimed lack of susceptibility to causal explanation also seem to me to be contemporary expressions of this program (see for example, the work of Abelson, 1977; Louch, 1966; Taylor, 1964). One also sees in Schafer's (1976) work – in the very notion of "action language" – the influence of these philosophers of action on a conception of psychoanalysis.

analysis. In recognizing this duality, Rubinstein has preserved one of Freud's core insights and one of the primary sources of creative tensions within psychoanalysis (see Holt, 1972, for a discussion of Freud's two images of humankind).

Rubinstein's writings and contributions cover a wide range. They include a conceptual analysis of psychoanalytic ideas such as unconscious mental events and defense; an elucidation of the nature of clinical inferences in psychoanalysis; the developement of a model of mental functioning that is compatible with both psychoanalytic accounts and neurophysiology; lucid discussions of the mind-body problem and how it relates to psychoanalytic theory; and a beautiful explication of the nature of metaphor and related phenomena and their relationship to certain psychoanalytic issues. (Rubinstein's 1972 paper on metaphor in particular is a wonderful combination of clarity of analysis and exquisite sensitivity to poetic and literary nuances.) In all these areas, Rubinstein substitutes for casual use of psychoanalytic concepts careful and detailed examination. For example, the notion of unconscious mental events is utilized in a casual fashion in the psychoanalytic literature without any apparent recognition of its ambiguity or the conceptual difficulties it entails. Similarly, psychoanlytic interpretations and inferences are typically made in the course of clinical work and in case history descriptions without any systematic attention to the nature of the evidence on which they rest or to their epistemic and explanatory status. Rubinstein's rare armamentarium of extensive psychoanalytic clinical experience, a thorough and deep knowledge of the psychoanalytic literature, and a high degree of philosophical sophistication permits him to subject such psychoanalytic concepts and methodology to careful conceptual analysis.

Since Rubinstein's work is so rich and complex, I can deal only with limited aspects of his work here. I will begin with a brief discussion of his demonstration of the dependence of the clinical theory for its validation on some form of metapsychology, or extraclinical theory (a term Rubinstein prefers because it avoids confusion with Freud's metapsychology). Rubinstein (1967) has shown that what he refers to as "general clinical hypotheses"—the hypotheses of "partial functional equivalence" or of "the persistent manifestation potential of unconscious motives" (Rubinstein, 1975, p. 13), for example—function as axiomatic assumptions in the formulation of specific interpretations and clinical hypotheses in a particular case. Thus, although we may infer unconscious motives in particular cases, we can "confirm their presence *only* if we presuppose the actual occurrence of processes by which the unconscious motives in question, if in fact present, have been rendered unconscious and being unconscious, are expressed in various, mostly indirect ways" (Rubinstein, 1980b, p. 13). But, Rubinstein also (1980a) notes, "the occurrence of these processes cannot be confirmed clinically" (p. 435). It is the *assumption* of their occurrence that permits the particular clinical inference. To confirm the existence of these processes requires the analyst to step out of the clinical context and look to nonclinical, including neurophysiological, evidence.

Consider another example of the dependence of clinical formulations on some form of metapsychology. We are justified, Rubinstein observes, in considering parapraxes and symptoms as motivated and in considering certain behaviors as substitute fulfillments because of the assumptions of persistent manifestation potential and of partial functional equivalence (including symbolic equivalence) among different behaviors. Now, there is simply no way one could ever confirm the hypothesis of persistent manifestation potential of unconscious motives solely on the basis of clinical data. Such a general assumption clearly requires nonclinical evidence for its confirmation.

This demonstration of the dependence of the clinical inferences and formulations on extraclinical theory indicates quite clearly the limitations, even the futility, of recent related attempts to define psychoanalysis solely in terms of its so-called clinical theory (e.g., Home, Klein, 1976; 1966; Shafer, 1976) and to conceptualize it as a hermeneutic discipline concerned only with interpretation and meaning.

Defining psychoanalysis as a hermeneutic discipline seems to represent, in part, an attempt to avoid the challenge of how to test and confirm the clinical inferences and interpretations the analyst regularly employs in clinical work. If psychoanalysis is only a hermeneutic activity, one need merely view clinical interpretations as "narratives" and "stories." What Rubinstein has shown, however, is that these interpretations are not "merely" stories, but are based on extraclinical axiomatic assumptions. If follows that the validity of these inferences and interpretations ultimately can be tested only if one steps outside the clinical context. The only self-sufficient clinical theory that can be developed is one which accepts that its clinical inferences and interpretations will remain untested and unconfirmed. The conceptualization of psychoanalysis as a hermeneutic discipline, limited only to "narratives," "stories," and other constructions seems to reflect an acceptance of this fate, insofar as it fails to come to grips with and brushes aside the question of the validity of clinical inferences.

One can attempt to dispense altogether with issues of validity and verdicality by limiting one's concerns to therapeutic effectiveness, taking the position that all that one claims for one's interpretations is that they provide the patient with a new, more helpful, and more constructive perspective on life. This position, stated explicitly or implicitly, is increasingly frequent these days. In its extreme relativism and utter dismissal of issues of validity and truth value, this position seems to run counter to the central values and outlook that inform Rubinstein's work. It also runs counter to the central psychoanalytic tenet that in the final analysis (no double entendre intended), the truth is liberating. Freud (1917) explicitly stated his belief that only interpretations that "tally with what is real" will be therapeutic. Although this may or may not be true, the question is central in the psychoanalytic outlook. When psychoanalysis is defined as a hermeneutic discipline, the question is, so to speak, legislated out of existence. As I have argued elsewhere (Eagle, 1980), most, if not all, patients who come for psychoanalytic treatment implicitly and explicitly expect, that they will learn the truth about themselves, not that they will be provided with "narratives" and "stories," however helpful they may be. And I strongly suspect that most psychoanalytically oriented therapists, whatever their philosophical position, believe that while they are doing clinical work they are helping their patients learn important truths about themselves rather than simply presenting helpful "stories." Indeed, I doubt that therapists who believe in presenting "stories" can be maximally effective.

Whatever patients and therapists believe, however, the claim that psychoanalytically inspired "stories" or "narratives" are therapeutic is (1) simply an assumption, and (2) itself a truth claim—it asserts that the proposition, "Stories or narratives constructed in the course of psychoanalytic therapy are therapeutic in such and such ways," is true. Attempts to validate or confirm this truth claim take one outside the boundaries of hermeneutics, just as, Rubinstein has shown, attempts to validate or confirm clinical inferences and interpretations take one outside the clinical theory as commonly understood. Furthermore, talk about new perspectives and liberating "narratives" takes place without any reference to systematic and controlled outcome studies that would give substance to at least the therapeutic claims made for these interpretive narratives.

Common to recent attempts to define psychoanalysis as a hermeneutic discipline, to the claimed independence of the clinical from the extraclinical theory, and to the failure to seriously consider, let alone implement, more systematic efforts to gauge outcome of treatment, is an implicit insistence on the self-sufficiency and autonomy of the clinical enterprise—as if this enterprise could somehow escape or is immune to issues of accountability on both the epistemological level of validation of clinical hypotheses and the pragmatic level of effects of treatment. These are disturbing developments, isolating and solipsistic in their effects. It is as if the response to the difficult and seemingly insoluble problems of validation of interpretations and clear determination of outcome is to declare them irrelevant and to aggressively hail the independent legitimacy of the clinical enterprise itself. This defiant proclamation of self-sufficiency seems to mask an underlying despair of being able to deal effectively with the complex problems generated by the clinical enterprise. In contrast to this position, Rubinstein has through the years doggedly attempted to unravel and reveal to us the inherent logic of clinical inferences and clinical hypotheses and the evidence and assumptions on which they rest (see, for example, Rubinstein, 1975).

Ironically enough, Rubinstein's (1975) description and defense of the clinical theory in psychoanalysis is more systematic and complete than that of those who argue for the self-sufficiency of the clinical theory. He demonstrates that it is at least possible to lend additional credence to both the general and the specific clinical hypotheses of psychoanalytic theory. In addition, his discussion of Popper's falsifiability in the context of confirmation of clinical hypotheses is a gem of lucidity and simple ingenuity, worth describing briefly. Popper (1962) argues against the scientific respectability of psychoanalytic theory by maintaining that it is "simply non-testable, irrefutable" (p. 37). According to Popper, only refutability rather than confirmation are tests of scientificity because "it is easy to obtain confirmations, or verifications, for nearly every theory – if we look for confirmations" (p. 36). Rubinstein shows that this argument can be turned into a defense of confirmation in the following simple and elegant way: The hypothesis (c) "He has an unconscious wish for A," although not falsified by the hypothesis (d) "He has an unconscious wish for non-A," *is* falsified by the hypothesis (e) "He does not have an unconscious wish for A." It seems clear that to falsify hypothesis (c) one would have to confirm hypothesis (e). But, Rubinstein (1975) notes: "Hypothesis (e) can only be confirmed by an *absence* of data confirming hypothesis (c). Accordingly, data confirming hypothesis (c) must be taken as valid in favor of this hypothesis. Popper's falsifiability criterion is fulfilled since, as is evident from the compatibility of hypotheses (c) and (d), the only condition for falsifying hypothesis (c) is the absence of data confirming it" (p. 46).[2]

It seems to me that an all too frequent recent response to criticisms of the scientific status of psychoanalytic theory is to declare that psychoanalysis is to be judged by criteria other than the rules of evidence and inference characterizing the sciences. Bowlby (1981) sees this response as a reaction of despair at dealing even adequately with these criticisms. Rubinstein's response, as the examples given here demonstrate, is to deal carefully and systematically with such criticisms and to try to make

---

[2]The letters of Rubinstein's passage have been changed to conform to my example.

explicit the kinds of evidence and inference that are critical in the testing of clinical hypotheses.

I will now turn to a concern that, in greater or lesser degree, permeates a good deal of Rubinstein's work—the mind-body problem. This problem seems never far from the center of Rubinstein's thoughts on psychoanalysis. Consider the themes and issues that have been detailed: persons and organisms, meanings and causes; clinical and extraclinical theory. All these relate in relatively clear fashion to the mind-body problem. I noted earlier Rubinstein's pervasive recognition of the duality of human existence. This should not be misread to mean that Rubinstein takes a dualistic position on the mind-body problem. On the contrary, he forcefully (and in my view, correctly) rejects any philosophical position or option which ignores the central fact that we are *embodied* beings, and whatever it means to be a person cannot be entirely separated from that embodied status. Rubinstein rejects not only a metaphysical dualism, which treats mental events as if their ultimate nature were made up of mental "stuff," separate and apart from physical matter, but also what can be called a methodological dualism, which claims autonomy for psychological explanation, whatever its relation (including one of contradiction) to explanation at the level of neurophysiological functioning. In either case, Rubinstein rejects the self-sufficiency of mind.[3] In his view, a psychological explanation or account, however clever and ingenious it may be, however intuitively or empathically correct it may seem, cannot be valid if it contradicts what is known about the principles of neurophysiological functioning. This will seem self-evident to many, but it is obviously not self-evident to those who take the position that the formulations and hypotheses of psychoanalytic theory are and should be entirely derived from the psychoanalytic situation, whatever the logical relationship of these formulations to other bodies of knowledge.

---

[3]It seems to me that the recent cluster of formulations including the hermeneutic vision of psychoanalysis, the autonomy of the clinical theory, and the exclusive emphasis on the psychoanalytic situation reveals an underlying attitude that implicitly proclaims the autonomy of the mental and that denies our embodied, material nature. This attitude, in part propelled by a reaction against the purported dehumanizing influence of the scientific weltanschauung, characterizes many recent intellectual developments, particularly in the social sciences. Ironically, although the failure to include and do justice to such essential psychological considerations as subjective experience and intentionality in an explanatory system may be dehumanizing, it is equally dehumanizing, though perhaps in a less obvious way, to fail to include and do justice to our embodied status. We certainly recognize in our clinical thinking that the isolation and separation of mind from body is alienating and dehumanizing. For example, Winnicott (1954) points to the role of excessive mentation and the separation of mind from what he refers to as the psycho-soma in schizoid conditions.

In rejecting a psychology that implicitly advocates the self-sufficiency of mind and ignores our embodiment, Rubinstein is being faithful to a core and critically valuable aspect of psychoanalytic theory. It is Freud's recognition of the central fact of our embodiment, as expressed in his instinct theory, that forms the foundation for psychoanalytic theory. Although many of the specifics of Freudian instinct theory may be deficient or mistaken, what remains valid is Freud's insistence that our basic motives and desires as well as our modes of behavior derive from biological imperatives and are intimately linked to our neurophysiological structure. In rejecting dualism and in keeping in the forefront the fact of our embodiment, Rubinstein is reminding us of that general insight.

It may seem strange to link Rubinstein to instinct theory. But what I am pointing to is Rubinstein's emphasis on our neurophysiological structure as the source of both our motives and the manner in which we go about dealing with these motives. In this sense Rubinstein preserves the insights that remain valid in Freudian instinct theory; and the rejection of these central insights characterizes attempts to separate psychoanalysis – either methodologically or substantively – from the facts of embodiment.[4]

Rubinstein's philosophical position on the mind-body problem is expressed in his discussion of the nature of unconscious mental events. What can it possibly mean, he asks, to speak of unconscious wishing, wanting, thinking, etc.? According to Rubinstein, unconscious mental events are theoretical terms that can be described in (1) the language of psychological observables; (2) the language of neurophysiology or "protoneurophysiology" (as in a *disposition* for conscious wishing);[5] and (3) "*as-if*" mental or phenomenal terms. With regard to the third description, by prefixing the term "unconscious" to ordinary mental terms such as "wishing," "desiring," and "thinking," we intend to convey the idea that the person is behaving and acting *as if* he or she were wishing, desiring, and thinking such and such, when in fact, in the ordinary sense of these terms, which includes the element of conscious experience, the person is not so behaving.

---

[4]I am not suggesting, as do some defenders of Freudian instinct theory, that all divergences from and criticisms of that theory are based on a rejection of the biological – of our embodiment. Indeed, some of these criticisms entail an expansion of the instinctual. For example, Bowlby's (1969) rejection of what he calls Freud's "secondary drive" theory of the infant-mother relationship is based on the positing of an independent instinctual attachment system. And Fairbairn's (1952) dictum that "libido" is object seeking" can be construed as positing an inborn response to objects. (See Eagle, 1981, for a further discussion of these ideas.)

[5]A disposition to behave (or think or feel) in a particular set of ways can be taken as the manifestation of a neural structure.

A further consideration of how terms such as "desiring" and "thinking" are used in ordinary discourse helps us make the transition to talking about unconscious desiring and thinking. In ordinary discourse, to say that one is desiring or thinking X does not necessarily mean that either content X or the activities of desiring or thinking continually occupy all of one's conscious experience. There is a dispositional element to many such psychological terms, by which I mean that someone consciously desiring X both behaves and is predisposed to behave in certain ways, whether or not, at any given moment, that person is consciously aware of X or of experiencing desire for X. In thinking, similarly, when we focus on a problem, for example, we are not necessarily aware of a continual stream of thoughts or of the uninterrupted experience of thinking. As is well known, one may arrive at a solution following a period in which one neither consciously experienced any relevant thoughts nor was aware of thinking. As Rubinstein (1977) and, more recently, Dennett (1978) note, during this period we, as persons, did not do anything. Rather, our brains did. I would add that we can get some idea of the structure of these brain events by noting the nature of the solution. In describing the solution and the structure it implies, we often allow ourselves to say that it is *as if* we engaged in conscious thinking of such and such a kind.

The point of all this is that even in ordinary discourse, mental terms such as "desiring" and "thinking" presuppose a more continual neural activity underlying the stochastic and sporadic nature of conscious experience. This observation was made by Freud and was certainly involved in his general conclusion that the major part of mental life goes on without awareness. Now, if the ordinary use of terms such as "desiring" and "thinking" imply neural activity plus a process in which aspects and portions of that activity are represented in conscious experience, it seems reasonable that *unconscious* desiring and thinking, which by definition do not include the element of conscious experience, would refer to neural activity.

Once having recognized that statements referring to unconscious mental events can be viewed as "as-if" statements that ultimately refer to neural events, a number of questions immediately arise. One basic question is whether the conception of unconscious mental events retains the intentionality (both in Brentano's [1960] sense and in the ordinary sense of the term) we have in mind when we speak about *mental* events. Let me comment here that philosophers are not necessarily entirely in agreement regarding what is meant by intentionality or the criteria by which a system is judged to be an intentional one. But for our purposes, we can agree that intentionality refers to such conscious properties as having purposes and goals, planning, and thinking. Freud's approach to this issue, which is entirely consistent with Rubinstein's, is that the essence of the mental is somatic (neural) processes. However, Freud (1915b) said, these unconscious mental processes "have abundant points of contact with conscious mental process. . . . They can be transformed into, or replaced by, conscious mental processes, and all the categories which we employ to describe conscious mental acts, such as ideas, purposes, resolutions and so on, can be applied to them" (p. 168). Hence, Rubinstein (1965) concludes, for Freud, unconscious mental events are neurophysiological events which are classified as mental on the two assumptions

> (a) that observed phenomena resembling the effects of such phenomenal events as wishing, intending, fantasizing, etc., are in fact the effects of these neurophysiological events, and
> (b) that the latter are in some ways transferable to the particular neurophysiological events that are correlated with the phenomenal events, the effects of which their effects resemble [p. 43].

Hence, when we say "Unconsciously, Harry wants to do X," although strictly speaking we are referring to a neural event, we generally mean that although Harry does not experience wanting to do X and will deny wanting to do X, he behaves (here behavior is widely defined to include thoughts, dreams, slips, and symptoms) *as if* he wants to do X. Such talk of unconscious mental events is serviceable and not simply an aberration or anomaly of language, as some philosophers have claimed (e.g., Field, Aveling, & Laird, 1922), because, as Freud noted, these events have points of contact with and are describable in terms of conscious mental processes.

We recognize that we can say little regarding the neural events underlying what we describe in the language of unconscious mental events. What we can do, however, is develop models in a *neutral* language that is compatible with both conscious experience and neurophysiological functioning. As we shall see, Rubinstein attempts to present just such a model. The challenge for any such model is to accomplish the necessary depersonification of ordinary psychoanalytic statements required by a scientific rendering and, at the same time, retain the intentionality contained by the ordinary statements. For example, in an increasingly scientifc rendering, a statement such as "Unconsciously, Harry wants to do X" must be depersonified, but in a manner that will not lose the intentionality that the original statement contains and that permits the use of "as-if" descriptions. Any depersonified scheme must reflect, as Rubinstein (1980a) puts it, "not the experience, but what we may regard as the phenomenological structure of wishing" (p. 438).

In a difficult but provocative paper, Rubinstein (1974) has presented a psychoanalytic theoretical model of mental functioning which, by virtue of being theoretical, is depersonified, but which nevertheless is intended to be consistent with the phenomenological structure of the activities of persons. It is also intended to be consistent with, or at least not contradict, what is known about neurophysiology. The model is presented in terms of classificatory processes and in a neutral language that is neither neurophysiological nor mentalistic.

One of Rubinstein's basic intentions is to construct a model in which the kinds of phenomena that psychoanalysts are interested in, such as motivated behavior and dream symbolism, are generated and elucidated by the *design features* of the system. Think of trying to build a machine that is so designed that it can perceive, recognize, engage in goal-directed behavior, and so on. Such a machine might yield some insight concerning the formal characteristics necessary to do such things as perceive, recognize, and so on. In this regard, Rubinstein's model is in the general tradition of artificial intelligence and computer simulation. Let me briefly describe the outlines of the model in order to give some idea of Rubinstein's attempt to link the psychoanalytic conception of mental functioning to current scientific thinking.

The model is mainly of motivational processes and the related processes involved in motivated activity, including perception, recognition, and imagery. Rubinstein's model of perception is based on the now commonly accepted central idea that perception is not a passive registration of external objects, but an active processing of input. This active processing is based on a hierarchically organized analysis of features. According to this view (e.g., Neisser, 1967), a percept is the result of an active synthesizing of analyzed features. Thus, the percept *orange* is achieved by synthesizing the features of its size, color, texture, smell, etc. And we recognize an orange by classifying it in accord with these various features. (It can be seen that in this view perception and recognition are closely related processes). Based on the idea of analyzed features, Rubinstein introduces the concept of *object classifier*. A classifier is made up of *subclassifiers*, each subclassifier corresponding to a different attribute or feature of the object. Subclassifiers are general properties or features such as "elongated object," "two syllables," "round," or "begins with the letter *s*." Hence, it can be seen that most subclassifiers will be common to many different object classifiers. It can also be seen that a percept is "constructed" out of subclassifiers or features, much like the title of a book or play is constructed in a game of charades.

It should be apparent that the notion of a classifier corresponds to the psychoanalytic concept of *object representation*. Obviously, a human object classifier will consist of many subclassifier features, including physical, aesthetic, psychological, and moral attributes. Looking at it this way, one can imagine the possibility that of a total set of subclassifiers that normally combine in a single percept or image, particular subsets can become functionally organized, yielding such representations as "good mother" and "bad mother". As Rubinstein notes, just as there are object classifications, there are also self-classifications, which probably interact in various ways with self-standards that we set.

Having elucidated the concept of object classifier, Rubinstein then turns to motivational processes and introduces the concepts of *goal-situation classifier* and *fulfillment-situation classifier* (which are combined into *goal-fulfillment-* or *GF-situation classifiers*) and *goal-act disposition*. A GF-situation classifier can be activated from within, which is analogous to the activation of an object classifier when we think about an object in its absence; from without, as is the case with situations we refer to as temptations; or spontaneously, as in the case of periodic fluctuations of sexual desire. A GF-situation classifier is activated by an existing goal situation much the way an object classifier is activated by the presence of the corresponding object. In both cases, the input is subjected to feature analysis, which then partly determines whether or not the classifier will be activated.

Rubinstein makes the assumption that once activated, a GF-situation classifier remains active at least until the motive is fulfilled. What activates a motive is a *mismatch* between GF-situation classifier and a particular perception of a situation. Normally, a mismatch will result in instrumental activity until *a match* is achieved (which will occur when, during the consummatory act, the situation is classified as a fulfillment situation). However, *a GF-situation fantasy* may be activated, particularly if instrumental action is "judged" not to be feasible. We may note the correspondence between this kind of fantasy and mental imagery (that is not related to a wish) of an object. In the case of mental imagery, the classifier activates features in the *feature storage* (rather than features of perceptual input); while in fantasy, the GF-situation classifier activates corresponding stored GF-situation features.

It should be noted that in this model, although a goal-situation percept can match a goal-situation classifier, it will *not* match the goal-fulfillment classifier. The latter is activated by the activation of the *goal-act disposition* and the release of the goal act. In ordinary terms, this is tantamount to saying that although one can experience a situation as an appropriate goal for one's motive, one will not experience fulfillment of that motive until the goal act is performed (unless one posits something like hallucinatory wish fulfillment). Such fulfillment is associated with pleasure and with a disintegration of the motive structure and its reversion to a mere disposition. There are motives that do not involve a consummatory act (Rubinstein's example is a motive such as the desire to be understood). In such cases, "fulfillment" of the motive is determined entirely by the goal-situation classifier.

I have given only the briefest sketch of Rubinstein's model and have omitted quite a number of details. We can obtain additional insights into the model by seeing how it accounts for certain phenomena of interest to psychoanalysis. Consider dream symbolism. The basic idea is that goal-situation (and object) classifiers break up into subclassifiers, with one or more operating independently to organize an image. For example, if a penis classifier is part of an active goal-situation classifier, the subclassifier or feature "elongated object" may operate independently and organize an image of a snake or baseball bat.

How does the model deal with repression? Briefly, certain active goal- and fulfillment-situation classifiers or a particular set of subclassifiers may match a superego classifier (that is, a classification of what must *not* be done, thought about, felt, etc.), which then prevents awareness of the motive as a motive and also, therefore, of all the subsequent steps that normally accompany awareness of a motive (such as instrumental action).

I want to remind the reader once again of Rubinstein's intention to construct a model in which the design features of the system can yield and account for the kind of motivational and intentional phenomena that are of greatest interest to psychoanalytic theory. Also to be stressed is that the terms of the model are in a *neutral* language that is neither mentalistic nor physiological but hopefully compatible with both. Finally, it is of utmost importance to Rubinstein that the model be not just verbal description, but falsifiable and discardable if it is not heuristic or is contradicted by the facts.

Returning to the issue of depersonification of explanatory schemes and theoretical models, Rubinstein (1976b) tells us that in talking about unconscious mental events we extend ordinary language applicable to persons or, more specifically, to "a sense-of-being-person-doing something" (p. 245). There is no harm in this, as long as we know that we are speaking in this "as-if," extended language. Strictly speaking, however, the unobservable and *unexperienced* activities referred to by unconscious mental events "are part of our everyday human world *in name only*" (p. 254). In fact, they refer to the depersonified natural science world of organisms. This fact tends to arouse in many deep-seated fears and suspicions toward a scientific enterprise which, in the process of concerning itself with human behavior, depersonifies it. However, it is important to keep in mind that, as noted earlier, such depersonification need not and must not eliminate such characteristically human features as intentionality (in the general sense of the term). Theoretical models need to describe and explain these features rather than eliminate or ignore them.[6] Having said that, however, it is important to note that theoretical models need not themselves employ the personal language of wants, wishes, and desires.[7] As I have argued elsewhere (Eagle, 1980) although wants, wishes, and desires serve an explanatory function in ordinary discourse, they are themselves phenomena to be explained in a scientific conception of humankind. One would hardly expect a scientific explanation to limit itself to the concepts that describe the very phenomena it aims to explain. This is something of what Rubinstein has in mind when he informs us in a highly condensed fashion that the scientific rendering of "Unconsciouly, Harry wants to do X" will necessarily involve the depersonification of that statement. Perhaps the most condensed description of why this is so is Rubinstein's (1977) reminder that "from a critical point of view it is illusory to regard a person as the subject—in the sense of being the agent—of an unconscious activity" (p. 13).[8]

---

[6]As Sellars (1963) puts it, ". . . to complete the scientific image we need to enrich it *not* with more ways of saying what is the case, but with the language of community and individual intentions, so that by construing the actions we intend to do and circumstances in which we intend to do them in scientific terms, we *directly* relate the world as conceived by scientific inquiry to our purposes and make it *our* world and no longer an alien appendage to the world in which we do our living" (p. 40).

[7]Indeed, even if such terms are used in a theoretical model, they will have meanings different from the ones they ordinarily have, as Rubinstein has shown is the case with unconscious wants, wishes, and desires. It is also possible, as Chomsky (1965) notes, that in giving a physical, depersonified explanation for such mental phenomena as wants, wishes, and desires "the very concept of 'physical explanation' will no doubt be extended to incorporate whatever is discovered in this [mental] domain, exactly as it was extended to accommodate gravitational and electromagnetic force, massless particles, and numerous other entities and processes that would have offended the common sense of earlier generations" (pp. 83–84).

[8]That one is not the agent of an unconscious activity or, more accurately, some variation of this insight, is undoubtedly one of the important considerations that lies behind Freud's division of the personality into id and ego. If one goes back to the original German terms this becomes clearer (see Bettelheim, 1982; Brandt, 1966). Thus, *Das Es* or "the it" (rather than the id) obviously represents those aspects of the personality that are not experienced as agent but rather as impersonal happenings; *Das Ich* or "the I" (rather than the ego) clearly is meant to include those aspcts of the pesonality that one experiences as personal agent. Although the concept of ego came to include more than this—unconscious defensive activities, for example—the fact remains that in Freud's tripartite division of the personality, that which is experienced as personal agent belongs to the ego. Freud's equation of id with instinct and his difficulty in deciding whether it was to be defined psychologically, biologically, or somewhere between the two (see Freud, 1915b, pp. 111–116) reflects the fact that Freud's id-ego division is, in part, body-mind distinction (see Eagle, 1984). As is the case with the concept of unconscious activity, in the concept of id, one is not the subject—in the sense of being the agent—of id strivings. And yet, also as in the case of un-

Implicit in Rubinstein's insistence that the existential referents for unconscious mental processes are neural events and implicit in Freud's belief that the essence of the mental is somatic processes is the seemingly strange idea that neural events themselves (or rather systems of neural events) possess at least some of the features we normally attribute to and by which we characterize conscious mental processes. I am not at all certain that one can justifiably speak of, let us say, the intelligence of neural events, except perhaps in a metaphorical sense. But, at least in a certain sense, they are intelligent—perhaps in the same sense that computers are intelligent. It has been customary to think of all physical processes as inherently "blind," that is, without intelligence or intentionality, and to locate these latter qualities in the mind and/or the person. However, there are certain perceptual and cognitive phenomena that imply often elegantly intelligent processes which are not and often cannot be represented in conscious experience. I will provide some examples.

Consider as the first example the dichotic listening situation in which subjects are presented with messages simultaneously on two different channels and are instructed to attend to and read aloud a message on one of these channels. Typically, they can report only gross physical features (for example, a male voice) from the unattended channel and cannot report the content. However, Lackner and Garrett (1973) have shown that messages in the unattended channel influence the particular interpretation given to ambiguous sentences presented in the attended and shadowed channel, even though subjects *could not report* what they heard in the former. As Dennett (1978) notes, "the influence of the unattended channel on the interpretation of the attended signal can be explained only on the hypothesis that the unattended input is processed all the way to a semantic level, even though the subjects have no awareness of this—that is, cannot report it." (p. 211).

As another example, consider an experiment by Lazarus and McCleary (1951) in which subjects are presented a series of words exposed tachistoscopically for a brief duration and are asked to report what they see. When the stimulus word is "raped," many subjects report

---

conscious activity, id strivings are nevertheless intentional and purposive. Because they are intentional, we want to attribute them to an agent. As Flew (1949) points out, in our habitual style of thinking we are accustomed to identify intentional and purposive with conscious and voluntary, not with unconscious, impersonal, and peremptorily involuntary. We are used to thinking of intentional activity as *doings* carried out by personal agents. However, as Dennett (1978) notes, subpersonal systems can be intentional systems. It seems to me that this point is implied in Freud's attribution of motivational aims to subpersonal structural components of the personality.

seeing "rapid." Their galvanic skin response (GSR) measurements, however, are of a magnitude associated with emotionally laden words such as "raped" rather than neutral words such as "rapid." As in the first example, some aspects of the subject's response indicate that the stimulus has been processed accurately, even though the subject is not aware of it and does not report processing the stimulus.

The next two examples are somewhat different from the first two. They focus on phenomena that reflect the problem-solving nature of perceptual processes which are not and cannot be represented in conscious experience. The first example is the well-known Ames room, in which the ceiling and floor are sloped in a manner unobservable to the viewer. A child standing in the corner of the room where ceiling and floor converge will look markedly taller than an adult standing in a corner where ceiling and floor diverge. This illusion is irresistible and persists even if the onlooker is told how the room is constructed. What is perceived seems based on a tacit inference that someone whose head is very close to the ceiling is obviously taller than someone whose head is not so close. Normally, ceilings and floors are parallel to each other, and this tacit inference or "rule" will be highly accurate and serviceable. In the context of the Ames box, that what is immediately perceived and experienced follows that tacit "rule" rather than what is consciously known. In fact, the immediate experience is, as noted, irresistible and not changed by one's conscious knowledge.

The second example in this area has to do with stroboscopic movement. If, let us say, the image of a triangle flashes at point A and then, after an appropriate interval, at point B, one will experience the triangle moving from A to B. As Rock (1970) notes, this perceptual experience is based on the tacit inference "that if an object is now here in this field and, a moment later, it is not there but elsewhere, then it must have moved" (p. 9). Indeed, Rock reports that the experience of movement can be eliminated "if, simultaneous with the flashing on of B, A reappears in its original location as well; in other words, if you flash A then A-B, then B then A-B and so forth, A need not be 'deduced' to have moved to B if it is still where it was a moment ago" (p. 9). The experience of movement can also be destroyed if a and b appear as two objects being successively uncovered and covered. As Rock notes, the experience follows the "impeccable logic" that "if the first object is covered over, it has not moved to location but remained where it is" (p. 9). Evidence such as this leads Rock to conclude that "perception turns out to be shot through with intelligence" (p. 10) and to support Helmholtz's (1962) rule that ". . . objects are always imagined as being present in the field of vision as would have to be there in order to produce the same impression on the nervous mechanism." (p. 5).

Finally, consider the seemingly simple phenomenon of experiencing vertigo after getting on an escalator that is not moving. One infers that the person experiencing such vertigo had unconsciously "expected" the metal stairs to move. That such unconscious expectations are different from ordinary, conscious expectations is evidenced by the fact that knowing beforehand that the metal stairs are not and will not be moving does not eliminate the vertigo. As Polanyi and Prosch (1975) note with regard to "tacit inferences" in general, such phenomena seem to be relatively immune to adverse evidence. To say that one unconsciously expected the metal stairs to move is, to Rubinstein's way of thinking, an "as-if" use of "expectation," which does no harm and is certainly useful insofar as it is structurally analogous with both conscious experience and the neural events for which it is an approximate description. However, as Rubinstein warns us, to give *existential* implications to unconscious expectations is erroneous. In a certain sense, there is no such thing as an unconscious expectation. It provides only a very approximately and vague linguistic window on certain neural events that intervene between getting on the stationary metal stairs and experiencing vertigo.

The ontological status of the processes involved in the phenomena described in these examples is difficult to pinpoint. At least since Helmholtz advanced his concept of "unconscious inference," there has been debate regarding the status of such processes. Helmholtz recognized that these processes have a cognitive, inferencelike property and yet are immediate and automatic and are not represented in conscious experience. The term "unconscious inference" was intended to capture both aspects of the process. Helmholtz's concept fell into disrepute, mainly as a result of the criticism that, by definition, inferences could not be unconscious and, therefore, the notion of an *unconscious* inference was an absurdity. However, the phenomena in our examples, attesting as they do to the inferencelike processes involved in perception, have led to a revival of the concept of unconscious inference.

It is instructive in this regard to consider the situation in so-called cognitive science. In that area, descriptions are given of inferred and hypothetical cognitive processes that are neither represented in conscious experience nor tied to specific brain events. Rather, the emphasis is on the *structure* of these cognitive processes. Similarly, one can say of the processes represented by Helmholtz's "unconscious inference" that they are not in conscious experience, nor can one specify the neural events to which they refer. What the concept does, however, is to inform us that leading up to some perceptual experiences are certain inferencelike processes—that is, they function *as if* they were making a conscious, logical inference of an if-then kind. Hence, Helmholtz's concept essentially reveals the (inferred) *structure* of certain processes that, at this point, cannot be further specified. One can interpret them as ontologically neutral. Similarly, Chomsky's (1965) concept of "deep structures" is also a structural description that is neither represented in conscious experience nor tied to specific neural events. It is meant to reveal some important things about the structure of the mind; however, it is embodied. It seems to me that in Rubinstein's way of looking at the concept of unconscious activity, an interpretation cast in the language of unconscious wishes or wants is a structural description that, despite their differences,[9] functions much like Helmholtz's "unconscious inference" and Chomsky's "deep structures."

It says something like: "Your behavior and associations are patterned *as if* you wish or want such and such," much like a statement of unconscious expectations says that one's vertigo is *as if* one expected the escalator to move. Casting statements about unconscious activity in the ordinary language of "narratives" about wishes and wants has the dual advantage of not only being potentially therapeutic, but also permitting one the freedom to describe patterns of behavior with as few constraints as possible. But Rubinstein's conceptualization of unconscious activity makes clear that these "narratives" ultimately have to answer to what is actually the case. That is, they must be consistent with what we know about the structure of neural processes. This single consideration seems to me to be a sufficient reason that a psychoanalytic theory that makes use of the concept of unconscious activity cannot be entirely construed as a hermeneutic discipline. As Rubinstein (1974) observes, ". . . no matter how apt an interpretation of a symbol in terms of its meaning, if the processes by which symbol formation is explained are improbable, we have no alternative but to discard the interpretation" (p. 105).

Keeping Rubinstein's clarifying comments regarding unconscious activities in mind, it would seem that the perceptual experiences in our examples are *as if* we were engaging in logical inferences. But such inferences or, more accurately, inferencelike processes, cannot be ascribed to a person insofar as the person is not aware of such activities. Hence, it seems to me that such intelligent, inferencelike processes must be ascribed to neural events and brain processes.[10] To state it generally, intelligence resides in subpersonal neural processes. I do not pretend to be able to explicate this notion much further, except to say that such neural processes must have been selected out in the course of evolution

---

[9]An essential difference is that whereas unconscious wishes or wants can become conscious, Helmholtz's "unconscious inference" and Chomsky's "deep structures" cannot, almost by definition.

[10]It should be clear that not all the implications I draw from Rubinstein's formulations would necessarily be shared by Rubinstein himself.

and to point to the work of others who have attempted to develop further this idea of subpersonal intelligence and intentionality (e.g., Dennett, 1969, 1978).[11]

It seems to me that the notion of subpersonal intelligence and intentionality is also implicit in some of Freud's basic formulations. This is seen in a number of ways. The very basic scheme of partitioning the personality into id, ego, and superego can be seen as implying subpersonal intelligence and intentionality. Strictly speaking, insofar as id, ego, and superego are unconscious processes, they are, ontologically, brain processes ascribable to an organism. However, as we have seen earlier, Freud (1915b) tells us that unconscious mental processes "have abundant points of contact with conscious mental processes" and can be described by the categories applicable to conscious processes. Hence, id, ego, and superego are not simply metaphors of what persons do, as is claimed, for example, by Schafer (1976) in his "action language," but are both (1) labels for particular constellations of neural events and brain processes and, (2) names for classes of wishes and dispositions to behave in certain ways and to have experiences of certain kinds. In other words, as with Rubinstein's classification model discussed earlier, one can think of id, ego, and superego as a *neutral* language description that will ideally capture something of the structure of both neurophysiological functioning on the one hand and behavior and conscious experience on the other.

If unconscious processes are, ontologically speaking, neural in nature and if, as Freud maintained, such processes constitute the basic psychic reality, then the seemingly peculiar conclusion one is led to is that psychic reality is neural! (See Nagel, 1974, for a further elaboration of this

---

[11]In the examples of perceptual phenomena, a subpersonal system such as the visual system has what Dennett (1978), borrowing from computer language, calls "computational access" to certain stimuli. What the person has access to, continuing with computer language, is some of the computational products of the visual system's processing. The latter are represented in conscious experience, whereas neither the stimuli to which the visual system has "computational access" nor the visual system's processing are so represented. One may also speculate, as Dennett does, that just as the visual system has access to certain stimuli, there is very likely an "affect" system within the person that has access to certain "inner" events (for example, hormonal secretion and hypothalamic stimulation). Continuing with the analogy, just as the products of the processing by the visual system are consciously experienced percepts, so the products of the hypothetical "affect" system are experienced as wants and desires. Finally, just as the individual "constructs" percepts when the product of visual processing is unclear, so one "constructs" reasons, desires, motives when the product of the "affects" system processing is unclear.

It should be noted that although I mention subpersonal intelligence and intentionality, the problems presented by each are not necessarily equivalent. Thus, the essence of certain machines is that they are intelligent, as the very term "artificial intelligence" indicates.

argument.) This conclusion is not as peculiar as it may seem. For what else can unconscious activities be but neural events? But they are at the same time *mental*, insofar as they are characterized by intelligence and intentionality. For Freud, it should be noted, what defined "mental" was not phenomenal experience but what I am referring to here as intelligence and intentionality. For Freud, conscious experience was not the essence of the mental but only a surface and sporadic representation of an ongoing underlying activity. Hence, when Freud writes that the ultimate and underlying psychic reality is unconscious, he is essentially saying that the underlying psychic reality is neural. Although Freud abandoned his attempt to implement in detail this point of view (in the *Project for a Scientific Psychology*, 1895), this general conception of psychic reality was never abandoned.

A critical question raised by the psychoanalytic conception of unconscious activity is how an unconscious want or idea becomes transformed into a conscious want or idea. If, as Rubinstein maintains, an unconscious want refers essentially a kind of neural activity, how does it ever get represented in conscious experience? This question has always been central to psychoanalysis. How does the unconscious become conscious, and how does it get to be represented in personal experience? I do not pretend to have even the beginnings of an answer to this question. But implicit in psychoanalytic theory and in some current conceptions is the idea that much of our behavior is guided by subpersonal intelligent and intentional processes and that only the products of some of these processes are represented, with varying degrees of distortion, in conscious experience. Conscious experience can be conceptualized as a selective and constructional rendering of products of underlying subpersonal processes. If, as Dennett (1978) suggests, there is a subpersonal system that processes "inner events," it is the products of such processing that are selectively represented in consciousness (just as it is the products of visual processing that are selectively represented in perceptual visual experience). Surely this is implied by Freud's belief that the major part of mental life goes on outside awareness.

The opportunities for defense and dissimulation arise in the representation and rendering of these subpersonal products. In strictly psychoanalytic language, this would be stated largely in terms of the degree to which conscious experience and the ego accurately represent unconscious instinctual aims.[12] If unconscious aims are only metaphorical descriptions of neural activity, the issue becomes the degree to which con-

---

[12]It is interesting and consistent with what I have been proposing that Gedo (1979) states as an important goal of psychoanalytic treatment the raising of biological aims and needs to the level of conscious awareness.

scious experience and the ego accurately represent the subpersonal neural activity we are really referring to when we talk about unconscious aims.

Another issue that has been central to psychoanalysis is the degree to which subpersonal aims are *integrated* into those structures we think of as consciousness and selfhood. Obviously, that which is not represented in these structures cannot be integrated into them. But it is possible for certain subpersonal aims to be represented in but not integrated into consciousness, as in the case of an ego-alien obsessive thought. Indeed, what we mean by a partial failure of repression is that the aim linked to the obsessive thought is rather clearly represented in consciousness, but in an unintegrated, ego-alien state—in contrast to a more complex repression in which the aim is only very indirectly represented or hardly represented at all.

In any case, the point here is that in psychoanalytic theory, a central aspect of personality integrity concerns not only representation but the successful integration of subpersonal tendencies and aims into a superordinate, higher-order structure identified as one's (largely conscious) self. This central idea is conveyed by the dictum "where id was, there shall ego be," which can also be translated as "where the impersonal 'it' was, there shall the personal 'I' be." Although the impersonal "it" has been equated with instinctual aims, it can also be interpreted as referring to all those unconscious subpersonal tendencies that are not but can become part of the "I," the personal self. If, however, the impersonal "it" is essentially neural activity (and it is difficult to see what else it can be), then Freud's dictum is tantamount to the assertion that one can claim or reclaim, so to speak, bits of neurology and transform them into psychology. Or, to put it somewhat differently, the self assimilates bits of the impersonal and transforms as well as integrates them into the personal, thereby expanding the realm and domain of the latter.

No wonder the mind-body issue is at the center of both Rubinstein's writings and of psychoanalytic theory! It may seem less strange to speak of transforming and integrating bits of neurology into psychology if one takes the perspective that every bit of conscious experience represents such a transformation. According to the logic of Freud's conception of psychic activity, every bit of conscious experience entails making the unconscious conscious. What is distinctive about the process when it is discussed in the therapeutic context is that active forces (i.e., repression) have both rendered certain contents unconscious (hence, the concept of the dynamic unconscious) and interfered with the smooth transformation of unconscious (neural) activity into conscious experience.

The picture of psychoanalysis that emerges from Rubinstein's (as well as Freud's) conception of unconscious mental events is radically different from the current conception of psychoanalysis as hermeneutics and from the current emphasis on "stories," "narratives," and related constructions. As I have already noted, for Rubinstein these "stories" and "narratives" ultimately depend for their validity on confirming through nonclinical means general hypotheses regarding our basic structure. Now, from the point of view of unconscious activity as neural events, to ascribe to the individual unconscious wishes, wants, and so forth is, in an approximate and metaphoric way, to describe the structure of that person's mind, with mind identified as an intentional but nevertheless neural system. Hence, it is not merely a matter of a "story" or "narrative" that makes sense, but of an account that cannot contradict what we do know about the structure of mind in general. In other words, implicit in Rubinstein's view is the idea that psychoanalytic interpretations regarding unconscious mental events, although cast in the ordinary language of desires, wants, and actions, are, in some cases, groping descriptions of brain processes and hence, not only must not contradict what we know about brain processes, but must actually reflect something about the structure of the latter.

The final issues I want to deal with in this discussion of Rubinstein's work emerge from contrasting his formulation with Schafer's (1976) "action language." By referring to all mental events, including unconscious activity, as action, Schafer makes it clear that in his view all the phenomena with which psychoanalysis deals are to be ascribed to the person. Unconscious motives are to be seen as disclaimed actions. One consequence of ascribing unconscious activity to the person (rather than ascribing such activity to the organism) is Schafer's conclusion that we are all responsible for such activity. (Thus, Schafer's cites with approval Freud's [1925] comment that we are responsible for our dreams). Schafer's conclusion does, indeed, logically follow from his premise. For, if unconscious activities are things we *do* to accomplish particular ends, then they fit the model of action and the practical syllogism that describes action; and, if these activities are actions, we are responsible for them. But Rubinstein's analysis of unconscious activities sensitizes us to such questions as how an activity, the goal or aim of which we are not consciously aware, can be an action. He points out that certain motives, particularly unconscious motives, function more as causes propelling activity than as reasons for action. Schafer does not deal with these issues, but rather attempts to resolve the conceptual difficulties inherent in the notion of unconscious activity merely through the verbal device of labeling such activity "action." As for our responsibility for unconsciously motivated behavior, Rubinstein's analysis suggests that this whole issue represents confusion between different universes of discourse. That is to say, the whole question of responsibility applies to the everyday world of persons and actions (and the social-legal-ethical contexts it generates), whereas talk about unconscious wants and desires, insofar as it is a metaphoric description of neural activity, belongs to the world of organisms.

There is a good deal of Rubinstein's work that has not been covered here, and what has been discussed has not had the rigor and details that characterizes Rubinstein's own work. That, of course, is inevitable in a chapter of this kind, but I believe that what I have discussed represents some of the more important and central themes of Rubinstein's work.

In summarizing some of the main related themes in Rubinstein's writings, first and foremost is Rubinstein's awareness of the dual perspective one can adopt toward human existence—that is, we are both persons in an everyday human world and organisms in a natural science world. This awareness—which, I believe, is also central to psychoanalytic theory—permeates much of Rubinstein's work. It permits him, for example, to understand the complementarity of meanings and causes rather than pitting one against the other.

A second theme is Rubinstein's relentless quest to understand the *relationship* between the world of persons and the world of organisms and to avoid confusion between the two worlds and contexts. This quest is reflected in his analysis and clarification of psychoanalytic concepts such as unconscious mental events and in his writing on the mind-body problem. It is also reflected in Rubinstein's attempt to develop a "neutral language" model of mental functioning that will be faithful to the worlds of both persons and organisms.

A third theme in Rubinstein's work is his elucidation of the logic and nature of clinical inference in psychoanalysis. More than any other psychoanalytic theorist, Rubinstein attempts to explicate clearly and, as I described it earlier, "doggedly" the nature of the evidence and inference rules that legitimate clinical inferences. His description of how particular clinical hypotheses are confirmed represents one of the few systematic attempts in this area. Also, his demonstration of the logical dependence of particular clinical formulations on general clinical hypotheses and the dependence of the latter on extraclinical sources of evidence represents the most effective argument against an overly narrow conception of psychoanalysis.

As important as such specific themes and contents, however, is the unrelenting intellectual honesty, clarity, and rigor of Rubinstein's thinking. I hope I have given the reader some idea of these qualities.

REFERENCES

Abelson, R. (1977). *Persons: A study in philosophical psychology*. New York: Macmillan.

Ames, A., Jr. (1946). *Nature and origin of perception*. Hanover, NH: Institute for Associated Research.

Bettelheim, B. (1982, March 1). Reflections: Freud and the soul. *New Yorker*, 52–93.

Bowlby, J. (1969). *Attachment and loss: Vol. 1. Attachment*. New York: Basic Books.

Bowlby, J. (1981). [Symposium on E. Peterfreund on Information and Systems Theory]. *Psychoanalytic Review, 68*, 187–190.

Brandt, L. W. (1966). Process or structure? *Psychoanalytic Review, 53*, 50.

Brentano, F. (1960). The distinction between mental and physical phenomena. (D. B. Terrell, Trans.). In R. M. Chisholm (Ed.), *Realism and the background of phenomenology* (pp. 39–61). Glencoe, IL: Free Press.

Chomsky, N. (1965). *Aspects of the theory of syntax*. Cambridge, MA: MIT Press.

Dennett, D. C. (1969). *Content and Consciousness*. London: Routledge & Kegan Paul.

Dennett, D. C. (1978). Toward a cognitive theory of consciousness. In C. W. Savage (Ed.), *Minnesota Studies in the Philosophy of Science: Vol. 9. Perception and Cognition: Issues in the foundations of psychology* (pp. 210–228). Minneapolis: University of Minnesota Press.

Dilthey, W. (1961). *Meaning in history*. (H. P. Rickman, Ed.) London: Allen & Unwin.

Eagle, M. N. (1980). Psychoanalytic interpretations: Veridicality and therapeutic effectiveness. *Noûs, 14*, 405–425.

Eagle, M. N. (1980a). A critical examination of motivational explanation in psychoanalysis. *Psychoanalysis and Contemporary Thought, 3*, 329–380. (Also in L. Laudan, Ed., 1983. *Mind and Medicine*. Berkeley and Los Angeles: University of California Press, pp. 311–353).

Eagle, M. N. (1980b). Interests as object relations. *Psychoanalysis & Contemporary Thought, 4*, 527–565.

Eagle, M. N. (1984). *Recent Developments in Psychoanalytic Theory: A Critical valuation*. New York: McGraw-Hill.

Fairbairn, W. R. D. (1952). *Psychoanalytic Studies of the Personality*. London, Tavistock.

Field, G. C., Aveling, F., & Laird, J. A. (1922). Symposium on Is the conception of the unconscious of value in psychology? *Mind, 31*, 413–442.

Flew, A., (1949). Psychoanalytic explanation. *Analysis, 10*, 8–15.

Freud, S. (1895). Project for a scientific psychology. *Standard Edition, 1*, 295–397.

Freud, S. (1915a). Instincts and their vicissitudes. *Standard Edition, 14*, 117–140.

Freud, S. (1915b). The unconscious. *Standard Edition, 14*.

Freud, S. (1917). Introductory lectures on psychoanalysis. *Standard Edition, 16*, 448–463.

Freud, S. (1925). Some additional notes on dream interpretation as a whole. *Standard Edition, 19*, 25–30.

Gedo, J. K. (1979). Beyond Interpretation. New York: International Universities Press.

Grünbaum, A. (1984). *Foundations of psychoanalysis: A philosophical critique*. Berkeley: University of California Press.

Habermas, J. (1971). *Knowledge and Human Interests* (J. J. Shapiro, Trans.). Boston: Beacon Press.

Habermas, J. (1979). *Communication and the Evolution of Society* (T. McCarthy, Trans.). Boston: Beacon Press.

Helmholtz, H. Von (1962). *Treatise on Physiological Optics* (Vol. 3; Translated from the third German edition). J. P. C. Southall, (Ed. & Trans.). New York: Dover.

Holt, R. R. (1967). [Editor's introduction.] In R. R. Holt (Ed.), Motives and thoughts: Psychoanalytic essays in honor of David Rapaport. *Psychological Issues, 5* (2/3, Monograph 18/19), 18–19.

Holt, R. R. (1972). Freud's mechanistic and humanistic images of man. In R. R. Holt and E. Peterfreund (Eds.), *Psychoanalysis and Contemporary Science*. New York: Macmillan.

Home, H. J. (1966). The concept of mind. *International Journal of Psycho-Analysis, 47*, 42–49.

Huxley, T. H. (1967). In P. Edwards (Ed.), *Encyclopedia of Philosophy, Vol. 3* (pp. 102–103). New York: Macmillan. (Original work published 1893–94).

Klein, G. S. (1976). *Psychoanalytic theory: An exploration of essentials.* New York: International Universities Press.

Kohut, H. (1954). Introspection, empathy aand psychoanalysis. *Journal of the American Psychoanalytic Association, 7,* 459–483.

Kohut, H. (1971). *The restoration of the self.* New York: International Universities Press.

Lackner, J. R., & Garrett, M. (1973). Resolving ambiguity: Effects of biasing context in the unattended ear. *Cognition, 1,* 359–372.

La Mettrie, J. (1912). *Man a machine.* La Salle, IL: Open Court Publishing Co.

Lazarus, R. S., & McCleary, R. A. (1951). Autonomic discrimination without awareness: A study of subception. *Psychological Review, 58,* 113–122.

Louch, A. R. (1966). *Explanation and human action.* Oxford: Blackwell.

Nagel, T. (1974). Freud's anthropomorphism. In R. Wollheim (Ed.), *Freud: A collection of critical essays* (pp. 11–24). New York: Anchor Books.

Neisser, U. (1967). *Cognitive psychology.* New York: Appleton-Century-Crofts.

Polanyi, M., & Prosch, H. (1975). *Meaning.* Chicago: University of Chicago Press.

Popper, K. R. (1962). *Conjectures and refutations.* New York: Harper, 1968.

Ricoeur, P. (1970). *Freud and philosophy: An essay in interpretation.* New Haven: Yale University Press.

Ricoeur, P. (1977). The question of proof in Freud's psychoanalytic writings. *Journal of the American Psychoanalytic Association, 25,* 835–871.

Rock, I. (1970). Perception from the standpoint of psychology. In *Perception and its disorders, Vol. 68* (pp. 1–11). Association for Research in Nervous and Mental Disease.

Rubinstein, B. B. (1965). Psychoanalytic theory and the mind-body problem. In N. S. Greenfield & W. C. Lewis (Eds.), *Psychoanalysis and current biological thought.* Madison: University of Wisconsin Press.

Rubinstein, B. B. (1967). Explanation and mere descriptions: A metascientific examination of certain aspects of the psychoanalytic theory of motivation. In R. R. Holt (Ed.), Motives and thoughts: Psychoanalytic essays in honor of David Rapaport. *Psychological Issues, 5,* 2/3 Monograph 18/19, 20–77.

Rubinstein, B. B. (1972). On metaphor and related phenomena. *Psychoanalysis & Contemporary Science, 1,* 70–108.

Rubinstein, B. B. (1974). On the role of classificatory processes in mental functioning: Aspects of a psychoanalytic theoretical model. In L. Goldberger & V. H. Rosen (Eds.), *Psychoanalysis and contemporary science, Vol. 3* (pp. 3–57). New York: International Universities Press.

Rubinstein, B. B. (1975). On the clinical psychoanalytic theory and its role in the inference and confirmation of particular clinical hypotheses. *Psychoanalysis & Contemporary Science, 4,* 3–57.

Rubinstein, B. B. (1976a). Hope, fear, wish, expectation, and fantasy: A semantic-phenomenological and extraclinical theoretical study. In T. Shapiro (Ed.), *Psychoanalysis and contemporary science, Vol. 5* (pp. 3–60). New York: International Universities Press.

Rubinstein, B. B. (1976b). On the possibility of a strictly clinical psychoanalytic theory: An essay in the philosophy of psychoanalysis. In M. M. Gill & P. S. Holzman (Eds.), *Psychology versus metapsychology: Psychoanalytic essays in memory of G. S. Klein* (pp. 229–264). New York: International Universities Press.

Rubinstein, B. B. (1977). On the concept of a person and of an organism. In R. Stern, L. S. Horowitz, and J. Lynes (Eds.), *Science and psychotherapy* (pp. 1–17). New York: Haven.

Rubinstein, B. B. (1978). Psychoanalytic hypotheses and the problem of their confirmation. In K. D. Irani, L. Horowitz, & G. Myers (Eds.), *Pathology and consciousness* (pp. 35–50). New York: Haven.

Rubinstein, B. B. (1980a). On the psychoanalytic theory of unconscious motivation and the problem of its confirmation. *Noûs, 14,* 427–442.

Rubinstein, B. B. (1980b). On the psychoanalytic theory of unconscious motivation and the problem of its confirmation. *Psychoanalysis & Contemporary Thought, 3,* 3–20.

Rubinstein, B. B. (1980c). The problem of confirmation in clinical psychoanalysis. *Journal of the American Psychoanalytic Association, 28,* 397–416.

Rubinstein, B. B. (1980d). [Review of *The self and its brain: An argument for interactionism,* by K. R. Popper and J. C. Eccles.] *Journal of the American Psychoanalytic Association, 28,* 210–219.

Rubinstein, B. B. (1981, January 27). *Person, organism, & self: Their worlds and their psychoanalytically relevant relationships.* Paper presented at a meeting of the New York Psychoanalytic Society, New York.

Schafer, R. (1976). *A new language for psychoanalysis.* New Haven: Yale University Press.

Sellars, W. (1963). *Science, Perception, and Reality.* London: Routledge Kegan Paul.

Taylor, R. (1964). *The Explanation of Behavior.* London: Routledge and Kegan Paul.

Winnicott, D. W. (1949). Mind and its relation to the psycho-soma. In D. W. Winnicott *Collected Papers: Though Pediatrics to Psychoanalysis.* New York: Basic Books.

5 Emanuel Peterfreund: The Information Revolution

Stanley R. Palombo, M.D.

When Emanuel Peterfreund's *Information, Systems, and Psychoanalysis* appeared in 1971, it posed a new and unusual challenge to traditional psychoanalytic beliefs. Peterfreund's work was not simply a development of ideas that were already competing within the ideological arena marked out by Freud's discovery of unconscious mental activity. More significantly, it presented a new framework of ideas within which the unique achievements of traditional psychoanalysis could be integrated with the profound conceptual changes currently taking place throughout the natural and biological sciences.

The effects of these changes are still only beginning to be felt, but they have already produced a picture of the universe quite different from that of Freud's time, a picture in which information has replaced energy as the central unifying concept. My primary objective in this essay will be to trace the significance of this changing world picture for psychoanalysis. *Information, Systems, and Psychoanalysis* has a central role in this inquiry. It raised many of the basic questions that must be answered if psychoanalysis is to maintain its position at the forefront of scientific thought.

Rubinstein (1975, 1980), whose investigations of psychoanalysis as a revolutionary episode in the history of science have cast a bright light on the conceptual problems inherited by psychoanalytic theory from the prepsychoanalytic past (1975, 1980), says in his preface to *Information, Systems, and Psychoanalysis:* "We are here on an adventurous journey, into what, from the viewpoint of most analysts, must appear as strange and exotic territory. But it is a journey that must be

109

undertaken. The alternative is a standstill, as a consequence of which current metapsychology will most likely become increasingly alienated from science generally and hence scientifically irrelevant" (p. 6). And, in a recent symposium on the significance of Peterfreund's work, Bowlby (1981) notes:

> The material of psychoanalysis, it is sometimes contended, is not a kind that can be dealt with by means of conventional scientific procedures: it needs special procedures of its own. An alternative reaction is to search the current scientific scene to discover whether any of the more recent concepts and theories that have been developed can be harnessed to provide a model for psychoanalysis better fitted to its subject matter. This is what Emanuel Peterfreund has done. (p. 187)

Reppen (1981), in his introduction to the same symposium, remarks: "It is curious that Peterfreund in his updating of Freud delivers another narcissistic blow to man's old view of himself as central in the universe. To Freud's earlier observation that man is not master in his own house must now be added the notion that man may be merely an automaton—one must hasten to add, perhaps to soften the injury, an incredibly complicated one" (p. 159). Reppen seems to be suggesting that this narcissistic injury was responsible in large part for the "considerable neglect" from which Peterfreund's work has suffered. This neglect has taken place, as Reppen notes, despite Peterfreund's training and origins in the mainstream of psychoanalysis. Peterfreund, who attended the City College of New York and the University of Chicago Medical School, trained at the New York Psychoanalytic Institute. He is an associate clinical professor of psychiatry at Mount Sinai Medical School as well as a member of the American Psychoanalytic Association.

The resistance to Peterfreund's revolutionary contribution to psychoanalytic theory illustrates the difficulties encountered by a scientific community when its investment in the past becomes an obstacle to further advancement. *Information, Systems, and Psychoanalysis* goes directly to the heart of the problem in the older theory. It provides a point of view, first of all, from which the conceptual inconsistencies of traditional metapsychology can be clearly inspected. It makes the cumbersome improvisations required to circumvent these inconsistencies visible for what they are.

As in the psychoanalytic process itself, the diagnosis is the beginning of the cure. A different kind of theory was needed, a theory at once simpler in its essentials and more advanced in its powers of implication, the kind of theory Copernicus offered to the tradition-mired astronomers. While many analysts were wondering whether the desperate remedy to the problem of theoretical obsolescence was to cut the remaining ties between psychoanalysis and the rest of the science, Peterfreund was showing that better science was the only real choice.

SCIENCE AND PSYCHOANALYSIS

Freud was fascinated by the emotional shock effects produced by sudden, radical changes in the scientific world view. He saw the massive resistance to Copernicus and Darwin as evidence that their discoveries had undermined a collective fantasy of human centrality and mastery. He believed that psychoanalysis was meeting the same massive resistance because his discovery of the unconscious had undermined that fantasy even further (Freud, 1914).

Freud showed how tentative is our control over our own minds and how much of what we ordinarily consider to be within our conscious control is better thought of as belonging to something external to our self-awareness, a "psychic apparatus" functioning outside our consciousness and our capabilities for rational decision making. But his imagery for representing the psychological opposition between what he called the "I" and the "it" was little more than a metaphorical letting loose in the human mind of the purely physical forces that had been tamed during the nineteenth century in the factory and the laboratory.

Natural science in Freud's time was dominated by the notion of energy. The conceptual vocabulary from which Freud created his metapsychology was formed by the great advances in the physical sciences during his own lifetime. The discovery of the various forms and manifestations of physical energy, their interchangeability, and the conservation of quantities through transformations from one form of energy to another, made it appear that the physical universe had been completely understood. The human mind seemed to stand outside this rush of physical transformations, as an interested but uninvolved observer.

Part of the shock effect of psychoanalysis resulted from its refutation of the myth of progress engendered by the advances in the physical sciences. This idea had been grasped by many as a replacement for the outmoded religious mythology that put humankind at the center of creation. But another aspect of the shock was its appropriation of the vocabulary of the physical sciences to reach its pessimistic conclusions about the power of the human mind. Freud's success in turning the myth of scientific progress against itself seemed to finish off whatever was left of collective human narcissism.

Nevertheless, the psychoanalysts who followed Freud developed a myth of their own, a myth that became an obstacle to further theoretical changes. If the discovery of the unconscious meant the ultimate deflation of human vanity and self-deception, then no further surprises about the nature of the mind could come from the other sciences. Any claim to that effect would have to be treated as a denial of the importance of the unconscious. The psychoanalysis of Freud's time would become the permanent basis for "a general psychology," even though its conceptual scheme had been inherited from nineteenth-century physics.

But, as *Information, Systems, and Psychoanalysis* repeatedly points out, science in our own time has moved in a direction that makes nineteenth-century physics increasingly irrelevant to psychology. Contemporary science is primarily concerned not with forces but with structures and procedures. Its subject matter is the accumulation of patterned information in complex systems, biological and otherwise. An organism is no longer thought of by biologists as a collection of chemical reactions, but as a hierarchy of organizational structures. Within this conceptual framework, the human mind takes its place as a system like others, differing in the degree of its complexity but not in its possession of unique attributes or qualities.

Despite Freud's repeated minimizing of the role of rational thought in determining human behavior, his model of the mind in conflict requires the presence of a rational human agency—the ego—striving through intelligent procedures to dominate the naturally occurring chaos of instinctual forces (Freud, 1923). Freud's attempt to derive the structure of the ego from an evolutionary process guided only by the clashing of these unstructured natural forces was brilliantly conceived but doomed to failure from the beginning. Without a scientific conception that included information and structure as essential features of all natural process, it could not succeed.

To complete Freud's project for understanding the origin and development of the ego as a sequence of natural events, it is necessary to see that the natural world includes not only the clash of unstructured forces but, even more important, a hierarchy of procedures for conserving and transforming information as well. Taking this approach, we are drawn inevitably to the idea that the large-scale intelligent procedures used by the human mind to do its work in the real world must be integrated systems of smaller and smaller intelligent subprocedures. These subprocedures, in turn, must exist independently in relatively simple nonhuman systems—in the genetic mechanisms of the living cell, for instance, and in intelligent computer programs.

Although psychoanalysis seems in retrospect to have been the first of the information sciences (Pribram & Gill, 1976), Freud's energic metaphor for the world of nature did not allow him to anticipate either the shocking realization that we share our sapience with microorganisms and machines or the freedom from anthropomorphic misconceptions that follows from the realization. By introducing psychoanalysis to the higher level of generalization made possible by concepts of information processing, Peterfreund restored the discovery of the unconscious to its proper place in the continuing sequence of disillusionments that must accompany the progress of science. Freud's momentous contributions were relieved of the burden of incredibility assumed by all final revelations.

The Privileged Ego

The realization that the executive ego is also an "it" has not yet penetrated very deeply into the psychoanalytic consciousness. Peterfreund showed that the privileged ego, exempt from the constraints that apply to all other natural systems, has been a refuge for psychoanalysts from the seriousness of Freud's scientific goals. Many analysts appear to believe that it would be "dehumanizing" to venture even a single step beyond the limit of Freud's personal achievement in unmasking the mechanical element in human mental life. Some have even insisted that subjective emotion, the most complex of integrative experiences, receives its due as an influence on human life only when it is represented with the poetic simplicity of a thunderstorm or a tidal wave. (The science of our grandparents' generation always seems soothingly humanistic when compared with our own.)

Information, Systems, and Psychoanalysis met this resistance head-on. Part 1, "A Critique of Current Psychoanalytic Theory," made the privileged ego the special target of its criticism. To the analyst who already thinks of the ego as an organizational concept rather than as the experiencing self, Peterfreund's proposal to remove this familiar term from the lexicon of psychoanalytic theory entirely may seem rather bewildering. But, despite the emphasis placed on this concept by the psychoanalytic ego psychologists, confusion on this point is still widespread in the psychoanalytic community. (Hartmann's [1950, 1952] attempts to integrate organizational concepts into a theoretical framework derived from the concept of energy could never be fully convincing, for reasons already discussed here.)

Peterfreund's proposal was intended to focus attention on the inconsistency that results when the ego is exempted from the chaotic imagery with which Freud depicted the rest of the psychic apparatus. By disregarding the role of the ego as an organizational structure in ego psychology, Peterfreund was deliberately sharpening the contrast between the inconsistencies of the older theory and the rigor promised by the new. As a tactic in the reform of psychoanalytic theory, this move may have misled many of the analysts he was trying to reach. As a statement that the structural attributes of the ego are not derivable from the energic axioms of the metapsychology, however, it has its own internal logic.

THE INFORMATION FRAMEWORK

Part 2 of *Information, Systems, and Psychoanalysis* (Peterfreund, 1971) "Basic Information-Systems Concepts," outlined the new frame of reference within which Peterfreund was locating psychoanalysis. Here, with the collaboration of Jacob Schwartz, a computer scientist, he presented a technically rigorous view of information

> [as] having to do with . . . patterns of physical events or the relationship between patterns of events. A pattern of one physical form can be transduced into a pattern of another physical form, and the latter in turn can be transduced into a pattern of still another physical form. What remains the same in this sequence is the information; it is the common factor in the sequence of changing patterns [p. 115].

What will seem strange to the psychoanalyst in this view is its neutrality with respect to the origin and meaning of the patterns being transduced or transmitted. Information is not necessarily "about" anything. It doesn't have to be a "message" from a "transmitter" to a "receiver." The motivation, if any, of the agents concerned, if any, is a separate problem to be taken up at another structural level. When a tree falls in the forest, a pattern of compression waves radiates through the surrounding atmosphere. This pattern constitutes information. Whether it falls on the ear of an organism, and whether that organism can interpret the information as the sound of a tree falling, are separate questions entirely. Peterfreund thus begins with the fundamental distinction in information theory. It separates the physical traces of events, the "evidence," from any possible interpretation of their meaning or significance. The sound of a tree falling is a function not only of the pattern of air waves radiating from the tree, but of the information contained in the ear and brain of the listening organism as well.

How can this distinction be useful to the psychoanalyst? The analyst is concerned precisely with questions about the highest levels of organization, questions about motivation and meaning. That the sound of middle C is heard when the air is vibrating at so many cycles per second is hardly relevant to the experience of the opera lover. In contrast to Peterfreund's position, Rosenblatt and Thickstun (1978) would restrict the use of the term "information" to the coded record of the physical events within the listening and interpreting organism or machine. This, they believe, would overcome the trivialization that might occur if "every nonrandom phenomenon in the observable universe" were considered to be information. But I think Peterfreund's point that the more general definition has greater power is a valid one, especially when psychopathology is concerned. The internally coded record of a physical event must in some essential respect be isomorphic with the actual event. For a particular listener or processor, how "nonrandom phenomena" are recognized as being both nonrandom and relevant to the listener's or processor's interests and needs, is still an important empirical question.

Peterfreund's formulation provides the useful reminder that in every hierarchical system, all constraints that apply at a lower level of the system also apply at all higher levels. We can substitute a patient relating a fantasy for the tree falling in the forest. What is heard by the listener is a function of the information contained in the listener's ear and brain as much as in the words and the tone of the speaker, but the listener must begin by responding to what is actually there in the patient's communication.

If the analyst hears what he or she considers to be evidence of a repressed infantile wish, the analyst's judgment must be tempered by specific information about the patient's state of mind at the moment and at crucial moments in the past, by general information about human development and the psychic mechanisms of repression and symptom formation, and, finally, by information about the analyst's own state of mind in the present and throughout his past. This information must all be internally consistent and it must all fit together to form the optimal interpretation.

Peterfreund points out that at any moment in a typical analysis much of this information is either unavailable or unverifiable. A major function of psychoanalytic theory in the clinical situation is to provide hypotheses to fill in temporarily for the missing information. When these hypotheses are themselves consistent they can be helpful to the analyst in organizing the information actually available and in identifying specific questions that still need to be answered. But if the analyst's hypotheses contain internal contradictions, they will necessarily produce distortions in what the analyst hears.

Because every theoretical formulation is the product of its own historical development, it will always be subject to further modification as new information becomes available. Information theory suggests a number of ways to minimize the consequences of having to work with a fallible theory. One is to be on the alert for inconsistencies between levels in the hierarchy of theories that supports the theory in question. This means that although biological and psychological theory cannot "explain" the particular phenomena with which the psychoanalyst is concerned, no hypothesis of psychoanalysis can be allowed to contradict what is known at the time about biological and psychological processes.

Perhaps the most dramatic example of a contradiction in the hierarchy of theories underlying psychoanalysis is the one that resulted from the discovery by Aserinsky and Kleitman (1953) that dreaming sleep occurs in a constantly repeated pattern of 10 to 20 minute periods occurring at regular 90-minute cycles throughout the night, regardless of the content of the dreams. This laboratory finding renders untenable the traditional psychoanalytic view that dreams are *caused* by the eruption of repressed impulses from the unconscious (Freud, 1900). It takes nothing away from the clinical observation that repressed wishes are *expressed* in the content of dreams, of course. But it does undercut the entire theoretical structure built on the assumption that impulses are capable of achieving expression without the cooperation of the executive apparatus.

In the case of dreaming, the executive apparatus is creating and delimiting the opportunities for repressed wishes to be expressed as dream contents. This implies that the expression of the repressed wishes is not the result of a self-initiated drive for discharge but part of an adaptive process for evaluating the urgency of the impulses being aroused by current life experience (Palombo, 1978, 1980). A consistent psychoanalytic theory will have to take these nonpsychoanalytic facts into account. This example illustrates the general point that every higher-level theory has embedded within it a host of lower-level theoretical assumptions. For this reason, psychoanalytic theory cannot be skimmed off the top of the human sciences and treated as if it were completely independent.

Without an explicit awareness of lower-level assumptions, it is difficult to specify what would constitute reliable evidence for or against a prediction made by a higher-level theory. Observations and predictions must each be formulated at the same level of precision to be useful in testing the validity of a prediction. For the psychoanalyst trying to match global theoretical conceptualizations with fragmented samples of the patient's intrapsychic experience, this can be critical. Information theory can be of considerable help here, because it requires the theorist to be clear about relationships between hierarchical levels and component subsystems.

The result is an opportunity to subdivide a problem as often as necessary for its components to match the scale of the phenomena being observed. John Clippinger's brilliant computer simulation of a patient's production in psychoanalytic therapy provides a dramatic demonstration of this method at work (1977). The simulation begins with a repressed sexual wish uncovered toward the end of a session. Five inter-acting structures transform this input by generating a formal expression for the wish, giving it a linguistic form, censoring it, revising it to conform to the censorship, and reintegrating the censored version with aspects of the original wish.

The output of the simulation is a passage that almost exactly matches the transcript of an earlier interaction during the hour in which the pa-tient's conflict was expressed in what seems like a random and aim-less digression. Of special importance is the network of connections among the five internal structures of the simulation that Clippinger calls Leibnitz, Calvin, Machiavelli, Cicero and Freud. Each of these structures has the power to interrupt and modify the output produced by some but not all of the others. The original wish passes through each of these structures many times. By dividing the processing among these interacting components, Clippinger was able to master the complexity of the patient's internal production of the text.

Peterfreund gives priority to what can be directly monitored in the therapeutic situation—the feedback loops that regulate the interaction of the patient and the analyst. The importance of feedback as an error-correcting procedure was recognized by Shannon and Weaver (1949) as early as 1942. Monitoring the differences between the current situation and the desired outcome was shown to be an essential feature of any complex problem-solving system by Newell, Shaw, and Simon (1957). Miller, Galanter, and Pribram (1960) applied this principle as a general tool for analyzing the behavior of organisms. They showed that every action performed by an organism presupposes a preexisting goal and a plan for reaching that goal. After an action has been completed, its suc-cess in reaching the designated goal is evaluated by the organism. Be-fore any subsequent action is to be taken, errors are identified and the plan modified to reduce them. The stream of behavior produced by the system is therefore the integration of many repetitive cycles of plan-ning, acting, evaluating, and correcting.

Analysts who understand only a part of what they need to know about a patient can add to their understanding by breaking down the patient's stream of behavior, identifying the patient's moment-to-moment goals, reconstructing the patient's plans for achieving them, and noting how the patient modifies the plans when they fail. To do this, analysts must continually test their own theoretical formulations for *their* success in helping to identify the *patient's* goals and to reconstruct his or her plans. From the analysis of these feedback loops, larger structures can be dis-covered. For example, it is quite likely that the patient has his or her own set of more general plans for modifying unsuccessful moment-to-moment plans. These more general plans may be either adaptive or defensive. If adaptive, they will enhance the flow of information through the patient-analyst system. If defensive, they will constrict the flow of information. The same may be said for analysts' procedures for dealing with discrepancies between their theoretical formulations and the patient's actual behavior. Most of this monitoring and processing takes place outside the analyst's direct awareness. It is usually referred to in noncognitive terms, as intuition, identification or empathy.

Peterfreund's argument suggests that there is nothing to lose and everything to be gained in making these procedures explicit. His new book, *The Process of Psychoanalytic Therapy* (1983), shows how ideas derived from information theory can make a critical difference in the technique of psychoanalysis. This important practical issue will be considered, along with this new work, later in this chapter.

The Self-initiating Impulse

The conceptual distinctions of information theory lead to significant theoretical differences with traditional psychoanalytic metapsychology. As I mentioned earlier, the idea of a self-initiating impulse has been radically undermined by the findings of the sleep laboratory. But this idea is also incompatible with the information theory point of view on very general grounds, as well as with the principle of psychic determinism, emphasized by Freud as a major discovery of psychoanalysis. Within the information-processing framework, the Freudian "impulse" is actually a compound formed by matching competing demands for the gratification of a need with competing plans for achieving a desired gratification. At any moment, priorities must be assigned to current needs and then an optimal plan chosen from the many possible plans available. The choice of a plan will depend on many determining factors. If the demand is an urgent one, for example, the corresponding action will very likely follow a preplanned routine designed to be set in motion on extremely short notice. A preplanned action of this kind will necessarily be simple, direct, nonspecific, and inflexible. These are the characteristics used in traditional psychoanalytic theory to support the notion that "impulses" are self-initiating, peremptory, and indifferent to the particular channel for discharge open to them at the moment. This, in turn, is taken to justify the radical separation of "impulses" from other forms of mental activity.

That neurotic patients see their impulses as alien objects breaking into their minds from outside is evidence that the mechanism of repression is at work, nothing more. Since the objective of psychoanalytic treatment is to overcome patients' needs for such dramatic misrepresentation of their own mental contents, it is surprising to find many psychoanalysts feeling that a scientific theory of the neuroses should adopt this subjective misperception.

A misunderstanding that comes up again and again in my conversations with other analysts about this issue is the belief that terms like "planning," "decision making," "goal seeking" and "problem solving" are anthropomorphisms inappropriate for describing the simplest expressions of biological and emotional need. When I point out that these operations can be carried out at any level of complexity and that very simple computer programs act in ways that can only be described in these terms, they tell me that the human mind is not logical like the computer. I asked one rather thoughtful senior colleague if she believed that the human mind is more like a pot of boiling water. After a moment's reflection, she nodded her head and, in all seriousness, said yes.

We are talking here about programming structures built up from conditional statements that take the following form: "If X is true, carry out the next instruction, Y; otherwise jump to instruction Z." The logical result of this procedure would be exactly the same as in the case of an "impulse" seeking discharge through one (preferred) channel but moving on to another if it finds that the first one is not accessible. The structure of the discharge channels and their gates is no less a logical structure than that of the computer program. The difference is not in the logic, but in the relationship between the logical elements and the activity of the system as a whole. In the computer program, as in the simplest organism, the logical structure is incorporated into the process that initiates, regulates, and terminates the activity of the system. For example, the X in the statement, "if X is true, do Y," is not usually a value fixed before the execution of the program, but rather is the result of a computation determined while the program is actually running. Interlocking feedback loops give the system the potential for combining simple logical structures to form more complex ones. The logical structure is flexible, active, and self-modifying.

In contrast, the logical structure that determines the discharge pathway of the "impulse" in traditional psychoanalytic theory is rigid, passive, and inert. Because the impetus for the act of discharge comes entirely from the impulse, the logical structure has no motivation to respond to the passage of the impulse or to modify itself as a result. It is simply not an interested party to the transaction. For this reason, it is often represented metaphorically as a hydraulic system of rigid channels and solid barriers.

It is difficult to imagine either how or why such a system would evolve into an executive ego capable of adapting itself to a complex external environment. "Reality" is supposedly the agent of change here, but, to my knowledge, neither a mechanism nor a source of motivation has ever been proposed through which such a system might be capable of organizing itself to interact with the outside world. This conceptual poverty is the price psychoanalysis has been willing to pay for a self-initiated "impulse" that operates outside the adaptive information-processing structure of the organism in which it resides.

HIERARCHICAL STRUCTURE

Part 3 of Peterfreund's (1971) *Information, Systems, and Psychoanalysis*, attempts to show how complex hierarchical structures that evolve naturally from simpler information-processing structures can give a comprehensive account of the subject matter of psychoanalysis with a significant gain in coherence. A critical issue is whether the systems of structures traditionally classified as "id" and "ego" can be distinguished through their relationship or lack of relationship to the outside world.

Peterfreund argues persuasively that a motivational structure, as the id is considered to be, must be able to direct its activity toward actual opportunities for gratification and not merely to rigid "discharge channels" (see Rosenblatt & Thickstun, 1977, 1978, for a fuller development of this theme). An immature and vulnerable organism cannot afford the luxury of self-initiating impulses lacking an adaptive function. The human infant is a little different in this regard from its phylogenetic ancestors. With the protection and support of its parents, it can afford, temporarily, the *fantasy* of an autonomous impulse life. But even if the infant could actually dispense with an adaptively functioning psychic apparatus in the earliest weeks or months of life, there is no possible scenario through which even a temporarily nonadaptive psychic apparatus could have survived the evolutionary struggle.

For similar reasons, there is no possibility that an adaptive ego could evolve ontogenetically from a primitive psychic apparatus that itself lacks the capacity to adapt. The Freudian id is a concept that ruptures the evolutionary sequence just at the point of its crucial transition from slow-motion information processing in the genetic mechanisms to high-speed information processing in the brain. Interposing a state of chaos between these intimately interactive stages of evolution is mythological thinking, supported, like all mythological thinking, by out-of-date science. It makes little difference that the out-of-date science in this instance is only a century old.

Peterfreund's proposals for a unified conceptual framework represent an important advance over the "continuum" of structures extending from id to ego suggested in 1963 by Gill. It replaces the one-dimensional continuum with a multiply branching hierarchy, in which id functions are distinguished from ego functions by their relative simplicity and more direct relationship to biological events, but not by a lack of adaptive significance.

Feeling and Function

The psychic apparatus in Peterfreund's theory is driven not by subjective feeling states, but by adaptive decision making. As we know, important decisions made in pathological states may have serious maladaptive effects. Peterfreund points out that this is often due to a deficiency in the quality or appropriateness of the information on which the decisions are based, because of repression and other information-degrading defensive operations. Alternatively, it may be due to developmental defects caused by failures of feedback at crucial stages of structure building. The subjective experience of an intruding impulse is a mental representation of the faulty outcome of a decision-making procedure. It is not an actual perception of the psychic apparatus at work.

Since this is a point that is difficult for many people to grasp, I think it is worth elaborating. A frequent complaint about information theory is that it does not "account for" the subjective experience of feeling or the motivating effects of feeling states. As we noted in the example of the falling tree, two very different kinds of theory are required to understand the nature of the information generated by an event and the interpretation of that information by a living observer. This is no less so when the event and the observation take place within a single person.

Although a systematic method of interpretation may produce substantial benefits (as Freud's system of dream interpretation does), it does not constitute a scientific theory if it explains only the subjective interpretation of events by the human mind and not the events themselves. Freud was aware of the importance of this issue when he tried to supplement his method of dream interpretation with a theory of dream construction. Now that many of the original assumptions of that theory have been refuted in the sleep laboratory, it is possible to see more clearly that the interpretive method is largely independent of it.

Maintaining this distinction can be helpful. It means that (1) the interpretive method will not be any less valuable if the old theory of dream construction loses its persuasiveness, but (2) the interpretive method is very likely to be improved if it is supported by a more accurate understanding of the psychological events underlying the subjective states of dreaming. "Psychological" in this context refers to the vast amount of information processing that normally takes place outside conscious awareness, even during sleep.

The sensory impressions experienced by the dreamer are something quite distinct from this underlying process. So, too, are the dreamer's affective states. Freud's psychic energy theory was a response to his realization that neurotic patients acted as if they were "feeling" something they were not subjectively aware of. The supposed transformations of psychic energy represented the unknown events underlying the otherwise inappropriate actions. The idea that these actions are the expression of "unconscious affects" is contrary to the spirit of Freud's attempt to support his observations with a noncircular scientific explanation. Information theory is a more rigorous approach to the underlying events that Freud was trying to reach.

Peterfreund shows that the traditional treatment of feelings in psychoanalytic discourse (not necessarily Freud's) is dualistic and inconsistent. The complaint that information theory is too complicated to explain the directness and simplicity of instinctual impulses is contradicted by the objection that it is not complicated enough to explain the subtlety and discriminative capacity of higher-level feeling states usually associated with the ego. These include, among many others, esthetic judgment, creative inspiration, and empathic identification.

These higher-level feeling states are usually described in two different and mutually exclusive ways, often at the same time. In the more traditional description, higher-level feeling states are considered to be cognitive processes that are simply accompanied by painful or pleasurable affective charges of varying intensity. Here the complaint that information theory is inadequate to explain these states is irrelevant from the beginning, because for this model there is no structural relationship of any kind between thought and feeling. Feeling is either painful or pleasurable. Any element of differentiation belongs to the cognitive rather than the affective order.

In the more current psychoanalytic approach, higher-level feeling states are derived from lower-level states through a process of internal differentiation and maturation, under the guidance of the developing ego. This idea is more consistent with the data of child observation accumulated over many decades. But the crucial point is that this process of differentiation and maturation cannot be described without the concepts of information theory. A simple thing cannot evolve into a complex one except through a reorganization of its original substance. Information theory is the science of organization. A simple feeling, like the pleasure of sex, and a complex feeling, like the mature love of a sexual partner, are somehow made of the same stuff, differently arranged and organized. That observation was and is still the underpinning of Freud's therapeutic method.

Both these descriptions of higher-level feeling states lead, if thought through independently, to information theory. The failure of one well-known attempt to circumvent this conclusion can be helpful in understanding why. Hartmann (1952) tried to derive the development of psychic structure from the process Freud called "neutralization." His idea seems to have been that when sexual and aggressive energies are mixed in the right proportions, their "active principles" react with each other to form a stable product. (We will overlook for the moment the absence of a mechanism for determining "the right proportions" or for regulating the process of mixing, whatever that is taken to be.)

The analogy is clearly with the chemistry of acids and bases. When solutions of an acid and a base are mixed, their ionic components, initially distributed at random in the solution, combine and precipitate out to form a crystalline structure lacking the corrosive properties of the original reagents. The salt formed in this way becomes the metaphor for the ego. But the structure of the salt is simply an endless repetition of a simple geometric form. It is an arrangement with no capacity to change in response to events or to incorporate any new information from its environment into its own structure. The "growth" of the crystal has nothing whatever to do with the maturation of the ego. As a metaphor for human development it is completely lifeless.

But a tolerance for dead metaphor as a substitute for missing theory is not uncommon in the psychoanalytic world. For some, a theory need not be any more than a recognizable word picture. Its purpose is to resemble the mind, rather than to explain it. Like my friend who thought that a pot of boiling water is a meaningful representation of the mind, they believe that a muddled theory is needed to do justice to the muddle of motivations contained in the unconscious.

The Persistence of the Primitive

This brings me to an important area in which Peterfreund's thinking needs to be supplemented by a further application of information theory. This is where he tries, unsuccessfully in my opinion, to deal with an important set of observations that motivates much of the dualism in psychoanalytic thought. One might call this issue "the persistence of the primitive."

As Peterfreund sketches the hierarchy of psychic functions, he stresses the dimension of complexity almost to the exclusion of other differences that may exist between lower- and higher-level functions. The picture he presents is one in which simpler functions appear to lose their individual identities as they are incorporated into or evolve into the more complex. In information-processing language, the levels of the hierarchy are "tightly coupled" (Pattee, 1973). An example in nature is the multicellular organism. This is a hierarchy in which the smallest units, the cells, combine to form the tissues; the tissues join to make organs; and, finally, the organs interact to constitute the complete organism. Only at the level of the organism as a whole is there anything that can be called an independent unit.

This might appear at first glance to be a natural model for the psychic apparatus, functioning as it does as the control system for an organism. Schafer (1976), for example, makes a point of insisting that only the hierarchical level of the whole person be acknowledged by the psychoanalyst. But in taking this position, Schafer disregards another of Freud's (1911) major discoveries, that at least two levels of the psychic apparatus – the primary and secondary processes – are, in functional terms, only "loosely coupled." Hierarchical levels that are loosely coupled function independently of one another. In the large-scale organization of matter, for example, stars and galaxies are very loosely coupled. Emergent properties often appear when a higher level is only loosely coupled with those below it, as when molecular properties emerge from atomic interaction or linguistic behavior from hominid intelligence. Living systems are loosely coupled with their physical environments, although tightly coupled within themselves.

Interesting questions arise when we try to determine the conditions under which tight couplings seem to change to loose couplings and vice versa. The origin of life is one of these, as is the separation of individual galaxies from the primordial mass of matter and energy. A possible definition of psychoanalysis might be "the study of the psychic conditions in which the coupling of primary and secondary processes changes from tight to loose and back again."

Peterfreund prepares us for the view of the primary process as a loosely coupled level of psychic organization when he speaks of it as an information-processing activity that takes place at a lower level of complexity than waking thought. For him, the critical question is the membership of the primary process in the hierarchy of adaptive functions. He tries to derive the functional properties of primary process activity from the features it has in common with more complex cognitive activities that have clear-cut information-processing functions.

This demonstration is persuasive, but it fails to answer a question that has drawn some public criticism to Peterfreund's work. This, once again, is the question of the persistence of the primitive. Why, if the primary process is simply a lower level of psychic functioning, does it take on a life of its own, both in dreaming and in other mental states, where it appears at times to intervene in the normal processes of waking thought? Why, under these conditions, is it only loosely coupled with the higher-level activities into which one might expect it to be absorbed? (We are putting aside for the moment the observation that the primary process is always at work behind the scene of waking consciousness, supplying memories and correspondences not accessible through the normal channels of logical or narrative thought. Under ordinary circumstances of waking life the primary process does function as if it were tightly coupled to the higher levels of mental activity.)

How are we to explain those occasions, most notably dreaming, in which the primary process appears to be very loosely coupled, if at all, with more advanced forms of cognitive activity? There is a simple and straightforward information-processing explanation. The primary process has its own cognitive function that is separate from, although necessary to, the functioning of higher-level processes. This explanation implies that the adaptive goals of primary process activity can and must be achieved independently of whatever further use the secondary process may make of them.

When we observe the primary process working to accomplish its own adaptive goals, as in dreaming, it is only loosely coupled to higher processes. When we observe the products of the primary process being utilized directly in the pursuit of goals of a higher order, as they are, for example, in the creative process, the two levels of mental activity appear to be tightly coupled. The "products" of the primary process I refer to are the uniquely individual associative links that combine to form the treelike structure of human long-term memory. These links connect the isolated elements of our experience across a range of contexts much wider than their original historical relationships. They provide the raw materials for all forms of reasoning by analogy, from simple problem solving to inspired acts of the creative imagination.

In dreaming we find the primary process doing its normal adaptive task of matching new experience with related experience of the past. The dream image is a composite of past and present events, a test, as in Galton's photographic method, of their "family resemblance." (Freud (1900) described how Galton had superimposed photographs of family members to find their common features. He suggested that the mechanism of condensation in dreaming is doing the same with events and experiences.) The process of dreaming is physiologically isolated from waking thought so that the full resources of the sensory projection mechanisms can be used for this task. (Palombo, 1976, 1978).

Loose coupling of the primary process is also characteristic of the neuroses. But the explanation for it in this case is not the same as it is in dreaming. In neurotic symptom formation, the uncoupling of primary and secondary processes is an artifact, the result of pathological defensive operations motivated by anxiety. It was one of Freud's (1894) earliest discoveries that this uncoupling of consciousness does not result, as intended by the defenses, in the exclusion of primary process input from the behavioral control mechanisms. Instead, the primary process input influences behavior directly, without passing through the normal sorting and filtering by higher-level cognitive processes.

This capacity for independent action is strong evidence that behavioral control did not pass automatically from the lower to the higher structures as the cognitive hierarchy evolved. The higher-level structures must be something much more like coordinating mechanisms than structures of direct control. Control actually remains distributed at all levels, perhaps most tenaciously at the lowest. It is the conscious illusion of control that makes neurotic patients vulnerable to sabotage by the products of their repressed and unintegrated primary process activity.

THEORY IN PRACTICE

How is the theoretical difference between the self-initiating impulse and loosely coupled lower-level information-processing structures applicable to the psychoanalytic treatment process? The traditional theory addresses itself to two kinds of therapeutic events, the release of dammed up psychic energy at the primary process level and the acquisition of insight at the secondary process level. Through the insight that comes from having the "unconscious made conscious," the released energy is said to be redirected into more adaptive discharge channels.

The problem with this model is that it fails to account for the building of new psychic structure during an analysis. It rests on the assumption that the therapeutic effect of psychoanalysis results exclusively from the removal of defensive barriers to the utilization of already existing structure. Developmental theory and object relations theory have moved far beyond this view of psychoanalytic therapy, but they have not supplied a rigorous theoretical alternative to it. Despite its enormous promise for psychoanalysis, for example, Piaget's information-processing approach to development has not yet been successfully assimilated by object relations theory. But even without new theory, the empirical evidence gathered in the analyst's office shows very little correlation between patients' conscious insight and the therapeutic benefit of analytic work.

It has become the custom in the psychoanalytic world to speak of analytic treatment as an integrative process that may become conscious to the patient in varying degrees. And it is customary to speak of the integration of the more primitive aspects of the patient's mental life into the larger structure of his or her ego. How this happens in the day-to-day work of the analysis remains a mystery for the traditional theoretical model, which does not provide the mechanisms for this transformation. Most particularly, it does not allow for the active participation of the primary process in the work of integration.

From the information-processing point of view, the treatment process is a series of coordinations or couplings that bring lower-level functions isolated by the defenses into a more collaborative relationship with higher-level functions within the hierarchical structure of the ego. The primary process is not merely a passive partner in this work, a source of energy to fuel the organizing activity of the ego. It supplies vital information about current needs and about the accumulated record of past events in which similar needs were acted on with varyingly successful outcomes.

As the analysis proceeds, defensively isolated associative structures are restored to functioning through the reopening of blocked connecting pathways. At the same time, new pathways are constructed and integrated into a reorganized set of more efficient higher-level structures, as required by the particular circumstances at each point in the patient's development. A vital part of every analysis is the discovery of these requirements. Nothing of the complexity of interaction among the multiple components of the patient's psychic apparatus is captured by (or comprehensible to) a theory that views all change as the simple rechanneling of impulses.

Peterfreund's long chapter on the treatment process in *Information, Systems, and Psychoanalysis* (1971) appears near the end of the book, but was actually written first. It describes the treatment process from a more intuitive position derived from an examination of the analyst's empathic identification with the patient as a feedback process that governs the progress of treatment. In a series of later papers (1973, 1975a, 1975b, 1978, 1980; Peterfreund & Franceschini, 1973), particularly in "How Does the Analyst Listen? On Models and Strategies in the Psychoanalytic Process," Peterfreund (1975a) refined and expanded this application of information theory to the treatment situation.

A Heuristic Approach to Psychoanalytic Treatment

These later ideas have been brought together in *The Process of Psychoanalytic Therapy* (Peterfreund, 1983). As in the earlier works, Peterfreund's emphasis is on the role of feedback processes in the moment-to-moment interaction between patient and analyst, rather than on the long-term buildup of psychic structure within the patient. This is a return to the problem of technique that originally motivated his interest in information theory. He mentions his concern that his efforts to promote the assimilation of a comprehensive new theoretical system into psychoanalytic thought may have diverted attention from his more concrete technical proposals.

The Process of Psychoanalytic Therapy attempts to circumvent this problem by separating the technical issues, as far as that is possible, from the theoretical. Traditional ideas are criticized in this work not because they are inconsistent or illogical, but because they impede the flow of information between the patient and the analyst. Although information-processing concepts underlie the technical approach, information-processing terminology is replaced for the most part by more familiar language. Questions of the scientific authenticity and historical development of psychoanalysis are relegated to the remote periphery of the discussion. Everything is subordinated to the single issue of clinical efficacy.

The result is a profoundly illuminating demonstration of the applicability of information theory to a central problem of clinical psychoanalysis. The book begins with a discussion of the analyst's use of theoretical knowledge in working with a patient. Peterfreund distinguishes between stereotyped and flexible approaches, which he compares with the "algorithmic" and "heuristic" methods of problem solving used by intelligent computer programs.

In the algorithmic method, a fixed sequence of procedures is designed that will guarantee the desired result if followed precisely. This way of doing things works only for very simple problems, where a limited number of possible outcomes can be evaluated within a reasonable time. In more complex situations, the problem solver must be able to search the enormous array of possible solutions by comparing the alternatives at each decision point according to the probable outcomes calculated from its previous experience with similar situations. It must also be able to back up from a disadvantageous position when past experience has failed to provide the required solution for the problem immediately at hand and return to the previous decision point to begin the search once again.

This method is heuristic because it allows the problem solver to find his or her way without knowing the exact dimensions of the problem in advance. The problem solver is discovering what the problem is in the process of solving it. ("Heuristic" comes from the Greek verb *heurein*, to find or discover, as in "Eureka!") This is, Peterfreund says, what analysts are required to do. When they approach a patient's problem heuristically, they use their own theoretical knowledge to evaluate the probabilities at the many decision points that must be traversed in the process of discovering the real nature of the problem. They must be able to judge whether their theoretical expectations have been fulfilled as the process continues and to back up and modify their expectations when they have not.

Analysts who are working stereotypically do not follow these steps. They allow themselves to think they understand the problem before having had the opportunity to investigate it. They then try to fit what the patient says in the office into their initial formulations and tend to ignore or misinterpret whatever fails to fit. Although this might seem like an easy pitfall for any well-meaning analyst to avoid, Peterfreund shows with examples taken from the psychoanalytic literature and from his own experience that there are many hidden traps for the unwary. Most important, he shows that the reductionistic bias of traditional theory encourages the tendencies to clinical stereotyping created by the paucity and distortion of information with which the analyst must always contend.

Over and over again, it becomes clear how the analytic interchange can be transformed from a feedback loop into a vicious circle if the analyst allows theoretical expectations to interfere with efforts to discover what really happened in the mind of the patient during development and current life situation. Problems can be resolved if the analyst cuts through the circularity of the patient's defensive operations and directs the patient's attention to the fact or feeling missing from the repetitive story he or she has been telling. Peterfreund reports his successful interventions and his missed opportunities with equal objectivity, using follow-up inquiries as well as retrospective reconstruction to pinpoint the critical turn in each case.

The idea of the self-initiated impulse reappears in this context as an obstacle to the therapeutic process. After Freud's (1905) disillusionment with his mistaken idea that hysterical patients had been seduced by their fathers, he began to see the actual events of his patients' lives (intrapsychic as well as interpersonal) as of only minor significance. The real sources of the patients' difficulties were their dominating instinctual impulses. These impulses could seize on and control any fragment of the patients' experience that suited them as a means to their expression or "discharge."

Patients' presentations were valuable pictures they provided as they had been those experiences. The specific details of that experience were somehow relevant to their illness, but could not be identified with their causes. The lack of coherence in the patients' life stories was evidence of conflict in dealing with their impulses, but the missing details of the stories were not expected to explain the nature of the conflicts.

Few analysts (certainly not Freud himself) have tried to model their conduct of analytic treatment exclusively on this rigid schema. But

Peterfreund shows how the idea of the self-initiating impulse can operate in the background as a justification for denying the analyst's need to know the specific details of the patient's life story. The two kinds of impulse, aggressive and libidinal, are a small but well-known quantity. It is not unreasonable to try to resolve uncertainties about the meaning of the patient's communications by appeal to the most primitive features of instinctual life. The extensive clinical examples in *The Process of Psychoanalytic Therapy* show that these assumptions can be fatal to the progress of an analysis.

Working Models

To describe his technique for bringing coherence to the patient's life story, Peterfreund adopts Bowlby's conception of "working models." These are, in Bowlby's (1969) words, "the internal worlds of traditional psychoanalytic theory seen in a new perspective" (p. 82). In Peterfreund's thinking, these models are like the stored programs used by a computer. They provide not only a representation of some limited area of experiences, but also a plan of action for operating within that area. Unlike the vast majority of computer programs currently in operation, however, working models are self-modifying in the light of further experience.

They are, in other words, component systems in the overall adaptive structure that generates and regulates the experience and behavior of the person. Many of these components are actually miniature versions of the entire system, functional representations of the system as a whole. They can be temporarily modified for the purpose of exploration and experimentation, so that they can perform what Freud called "trial actions" with minimal risk.

None of these miniature representations is complete, of course. They are simulations, constructed from a variety of simplifying assumptions. For this reason, a great many of them are required to represent the overall system to itself, including its various modalities of interaction with the outside world. Conflict between the models is not only possible but inevitable. Leibnitz, Calvin, Machiavelli, Cicero, and Freud in Clippinger's (1977) simulation are each working models within the larger working model of the main program itself.

Peterfreund lists eight major working models employed by the analyst. The first is the analyst's knowledge of the world in general, as it operates in normal circumstances. Second is the analyst's model of his or her own personal history and the stable elements of his or her own self-representation. Third is the normal developmental sequence of cognitive and emotional experience. Fourth is the phenomenology of the analytic process. Fifth is the analyst's general clinical experience. Sixth is the analyst's model of the particular patient as a "total experiencing human being." The seventh model includes two theoretical metamodels, one a theory that explains psychopathological mechanisms, the other a theory that accounts for the therapeutic effect of the analytic process. Finally, there is an eighth model, a higher-level metamodel that integrates the explanatory concepts generated by all the others. There are obviously a great many component models at all levels with varying degrees of independence and interdependence. When the analyst processes the information provided by the patient, he refers it to each of his own relevant working models. The analyst then begins the sometimes arduous labor of reconciling inconsistencies that develop among the various models as they are updated by the new information.

Most of *The Process of Psychoanalytic Therapy* is devoted to a discussion of clinical cases in which the reconciliation of these inconsistencies required both flexibility and insight from the analyst. Peterfreund's illustrations are themselves models of the therapeutic process at work. It would be a grave injustice to try to condense them into a few words in a brief essay such as this one. Suffice it so say that *The Process of Psychoanalytic Therapy* is probably the best book of its kind available to teachers and students of psychoanalytic therapy today.

Beyond this major work of Peterfreund's, one can see still another contribution of information theory to clinical psychoanalysis. This will be a rigorous account of primary process activity as it relates to the therapeutic process. The patient's primary process thought is, in fact, the primary source of information about the patient's earliest experience in dealing with his or her needs and wishes. The primary process of the analyst functions in the therapeutic situation by matching his or her internal models of the patient's mental life with the derivative representations of that early experience communicated to the analyst by the patient.

Peterfreund (1983) brings us to the edge of this conception when he says, for example:

> All working models are changed by the very information received. They must be constantly updated, adapted, readapted, checked and rechecked for consistency—both for internal consistency as well as for consistency with other models. Such processes are basic aspects of learning and are apparently in large part associated with the phenomena we call "consciousness" or "awareness" [p. 83].

The "larger part" not associated with consciousness or awareness has attracted the puzzled attention of psychoanalysts for a very long time.

Peterfreund's translation of "empathy" into a system of working models is an important step toward the solution of the puzzle.

CONCLUSION

The movement of history has carried psychoanalysis beyond the limits of Freud's extraordinary achievement. Peterfreund's contributions mark the entrance of psychoanalysis into a new era of scientific thought. As with all pioneers, he leaves many tasks of exploration and consolidation to be done. But he has established the broad outlines of a comprehensive new framework within which traditional psychoanalysis can be safely embedded.

Scientific revolutions, no matter how long postponed, have an inevitability about them. They succeed by sheltering the living tradition within a reconceptualization of greater power and comprehensiveness. Copernicus' first concern when he turned the solar system inside out was to save the phenomena of astronomical observation. Peterfreund's work has already fulfilled the promise of information theory to extend the conceptual universe of psychoanalysis while making its day-to-day observations clearer and more precise.

REFERENCES

Aserinsky, E., & Kleitman, N. (1953). Regularly occurring periods of eye motility and concomitant phenomena during sleep. *Science, 118:* 273–274.

Bowlby, J. (1969). *Attachment and loss: Vol. 1. Attachment.* New York: Basic Books.

Bowlby, J. (1981). [In J. Reppen (Ed.), Symposium on Emanuel Peterfreund]. *Psychoanalytic Review, 68:* 187–190.

Clippinger, J. H. (1977). *Meaning and Discourse: A computer model of psychoanalytic speech and cognition.* Baltimore: Johns Hopkins University Press.

Freud, S. (1894). The neuro-psychoses of defense. *Standard Edition, 3:* 45–61.

Freud, S. (1900). The interpretation of dreams. *Standard Edition,* 4–5.

Freud, S. (1905). Three essays on the theory of sexuality. *Standard Edition, 7,* 130–243.

Freud, S. (1911). Formulations on the two principles of mental functioning. *Standard Edition, 12,* 218–226.

Freud, S. (1914). On the history of the psychoanalytic movement. *Standard Edition, 14,* 7.

Freud, S. (1923). The ego and the id. *Standard Edition, 19,* 12–66.

Gill, M. (1963). *Topography and systems in psychoanalytic theory.* New York: International Universities Press.

Hartmann, H. (1950). Comments on the psychoanalytic theory of the ego. *The Psychoanalytic Study of the Child, 5,* 74–96.

Hartmann, H. (1952). The mutual influences in the development of ego and id. *The Psychoanalytic Study of the Child, 7,* 9–30.

Miller, G. A., Galanter, E., & Pribram, K. H. (1960). *Plans and the structure of behavior.* New York: Holt.

Newell, A., Shaw, J. C., & Simon, H. A. (1957). Empirical explorations of the logic theory machine: A case study of heuristics. *Proceedings of the Joint Computer Conference* (pp. 218–230). Washington, DC: Spartan Books.

Palombo, S. R. (1976). The Dream and the Memory Cycle. *International Review of Psycho-Analysis, 3:* 65–83.

Palombo, S. R. (1978). *Dreaming and memory: A new information-processing model.* New York: Basic Books.

Palombo, S. R. (1980). The Cognitive Act in Dream Construction. *Journal of the American Academy of Psychoanalysis, 8,* 186–201.

Pattee, H. H. (Ed.). (1973). *Hierarchy theory: The challenge of complex systems,* New York: George Braziller.

Peterfreund, E. (1971). Information, systems, and psychoanalysis. *Psychological Issues, 7* (1/2, Monograph 25/26). New York: International Universities Press.

Peterfreund, E. (1973). On information-processing models for mental phenomena. *International Journal of Psychoanalysis, 54,* 351–357.

Peterfreund, E. (1975a). How does the psychoanalyst listen? On models and strategies in the psychoanalytic process. In D. P. Spence (Ed.), *Psychoanalysis and contemporary science,* (Vol. 4, pp. 59–101). New York: International Universities Press.

Peterfreund, E. (1975b). The need for a new general frame of reference for psychoanalysis. *Psychoanalytic Quarterly, 44,* 534–549.

Peterfreund, E. (1978). Some critical comments on psychoanalytic conceptalizations of infancy. *International Journal of Psycho-Analysis, 59,* 427–441.

Peterfreund, E. (1980). On information and systems models for psychoanalysis. *International Review of Psycho-Analysis, 7,* 327–344.

Peterfreund, E. (1983). *The process of psychoanalytic therapy.* Hillsdale, NJ: The Analytic Press.

Peterfreund, E., & Franceschini, E. (1973). On information, motivation and meaning. In B. B. Rubinstein (Ed.), *Psychoanalysis and contemporary science* (Vol. 2). New York: Macmillan.

Pribram, K. H., & Gill, M. (1976). Freud's "Project" reassessed. New York: Basic Books.

Reppen, J. (Ed.). (1981). Symposium on Emanuel Peterfreund, *Psychoanalytic Review, 68,* 159–161.

Rosenblatt, A. D., & Thickstun, J. T. (1977). Energy, information and motivation: A revision of psychoanalytic theory. *Journal of the American Psychoanalytic Association, 25,* 537–558.

Rosenblatt, A. D., & Thickstun, J. T. (1978). Modern psychoanalytic concepts in a general psychology (Parts 1 & 2). *Psychological Issues, 11* (2/3 Monograph 42/43), New York: International Universities Press.

Rubinstein, B. B. (1971). Preface. In E. Peterfreund, Information, Systems, and Psychoanalysis. *Psychological Issues, 7* (1/2, Monograph 25/26). New York: International Universities Press.

Rubinstein, B. B. (1975). On the clinical psychoanalytic theory and its role in the inference and confirmation of particular clinical hypotheses In D. P. Spence (Ed.), Psychoanalysis and contemporary science (Vol. 4. pp. 3.57). New York: International Universities Press.

Rubinstein, B. B. (1980). The problem of confirmation in clinical psychoanalysis. *Journal of the American Psychoanalytic Association, 28,* 397–417.

Schafer, R. (1976). *A new language for psychoanalysis.* New Haven: Yale University Press.

Shannon, C. E., & Weaver, W. (1949). *The mathematical theory of communication.* Urbana: University of Illinois Press.

6 Merton M. Gill: A Study in Theory Development in Psychoanalysis

Irwin Z. Hoffman, Ph.D.

Merton Max Gill was born in Chicago in 1914. He was the second of three boys. For business reasons, the family soon moved to Milwaukee. In high school, Gill was among the top performers in an oratory club. He was an excellent student and graduated first in his class.

Gill received his Ph.B. (Bachelor of Philosophy) from the University of Chicago in 1934, having majored in psychology. His interest in psychoanalysis developed quite early, inspired, in part, by a reading of Freud's *Introductory Lectures*. By the time he entered medical school at the University of Chicago, he was certain that he wanted to become not only a psychiatrist but also a psychoanalyst. Gill received his M.D. from the University of Chicago in 1938 and went on to do his internship at Michael Reese Hospital from 1939 to 1941.

In 1941, Gill began his residency at the Menninger Clinic in Topeka, Kansas. Here his psychoanalytic career was launched under the influence of such notable psychoanalysts as Karl and William Menninger and Robert Knight. The most important intellectual influence was that of David Rapaport, the head of the Department of Psychology and subsequently of the Department of Research, with whom there quickly developed a very strong reciprocal bond. Gill became involved initially, along with Roy Schafer, in Rapaport's work on diagnostic psychological testing (Rapaport, Gill, and Schafer, 1945–46, 1968). Later, he collaborated closely with Rapaport on the development of psychoanalytic metapsychology. At Topeka, Gill was also introduced by Margaret Brenman to hypnosis, a technique that was useful in treating the many war-related cases of traumatic neurosis at that time. This was the beginning of a 16-year collaborative investigation of hypnosis and related phenomena. Gill also met George Klein and Robert Holt, among others, at the Menninger Clinic.

After graduating from the Topeka Psychoanalytic Institue in 1947, Gill, along with Rapaport and Brenman, moved to Stockbridge, Massachusetts, to join Knight who had become the director of the Austen Riggs Center. At Riggs, between 1948 and 1950, Gill continued his work on hypnosis and on metapsychology. From 1950 to 1953, Gill was at Yale where he collaborated with Newman and Redlich in writing *The Initial Interview in Psychiatric Practice* (1954). While at Yale, he was appointed training analyst at the Western New England Psychoanalytic Institute.

Gill moved to Berkeley, California, in 1953, where he had a private practice and an appointment as training analyst at the San Francisco Psychoanalytic Institute. Supported by a grant from the Foundations Fund for Research in Psychiatry, Gill continued his collaboration with Brenman (Gill & Brenman, 1959) and with Rapaport (Rapaport & Gill, 1959). He met with Rapaport three or four times each year to exchange ideas and to go over papers and drafts of chapters for the book they were writing. Gill also teamed up with Timothy Leary to do research on psychotherapy, an effort that led to a coding scheme designed to give a comprehensive account of the psychotherapeutic process (Leary & Gill, 1959). Toward the end of this period in California, Gill collaborated with the neuropsychologist Karl Pribram in a study of Freud's *Project for a Scientific Psychology*. This work was shelved, however, and was not prepared for publication until many years later (Pribram & Gill, 1976).

Rapaport's untimely death in 1960 was a great personal loss for Gill. Soon after, Gill completed the monograph they had begun together (Gill, 1963) and began collecting Rapaport's papers (Rapaport, 1967). With George Klein, he also wrote a summary of Rapaport's contributions (Gill & Klein, 1964). Later he contributed a paper on the primary process to Robert Holt's collection of essays in Rapaport's honor (Gill, 1967).

In 1963, as the recipient of a lifetime Research Career Award from the National Institute of Mental Health, Gill moved to Brooklyn, where he became Research Professor in Psychiatry at the Downstate Medical Center of the State University of New York. He also began in earnest to record psychoanalysis for research purposes, although he had done a good deal of recording previously in his studies of hypnosis and psychotherapy.

From 1968 to 1971 Gill was a Fellow at the Research Center for Mental Health at New York University. Here, Gill rejoined Klein and Holt, both of whom further influenced Gill's thinking on psychoanalytic metapsychology.

In 1971, soon after Klein's death, Gill returned to Chicago where he became professor of psychiatry at the University of Illinois at the Medical Center and a supervising analyst at the Chicago Institute for Psychoanalysis. With Leo Goldberger, he edited George Klein's book for publication (Klein, 1976). In 1976, he and Philip Holzman edited a collection of papers in Klein's memory dealing with the controversy that surrounded psychoanalytic metapsychology. In this volume, Gill (1976) published his own full-scale critique of metapsychology, calling into question much of what he himself had written over the years. In Chicago, changes in Gill's thinking about the psychoanalytic process were further stimulated by Samuel Lipton's ideas, particularly Lipton's distinction between the personal relationship in psychoanalysis and technique (Lipton, 1977a) and his close attention to various forms of resistance to the transference (Lipton, 1977b). Here, Gill (1979, 1982) crystallized his own revised view of psychoanalytic technique and the beginnings of a method for systematically studying its application (Gill and Hoffman, 1982b).

Among the most important influences on Gill's thinking were his own experiences as a patient with several analysts. These experiences left him with a deep sense of the difference that the personality of the analyst can make in the analytic process, as well as of the differences attributable to varying points of view on technique. Gill's convictions have been informed and inspired by a wide range of experiences as an analyst, as an analysand, and as an intimate co-worker with many of the most seminal psychoanalytic thinkers of our time.

THE SCOPE OF GILL'S CONTRIBUTIONS

Merton Gill's contributions to psychoanalytic thought encompass a wide range of interrelated issues that are fundamental to the development of psychoanalysis as an intellectual and professional discipline. One of the extraordinary things about the corpus of Gill's work is that it embodies some of the major tensions in the field, with Gill himself standing among the leading spokespersons on both sides of a fundamental controversy. Thus, it is not unusual for Gill in 1984 to find himself differing sharply with someone who cites "Gill, 1954" to buttress his or her own position. Similarly, no critique of the earlier Gill is more thorough-going and unsparing than that which is stated or implied in Gill's later contributions.

At the heart of this movement in the history of Gill's ideas lies the renunciation of psychoanalytic metapsychology. In this respect, Gill's intellectual history is closely related to those of other students and colleagues of David Rapaport who moved away from the perspective of this extraordinary, charismatic teacher even while continuing to reflect his inspiration in the energy, rigor, and imagination of their own work (Holt, 1965, 1976; Klein, 1976; Schafer, 1976). Despite the striking commonalities among the members of this group, Gill's intellectual metamorphosis is especially noteworthy because he was probably the closest to Rapaport of his students. It was Gill who took it upon himself to collect Rapaport's papers (Rapaport, 1967). It was also Gill who completed the ambitious theoretical project that began with the landmark paper on the metapsychological points of view that he and Rapaport wrote together (Rapaport and Gill, 1959) and that culminated with the publication of *Topography and Systems in Psychooanalytic Theory* (Gill, 1963), most of which was written by Gill himself after Rapaport died. With Klein, as noted earlier, Gill also wrote an extraordinary summary of Rapaport's contributions (Gill & Klein, 1964). It is a tribute to Gill's intellectual independence and courage that he, too, finally broke with Rapapport and became one of the most thoughtful and careful critics of psychoanalytic metapsychology.

In this essay, Gill's contributions are reviewed in relation to three fundamental tasks or challenges that are critical for psychoanalysis and that are brought into sharper focus in Gill's work. The first is the challenge of determining and describing the nature of psychoanalysis as a discipline. I include under this heading Gill's contributions to metapsychology as well as his later critique of metapsychology and his argument against the natural science framework that psychoanalytic metapsychology utilizes. To include Gill's early contributions under this heading is to take a questionable liberty, since Gill was not raising questions about psychoanalysis as a discipline while he was immersed in elaborating its theoretical structure within a natural science frame of reference. Only with hindsight can one argue that seeds of the later critique were sown, paradoxically, by the very thoroughness of the earlier work. In this respect I am taking my cue from Gill (Reppen, 1982) himself, who has said of Rapaport: "It was the clarity, brilliance, and persistence with which he pursued the implications of metapsychological theory that exposed its structure and problems" (p. 169).

The second challenge is that of defining the nature of the psychoanalytic situation itself and the optimal psychoanalytic technique. What are the distinguishing features of psychoanalysis as compared with other therapies? How does psychoanalytic theory of technique take account of the fact that the analyst is a person who inevitably bears a personal relationship to the patient? This concern has been central for Gill throughout his career, as has a variant of this question, one which lies on the interface of the metatheoretical and the clinical-theoretical areas, namely, what are the implications of the fact that psychoanalysis is a discipline in which the human mind is simultaneously the subject and object of investigation? In his clinical contributions, too, we find a major shift in Gill's position. Unlike the shift in his metatheoretical perspective, however, there are relatively clear and direct precursors of Gill's later ideas on psychoanalytic treatment in his earlier work.

Finally, we have the challenge of subjecting psychoanalysis as a mode of therapy to some kind of systematic observation and empirical test, despite the requirements of confidentiality and the enormous complexity of the whole phenomenon. On this matter, Gill has been unwavering throughout his career, insisting that the propositions of psychoanalysis must be verifiable according to the usual criteria of science. To reject the notion that psychoanalysis is a natural science, Gill has insisted, is by no means to reject the notion that it is indeed a science. Or, approaching the matter from the other side, to espouse the notion that psychoanalysis is a hermeneutic discipline is not to relinquish its scientific accountability.

It is somewhat artificial to separate Gill's contributions into these three areas because of the extent of their interrelationship. This is particularly true with respect to Gill's later work. Over the years, Gill's ideas have developed into an increasingly coherent and internally consistent position. His metatheory, his clinical theory, and his attitude toward research have developed into a unified perspective on psychoanalysis. What Gill now has to say about research in the psychoanalytic situation follows logically from what he has to say about the nature of the psychoanalytic situation itself and about the essence of psychoanalytic technique. The latter, in turn, bears a close relationship to his critique of metapsychology and his espousal of a rigorous hermeneutic position for psychoanalysis. This conceptual integration was absent in Gill's earlier work; the contributions to metapsychology were either unrelated to the concurrent clinical contributions or bore a strained relationship to them. Similarly, the research focus was only partially related to the metapsychological investigations or to clinical psychoanalysis.

As noted earlier, Gill's current perspective amounts to a telling critique of his earlier ideas. In this overview of Gill's contributions, a bias will be evident in that the earlier work will be considered in the light of its relationship to later developments in Gill's thinking. This approach automatically risks denigrating the intrinsic value of certain earlier positions and contributions because they will appear either as germinal vis-à-vis what comes later or as unworthy of further development in their own right. No history is unbiased, however, and this author would be hard pressed to look at Gill's earlier work in any other way because I share his later perspective and have had the good fortune to collaborate with him on some aspects of its development. What follows is a selective review of Gill's extensive writings, drawing primarily on books and papers that seem to represent culminations or crystallizations of phases of his work and thought.

CONTRIBUTIONS TO PSYCHOANALYTIC METATHEORY

Gill's Immersion in Metapsychology

Rapaport and Gill (1959) set out to complete a program that they believed Freud left unfinished, namely, the spelling out of "that minimal set of assumptions upon which psychoanalytic theory rests" (p. 1). They group these assumptions under five headings that, they propose, constitute the basic *points of view* of psychoanalytic metapsychology. These points of view are at the highest level of abstraction in the theory (Gill, 1963, p. 153). Presumably, to be complete, a psychoanalytic explanation of any psychological phenomenon must include reference to all five points of view. According to Rapaport and Gill, these points of view are the *dynamic* (having to do with force), the *economic* (having to do with energy), the *structural* (having to do with "abiding psychological configurations"), the *genetic* (having to do with origins and development), and the *adaptive* (having to do with relationship to the environment). The genetic and adaptive points of view are additions to those explicitly formulated by Freud. The structural point of view refers specifically to the division of the mental apparatus into the systems of id, ego, and superego, and replaces the topographic point of view insofar as the latter refers specifically to the division of the mental apparatus into the systems of unconscious (Ucs.), preconscious (Pcs.), and conscious (Cs.). Rapaport and Gill (1959) argue that, although he moved in this direction, "Freud never explicitly replaced the topographic point of view of metapsychology by a structural one" (p. 2).

The Elucidation of Theoretical Inconsistencies. Gill's contributions to psychoanalytic metapsychology bear the stamp of Rapaport's influence both in style and substance. In *Topography and Systems in Psychoanalytic Theory* (1963), Gill's most extensive metapsychological work (see Ross, 1965, and Spence, 1964, for synopses and reviews), we find a scrupulous attention to Freud's writings. Often, quotations and page citations on some aspect of the subject are followed first by a highlighting of internal inconsistencies and then by a creative attempt at integration, including whatever reformulation seems necessary or useful. This kind of careful exegesis of Freud's writings, one of Rapaport's legacies (Gill & Klein, 1964), invariably underscores the complexity of Freud's thinking and the elusiveness of what Freud "really meant" by various terms, such as "ego," "id," "primary process," "secondary process," and even "metapsychology" itself. This very elusiveness is a tribute to Freud's scientific temperament and his refusal to become comfortable with formulations that are simplistic, incomplete, or inconsistent with other theoretical propositions and with clinical data.

Apfelbaum (1966) is critical of Gill for implying that the contradictions in Freud are avoidable and that it is, in principle, possible to develop a more coherent and internally consistent account of the systems of the mind. He writes:

> One aim of Gill's monograph is to give the *coup de grace* to the topographic model, so as finally to settle the issue from what point of view the mental systems are to be established. Gill finds in Freud's unwillingness to drop this model a difficulty of Freud's rather than a difficulty inherent in the structural approach itself [p. 467].

In point of fact, however, Apfelbaum does Gill something of a disservice here in that Gill's monograph, quite in the spirit of Freud's writings on the subject, raises as many if not more questions than it answers about psychic structures.

Indeed, Gill's discussion shatters any illusion one might wish to maintain that the replacement of the topographic model by the structural model does away with internal inconsistencies within the various subsystems of the mind. Gill diligently follows Freud in his attempt to localize various properties of mental content in one or another subsystem. He examines each of the dimensions with which Freud was struggling: the relationship of contents to consciousness, the condition of their energy, their mode of functioning, whether or not they employ neutral energy, and, finally, whether they are associated with the repressed or the forces of repression. For the sake of scientific elegance, it would have been convenient if unconsciousness, free energy pressing for immediate discharge, primary process (that is, drive-organized ideas), absence of neutral energy, and contents that are considered to be repressed could all have been located in one system. Conversely, consciousness, inhibited or bound energy, the secondary process, neutral energy, and the forces of repression, ideally, would all be correlated and form a second major system. The fact that the repressing forces—that is, the defenses—could themselves be unconscious was decisive in leading Freud to partially discard the topographic model, that is, the criterion of consciousness for defining systems. Instead, Freud chooses to group together the repressed in the system-id and the repressing forces in the system-ego. However, as Gill (1963) notes:

> Freud's solution of the difficulties of the topographic system leaves unresolved a number of issues relating to these difficulties. Even if the relationship to consciousness is dropped as a criterion of mental systems, it is still necessary to account for the exceptions to parallelism between the relationship of contents to consciousness and their mode of organization and kind of cathexis; and a division of the repressed and repressing into id and ego fails to account for the similarity between them indicated by the fact that they are both dynamically unconscious [p. 51].

It is noteworthy that Gill's extraordinary effort to reconcile these contradictions ends up with his raising a significant question about the validity of the structural model itself insofar as it connotes a set of internally consistent, relatively well-demarcated systems of the mind. There seem to be no end to the "exceptions to parallelism" that are exposed by clinical experience. Perhaps one of the most important and bold contributions of Gill's (1963) monograph is the blurring of the distinction between id and ego:

> I favor, then, a definition in which id and ego are conceived of as a hierarchical continuum of forces and structures existing at all levels of the hierarchy.

> Such a solution argues that Freud's resolution of the fourth difficulty of the topographic systems was *not a good one*, because, by putting force into one system and counterforce into another, it obscured the existence of a hierarchy of force-counterforce integrations, and while conceptualizing counterforce in structural terms, did not do the same for force. The recognition of this hierarchy, furthermore, makes it clear that, on any particular level of the hierarchy, force and counterforce, despite their antithesis, show similarities in mode of functioning, energy employed, and energy regulated [pp. 146–47; italics added].

Gill's emphasis on continua of types of mental activity throughout might be regarded as a forerunner of his later holistic approach, which places the whole person at the center of the theory. This will be discussed further later on. The main point I wish to make here is that one comes away from *Topography and Systems* with anything but the sense that the whole notion of systems has been salvaged and clarified. Indeed, whether it is useful to think at all in terms of discrete psychological systems, at least in accord with the various criteria that Freud was juggling, seems questionable and is explicitly challenged by Gill.

The Depreciation of Consciousness. In *Topography and Systems,* Gill (1963) discusses the considerations that argue for discarding the topographic perspective as a metapsychological point of view. Central to his thesis is the idea that "the relationship [of contents] to consciousness can be subsumed under the five metapsychological points of view" (p. 159). Gill takes pains to emphasize that to demonstrate that "a topographic point of view in metapsychology is unnecessary" and is not intended to "belittle the importance of the relation of contents to consciousness and of consciousness as such." On the contrary, topographic conceptions retain "an important place in psychoanalysis, both clinically and theoretically" (p. 148).

However this disclaimer is unconvincing. To say that the topographic status of a mental event, which encompasses its phenomenological status, can be "subsumed under" (p. 159) the other points of view, or is "explicable in terms of the more basic hypotheses" (p. 159) associated with them, or can be "accounted for" (p. 61) in their terms *is* to denigrate consciousness as a source of explanation in the theory. Elsewhere, Gill and Klein (1964) indirectly acknowledge as much when, speaking of Rapaport, they state that "he observed that with the replacement of Freud's topographic systems by the tripartite model of ego, id, and superego, consciousness was reduced in importance" (p. 493). Applying Gill's (1976) own critique of metapsychology, I believe that the idea that topographic considerations are reducible to the other points of view follows from the mistake of assuming that quasi-neurophysiological concepts describable in terms of the dimensions of natural science are of a higher order or are more abstract than psychological concepts. That this is the mistaken assumption underlying the exclusion of a topographic point of view may be obscured by the fact that the view itself can be framed largely in natural science terms. However, such terms are applicable primarily to the preconditions for the emergence of conscious experience, not to the impact of consciousness itself on the organization of experience and behavior. We can see this clearly if we examine the terms of Gill's (1963) discussion of the clinical importance of consciousness (chapter 9) and compare it with the terms of his argument against the inclusion of the topographic perspective among the basic metapsychological points of view (chapter 10). In the first discussion, for example, Gill speaks of the hypothesis that "insight plays a vital role in changing behavior" (p. 151). In the second discussion, Gill argues that "access to consciousness is determined by competition among external forces, among internal forces, and between external and internal forces" (p. 155). Applying Gill's later critique (1976, 1977a), the first of these statements is framed in psychological terms, whereas the second is framed in quasi-neurophysiological terms. According to Gill in 1976, only the first is relevant to psychoanalytic theory, but in 1963 the first statement was regarded as subordinate to the second in line with the assumption that psychological phenomena must be explained by antecedent neurophysiological conditions.

One is left then with this non sequitur: the *preconditions* of consciousness can be described in terms of the economic, structural, dynamic, genetic, and adaptive points of view. Therefore, the difference that consciousness *makes* in experience and behavior is subsumable under these points of view. The rejoinder may be that even the changes that follow from consciousness or, more particularly, from insight, may be describable in terms of the other points of view. We find such a formulation in the following statement by Gill (1963): "The sense organ Cs. plays the highest role in the hierarchy of regulations of psychic functioning, increasing the cathexis of contents to which the attention cathexis is directed, bringing about an advance in synthesis of the contents which excite it, and making possible the cathecting even of contents which give rise to unpleasure" (p. 158).

The weakness of this argument is transparent, since consciousness is reduced to some sort of sensory apparatus, and it is not at all clear how a sensory apparatus can "direct" anything. Moreover, to the extent that it does direct ensuing processes, it is not all evident how this element of control could be described without reference to consciousness itself, that is by referring only to the interactions among various other forces. The fact is that the directive properties of the system Cs. carry us inescapably into the realm of human intention and into the universe of discourse in which intention, meaning, and self-conscious reflection have their proper place. Among the critics of psychoanalytic metapsychology, Klein (1976) probably has been the clearest and most emphatic on this issue.

The restoration of consciousness in psychoanalytic theory does not in any way imply a denigration of the crucial role of unconsciously motivated actions. However, terms like "intention" and "meaning," which Gill now believes are the proper terms for psychoanalytic discourse, are, to begin with, categories of conscious experience. These categories are then attributed to phenomena that lie outside the realm of conscious experience but that nevertheless act to a significant degree "as if" they were conscious. As Gill (1977a) has written: "Let it be recalled that Freud insisted that only on the assumption that unconscious psychological processes must be understood in the same terms as conscious ones, except for the fact of consciousness itself, could one fill in the gaps in conscious life and construct a coherent, meaningful psychological continuity" (pp. 585–586).

In the end, Gill himself equivocates about the demotion of the topographic perspective from the level of formal point of view to the level of clinical theory. He concludes *Topography and Systems* (1963) with a telling disclaimer: "It is of course also possible that with some future redefinition or reclassification of the metapsychological points of view a topographic point of view will be included. The issue is, after all, one of definition" (p. 159). Nevertheless, it is a measure of the degree to which Gill uncritically adopted the natural science frame of reference of metapsychology that in his major theoretical contribution to metapsychology he slights the point of view that is most useful clinically and that is closest to the data of the psychoanalytic situation and of interpersonal experience generally. Implicit in the holistic "person point of view" that Gill (1983b) was later to adopt as the supraordinate point of view of psychoanalysis and implicit also in the theory of technique that Gill came to advocate is a recognition of the fundamental importance of the topographic point of view and of consciousness in psychoanalytic explanation.

The Depreciation of Object Relations. Another indicator of the depth of Gill's immersion in metapsychology was his relative neglect of internal and external objects in his discussion of the systems of the mind. Freud's superego provides the basis for a bridge from the mechanistic model in which the forces of the id are harnessed by the apparatuses of the ego to one in which the person's experience is seen as shaped by his or her interactions with others. Yet not only is the person as such virtually absent from Gill's account of mental processes in 1963, but so are other persons, which is merely the other side of the same coin.

The systems of the mind, in the framework of classical metapsychology, house and process various stimuli from within and from without. Presumably, the stimuli that are associated with encounters with other human beings, who are perceived eventually as whole persons, are the most important in determining the quality of experience, behavior, and development. Freud's concept of the superego (even though it may derive its power from the forces of the id) theoretically requires attention to object relations – that is, to the meaning of interpersonal encounters as opposed to impersonal stimuli as they impinge on the individual. As Apfelbaum (1966) points out, ego psychology tended to systematically underemphasize the superego precisely because it is not readily accounted for in a mechanistic model:

The omission of the superego on a level of formal theorizing by Hartmann, Rapaport and Gill further illustrates the point that the structural approach, as they have developed it, no longer refers to the study of the interrelations of id, ego and superego, but to formulations having to do with "the control of structure over drive." To put this another way, the structural approach now refers to the construction of a psycho-analytic model which relies wholly on explanation in terms of energy and structure. A dynamic conception such as the superego is not congenial to this model since it cannot be rendered in these terms [pp. 460–461].

Apfelbaum goes on to praise Melanie Klein, Erikson, Zetzel, and Winnicott for their focus on the superego and the corollary understanding that "the nature of the ego is determined at all times by its relations with internal and external objects" (p. 461). This view is consistent with Gill's later critique of metapsychology, which grows out of a hermeneutic position. This position, for Gill, is inseparable from an object relations perspective.

The Seeds of the Later Critique. Gill's metapsychological contributions pull simultaneously toward the deepest possible immersion in a natural science framework and toward the extrication of psychoanalytic theory from it as an inappropriate universe of discourse. As counterpoint to Gill's depreciation of consciousness and his underemphasis of object relations, we find a surfacing of fundamental questions that jeopardize the entire way of thinking entailed by psychoanalytic metapsychology. In the first place, the internal contradictions are so cumbersome and the moves necessary to resolve them so convoluted and so distant from the data that they allegedly comprehend that the viability of the whole project seems precarious. In the end, as we have seen, Gill's proposals are actually quite radical in that they challenge the validity of existing attempts to define clearly demarcated subsystems in the mind and argue instead for an emphasis on continua (see also, Gill, 1967). Freud (1923) himself said that "the ego is not sharply separated from the id; its lower portion merges into it" (p. 24). Gill (1963, p. 141) goes beyond Freud, however, encouraging an almost complete erosion of the boundaries between the two systems. His position actually foreshadows a retreat from the notion of a primary source of energy and force having a prepsychological, quasi-organic basis. *The infusion of the id with the properties ordinarily reserved for the ego represents a pull away from drive theory as conceptualized in traditional metapsychological terms. At the same time, the infusion of the ego with the motivational properties ordinarily reserved for the id pulls away from the notion of a rational agency in the mind that has access to the outside world uncontaminated by subjectivity.* Thus, although it was clearly not part of his intent, Gill, in 1963, had already laid the groundwork for the dissolution of the sharp dichotomy of subjectivity and objectivity that characterized Freud's epistemology and that so colored his clinical theory. Moreover, Gill's redefinition of the id represents a precursor of his later attack on the "energy-discharge point of view" as distinct from the "person point of view" in psychoanalysis (Gill, 1983b).

The Repudiation of Metapsychology

Gill's movement away from metapsychology had to be a painful process, given his closeness to Rapaport. He did, however, have the support of Schafer and Klein among others. Klein, in particular, had a strong influence on Gill's thinking. Gill's (1976) critique of metapsychology further develops Klein's (1973) original notion that psychoanalytic theory is characterized by a mingling of terms from two universes of discourse, the psychological and the biological, and that the two must be disentangled before psychoanalytic theory can develop in any useful way.

The reversal of Gill's position on the value of classical metapsychology for psychoanalysis is reflected in a dramatic way in the book he wrote with Pribram on Freud's *Project for a Scientific Psychology* (Pribram and Gill, 1976). Here, Pribram and Gill elaborate on metapsychology as a theoretical model for neuropsychological investigations. In a certain sense, this effort is in keeping with Gill's claim that metapsychology is, in fact, in a different universe of discourse than psychoanalytic psychology. However, it also carries the implication that the development of psychoanalysis itself will be promoted by investigations that focus upon "brain-behavior-experience interfaces" (p. 168). In a conclusion that was added around the time of publication, more than ten years after much of the collaborative work was completed (M. M. Gill, personal communication), there is an unusually candid statement of sharp disagreement on this issue between the two authors. The book concludes with this provocative comment: "Where we differ is that Gill feels that psychoanalysis must go its own way and that means purging it of its natuural science metapsychology, while Pribram welcomes psychoanalysis back into the natural sciences. Pribram doubts that the differing views of the two authors are really, in the long run, incompatible, while Gill finds them irreconcilable" (p. 169).

The format of Gill's tour de force on metapsychology (Gill, 1976) is once again, in the Rapaport tradition in that it begins with a detailed examination of Freud's writings in order to clarify the implications of Freud's theoretical propositions. In particular, Gill does psychoanalysis an inestimable service by documenting Freud's continuing tendency to gravitate toward neurophysiology despite his many disclaimers and his acceptance, at times, of psychoanalytic psychology as a science in its own right. Repeatedly, as Gill shows, Freud betrays an underlying feeling that the phenomena of psychology must be explained by neurophysiology.

It is important to emphasize that Gill is not rejecting theory as such, including the whole hierarchy of concepts that characterizes a fully developed theory, ranging from concepts that are close to the data to those that are more distant and more abstract. This is a common misunderstanding that goes hand in hand with the idea that the survival of Freud's metapsychology is equivalent to the survival of analytic theory itself. Rather, Gill is arguing that concepts having to do with space, force, energy, and the like are not on a higher level of abstraction than those that are clinically derived and that are framed in strictly psychological terms. Instead, the former are hypotheses about the neurophysiological correlates of psychological phenomena. What is wrong here is not only that they happen to be bad neurophysiology (Holt, 1965), but that they are intended as higher-order concepts than those of the clinical theory.

In fact, Gill is not even entirely rejecting the metapsychological points of view. He argues, for example, that although the terms of the economic point of view so consistently reify the notion of quantities of energy and force that they should be discarded, the other points of view, especially the structural and dynamic, might be salvageable if reformulated in psychological terms. In fact, Gill (1976) concludes his critique of metapsychology with a statement that is much milder than the title, "Metapsychology is Not Psychology," suggests:

> Metapsychological propositions and clinical propositions that are purely psychological must be disentangled and examined on their appropriate grounds. For this reason, despite the argument that there is no direct connection between metapsychology and psychology, the present state of affairs in psychoanalytic theory is such that it makes no sense to say globally that one accepts or rejects metapsychology [pp. 103–104].

Following Klein and Schafer, Gill insists that not only is the quasi-neurophysiological theory of metapsychology detrimental to the development of psychoanalysis, but so is any "metatheory" that implies that psychological phenomena must be explained in terms of mechanisms known from another universe of discourse. Thus, it is not surprising that Gill rejects the attempt to substitute the model of the computer and information theory (Peterfreund, 1971) for traditional metapsychology. Information theory is seductive because it seems, on the surface, to be addressing the problem of meaning itself, thereby avoiding the pitfall of traditional metapsychology. However, Gill (1977a) claims that the terms of information theory are either being used in an informal, nontechnical way, in which case they amount to "no more than a restatement of psychoanalytic propositions in technical sounding terms like 'feedback' and 'match and mismatch' " (p. 591), or else they are being used in a technical sense, which means they are located in a natural science frame of reference. Once again, in other words, the assumption is being made that psychoanalytic theory building must subsume the phenomena of self-conscious human experience under the rubric of an allegedly more general set of phenomena in which the person as agent is absent. Gill's point is that the very exclusion of the person identifies information theory as one that deals with a different universe of discourse than psychoanalysis rather than as one that is at a higher level of abstraction.

Gill (Reppen, 1982) is arguing for a theory that assumes the existence of the person as "a unitary human agent conceived of as initiating and in that sense responsible for pursuing humanly meaningful aims" (p. 179) and that proceeds to identify patterns and regularities among such aims and the adaptations that accompany them. To a certain extent, especially with respect to the content of basic human motives, Gill has left open the question of what will evolve from a purely clinical, person-oriented psychoanalytic theory. Gill (1977a) has been loathe to give up the central importance of drives in development:

> The close association in our literature between the concept of peremptoriness, instinctual drives, and psychic energy apparently leads many to believe that the abandonment of the concept of psychic energy amounts to giving up the idea of instinctual drives. That is simply not true. What is true is that the biological phenomena related to instinctual drive cannot be directly translated into the realm of psychoanalytic psychology, but become relevant there only in terms of their meaningfulness [p. 593].

There are indications in Gill's writings, however, of a questioning of the concept of the primacy of instinctual drives, even if recast in psychological terms. Thus, for example, he has described as "fateful" the theoretical step Freud took when he conceptualized conflict between the systems of the mind in terms of forces seeking expression and those opposed to such expression. Gill (1978) explains that this step "opened the way to designate a special class of motivations as the ones seeking expression in contrast to that class of motivations which sought to keep them from expression. The class seeking expression was referred to as the instinctual impulses and those were in turn related to bodily needs, in particular sexual" (p. 484). The emergence of the structural theory did nothing to change this basic distinction between the two types of motivation, Gill continues:

> Though [Freud] had thus disposed of the error of assuming that defensive processes had ready access to consciousness while the processes de-

fending against did not, he was still left with a class distinction between processes seeking expression and processes seeking to prevent such expression.

An alternative scheme would have been to conceptualize the contending processes as equally striving for expression and to sever the idea of processes seeking expression from any special relationship to the body, but such a scheme would have violated his conception of a hierarchy of psychic processes with the base of the hierarchy constituted by the somatic "drives" [pp. 484–485].

Although Gill does not explicitly draw the implications, his position certainly is consistent with the kind of theorizing that George Klein (1976) undertook. Freed of the encumbrance of metapsychology, Klein set forth a revised view of human sexuality and proposed other types of "vital pleasures" that have a kind of irreducible status.

Gill's New Metatheory: An Epistemological Position

It is true, nevertheless, that Gill himself has refrained from formulating specific notions of the fundamental motives that organize behavior and experience. Gill has devoted most of his attention to psychoanalytic theory of technique, complete with lower-level concepts, such as types of communications by the patient and types of interventions by the analyst (Gill, 1982; Gill & Hoffman, 1982b), and higher-level concepts, such as resistance to awareness of transference, resistance to the resolution of transference, and propositions about the interrelationships among all of these (Gill, 1979, 1982). At the highest level of abstraction we find a bridge to the new metatheoretical perspective that Gill has adopted. Although in some of his writings Gill has equated metapsychology with Freud's energy discharge model, Gill (1983b) recently stated that he regards as a "cogent objection" the idea that "any system of thought must have a 'meta' organizing principle, whether implicit or explicit" (p. 525). The organizing principle that Gill believes should replace Freud's basic concept of energy discharge is "the person point of view." For Gill, the term "person" connotes both the *agency* of the subject of analytic investigation and treatment and the subject's *social* nature.

What appears to be left out of Gill's theory of technique are propositions about the content of the issues that one would expect to be sources of conflict for the individual and that would become the objects of resistance. Gill's theory of technique, in this particular sense, is content free. But it is important to recognize that this absence of attention to content is not merely the reflection of Gill's particular area of interest.

There is, rather, something intrinsic to Gill's position that is resistant to generalizations about the content of human motivation. This feature lies at the heart of what has evolved as Gill's epistemology and, at the same time, is the organizing principle at the apex of the hierarchy of concepts that constitute his theory of technique. This is the principle of perspectivism or constructivism: The meaning of any emotionally significant experience is actively organized by the person according to a particular perspective that he or she brings to bear in interpreting it. This position is necessarily skeptical of or actively critical of propositions about universal motives, since such propositions may imply a transcendence of perspectivism—a revelation, one might say, of the motivational factors that generate perspectives in the first place. A perspectivist position, by definition, does not allow for the possibility of such transcendence. This is not to say that perspectivists may not, for heuristic purposes, posit the existence of certain basic motives, but they would naturally be skeptical about the applicability of such motives in any particular culture, subculture, individual, or individual at a certain moment in time.

The definition of perspectivism just given does not refer explicitly to one important feature of the principle—its social basis. Peoples' perspectives develop and are sustained or eroded in the context of their interactions with other persons. In analysis, according to Gill, one never reaches a point where one discovers something that comes solely from the patient, independent of the influence of other persons. Instead, one finds specific interactions, out of which certain perspectives emerged that were to color subsequent interactions. In these interactions, the patient, with the participation of the other persons involved, constructed an identity, a social world, and a way of living with other people, which the patient perpetuates in subsequent encounters. This way of being with others is not the only way available to the patient, although he or she may subjectively experience it as such.

There is one basic human tendency or motive that Gill's perspectivism can accommodate, and that is the universal human tendency to make sense of experience in an interpersonal context. The need for meaning and the need for other people are inextricably intertwined. In his most recent writings, Gill has gravitated toward theories, such as Bowlby's, that emphasize human attachment as the basic motive in the hierarchy of human motives (Gill, 1983b; cf. Eagle, 1981). Gill has shied away from considering the seeking or construction of meaning as primary motives (cf. Basch, 1977) because interpersonal human relatedness for Gill is paramount. However, Gill's epistemology and his emphasis on human interaction can readily be integrated.

Gill's theory of technique can be viewed, in effect, as the clinical application of his epistemology. This is not, of course, a reflection of the way in which the theory of technique evolved. On the contrary, Gill moved from particular clinical experiences, as an analysand and as an analyst, toward a deep conviction about a way of working with people that he felt would be most conducive to change. If anything, his epistemology grew out of his clinical theory. Once the epistemology is articulated, however, it is not difficult to go back and see its reflection in the theory of technique.

Gill sees the psychoanalytic situation as one in which two people interact and continually try to establish the meaning of that interaction as one of them experiences it. Gill's focus on the here and now could be viewed, in part, as an intensive molecular study of the process by which meaning gets constructed by one human being—the patient—in interaction with another—the analyst. This process is understood to be liberating precisely because it entails a movement by the patient from an absolute view of his or her predicament, which is dominated by the neurotic or obstructing transference, to a perspectivist view, which allows for the realization of latent potentialities. This change is born out of an emotionally meaningful interpersonal experience in which patient and anlayst work together to extricate themselves from the repetitive patterns that the neurotic transference and countertransference impose, as if these patterns defined the only ways in which the two participants could relate. Before giving a fuller account of Gill's current theory of technique, let us go back and review the clinical contributions that antedate it and that, in varying degrees, contain the seeds of its development.

THE CLINICAL CONTRIBUTIONS

As noted earlier, unlike the integral relationship between his current theory of technique and his current metatheoretical position, there is only a partial connection between Gill's earlier clinical contributions and his metapsychological contributions. In discussing this second aspect of Gill's work, I will focus on three main areas of clinical contribution: hypnosis, the initial psychiatric interview, and psychoanalytic technique.

Studies of Hypnosis and Related States

Gill's research and writing on hypnosis bring together many of his major areas of interest. Unlike his work on the initial interview (Gill, Newman, & Redlich, 1954), which maintains a strictly clinical focus throughout, Gill's discussion of hypnosis includes the ambitious attempt to synthesize empirical observations and clinical theory, on the one hand, with classical metapsychology, on the other. Consistent with a value that runs through all of Gill's professional life, however, the work on hypnosis was inspired by an interest in developing an approach that could be applied usefully to deal with a pressing clinical problem – in this instance, that of traumatic neurosis during World War II.

The publication of *Hypnosis and Related States* (Gill & Brenman, 1959) represented the culmination of his collaboration with Brenman on a wide range of studies, which involved the participation of many outstanding clinicians, including Knight, Karl Menninger, and Schafer. Over time, the authors' interest in the clinical application of hypnosis evolved into a much broader task, which was to understand regressive states generally, including those encountered in the usual psychoanalytic situation.

The entire complex project utilized a combination of methods, including observation of hypnosis in psychotherapeutic situations, experimental procedures, and even the use of anthropological data gathered by Bateson and Mead (1942) in their study of trance states in Bali. The work by Gill and Brenman is a model of clinical research; not only are many methods used and systematically compared, but the authors are extraordinarily diligent in openly discussing the process of the research and the thinking that went into each piece of work that they undertook. Hypotheses and findings are always accompanied by candid discussion of uncontrolled variables affecting the authors' sense of confidence in their own hunches and conclusions. Systematic quantitative studies are supplemented by a wealth of rich clinical material throughout.

The studies of hypnosis include a fascinating oscillation between the poles of the strictly psychological and the biopsychological. Significantly, and in accord with Gill's later work, Gill and Brenman (1959) state: "For many years we found ourselves accumulating two apparently independent bodies of data from our observations of the hypnotic state, but were unable to discern any theoretical bridge between them. The observations of 'altered ego function' and of 'transference phenomena' seemed to us to be in quite separate realms of discourse" (p. xix).

However, in sharp contrast to Gill's current psychoanalytic focus, which is deliberately confined to the realm of "transference phenomena" in the broad sense (that is, the realm of the interpersonally meaningful), Gill and Brenman considered the integration of the two realms of discourse to be of great importance. Although, to be sure, the subject matter in this instance was hypnosis and not psychoanalysis or psychoanalytic theory per se, the authors were operating with a psychoanalytic perspective and the work itself was undertaken in the spirit of a psychoanalytic investigation, as the subtitle, *Psychoanalytic Studies in Regression*, makes clear. Thus, it is legitimate to contrast Gill's implicit perspective on psychoanalysis as a discipline in this book with his current viewpoint. The earlier work epitomizes a contribution born out of the view that psychoanalysis can and should be a general psychology. What makes this possible, Gill and Brenman (1959) argue, is the development of ego psychology as represented in the work of Hartmann, Kris, Loewenstein, and Rapaport (p. xxi). As a result of the efforts of these theorists, it is possible, the authors claim, to investigate the effects on the ego of various kinds of environmental factors, including the presence or absence of various quantities of "stimulation." The authors state the "basic theoretical premise of their book" as: "hypnosis is a particular kind of regressive process which may be initiated either by sensory motor-ideational deprivation or by the stimulation of an archaic relationship to the hypnotist" (p. xx). It is not that Gill would now argue that only the meaning of the relationship to the patient is necessary to describe or explain the phenomenon of hypnosis, and that the effects of stimulus deprivation as such are unimportant. He would assert, however, that an investigation defined as *psychoanalytic* would be confined to and would be designed to maximize what could be understood about that aspect of the phenomenon having to do with its meaning to the participants.

Another issue that sharply divides Gill's point of view in his work on hypnosis from his current perspective is the role of regression in the psychoanalytic process. For Gill in the 1950s, there was little doubt that an induced regression lay at the heart of the psychoanalytic process. His intensive investigation of hypnosis and related regressive states was undoubtedly fueled in part by the assumption that anything learned about regression in hypnosis would not only have clinical utility in itself, but would also further the understanding of psychoanalytic treatment. Gill and Brenman (1959, pp. 117, 134–135, 329) cite and agree with Macalpine's (1950) conceptualization of the psychoanalytic process as a kind of slow-motion hypnotic procedure. Hypnosis also has in common with psychoanalytic treatment the fact that, ideally, the regression is not a total one ("regression proper") but rather a partial one, which "a subsystem of the ego" undergoes in keeping with Kris' concept of regression in the service of the ego. This regression is brought about in hypnosis as well as in analysis by a combination of impersonal factors (such as stimulus deprivation) and interpersonal factors (such as promotion of a submissive, dependent attitude). Although the regression itself, in either case, is not spontaneous but induced, the particular form that the regression takes bears the stamp of each patient's history and neurotic conflicts. Important points of agreement and disagreement between Gill's earlier view of transference and his current view are well illustrated in the following statement from *Hypnosis and Related States*:

> We know in general that when a "transference interpretation" is made, it should in fact be an interpretation which shows the patient that his response is not appropriately geared to the actual behavior of the therapist, but is in fact an expression of something ancient in himself which he has brought to the situation. We must now ask ourselves what is our position in this connection if we introduce a technique (hypnosis) which implicitly states, "By dint of what I am doing you will find yourself able to do things you otherwise cannot and unable to do things you otherwise can." In short, if we take a position which implies superior power, how can we ask the patient to analyze the *irrational, transference* aspect of his being hypnotizable at all? Yet we have done this, usually in the face of bitter resistance from our patients, some of whom, as we have seen, said they would prefer to give up the use of hypnosis entirely rather than analyze its meaning for them. As one might expect, despite what one might call the "reality provocation" of inducing hypnosis, it has been possible to tease out the specifically personal projections of each individual and, on the basis of what the hypnotic relationship seemed to mean to him, to make use of these in the treatment.
>
> Yet is this *qualitatively* different from the non-hypnotic standard psychoanalysis where we ask the patient to lie down while we sit up, where we arrogate to ourselves the privilege of responding or not as we see fit, where we ask the patient to let us see him completely though he cannot see us, and finally where from time to time we tell him what is "really" going on? Does not all of this too imply that we regard ourselves as "in charge" of the situation in a uniquely powerful way? Indeed, how commonly this is the lament of the analysand. Yet, the fact remains that each analysand reacts in his own way to this "provocation" too, and reveals his archaic and established patterns of feeling and behavior as transference phenomena [pp. 369–370].

Clearly, then as now, Gill was concerned about the influence of the analyst's behavior on the patient's experience of the relationship. Indeed, the *strained* quality of his effort to reconcile the classical view of transference with his appreciation of the influence that the analyst exerts is striking and seems to almost beg for the new resolution he was later to achieve. Gill no longer defines transference, even with its particular idiosyncratic nuances, as divorced from the way in which the analyst participates in the process. Also, in accord with the perspectivist position he has developed, Gill no longer divides the patient's experience into an aspect appropriate to the present circumstances and one grossly inappropriate to them which comes entirely from the past.

In a major departure from his earlier views, Gill no longer considers the deliberate attempt to induce a regression to be essential or even desirable in the psychoanalytic situation. Gill now objects, in principle, to any intentional manipulation of the patient regardless of its purpose. At the core of the psychoanalytic process is the exploration of the ways in which the patient is assimilating the advertent and inadvertent influences that the analyst exerts via the analyst's inevitably significant emotional participation in the interaction (Gill, 1982, 1983a). For Gill now, a molecular analysis and explication of the patient's conscious and preconscious way of constructing and construing the immediate interaction with the analyst has replaced the induction of a state of mind that is allegedly closer to that of the primary process and the unconscious. Thus, there is no question that Gill has abandoned the effort to investigate in a direct way, in the psychoanalytic situation or in any other context, those mental states that appear to be discontinuous with familiar, secondary process modes of thought. The condensed, often uncanny symbolic richness of the material represented in many of the vignettes in *Hypnosis and Related States* seems to be absent from much of the clinical material Gill has published recently to illustrate his current view of analysis of transference (e.g., Gill & Hoffman, 1982a).

It is clear that Gill has turned away from the mysteries of hypnotic states, dreams, fugue states, and so on in favor of the more readily accessible nuances of interpersonal interactions. It would be easy, but also a mistake, to assume that Gill's course represents a flight from a dangerous and foreign world to a more familiar and safe one. The fact is that although the content and modes of organization of thought in the psychoanalytic discourse that Gill now encourages may seem familiar or mundane, the type of interaction he seeks is rare indeed, and the route toward its achievement is not without its own special psychological perils. Gill would be inclined now to suspect that being caught up with the psychodynamic meaning of symbolic material may represent an escape from the greater anxiety associated with directly confronting what the patient and the analyst are experiencing in their immediate interaction but which is unformulated or unspoken.

It is important not to leave this area without underscoring the important lines of continuity between the ideas presented in Gill's work on hypnosis and his current viewpoint. To begin with, there is the notion of two universes of discourse, as noted earlier, which remain separate throughout *Hypnosis and Related States* despite the authors' determination to integrate them. Second, there is an emphasis on the importance of the relationship throughout and on the element of mutuality in the process. Gill and Brenman (1959) take the position that "hypnosis is at least in part a dovetailing of the unconscious fantasies of the two people involved, and that strictly speaking one should not speak of 'the hypnotic state' but rather of 'the hypnotic relationship' " (pp. 60–61). They spell out the specific form that this reciprocity of roles takes:

From analysis of the two sets of data, on subject and on hypnotist, it appears to us quite clear that hypnosis is a complex dovetailing relationship between the two participants wherein the overt role taken by the one is the covert fantasy of the other. Thus, while the hypnotist is *overtly* being the powerful figure, whether as a domineering tyrant or a boundless source of "supplies" he is *covertly* on the receiving end of this power and/or bounty in his fantasy. . . .

As we have seen, on the other side of this coin, the hypnotic subject takes *overtly* the role of the obedient, super-compliant puppet; *covertly* he is not only sharing in the hypnotist's presumed omnipotence, but is pushing this in fantasy to the point of the hypnotist's having to abdicate completely [p. 98].

Here we have just the kind of emotional reciprocity that Gill would now be on the alert for in his work as an analyst, in which the interpretation of the transference always includes reference to the patient's plausible ideas about the analyst's countertransference response.

Toward the end of the book, Gill and Brenman discuss the reasons why many therapists often give up the use of hypnosis even as an adjunctive technique. Among the reasons they give is the growing awareness of the unconscious wish to assume the role of the omnipotent parent or, covertly and vicariously, of the helpless, regressed child. Whatever personal factors were involved, Gill left hypnosis behind both as a treatment technique and as an instrument for investigation of psychological phenomena. Instead of the unabashed exercise of psychological power that hypnosis epitomizes but which is more subtly represented in standard psychoanalytic technique, Gill has opted for a rigorous, critical understanding of interpersonal influence in the psychoanalytic situation as a means of liberating the patient from closed and repetitive patterns of interaction with others.

The Initial Psychiatric Interview

During his relatively short stay at Yale between 1950 and 1953, Gill collaborated with Newman and Redlich on *The Initial Interview in Psychiatric Practice* (1954), a book that is remarkable for the extent to which it anticipates Gill's later perspective. In the first place, the book is based on three transcribed sessions, reflecting Gill's commitment to recording, which had already taken hold in the mid-1940s. In the second place, the book is a critique of the medical model as it is generally applied in psychiatric diagnostic interviewing—a critique that foreshadows Gill's (1976, 1977b) later repudiation of both biologistic psychoanalytic theorizing and medically tinged conceptualizations of psychoanalytic technique that emphasize the analyst's detachment rather than participation in the process.

The rejection of the medical model in this early work bears some special attention. Gill and his collaborators object to the prevalent practice of gathering information from the patient under various headings instead of following the patient in a relatively open-ended fashion. Of special interest, in view of what comes later, is the authors' rejection of history taking as the necessary way to arrive at a valid diagnosis. This position has continuity, of course, with Gill's later concern that analysts are often interested in genetic reconstruction at the expense of understanding the patient's experience of the relationship in the here and now.

There are, of course, important differences between Gill's current theory of technique and his approach to interviewing in 1954. Although some of these may be explained by the fact that the two types of clinical situations are not fully comparable, I think Gill's current position regarding technique does entail principles that he believes can and should be extended to diagnostic interviewing. For Gill, what is of central importance diagnostically is the way in which a person relates in the here and now, including the patient's capacity to reflect upon the meaning of his or her immediate experience with the interviewer. Other considerations may also be important, but they are secondary. What we do not yet see in *The Initial Interview in Psychiatric Practice* is the full emergence of the focus on the relationship, including the technique of systematically searching for and interpreting disguised allusions to the transference, even at the beginning of the treatment (Gill & Muslin, 1977).

There are many examples in *The Initial Interview in Psychiatric Practice* of Gill's early conviction that the immediate process should take priority over collection of content. Concerning departures in interviewing from a "psychiatric copy of medical schedules" Gill and his collaborators (1954) wrote: "Probably the most important [departure] was the psychiatrists' realization of the significance of the patient-therapist relationship as the very framework within which the nature and meaning of the patient's productions must be understood" (p. 19).

Gill wrote in 1954 as though the mental status exam and other aspects of traditional, medically oriented interviewing were already passé, but what he had to say then is still quite germane considering contemporary zeal about ferreting out the biological factors in mental disorders. Foreshadowing his later sharp distinction between a psychological realm of discourse and a biological realm, Gill makes clear that the assessment he is talking about is one of psychological (that is, interpersonal) functioning, not of biological factors. This is not to say that the latter are not relevant to a complete understanding of the patient's functioning, but only that assessing psychological factors is something separate and apart, something requiring the adoption of an attitude that is not compatible with the type of diagnostic attitude associated with assessment of organic factors. As Gill, Newman, and Redlich (1954) put it: "In the psychiatric interview the interpersonal relationship is focal. The psychiatrist must deal adequately with this relationship to insure that the desired communication between patient and therapist shall take place. Should there be any indication of a somatic disorder, the patient must be further studied *by techniques which are not our concern here*" (p. 65; italics added).

One of the reasons these authors gave for the persistence of the "old-fashioned mental status examination" was the psychological function it served for the interviewer:

> The second reason for the "deaf and dumb" quality of the older examination lies in the psychiatrist's need to retain his equilibrium by demonstrating his superiority. The inquisitory technique is used, then, as an unconscious defense against the threatening content of the experience of his disturbed patient, and against an emotional relationship with the patient—particularly against the patient's emotional demands [p. 23].

Here, again, we find a foreshadowing of Gill's later emphasis on the inescapable fact that whatever an analyst's or therapist's behavior, it carries meaning that derives from his personal participation in the process. Gill might well say the same today about the function of silence and other allegedly neutral postures that an analyst may adopt. Similarly, Gill, Newman, and Redlich (1954) wrote of the inevitability of the reciprocal influence of patient and interviewer: "Reactions of both doctor and patient will of course change as each meets the reactions of the other in that progressive redefinition which is the essence of any developing relationship" (p. 66–67).

As a final example of this early conviction, consider the following comment, which so clearly anticipates Gill's current emphasis on the here and now in psychoanalysis and his relative deemphasis of historical reconstruction if undertaken without reference to a reliving in the transference: "It has naturally occurred to us that we may be trying to push too far the idea of abandoning the collection of historical data in order to emphasize current interaction. But we are persuaded that doubts about our technique are caused by our inability more completely to divest ourselves of long-established and anxiety-reducing habits of professional practice" (p. 412).

It is also of interest to note that of the various influences on the development of their own orientation, Gill and his co-authors consider Sullivan's to be the strongest, although they note that Sullivan does not go as far as they do in giving up adherence to a "relatively formal 'reconnaissance' and 'detailed inquiry'" (p. 62). Significantly, Gill has recently immersed himself in Sullivanian literature and has written about the continuity of his own ideas and those of Sullivan as well as about important differences between them (Gill, 1983a).

There are many examples in the commentary on the transcribed sessions, the phonograph recordings of which were also published, in which the authors commend or criticize the interviewers depending on whether they follow the patients' leads or retreat defensively to some agenda of their own. Where the advocated technique and mode of listening depart from Gill's current view is in the failure to systematically interpret or even identify disguised allusions to the transference. I believe that if Gill were to criticize the interviews and the authors' commentaries on them now, he would point out that although much emphasis is apparently placed on the interaction, in practice, the approach fails to follow the patient's experience of the relationship in a systematic way, one that would require constant attention to disguised allusions to the transference in the patient's associations (Gill, 1982, 1983a, 1984a; Gill & Hoffman, 1982a, 1982b).

Psychoanalytic Technique

Probably the most carefully elaborated statement on psychoanalytic technique that Gill made while he was still immersed in psychoanalytic metapsychology and writing on hypnosis is found in the paper, "Psychoanalysis and Exploratory Psychotherapy" (Gill, 1954), published in an issue of the *Journal of the American Psychoanalytic Association* devoted entirely to papers on technique. It is useful and illuminating to compare Gill's views as represented in that paper with his current ideas (1979, 1982, 1983a), keeping in mind always that Gill's point of view in 1954 is probably representative of much that is still in the mainstream of classical psychoanalytic thought. Gill himself has written a paper (1984a) that undertakes such a comparative analysis.

Gill's definition of psychoanalytic technique in the 1954 paper is well known and often cited: *"Psychoanalysis is that technique which, employed by a neutral analyst, results in the development of a regressive transference neurosis and the ultimate resolution of this neurosis by techniques of interpretation alone"* (p. 775). The definition has three main elements, which Gill goes on to elaborate: the neutrality of the analyst, the necessity of regression, and the importance of relying on interpretation alone to resolve the transference neurosis.

Gill's (1984a) recent comparison of the classical position as he himself formulated it in 1954 and his current view emphasizes the differences between the two. In light of Gill's own emphasis on the contrast, a reader of the 1954 paper may be somewhat surprised at the points of continuity between the ideas Gill had then and those he has now. It is important to recognize, however, that although Gill may sometimes underestimate the element of consistency in his ideas about technique and, perhaps even more so, the element of continuity in the kinds of issues that have concerned him, the ways in which his ideas have changed are very important and substantial. Even the apparent points of agreement pale when considered in their total context. The changes are associated with the paradigm shift noted earlier, and Gill is justified in regarding them as "radical."

One apparent point of agreement is the irrelevance of the arrangement – either the frequency of visits or the use of the couch – to the definition of the technique. On this matter, Gill could hardly be more emphatic now than he was in 1954 when he labeled as "foolish" and "ridiculous" the tendency to regard such "outward trappings" as essential (pp. 774–775). However, this position has a very different meaning in the context of Gill's current overall point of view than it had then. In 1954 these "trappings," although disdained as part of the definition of technique, were nevertheless consistent with the attempt to "enforce" a regression; an attempt which *was* a defining feature of psychoanalytic treatment (pp. 778–779). In 1984 these trappings have lost this connection to the essence of the technique Gill advocates.

A second apparent point of agreement is the fact that neutrality does not mean the absence of any emotional involvement on the part of the analyst. Gill already recognized in 1954 that the analyst was a participant in the process and not just an observer and that there was room in the psychoanalytic situation for the analyst to feel and even to show a range of emotional responses, including amusement, irritation, and sadness (p. 780). Moreover, then as now, what separated an analysis from psychotherapy was not the absence of any interpersonal influence or suggestion in the process, but the attempt in the long run to "resolve the suggestive influence of the therapist on the patient" by means of interpretation (p. 790).

However, in 1954 Gill also wrote: "The clearest transference manifestations are those which occur when the analyst's behavior is constant, since under these circumstances changing manifestations in the transference cannot be attributed to an external situation, to some changed factor in the interpersonal relationship, but the analysand must accept responsibility himself" (p. 781). Gill would never make such a statement today since he sees the analyst as implicated on a moment-to-moment basis in the nuances of the transference as they emerge. On the other hand, he would agree that the aim of analysis includes a heightened appreciation by patients of their share of the responsibility for the quality of the interaction as they experience it. The relationship between these points of agreement and disagreement might be clarified if we realize that what was a main point with regard to technique in 1954 becomes a qualification in 1984 and vice versa. Thus, for example, the 1954 position on neutrality might be paraphrased as follows: Although there is always an element of suggestion in every analysis, *the analyst should try to maintain a relatively constant demeanor in order to be able to demonstrate to patients that the responsibility for their experience of the relationship lies primarily within themselves.*

The 1984 position would have the emphasis reversed, so that the attitude encouraged is quite different, that is: Although one of the goals of analysis is to enhance patients' appreciation of their responsibility for their experiences of themselves and others, and although it is important that the analyst avoid being so active or intrusive as to prevent this realization from emerging, *on a moment-to-moment basis, the analyst must pay attention to the ways in which he or she is contributing to the patient's experience and should include reference to these contributions, as they are plausibly construed by the patient, in his or her interpretations.*

In line with this important difference, Gill's main recommendation in 1954 to practitioners of "intensive psychotherapy" is that they be less directive, in order to bring the process closer to an optimal psychoanalytic one. His principle recommendation in 1984 to the same end is that they systematically analyze the transference—it being understood, of course, that analyzing the transference has a different meaning for Gill in 1984 than it had for him in 1954 and than it has for most classical analysts.

The principal differences between Gill's position on technique in 1954 and his current one center on the following issues: (1) the type of influence that the analyst intentionally exercises; (2) the extent to which the transference itself is understood and interpreted as a plausible construction on the patient's part; and (3) the optimal frequency of transference interpretations.

With regard to the first issue, in 1954 Gill believed, following Macalpine (1950), that inducing a regressive transference neurosis was an essential feature of technique. As noted earlier, Gill has abandoned this view. He no longer considers the achievement of any particular regressive state, beyond what the patient brings to the analysis, necessary or desirable. The work is no less analytic if the issues explored reflect high levels of ego functioning than if they are more overtly primitive, and there is no requirement that they become more primitive for the process to be called an analysis. Perhaps even more to the point, he is opposed to manipulating patients in a manner that does not in itself become a subject of analytic investigation. Instead, the analyst ought to openly encourage patients to explore their experience of the relationship, understanding that this encouragement may also have repercussions that require exploration.

Consistent with the creative, dialectical nature of Gill's thinking throughout his career, even with regard to the matter of regression, the 1954 discussion includes a foreshadowing of his later views. He argued then that theoretical advances in ego psychology lent greater weight to the importance of intrasystemic conflicts in the ego that achieve relative autonomy as opposed to the intersystemic id-ego conflicts from which they derived. He also reminds us that Freud himself (1926, p. 83) raised a question as to whether, in Gill's (1954) words, "after repression the original impulse necessarily persists in the unconscious" (p. 794). Gill suggests that the derivative conflicts may "exist in a form which allows a relatively firm resolution," particularly when psychotherapy takes on more of the character of psychoanalysis by being "more intensive and less directive." Moreover, he argues that "this may result in a quantitative shift which may not be so completely different from what often happens in psychoanalysis" (p. 793).

With regard to the second issue, the differences are both subtle and critical. It is clear that Gill recognized in 1954 that the general phenomenon of regression in analysis was not spontaneous but rather induced (e.g., pp. 778–779). However, the particular form that this regression took was one that was relatively free of the analyst's influence, which Gill (1954) described as "a nonspecific, steady, unremitting regressive pressure" (p. 780). The analyst, as noted earlier, could put himself or herself in a position that would enable him or her to show the patient that the *particulars* of the transference were coming from the patient alone.

In contrast to this view, and in keeping with his perspectivist orientation, Gill now sees the analyst as implicated in the transference in highly specific ways, since the transference is associated with continual plausible speculations on the patient's part about the analyst's inner state. Thus, the best transference interpretations generally refer to some way in which the analyst could plausibly be understood to have contributed to the patient's experience. To say this is not to abandon leverage for demonstrating the responsibility of patients for their own experience. Ultimately, the analysis leads to patients' heightened awareness of the repetitive patterns of interaction to which they are prone. The point is that they repeat patterns of *interaction*, and patients have reason to believe that the analyst's inner experience and outward behavior are colored by the pressure they exert to make the relationship repeat those patterns.

This shift is apt to be confused with the more common emphasis on the "real" influence of the analyst. This emphasis is often presented as an alternative to the view that the analyst functions only as a screen for the transference and as a technical instrumentality. As noted earlier, Gill has moved to a perspectivist view of reality, especially of emotionally significant interpersonal reality. From this point of view, the patient's ideas about the analyst are usually neither simply veridical nor simply groundless fantasy.[1] Gill's views are similar in some respects to those of Racker (1968), Levenson (1972), and Sandler (1976), among others. What these theorists – nominally, a Kleinian, a Sullivanian, and a Freudian – have in common is the idea of an inevitable degree of interlocking of transference and countertransference and a conviction that empathic transference interpretations must take this interplay into account (Hoffman, 1983).

The third difference noted in Gill's position on technique has to do with the frequency of transference interpretations that his current theory seems to encourage. Although Gill has emphasized that considerations of tact and timing are exceedingly important, and although he has recognized the importance of allowing the patient to have the initiative and to develop his or her own thoughts, the overall thrust of his position nevertheless encourages a generally more interactive stance and certainly more frequent interpretations of allusions to the transference than standard technique would recommend.

To some extent, this emphasis on regular interpretation follows from the fact that Gill is no longer interested in facilitating a mode of experiencing and communication that is remote from secondary process thinking. The conversation between analyst and patient is a special kind, to be sure, but there is no technical principle, such as the induction of regression, that is opposed on a moment-to-moment basis to the principle of analyzing the transference. In fact, instead of inducing regression by depriving the patient, Gill now feels that the transference should be "encouraged to expand" by continually explicating its immediate direct and indirect manifestations (1979, 1982).

A second consideration that is consistent with more frequent interpretations is Gill's emphasis on the "ubiquity" of disguised allusions to the transference (1982, pp. 69–79). Gill (1982, p. 80) differs with the following statement by Freud, (1913) especially with the first part to which Freud gave special emphasis: "*So long as the patient's communications and ideas run on without obstruction, the theme of transference should be left untouched.* One must wait until the transference, which is the most delicate of all procedures, has become a resistance" (p. 139). Gill believes that Freud failed to consistently recognize resistance in indirect references to the transference. Gill's review of Freud's ideas about

---

[1]Since Gill's views have been changing, some of his recent writings show remnants of his earlier, more traditional stance that are inconsistent with his newer ideas. Thus, for example, in his recent monograph on technique (1982), Gill sometimes divides the patient's experience into transferential and realistic components (e.g., pp. 94–96), although beginning with chapter 7, he adopts a more consistently perspectivist position.

transference (1982, pp. 139–175) is thorough and illuminating, re-vealing Freud's tendency, despite some important statements to the contrary, to see the analysis of the neurosis as primary and to see the transference as an obstacle that has to be dealt with when it obstructs the analysis of the neurosis. Gill (1982) believes, instead, that the neu-rosis will find its way into the transference in one way or another, either in transference of wish or defense (p. 32), and that the transference can be usefully interpreted in a relatively molecular way throughout the analysis. Moreover, Gill is not concerned that interpretation of transfer-ence per se will interfere with the therapeutic alliance (p. 84). On the contrary, tactful interpretation of transference from the first session on will promote the alliance[2] since it addresses issues that are troubling the patient in a very immediate sense but that the patient resists speaking of or thinking of explicitly for fear that they will not be accepted or un-derstood. Instead of being concerned about managing his own behavior so as to promote a nonspecific regression on the one hand, and a sponta-neous specific transference on the other, Gill's attention as a clinician is devoted to identifying the various disguised expressions of transfer-ence, such as displacement and identification. Citing Lipton's (1977b) discussion, Gill (1982, p. 170) finds that familiarity with identification, which is less commonly recognized than displacement (or, I might add, projection) as a vehicle for indirect communication, greatly expands the range of associations in which it is compelling to infer that there is an im-plication for the transference.

Despite his encouragement to the analyst to regularly interpret dis-guised allusions to the transference, Gill certainly allows latitude for a wide range of frequency, depending on the patient, the type of material that is coming up, and the style of the analyst. It is a mistake to regard frequency of interpretation per se as the crux of the difference between Gill's position and the classical one. Indeed, it is quite compatible with Gill's ideas to be critical of overzealous interpretation of transference, a perversion to which Gill's theory of technique may be prone but which certainly is not required by it. More at the core of Gill's departure from the classical model, in my view, are the changes associated with the first and second issues I have cited, namely, the opposition to deliberate ma-nipulation and the understanding and interpretation of transference as a plausible construction, given the inevitability of the analyst's personal participation in the process.

---

[2]Although Gill sometimes uses the term "alliance," he agrees with Lipton (1977a) that the concept is objectionable insofar as it denotes or connotes something that should be de-liberately fostered with special techniques and that is uncontaminated by transference (see Gill, 1982, pp. 96–106; Reppen, 1982, pp. 173–174).

All that I have said here pertains to what Gill (1979, 1982) calls "interpretation of resistance to the awareness of transference," as distinct from "interpretation of resistance to the resolution of transference." There is no question that Gill gives priority to the former as a matter of technique, feeling that a good deal of resolution of transference will follow spontaneously from its explication in the here and now. The patient will come to recognize that, for example, he or she paid selective attention to the features of the analyst's behavior that he or she had previously disavowed entirely. Also, the patient will spontaneously recall experiences from childhood that will help to show that his or her perspective has particular historical origins. Gill (1982) is very concerned that genetic interpretations may be used as a flight from the here and now, but he also recognizes their importance and the importance of other kinds of interpretation for the resolution of the transference:

> It is important that the analyst not be tied to some rigid rule that he should make only transference interpretations. Not only can extra-transference interpretations be useful, but the spontaneity of the analyst's behavior is essential for the conduct of an analysis. If an extra-transference interpretation occurs to the analyst as a plausible clarification, he should make it. At the same time, he should be alert to its possible repercussions on the transference—but then he should be alert to the repercussions on the transference of a transference interpretation too.

> I conclude that while extra-transference interpretations play a role in analysis—and extra-transference clarifications certainly must—priority, in both time and importance, should go to transference interpretations. This principle may be more readily accepted if I emphasize that attention to resistance to the awareness of transference should come first and that, even though priority in interpretation designed to resolve the transference should go to interpretation within the analytic situation, working through requires extra-transference, transference, *and* genetic transference interpretations [pp. 125–126].

Gill speaks of the person paradigm or point of view, the interpersonal paradigm, and perspectivism almost interchangeably, because for him each implies the others. Gill's more specific ideas about the analytic situation follow directly from these supraordinate concepts. In the old metapsychology, according to what Gill (1983b) calls the "energy discharge" point of view, the patient was encouraged to regress in order to arrive at the underlying infantile neurosis that would bear the stamp of the patient's bodily urges, relatively independent of environmental influences. In the old paradigm it was thought that "free association and regression will in time lead to the relatively direct expression of bodily urges little related to interpersonal interaction, whether with others in the past or with the therapist in the present" (p. 546). These urges are the decisive factors underlying the transference and the distortion of reality the transference entails. In other words, the emphasis on the past is linked with the idea of a somatic drive that precedes and determines interactions with others. But for Gill, there is nothing unearthed or reconstructed in psychoanalysis that antedates interactions. The present interaction, moreover, is the *best* place to look for the person's fixed ways of organizing interpersonal experience. Transference is redefined as a way of looking at things and as a way of being with other people—not a distorted way in any simple sense, but a rigid way that cuts off alternative potentials. The analyst always interprets in the spirit of acknowledging the plausibility of the patient's perspective. There is no absolute reality to which the analyst has access but to which the patient is blind because of the transference. In fact, the patient's transference perspective may shed light on some aspect of the analyst's own participation (overt and covert), which the analyst resists. Neither participant has a corner on the truth, and yet they try to hammer out an understanding that makes sense to both of them and that has the feel of cogency. Even as they are doing so, the analyst must take the lead in turning a critical eye on what they have decided and how they have decided it. That is why historical exploration cannot get very far without being interrupted by a question as to its purpose right now. To raise this question does not preclude returning subsequently to reconstructive work.

This continual scrutiny of the relationship is, in the ideal, not an intellectual exercise, but rather a moving, new interpersonal experience that represents and promotes personal growth (Gill, 1982, pp. 118–120). The new experience associated with the analysis of the transference rests in part on the analyst's openness to the possibility that, wittingly or unwittingly, he or she has been the patient's accomplice in the perpetuation of the old, fixed patterns of interaction that the transference represents. At the very moment in which this openness is conveyed to the patient, the analyst stands a good chance of extricating himself or herself from the role of accomplice. Gill is fond of citing Strachey's (1934) and Loewald's (1960) classic papers on the therapeutic action of psychoanalysis in which both of them state that analysis cures because the analyst offers himself or herself not only as a technical instrumentality but as an object with whom the patient can have a new kind of experience. What Strachey and Loewald omit or underemphasize is the element of mutuality in the shaping of the transference and the countertransference on a moment-to-moment basis.

With psychoanalytic techique redefined in a manner that encourages more active engagement of the patient and that demands more systematic exploration of the patient's immediate experience of the interaction, the whole question of analyzability is thrown open. Gill's views now on assessment of analyzability parallel those of Freud in calling for a "trial analysis" as the best way to begin. Gill does not have fixed ideas on who can benefit from a rigorous psychoanalytic approach based on standard types of classification. He feels that too many patients are written off as "unanalyzable" because they cannot adapt well to the couch and to a relatively silent and remote analyst who is systematically trying to induce a regression (1984a). For Gill, this procedure is misguided, and a patient's refusal or inability to comply with it could be a sign of strength. Analyzability for Gill has to do with a patient's ability to engage in and reflect upon a relationship with an analyst who is emotionally available and who thinks of himself or herself as a co-participant in the process. Gill (1983a) mocks the standard view of analyzability, stating that "an analyzable patient is a patient with whom the analyst can maintain the illusion of neutrality" (p. 213). In fact, there may be relatively healthy patients with particular temperaments who could not tolerate standard technique but who would respond well to Gill's approach. Similarly, there may be some very sick patients who are automatically written off because of their inability to adapt to the standard psychoanalytic situation but who may be able to respond relatively well to the more active focus on the here and now that Gill espouses.

RESEARCH IN PSYCHOANALYSIS

As noted earlier, Gill has been unwavering throughout his career on the necessity of systematic research on the psychoanalytic process, the third aspect of Gill's work that I will discuss here. He has never accepted the common psychoanalytic view, which Freud himself promulgated, that the case study method, however much it has contributed to theory and practice, can obviate the need for a more rigorous application of scientific methods to the gathering and analysis of psychoanalytic data. Perhaps Gill's most important contribution to the development of psychoanalysis as a science has been his pioneering effort to make the raw data of psychoanalysis available for study by independent observers through audio-recordings of psychotherapeutic and psychoanalytic sessions. Inspired partly by Carl Rogers and others of the client-centered school, who made recording and research a central part of their practice from the start, Gill, along with a few others, began recording psychotherapy at the Menninger Clinic as early as the middle 1940s. The advent of tape recording greatly facilitated this effort. Over the years, Gill has collected samples from each of a number of tape recorded analyses, some conducted by himself and some by the relatively few other analysts who were willing to contribute.

Recording was instrumental in Gill's research on hypnosis during the 1940s and 1950s—for example, in a study of spontaneous fluctuations in the depth of the hypnotic state during sessions of psychotherapy (Brenman, Gill, & Knight, 1952). In this study, ego functioning around the time of the fluctuation was assessed by having independent judges examine associations surrounding statements such as "I'm going deeper" or "I'm coming up lighter." The method itself provided a model that was later adapted by Luborsky (1967) in his studies of momentary forgetting in psychotherapy. The model also evolved into the broader "symptom context method" for investigating the appearance of physical and psychological symptoms during psychotherapy sessions (Luborsky and Auerbach, 1969).

In the 1960s, Gill and his collaborators (Gill, Simon, Fink, Endicott, & Paul, 1968) wrote a landmark article on recording and psychoanalysis, in which they take up and challenge many of the common sources of resistance to recording, some personal and some more clinical or theoretical. On the personal side, for example, there is fear of exposure and criticism. Gill (Reppen, 1982) recognizes that for some patient-analyst pairs, recording may pose insurmountable difficulties (p. 171). In general, however, he feels that the fear of exposure and criticism, both on an individual and institutional level, must be overcome if analysis is to have any hope of growing or even surviving as a scientific discipline.

Objections on the clinical side to recording for research purposes include concern about compromising confidentiality as well as about introducing another purpose into the analytic situation that is extraneous to the analytic work itself and to the immediate interests of the patient. There is no question, of course, that patients will react in various ways to these circumstances. However, Gill (Reppen, 1982; Gill et al., 1968) argues, it does not follow that they preclude a successful analysis. Here Gill's point of view on technique dovetails with his attitude on recording. The transference does not develop in a vacuum. However the analytic situation is set up, its transference repercussions must be explored in the spirit of recognizing the element of plausibility in the patient's view of the situation. In the first place, the research situation is not so different from other analytic situations in which confidentiality is compromised or in which the analyst's self-interest is readily apparent. When, for example, an institute candidate sees a patient as part of training, confidentiality is not inviolate, and the patient has cause to feel used. These circumstances are generally understood to be important complications that need to be explored, but not of such a magnitude that they preclude a successful analysis. In the second place, even when the patient has reason to believe that confidentiality is strictly maintained, the situation is likely to have particular meanings that must be investigated. In what might be regarded by many as the optimal analytic setting, the promise of strict confidentiality, the strong recommendation that the frequency of sessions be four times per week or more, the use of the couch, the analyst's fee, and the analyst's silence are all very powerful stimuli, which the patient construes in plausible and yet also personally expressive and, in principle, analyzable ways (Gill, 1984a).

Gill's theory of technique is also congenial to research on the psychoanalytic process in that it invites attention to each analytic hour as a unit that has a certain integrity of meaning. In the classical paradigm, in which the intent is to foster the unfolding of a regressive transference neurosis over a long period of time, it would be difficult to assess the quality of the analyst's technique as well as other variables because the context of each event is so temporally broad and so difficult to know and take into account. Although Gill is fully aware of the importance of context and knows that the analyst may be in a position to take it into account more than an external observer who has only a small sample of the data, Gill's molecular focus on the analysis of transference in the here and now lends itself to investigation of smaller and more manageable units of data. One of the fruits of Gill's commitment to systematic research has been the development of a coding scheme (Gill & Hoffman, 1982b), which permits classification of various kinds of patient communications and analyst interventions. The highlight of the scheme is the delineation of criteria for identifying disguised allusions to the transference in associations not manifestly about the transference. The research judge cannot claim that such an allusion has occurred without giving a specific basis for this inference. The basis may have the form of a previous statement by the patient that is explicitly about the relationship, or it may have the form of some readily recognizable event in the interaction about which neither of the participants has spoken. These criteria for coding allusions to the transference have clinical utility as well, because they set up at least partial guidelines to indicate when a transference interpretation might be called for and when it might not— guidelines that have been vague or lacking in clinical theory.

Gill recognizes that the development of this coding scheme is only a small first step toward a more comprehensive program of systematic research on the analytic process as he conceives of it. In the long run, Gill would want to see variables defined and operationalized and methods developed so that it would be possible to study, on a molecular level, the differential effects of various types of intervention on the process and, on a molar level, the relative efficacy of one treatment approach or another.

Gill's commitment is not to research for the sake of research but to clinical research that deals with theoretically meaningful variables. It is a commitment to the scientific study of human intention and meaning, including the interpersonal conditions that promote change and growth. In this sense, psychoanalysis for Gill is a hermeneutic science, a contradiction in terms for some (Blight, 1981; Eagle, 1980) but for Gill a category that connotes the special combination of values he feels should characterize psychoanalysis as a discipline.

CONCLUSION

As we have seen, Gill's point of view has changed radically over the years. His ideas have continued to evolve. Any attempt to capture the thrust of his position at a given time is unlikely to do justice either to various important qualifications that he has proposed or to new ideas and revisions of theory that are still germinal in his thinking. For example, recently Gill (personal communication, November, 1984) has been wrestling with several questions. Are there, after all, universal conflicts that play a role in every analysis, and, if so, what are they? As noted earlier, Gill has been considering the conflict between attachment and autonomy as a primary issue of this kind. With regard to theory of technique, does the elimination of the principle of deliberately inducing a regression leave a gap that invites, instead of excessive restraint, overzealous interpretation of transference? What provision is there in the theory, formally speaking, to prevent the *reductio ad absurdum* that would have the analyst forever interpreting the transference repercussions of overzealous interpretation? Is it enough to emphasize the importance of common sense, tact, and timing, or to say that one does not interpret until one has a compelling sense of a latent transference meaning in the patient's associations? Or is it necessary to formulate another principle of technique to balance the principle of analysis of transference? Perhaps for Gill this principle would be supraordinate to the analysis of transference and would, in the most general terms, have to do with promoting a certain quality of interpersonal experience. This experience might be most powerfully served by the analysis of the transference but, presumably, could also be undermined by it at times. What this quality of experience would be, of course, needs to be spelled out. It would also have to be located in relation to other conceptualizations in the literature of the interpersonal experience in analysis, such as Gill's own concept of the new experience that accompanies the analysis of the transference, Zetzel's therapeutic alliance, Winnicott's holding environment, Kohut's self-selfobject tie, and Schafer's more generic atmosphere of safety.

Gill's intellectual style is to steadfastly pursue the logical implications of a particular line of thought without shrinking from their consequences for entrenched tradition. At the same time, in dialectical relationship with this tendency, his convictions about theory, research, and practice are united by his readiness to turn a critical eye on his own perspective and to consider other points of view. Thus, despite the vigor with which he has advocated and defended his position, Gill has also actively explored the points of convergence and divergence of his own views and those of Gedo (Gill, 1981), Melanie Klein (Gill, 1982, pp. 129–137), Kohut (Reppen, 1982, pp. 183–186), Sullivan (Gill, 1983a), and Langs (Gill, 1984b), among many others. The very fact that he is actively engaged in dialogue with exponents of these diverse perspectives (as reflected in his publications, speaking engagements, and extensive correspondence) testifies to the bridge-building role that Gill now occupies in the field. I believe that such a role is congenial to him because of his disdain for parochialism; he has a deep conviction that psychoanalysis will survive and grow only if exponents of diverse viewpoints engage each other in an ongoing process of reciprocal, constructive criticism and ultimately submit their differences to the arbitrating power of systematic clinical research.

REFERENCES

Apfelbaum, B. (1966). On ego psychology: A critique of the structural approach to psychoanalytic theory. *International Journal of Psycho-Analysis, 47,* 451–475.

Basch, M. F. (1977). Developmental psychology and explanatory theory in psychoanalysis. *Annual of Psychoanalysis, 5,* 229–263.

Bateson, G., & Mead, M. (1942). Balinese character: A photographic analysis. *Special Publications of the New York Academy of Sciences, 2.*

Blight, J. G. (1981). Must psychoanalysis retreat to hermeneutics? Psychoanalytic theory in the light of Popper's evolutionary epistemology. *Psychoanalysis & Contemporary Thought, 4,* 147–205.

Brenman, M., Gill, M. M., & Knight, R. P. (1952). Spontaneous fluctuations in depth of hypnosis and their implications for ego-function. *International Journal of Psycho-Analysis, 33,* 22–34.

Eagle, M. N. (1980). A critical examination of motivational explanation in psychoanalysis. *Psychoanalysis & Contemporary Thought, 3,* 329–380.

Eagle, M. N. (1981). Interests as object relations. *Psychoanalysis & Contemporary Thought, 4,* 527–565.

Freud, S. (1913). On beginning the treatment: Further recommendations on the technique of psycho-analysis. *Standard Edition, 12,* 147–156.

Freud, S. (1923). The ego and the id. *Standard Edition, 19,* 12–66.

Freud, S. (1926). Inhibitions, symptoms and anxiety. *Standard Edition, 20,* 87–172.

Gill, M. M. (1954). Psychoanalysis and exploratory psychotherapy. *Journal of the American Psychoanalytic Association, 2,* 771–797.

Gill, M. M. (1963). Topography and systems in psychoanalytic theory. *Psychological Issues, 3* (2, Monograph 10). New York: International Universities Press.

Gill, M. M. (1967). The primary process. In R. Holt (Ed.), Motives and thought: Psychoanalytic essays in honor of David Rapaport. *Psychological Issues, 5* (2/3, Monograph 18/19), 260–298.

Gill, M. M. (1976). Metapsychology is not psychology. In M. M. Gill & P. S. Holzman (Eds.), Psychology versus metapsychology. Psychoanalytic essays in memory of George S. Klein. *Psychological Issues, 9* (4, Monograph 36), 71–105.

Gill, M. M. (1977a). Psychic energy reconsidered: Discussion. *Journal of the American Psychoanalytic Association, 25,* 581–598.

Gill, M. M. (1977b). The two models of the mental health disciplines. *Bulletin of the Menninger Clinic, 41,* 79–84.

Gill, M. M. (1978). Freud's concepts of unconsciousness and the unconscious. In A. S. Prangishvilli, A. E. Sherozia, & F. V. Bassin (Eds.), *The Unconscious* (Vol. 1). Tbilisi, U.S.S.R.: Metsniereba Publishing House.

Gill, M. M. (1979). The analysis of the transference. *Journal of the American Psychoanalytic Association, 27* (Supplement), 263–288.

Gill, M. M. (1981). The boundaries of psychoanalytic data and technique: A critique of Gedo's *Beyond Interpretation. Psychoanalytic Inquiry, 1,* 205–232.

Gill, M. M. (1982). Analysis of transference: Vol. 1. Theory and technique. *Psychological Issues* (Monograph 53).

Gill, M. M. (1983a). The interpersonal paradigm and the degree of the therapist's involvement. *Contemporary Psychoanalysis, 19,* 200–237.

Gill, M. M. (1983b). The point of view of psychoanalysis: Energy discharge or person. *Psychoanalysis and Contemporary Thought, 6,* 523–551.

Gill, M. M. (1984a). Psychoanalysis and psychotherapy: A revision. *International Review of Psycho-Analysis, 11,* 161–179.

Gill, M. M. (1984b). Robert Langs on technique: A critique. In J. Raney (Ed.), *Listening and interpreting: The challenge of the work of Robert Langs.* New York: Jason Aronson.

Gill, M. M., & Brenman, M. (1959). *Hypnosis and related states: Psychoanalytic studies in regression.* New York: International Universities Press.

Gill, M. M., & Hoffman, I. Z. (1982a). Analysis of transference: Vol. 2. Studies of nine audio-recorded psychoanalytic sessions. *Psychological Issues* (Monograph 54).

Gill, M. M., & Hoffman, I. Z. (1982b). A method for studying the analysis of aspects of the patient's experience of the relationship in psychoanalysis and psychotherapy. *Journal of the American Psychoanalytic Association, 30,* 137–167.

Gill, M. M., & Klein, G. S. (1964). The structuring of drive and reality: David Rapaport's contributions to psychoanalysis and psychology. *International Journal of Psycho-Analysis, 45,* 483–498.

Gill, M. M., & Muslin, H. (1977). Early interpretation of transference. *Journal of the American Psychoanalytic Association, 24,* 779–794.

Gill, M. M., Newman, R., & Redlich, F. C. (1954). *The initial interview in psychiatric practice.* New York: International Universities Press.

Gill, M. M., Simon, J., Fink, G., Endicott, N. A., & Paul, I. H. (1968). Studies in audio-recorded psychoanalysis: 1. General considerations. *Journal of the American Psycho-Analytic Association, 16,* 230–244.

Hoffman, I. Z. (1983). The patient as interpreter of the analyst's experience. *Contemporary Psychoanalysis, 19,* 389–422.

Holt, R. R. (1965). A review of some of Freud's biological assumptions and their influence on his theories. In N. S. Greenfield & W. C. Lewis (Eds.), *Psychoanalysis and current biological thought* (pp. 93–124). Madison: University of Wisconsin Press.

Holt, R. R. (1976). Drive or wish? A reconsideration of the psychoanalytic theory of motivation. In M. M. Gill & P. S. Holzman (Eds.), Psychology versus metapsychology: Psychoanalytic essays in memory of George S. Klein. *Psychological Issues, 9* (4 Monograph 36).

Klein, G. S. (1973). Two theories or one. *Bulletin of the Menninger Clinic, 37,* 102–132.

Klein, G. S. (1976). *Psychoanalytic theory: An exploration of essentials.* New York: International Universities Press.

Leary, T., & Gill, M. M. (1959). The dimensions and a measure of the process of psychotherapy: A system for the analysis of the content of clinical evaluations and patient-therapist verbalizations. In E. A. Rubinstein & M. B. Parloff (Eds.), *Research in Psychotherapy.* Washington, D.C.: American Psychological Association.

Levenson, E. (1972). *The fallacy of understanding.* New York: Basic Books.

Lipton, S. D. (1977a). The advantages of Freud's technique as shown in his analysis of the Rat Man. *International Journal of Psycho-Analysis, 58,* 255–273.

Lipton, S. D. (1977b). Clinical observations on resistance to the transference. *International Journal of Psycho-Analysis, 58,* 463–472.

Loewald, H. W. (1960). On the therapeutic action of psychoanalysis. *International Journal of Psycho-Analysis, 41,* 16–33.

Luborsky, L. (1967). Momentary forgetting during psychotherapy and psychoanalysis: A theory and research method. In R. R. Holt (Ed.), Motives and thought: Psychoanalytic essays in honor of David Rapaport. *Psychological Issues, 5* (2/3, Monograph 18/19).

Luborsky, L., & Auerbach, A. H. (1969). The symptom-context method: Quantitative studies of symptom formation in psychotherapy. *Journal of the American Psychoanalytic Association, 17,* 68–99.

Macalpine, I. (1950). The development of the transference. *Psychoanalytic Quarterly, 19,* 501–539.

Peterfreund, E. (1971). Information, systems, and psychoanalysis. *Psychological Issues, 7* (1/2, Monograph 25/26).

Pribram, K.H., & Gill, M. M. (1976). *Freud's "Project" reassessed.* New York: Basic Books.

Racker, H. (1968). *Transference and countertransference.* New York: International Universities Press.

Rapaport, D. (1967). *The collected papers of David Rapaport* (M. M. Gill, Ed.). New York: Basic Books.

Rapaport, D., & Gill, M. M. (1959). The points of view and assumptions of metapsychology. *International Journal of Psycho-Analysis, 40,* 1–10.

Rapaport, D., Gill, M. M., & Schafer, R. (1945–46). *Diagnostic psychological testing* (2 vols.). Chicago: Year Book Publishers.

Rapaport, D., Gill, M. M., & Schafer, R. (1968). *Diagnostic psychological testing* (rev. ed.; R. Holt, Ed.). New York: International Universities Press.

Reppen, J. (1982). Merton Gill: An interview. *Psychoanalytic Review, 69,* 167–190.

Ross, N. (1965). [Review of *Topography and systems in psychoanalytic theory,* by M. M. Gill.] *International Journal of Psycho-Analysis, 46,* 254–256.

Sandler, J. (1976). Countertransference and role-responsiveness. *International Review of Psycho-Analysis, 3,* 43–47.

Schafer, R. (1976). *A new language for psychoanalysis.* New Haven: Yale University Press.

Spence, D. P. (1964). [Review of *Topography and systems in psychoanalytic theory,* by M. M. Gill.] *Journal of Nervous and Mental Disease, 139,* 401–403.

Strachey, J. (1934). The nature of the therapeutic action of psychoanalysis. *International Journal of Psycho-Analysis, 15,* 127–159.

7 Robert Langs: The Communicative Approach

Zvi Lothane, M.D.

Expounding is propounding: It is not possible to expound another person's views without, at the same time, propounding one's own. This has been true of expositions of Freud and applies to those, such as the theorists in this volume, who went beyond Freud.

"Going beyond" is a spatial metaphor, which implies being in one place and then going somewhere else or toward something else. Psychologically, it means an identification with and a departure from. Thus, an exposition of thinking beyond Freud requires a preliminary exposition of Freud. But here, too, both the analytic and the lay expositions of Freud are face to face with the ever-present question: How to read Freud? For Freud is a protean thinker. Like Proteus, the Greek god of prophecy who, when consulted, refused to give answers but instead assumed various shapes, so Freud constantly eludes the attempt to give a definitive reading of his text. He has been claimed by many domains, from the biological (Sulloway, 1979), to the theological (Homans, 1970). Who can truly proclaim what Freud *really* said? Many of those who made such a claim have created the most hair-raising revisions (Lothane, 1983b). What the Italians say about translations applies here: *traduttore, tradittore* (the translator is a traitor).

Robert Langs began as a Freudian analyst before he developed his communicative approach. Therefore, I shall present my reading of Freud and show what he took over from Freud and where he took off.

Freud the methodologist, rather than Freud the ideologist or metapsychologist, is my focus in reading Freud (Lothane, 1980, 1981a, 1981b, 1982a, 1983a, 1984b). The methodological focus is operational: it studies what mind does as against what mind is. From this vantage point, Freud's was from the outset a *depth* psychology, which was *dynamic, dialectical,* and *dualistic* – that is, concerned with the conflict of strivings and actions both between man and man (interpersonally) and within man himself (intrapersonally).

Freud's psychology encompasses the following varieties of dynamics and dialectics:

1. The dialectics of the surface versus the depth, of the conscious versus the preconscious, of the manifest versus the latent, of the remembered versus the forgotten, of the explicit versus the implicit.

2. The dynamics of defense, originally repression but later including other modes of defense (also referred to as resistance, both intrapersonally and interpersonally).

3. The dynamics of dream thinking versus waking modes of thought.

4. The dynamics and dialectics of transference versus love and self-love.

5. The dynamics and dialectics of emotion and desire, including sexual desire.

Historically, during the first two decades of his psychoanalytic work, from 1895 to 1915, Freud was concerned with method and clinical theory. Thereafter he became increasingly concerned with metapsychology. The gist of the method is given in the *Studies on Hysteria* (1895d) and *The Interpretation of Dreams* (1900a). Both the psychological symptom and the dream are seen as similarly constructed: They show the same correspondence between the way they were caused and the way they were cured. The memory of a painful (traumatic) or conflictual event in the past is transformed by the silent (unconscious) operation of defense (repression) into a symptom. The cathartic method (the technique of hypnosis) creates the conditions of widening of consciousness and the emergence of memories in pictorial (imagic) forms and in words. Overcoming defense (resistance) facilitates this process and thus erases the pathogenic sting of memory. To be sick is to reminisce. To be cured is to recall and erase the record. Similarly, the painfully or conflictually experienced event prior to the dream – the day residue – evokes a psychological reaction: the latent dream thoughts. Under the influence of the censor and through the silent (unconscious) operation of dream work, the latent thoughts are transformed into the manifest content, or the dream as remembered. The cathartic method is now replaced by the psychoanalytic method. It is a homologue of the hypnotic technique and of the preconditions for dreaming. The withdrawal of attention from goal-directed pursuits and critical selection creates an altered state or frame of consciousness and fosters the emergence of pictorial modes of thought: images of memory, of imagination, of dreams and hallucinations. The combination of spontaneous free association and of directed free association to the separate elements of the manifest dream content leads to a retrieval of the day residue and the antecedent thoughts and feelings that were the reaction to the day residue. The central conception here is that action, whether symptom or dream, is determined by external reality (Lothane, 1983a). Both the symptom and the dream are a personal response to and a commentary on an episode of lived reality. Rapaport (1960) called this the adaptive point of view. I would like to refer to it as the action-reaction conception of the symptom and the dream.

What is being reemphasized here is that Freud's depth psychology is also a conflict psychology, and it is meant to explain inhibitions and distortions of memory and of sense perception. Both the symptom and the dream are shaped by defense in all its varieties and by the dream work in all its varieties. In this sense, the symptom is a return of the repressed and the dream a transformation of the latent content into the manifest content. Both are strange and puzzling manifestations and require a solution. To recall the memory that caused the symptom means to analyze, or dissolve, it; to trace the latent content from the manifest content is to interpret a dream, or solve it. As Freud (1900a) writes:

> The [latent] dream thoughts and the [manifest] dream content are given to us as two *depictions* [*Darstellungen*] of the same content in *two different languages*. . . . The dream content is expressed, so to speak, in a picture [hieroglyphic] script whose signs have to be translated, one by one, into the language of the [latent] dream thoughts. We would obviously be led into error if we were to read these signs according to their picture value instead of according to what the signs refer to. . . . [pp. 283–284; author's translation, italics added; see also Freud, 1900a, pp. 277–278].

The transformation wrought by the dream work can be undone by the activity which, Freud (1901) says, is "the counterpart of this [dream] work, which brings a transformation in reverse, which I already know of *analysis-work*" (p. 645; author's translation, italics Freud's). This original text, the first consciously registered reaction to trauma, is the cause of the second, edited text. The first text is now unconscious and replaced by the now conscious second text, which is a derivative, disguised, displaced, condensed, dramatized, pictorial, or *encoded* version of the first text. To analyze a dream, or a symptom, is *not* to read it cognitively or literally, according to the picture value, but to *decode* it. Such decoding can only be accomplished by a recourse to the special dynamics of the psychoanalytic situation: undoing of repression, fostering of images and

memories, and tracing the associative chains of reference from the signifier (the manifest content) to the signified (the latent content). The
emergence of imagic forms of thought proceeds hand in hand with a shift
in the dynamics of repression. Just as the conditions of sleep and
dreaming decrease waking vigilance, undo repression, and facilitate the
emergence of the repressed, so the psychoanalytic situation also fosters
just that; to the extent that waking, conversational give-and-take is decreased, the repressed memories, attitudes, and expectations have a
chance of emerging. In this way the psychoanalytic-therapeutic situation provides the conditions for a dynamic (undoing of repression) and
associative (emergence of images) unfolding and decoding of the patient's story.

Both repression (defense) and the dream work are unconscious, or silent, processes. The emphasis is on unconscious as an adjective quali-
fying the nature of this mental activity, *not* on the reified unconscious
and its various connotations. The reason for this emphasis is twofold: (1)
to underscore the dynamic-reactive nature of this activity in response to
a reality stimulus; and (2) to hold to the conception of a continuous counterpoint between direct modes of memory and perception and indirect,
or distorted, modes. Freud provides his own emphasis in these words in
a footnote added in 1928 to *The Interpretation of Dreams* (1900a):

> I used at one time to find it extraordinarily difficult to accustom readers to
> the distinction between the manifest content of dreams and the latent
> dream thoughts. . . . But now that analysts at least have become recon-
> ciled to replacing the manifest dream by the meaning revealed by its inter-
> pretation, many of them have become guilty of falling into another confu-
> sion. . . . They seek to find the essence of dreams in their latent content
> and in so doing they overlook the distinction between the latent dream
> thoughts and the dream work. At bottom dreams are nothing other than a
> particular *form* of thinking made possible by the conditions of the state of
> sleep. It is the *dream-work* which creates that form and it is alone the es-
> sence of dreaming – the explanation of its peculiar nature [pp. 506–507;
> italics Freud's].

The action-reaction paradigm is from the start opposed by another
line of thought in Freud: the role of sexuality. At first, sexuality was
considered as an aspect of external reality, and in the form of seduction
it played the role of an external traumatizing event, evoking its proper
response. The overthrow of the seduction theory by Freud went hand in
hand with another development: the concept of the dream as wish fulfillment. These two ideas pave the way for the final conception of the body
as an internal source, distinct from external reality, which generates
two kinds of movers of human action: the drive and the (dream-) wish.

With this new emphasis on action in response to inner sources of stimulation goes a deemphasis of the environment as a stimulus to action in the service of adaptation.

A most important corollary to this new orientation is the attitude toward the dream and daydream, or fantasy. Fantasy is no longer, via the dream work, a reaction to and commentary on events in external reality but an internally generated action. This reformulation of the dichotomy of internal-external creates a new approach to defining paradigms of cause (pathology) and paradigms of cure (analytic technique). One example is the so-called structural theory and the preponderant preoccupation with metapsychology. Although a fuller discussion of these is beyond the scope of the present essay, the central implication of this ideological shift was a tendency among analysts to embrace scholastic debates about internality, the remote infantile past, hybrid concepts, and theories removed from the realities we live in.

The internal-external dichotomy rears its head once again with the full blooming of the concept transference, first defined in Freud's *Studies of Hysteria* (1895). Although the notion of internally generated drives and fantasies only presupposes an object, the transferece actualizes it; in the psychoanalytic-therapeutic situation, the other person is experienced simultaneously as a real and an imaginary other. Thus the one-person psychology of drives and wish fulfillment becomes the two-person psychology of the interpersonal realm—of dialogue, communication, and interaction. Of the many aspects of transference, in addition to its traditional definition as reenactment of the past, two others are immediately relevant to the present argument: (1) its relation to dreaming (Lothane, 1983a), and (2) its relation to the dichotomies truth/error and reality/delusion. The one-person psychology and the intrapersonal dynamics of drives and internally derived fantasies had this effect on the concept transference: They tended to convert it into a monadic instead of a dyadic reality, divorced from the reciprocal personal influences between the participants in the psychoanalytic dialogue.

These trends have resulted in a curious double standard in the analytic profession. Although the ruling theories (metapsychology) have been formulated largely in terms of a one-system, one-person psychology and mechanism, the clinical practice has been rolling along in the context of interpersonal relations, conversation, and interaction. On the one hand, the one-system orientation created its dogmatics (Hartmann) and schismatics (Schafer) and bitter theological warfare within the psychoanalytic movement. On the other hand, the interpersonal approach has remained bereft of a systematic theory. Against this background, we can now proceed to examine the contribution of Robert Langs. I met Langs in 1980 as a result of having published a review of his *The Lis-*

tening Process (Langs, 1978a; Lothane, 1980). I later joined the faculty of the Lenox Hill Hospital Psychotherapy Program, of which Langs is the founder and director. In the exposition that follows, however, I have limited myself to the use of published material so that my assertions can be checked against verifiable sources and debated accordingly.

Robert Joseph Langs graduated from the Chicago Medical School in 1953. He later became a psychiatrist and graduated from Downstate Psychoanalytic Institute (now the New York University Institute). He joined the faculty there and was enrolled as member of the American Psychoanalytic Association. By 1971 he had become active in the practice of psychotherapy and psychoanalysis in clinical research and was on the staff of the Long Island Jewish and Hillside Hospitals. He had published clinical and research papers (Langs, 1978b). His first major psychoanalytic paper, "Day Residues, Recall Residues and Dreams: Reality and the Psyche," appeared in 1971. It contains the germ of his future views and "proved to be a fateful beginning" (Langs, 1978, p. 6).

In this paper Langs rediscovered external reality and its relevance for fantasy life, past and present. The clinical fact that led to this rediscovery was that the day residue–that is, events in external reality–was crucial to the understanding of the dream. As shown earlier, this was Freud's own perennial insight, which was replaced by formulations about the varieties of intrapsychic movers (the id, "the" unconscious, and unconscious fantasies). Toward the end of the paper, Langs (1971) argues for a

> reassessment of Freud's thinking regarding infantile seduction. In essence, we can see that Freud was actually correct in both of his formulations regarding the role of reality in the formation of neurosis: real seductions do occur on many levels, while unconscious fantasies are also constantly being created and revised from both experiencing and imagining. Together, interacting, creating a totality, they lead to the anxieties and conflicts out of which neurosis develops [p. 521].

In this, Langs anticipated the recent surge of interest in seeing the original seduction theory reinstated (Klein & Tribich, 1979; Lothane, 1983a; Musson, 1984; Swales, 1982).

This then is Langs' fundamental idea, the foundation on which the Langsian approach rests: The day residue is the stimulus to which the dream is a response. If for the day residue we substitute the psychoanalyst, the analyst's actions and conduct, and the way they affect the patient, we obtain the gist of Langs' method. Every sequence of the psychoanalytic session shows an *adaptive context,*, that is, the action of the analyst, the reality trigger, and the patient's double-layered reaction. This reaction has its manifest content and its latent content, what Langs

(1978b) termed the "specific unconscious fantasies and memories contained in derivative and disguised form in the manifest material" (p. 10).
This seminal idea has subsequently led Langs to a number of extrapola-
tions, which are both an extension of Freud's method and a departure
from it. We shall have a closer look at these issues later.

The next stage in the evolution of Langs' ideas is seen in the two
volumes of *The Technique of Psychoanalytic Psychotherapy* (1973,
1974) as well as in a clinical paper, "A Psychoanalytic Study of Material
from Patients in Psychotherapy," (1972). The two volumes of *The Technique of Psychoanalytic Psychotherapy* constitute a textbook that
reflects the best in the classical psychoanalytic tradition. They show
Langs to be a seasoned psychoanalytic clinician who writes lucidly and
persuasively.

Continuing the line of thought about day residues and dreams, Langs
(1973) places central emphasis on

> human adaptation in neurotogenesis. . . . Functioning, responding, and
> adapting are set off by environmental alterations . . . [the] environmental
> stimulus may, in general, be positive and supportive or negative and trau-
> matic. Most crucial for the development of neurotic disturbance are the
> intrapsychic responses to traumatic stimuli. It is these major, currently
> disruptive stimuli which have the potential to set off inappropriate or
> maladaptive (neurotic) responses that I have identified as the primary
> adaptive task [pp. 281–282].

This is in the spirit of Freud in the *Studies on Hysteria*. The traumatic
reaction is the paradigm of disease, and identifying the trauma is the
cure. Such identification is barred by the patient's defensiveness, which
must be analyzed first. But the traumas are not limited to intercurrent
reality events in the patient's extra-analytic life. A major event may be
the previous session, "the therapist's interventions or lack of them,
which may have traumatized the patient and evoked responses in him"
(p. 284).

The extension of the traumatizing event to include the actual behavior
of the therapist is the beginning of the specific Langsian emphasis.
Iatrogenic trauma, injury caused by the doctor's actions, is a medical
commonplace. Speaking of the dangers of hypnosis, Freud (1895) states:
"Where I caused damage, the reason lay elsewhere and deeper." (p. 266).
Many analysts have acknowledged the potential of the therapist to
cause harm by countertransference. But no analyst before Langs has
defined the therapist as an ever-present traumatizing agent, and none
has made this point of view into a system, as Langs has. This topic will
be discussed further.

In this textbook, Langs also develops the other methodological idea of
Freud's first two decades, the idea of the manifest and latent content.

This cardinal concept of dream psychology is conjoined by Langs with the idea of the adaptive task. In this way, a new methodological tool has been created for getting hold of the meaning of the patient's communications.

To understand a communication in context is different from understanding it in isolation. Freud addressed this issue squarely in *The Interpretation of Dreams*, where he contrasted the reading of a dream according to a universal symbol key with reading it in reference to a specific day residue and a specific decoding or tracing of the manifest dream thoughts to their latent antecedents. With the growth of the assorted psychoanalytic causal doctrines and ideologies, analysts have developed a fondness for stock formulas and clichés, used in the manner of what Freud called the "Egyptian dream book." Notions like castration anxiety, penis envy, the Oedipus complex, identity, and separation became the stock-in-trade of what Sandor Feldman (1958) called "blanket" interpretations. Otto Isakower (1968, 1971) warned, similarly, against the habit of diagnosing set patterns and trends in a given sequence of an analytic session rather than getting the drift of the actual mental images and their role in the communication. Like many others, Langs was faced with the sterility of the analytic clichés and chestnuts and went in search of the truth of the given moment in the lived experience.

Freud's idea of the manifest and latent was not limited, however, to the transformation wrought by the dream work. His depth psychology also addressed the issue of honesty versus hypocrisy in human communication, the difference between what is *said* and what is *intended* or meant. The *content* aspect of "meaning" has had a greater hold on both the popular and the professional imagination than the *intent* aspect. Although alive to the importance of intention, Langs has followed established habit in using the shorthand "unconscious fantasy" to refer to the deeper, implied, indirect, concealed intentions in communication. The manifest content is seen as a hidden, disguised, allusive reference to the direct idea or intention that lies latent in the manifest material and manifests itself as a *derivative* of the antecedent direct idea. Thus, any piece of material may be read not naively and at face value, but as a derivative pointing to deeper-lying truths. This seminal Freudian idea underwent some transformations in Langs' writings, which will be examined later.

It should be sufficient to note at this point that the use of the term "unconscious" is liable to certain pitfalls related to the tendency among analysts to reify the concept of the unconscious. Another tendency is, as in Freud's caution quoted earlier, to sacrifice the manifest content to the latent content, as if the manifest were second hand goods to be bypassed on the way to the latent content. Here Langs (1973) notes that "manifest content screens or conceals, but also reveals some of what lies beneath it" (p. 296). To deny the manifest would imply a wholesale repudiation of all art. For what is art but the giving of artful, or derivative, expression, that is, in various guises and disguises, to what can be more simply and directly expressed?

Two central conclusions emerge from this for Langs: (1) what to listen for in the material of the hour; and (2) the order of priorities in such listening. Regarding the first, every hour revolves around two contexts: the therapeutic context, that is, the manifestations of the patient's psychopathology as reported, and the adaptive context, as defined earlier. Both these are listened to on both the manifest and latent, conscious and unconscious levels. The highest priorities in listening in preparation for intervening, however, Langs concludes are indeed these "reactions to errors by the therapist and acute symptomatic crises" (p. 364). The other aspects, in order of decreasing priority, are "disturbances in the therapeutic alliance arising from sources other than the therapist's errors; other resistances; current intrapsychic conflicts and unconscious fantasies related to them; the genetic basis for the patient's reactions to the therapist and for his present symptoms and inner conflicts; reality issues and problems" (p. 364).

This exposition contains the essence of Langs' thought. It is on the one hand firmly rooted in the classical psychoanalytic tradition, and it marks a departure from it, on the other. The point of departure is the transition from a one-system, intrapersonal conception to a two-system, interpersonal or interactional conception. It should be noted that Langs has not completely given up the intrapersonal habit of conceptualizing. His clinical theories of symptom formation and the role of memory and fantasy are traditionally intrapersonal (intrapsychic). At the same time, his interpersonal formulations differ in this respect from those encountered in the classical literature: The delineation of the adaptive context has from the beginning led Langs to a consideration of the analyst, or therapist, as an ever-present traumatogenic agent. This one idea has been driven by him relentlessly to its logical limit. Let us examine this more closely.

The adaptive context emerges as the final common strand that gathers into itself all of the following threads: (1) how one *listens* to the session, how one discovers the sense, the point, the *central message* of any given session; (2) the *reciprocal action* of the patient and therapist upon each other, each manifesting a response to the other; (3) the two-layered *derivative* structure of each communication: the conscious/unconscious, latent/manifest, explicit/implicit (subsequently defined as truth/lie) levels of each utterance.

A convenient mid-point in the evolution of Langs' ideas is his book, *The Listening Process* (1978a), which I have discussed elsewhere at some length (Lothane, 1980). In it he spells out clearly the interweaving strands of the adaptive context.

The classical view stressed the *thematic content* of the patient's utterances in the psychoanalytic-therapeutic situation. The themes in the patient's narrative were related to the patient's memories, past and present-day realities. Initially, in the *Studies on Hysteria*, the analyst understood – that is, interpreted – these themes the same way a reader understands or interprets a told or printed story: by becoming aware of its meanings, messages, references. But in the *Studies on Hysteria*, Freud had already become aware of a story within a story, a drama within a drama: the emergence of transferences, or the effect of the patient-doctor interaction on the story as told. Thus, whereas at first memory was subjected to the same dispassionate scrutiny in the therapeutic session as was the histologic section under the microscope, it soon became evident that such scrutiny had to be tempered by clarifying the personal equation. Thus, the evidential status of the seduction stories was reevaluated as an attempt on the part of the patients to fake such stories in order to have a personal effect on the listener. Even with the recognition of the distorting potential of the here and now on the there and then, however, the latter was still viewed as a result of the *intrapersonal* dynamics of the patient, with the therapist remaining the dispassionate observer and interpreter of the patient's inner drama as remembered and enacted in the analytic situation.

As I have argued elsewhere (Lothane, 1983a), Freud replaced the trauma and dream paradigms of the symptom with the concept of intrapsychic dynamics of instinctual drives and defenses and intrapsychic determinism, as consistent with a one-system psychology. However, the fact remained that the analyst was not only a *naturalistic observer* from above of the goings on within the patient, a diagnostician of symptom complexes and mechanisms of defense; the analyst was also a *participant observer*. This placed an insoluble strain on the one-system conception. For whereas it takes one person to remember or to dream, it takes two to talk. Speaking and listening are in their very nature interpersonal and interactional. The basic one-system orientation persisted with the emergence of the concept of transference. The analyst in the transference was seen as an inert screen onto which dreams and memories were projected. And such projecting does exist. This mode of functioning of the psychoanalytic interaction is still valid as an instrument for the clarification of the there and then. But it is insufficient for the understanding of the here and now, the actual goings on in the living doctor-patient encounter.

This emphasis on the here and now and the present-day relationships as opposed to the there and then and past relationships first began with Ferenczi (see Lothane, 1983a). It was followed independently by Sullivan (see Lothane, 1984), Wilhelm Reich (1949), Szasz (1961), and now, among others, by Langs. In this connection, however, it should be appreciated that Freud's concept of the hysterical symptom was interpersonal from the start; the symptom was a statement with meaning that was intended for another person and thus could be decoded by an observer or listener.

It is the *theories* that were either intrapersonal or interpersonal, *not* the phenomena in question. Similarly, the doctor-patient relationship was viewed as a personal relationship from the very start, in the *Studies on Hysteria*. It is only the politics and ethics of this personal relationship that were not spelled out till some 20 years later in Freud's (1912–15) papers on technique. Thus the often-touted achievement of the so-called object relations theorists is not a finding but refinding of a truth already present in Freud.

To return to the main thread of this exposition, the gist of Langs' communicative approach (the latest designation of what was formerly called the adaptational or interactional approach) is these two ideas: the *adaptive context* (Freud's trauma paradigm) and *derivative communication* (Freud's dream language paradigm). Having explained the idea of the adaptive context, let us now turn to the concept of derivative communication.

The notion of derivative is in Freud. He defined derivative in the context of intrapersonal dynamics; Langs has redefined it in the context of the dialogue, in a specific way. Freud used the idea of derivative to refer to something observable that was seen as arising or formed from something else and prior to it. The notion of derivative is basic to Freud's method of determining causes and origins of phenomena. In linguistics a word derives from an earlier word. In chemistry one compound is a derivative of another. Freud (1915) used the word *Abkömmling* (literally, offspring), to state, for example, that "repression *proper* concerns *psychical derivatives* [*psychische Abkömmlinge*] of the repressed [instinctual drive] representation, or such trains of thought which, arising elsewhere, become related to it through association" (p. 250; author's translation, second italics added). Symptoms and dreams are psychological derivatives of trains of thought that are hidden, repressed, or warded off. Freud's psychology thus necessarily implies a surface and a depth. His depth psychology is based on the manifest and latent dichotomy.

The concept of derivative thus implies two basic judgments: a judgment about cause and origins, and a judgment about what is primary and what is secondary. A formulation about the dynamics of a case history, or of a sequence in a session, will thus entail a discussion of all sorts of derivatives.

The idea of the derivative is another centerpiece in Langs' communicative method. It is locked into the idea of an adaptive context and the two are an indissoluble whole. Langs (1978a) made the following distinctions:

> [In] clarifying the types of communication from the patient and the ways in which the analyst could organize and conceptualize the material . . . on the first level, a patient's associations could be organized around their *manifest contents*. This approach, which is essentially nonanalytic since it totally rejects all notions of unconscious process and content, confines itself to the surface of the patient's communications.
>
> On the second level, the analyst organizes material from the patient by attending to the manifest associations, isolating various segments of this material and imputing to each a specific unconscious meaning; I term these inferences *Type One derivatives*. Here the manifest content is addressed in relative isolation and the latent content–the unconscious communication–is determined by the recognition of obvious displacements, the use of symbols, the intuitive understanding of underlying meanings and a knowledge of a given patient's communicative idiom.
>
> A third level of organizing the material from the patient is feasible through the use of an adaptive context as the dynamic organizer of the patient's associations; this yields *Type Two derivatives*. The model here is that of the day residue and the manifest dream, the latent content of which is fully comprehended only with the knowledge of the dream's precipitant and the related associations. . . .
>
> Each adaptive context itself has both manifest and latent meanings. . . . A true understanding of the nature of an adaptive stimulus and of the responses it evokes (associations and behaviors) is founded on the self-knowledge of the analyst–his sensitivity to the conscious, and especially, unconscious meanings and projections conveyed in his verbal interventions, silences, and efforts to manage the frame.
>
> Type Two derivatives, then, are always viewed dynamically and as responses to adaptive stimuli. As a rule, they imply that virtually all of the communications from the patient must, on this level, be appended or related to the analytic interaction–those representing perceptions and introjections as well as fantasies and distortions. At this level, many seemingly divergent and relatively indecipherable associations accrue significance in the light of the recognized adaptive content [pp. 562–563].

"The efforts to manage the frame" are the most important doings and sayings of the therapist and the most telling impingements on the patient. This is the crux of Langs' interactionist emphasis. Consequently, the realm of the ground rules of the therapeutic situation is viewed as the prime arena of interaction. It comes to this: Any action by the therapist or the patient intended either to make or break the "frame," or the ground rules, will create a most important reality stimulus. The reaction to this stimulus is the adaptive context, expressed in an encoded form, or in Type Two derivatives.

The above defines a model of disease and a model of cure. Neurosis is an interactional or communicative creation, and its treatment, or resolution, is also interactional and communicative. The treatment, is a series of ever-evolving interactions and communications, but all betray a basic pattern of action and reaction. At all times the stimulus emanating from one person produces both a conscious or manifest level and an unconscious or latent level of reaction in the other person. The conscious or direct message is only the misleading surface of the communication. The true and valid level is the latent, encoded, derivative, embedded, or hidden message. The manifest message has to be decoded, unmasked, driven from its hiding place of disguise and exposed to yield the hidden message. All is in the interaction and in the here and now, and therapy means decoding the latent meanings of this interaction. All else is secondary. The most mature expression of this idea is given in Langs' latest systematic exposition of the communicative approach, *Psychotherapy: A Basic Text* (1982), and in a recent paper (1981).

It is essential to appreciate Langs' insistence on derivative, or encoded, communication, and the distinction between manifest content, Type One derivatives, and Type Two derivatives and formulations (Langs, 1981, 1982). In this distinction, Langs remains rooted in the classical analytic tradition but develops a new emphasis. The traditional way is to view neurosis as confined to one person who relives the memory of his past in the form of symptoms, dreams, and daydreams. Langs (1981), following Freud, refers to this as the unconscious fantasy constellation. The traditionally oriented therapist will treat these constellations as self-contained products and apply to them, in Langs' (1981) words, to the

familiar avenues of affective cognitive insight, through which the nature and effects of the unconscious fantasy constellations are interpreted to the patient, who then affectively understands them and works through them. This procedure, on all evidence clinically prevalent today, frees the patient's ego for growth and the development of relatively flexible and adaptive resources with which to cope with and resolve intrapsychic conflicts, and to modify pathological aspects of the unconscious fantasy constellations.

The one-person emphasis is characterized by Langs as resting on two misleading and interrelated approaches: (1) concentrating on the manifest content of the patient's consciously expressed thoughts and the manifest themes; and (2) formulating Type One derivatives. The manifest content approach takes the patient's statement at face value and the analytic relationship is addressed on its surface only (Langs, 1981). Type One derivatives, related to such conscious thoughts and themes, are the traditional dynamic and genetic formulations applied to such material. But this is tantamount to throwing the book at the patient. Such Type One derivatives exist in a vacuum, and they do not become useful until activated in response to a stimulus from the therapist. The manifest content and Type One derivative approach, furthermore, implies that "the burden of pathologicaal inputs is placed almost entirely on the patient and the sources of his seemingly distorted communications are seen to reside exclusively with his own unconscious fantasy constellations" (Langs, 1981). Langs will not deny that the manifest unconscious fantasy constellation is in itself a derivative. But here is the crucial point of departure: Since Langs (1981) goes for interaction, he chooses to emphasize interactional, or Type two, derivatives, over all alse: "This lays the foundation for the second avenue of symptom resolution [which] involves the object relationship between patient and analyst, the nature of their unconscious communicative transactions and projective and introjective identifications of each."

Once again, Langs invokes Freud's notion that the manifest content of the dream is a disguised edition of the latent content and of perception in external reality. In the context of the interaction, the patient's reaction to the therapist's impact upon him or her is not expressed directly, but in a derivative, that is, disguised and allusive, manner. In ordinary social intercourse, hypocrisy is more common than honesty. Like the king's jester, the patient disguises his or her true reaction to the therapist. Like Pinel, who came to the rescue of the insane, Freud went out to rehabilitate the worth of the opinions of neurotics. Similarly, Langs makes a case for the patient's correct and astute perceptions of the therapist's mistakes, foibles, lies, evasions, and abuses. The rigid therapist, like the authoritarian parent, may think he or she is above criticism and be quick to attribute the patient's complaints to "transference," "sickness," or "acting out." The correspondingly cowed patient might talk in allusions, or, as Langs puts it, in derivatives. Langs (1981), however, generalizes an indirectness to *every* patient and every interaction:

> In essence, every association and behavior by the patient is analyzed in the light of the stimulus or *adaptive context* that provoked it. Extensive empirical evidence suggests that these precipitants are almost without

exception the silences and interventions of the analyst. . . . All other stimuli, whether from within the patient himself or from traumatic outside relationships, are seen as secondary adaptive contexts and are, as a rule, linked to primary adaptive contexts within the therapeutic experience. On this level, the patient's material is given specific organization and meaning in the here-and-now as derivatives that must be understood in the light of the stimulating adaptive context, a concept modelled on Freud's conception of the day residue for the dream. . . . Listening at this level consistently addresses all manifest associations as derivatives of unconscious contents and processes, a term of both *fantasies* and *perceptions* [italics added] . . . [of] the extensive pathological communications contained in the therapist's and analyst's erroneous interventions and mismanagements of the framework. With remarkable consistency, patients unconsciously perceive and introject the implications of these errors. Similarly, when the analyst intervenes properly, representations of a positive introject and Type Two derivative validation ensue. . . . Making use of Bion's discussion of lies, liars, and the thinker (1970) we might advance the flowing postulate: truth as it pertains to the patient's neurosis within the psychoanalytic situation can be identified only by taking into account the unconscious communicative interaction between patient and analyst as this relates to the manifestations of that neurosis on the one hand, and to the central adaptive contexts for both patient and analyst on the other (Langs, 1980a, b). Truth must include a recognition of introjective and projective processes, transference and non-transference, countertransference and non-countertransference, and the valid and disturbed functioning of both participants. Any formulation which excludes any aspect of this totality, or which makes use of one part of the total picture as a means of denying or excluding the rest, should be viewed as a barrier to the truth. On this basis it becomes possible to distinguish truth therapy from lie therapy, and to develop a conceptualization of distinctive modes of symptom alleviation.

Langs (1982) also notes: "The distinction between Type One and Type Two derivative listening shows the need for a basic revision in the nature of psychoanalytic listening in the direction of adaptive context formulations." This claim makes the current milestone of the fruition of a seminal idea. Starting with a reaffirmation of the importance of reality, via clinical investigations of the role of day residues in dreams, Langs found the importance of the reality impact of the analyst. The focus on the actions of the analyst upon the patient, on the here and now interaction between the participants in the analytic encounter, then shaped two major areas of concern: (1) concern with the *content* and *form* of the communication, inspired by dream psychology, such that the patient's stream of consciousness is read for covert allusions to his or her thoughts and feelings about the therapist, even though the patient is overtly talking about his or her present and past life; and (2) a concern with the *ground rules* – the ethical norms governing the therapist's professional conduct.

Langs' emphasis has brought about a transvaluation of the traditional objects of analytic exploration. The patient's life, past and present, life's events and crises, and the time-hallowed transference are all viewed as secondary to the here and now and as merely a vehicle for the patient's reactions to the therapist's impact upon him or her.

Langs' innovation is evidently of great heuristic usefulness. It raises our consciousness to the actual and real inputs of the therapist and shakes our complacency about them. At the same time, in spite of Lang's repeated claims, it does not achieve a definitive degree of certainty about the intent of a given communication. In a given moment, who is the patient *really* talking about – the patient or the therapist? Entertaining a silent hypothesis about the intent, not merely content, of a communication can only lead to *presumptive,* not *conclusive,* inferences. We are dealing with interpreting matters of degree, intensity, accent. Such matters are in the realm of opinion. As such, they become open to debate and create debate. Their ultimate validation is subject to developments in time – to the judgment of history.

It is useful to invoke at this point the dialectic of content and form. This dialectic, and the varying emphasis on now one, now the other aspect of the content-form unity, has been in evidence from the very beginning of psychoanalysis. At first the idea predominated – the *what* (content) of the communication; for example, hysteria was defined as ideogenic, an idea persisting in time. Later Freud discovered the *how* (form) of the communication – the mood of dreaming, latent and manifest content, and free association. As dream psychology and interest in content waned, form came more and more to the fore, first as the emphasis on *manners of disguise and encoding,* later as transference and especially transference-resistance. This focus on resistance then led to two further developments: a shift of interest from *communication* to *conduct,* from the what to the how, and from the how to the what-for – that is, a shift from *content* to *intent* (Lothane, 1983a). Consequently, there was a greater stress on the *contract* aspect of the conduct of the two people, on their interactions in the here and now rather than on events in the there and then, and on the ethical norms governing this conduct. This development was traversed by Freud in his movement from his works on hysteria and dreams to the 1912–15 papers on technique. Along this path Freud gave his attention to two basic sorts of form: (1) the depth-surface, latent-manifest, straight-encoded forms of *communication* and conduct revealed by dream psychology; and (2) the honest-dishonest, cooperative-resistant, love-hate, gratification-abstinence forms of *conduct* reflected in the observance of the analytic contract. Langs has traced a similar course. On the one hand, he defined what to listen to in the communication (identifying the adaptive context) and how to listen for it (decoding derivatives). On the other hand, he has defined the ground rules (the frame). Over the decades, analysts have debated and battled about both these aspects of the analytic encounter.

Having given what is hoped is a balanced critical exposition of Langs' views, I shall now proceed to quote two reactions to Langs in the literature. To date, the orthodox analytic establishment has ignored Langs totally. To this, the reaction of Leo Stone, is both a unique and instructive exception. Searles has always been a maverick, himself viewed with suspicion by the orthodox.

In two dialogues of Langs with Leo Stone (Langs & Stone, 1980) and Harold Searles (Langs & Searles, 1980), there are expressed many interesting opinions, agreements, and disagreements. In both dialogues the disagreements are not so much in the realm of the frame of communication but in the realm of conduct.

Stone comes across as a pillar of the orthodox analytic establishment, a man both humane and urbane, who believes that the situation is more important than the rules. The Sabbath is made for human, not human for the Sabbath. He admits to having been influenced by Ferenczi (via his first analyst) and espouses an approach to the patient marked by common sense, justice, reasonableness, flexibility, and a modicum of gratification in the relationship. In this dialogue, Langs espouses a fundamentalist position on ground rules and their rigid application. He takes Stone to task for giving a patient an extra session when the patient requested pills to calm his anxiety. The patient's subsequent dream of the pills slightly chewed up and accompanied by an image of two worms was read by Langs as indicating the patient's view of the extra hour as "a dangerous contaminated gratification" (Langs & Stone, 1980, p. 173). Stone, pressed by Langs to concede the point, defends himself by seeing Langs' position as "Calvinist" and prohibitionist.

This brief vignette highlights the perennial problem of interpreting a record of a live text, especially when its author is not around. The interpreter can never be certain about the exact referents of an author's content or intent; the interpreter can only offer a plausible hypothesis. In this case, furthermore, the debate is not so much about the dream's meaning as a proposition as about the dream as the patient's *judgment* of the usefulness or helpfulnesss of the analyst's conduct. As such, it is less a matter of logic and more a matter of love. But the canon of love differs essentially from the canon of logic. Yes and no, true and false have different implications in love; they mean acceptance or rejection, like or dislike, preservation or annihilation. In logic it is possible to achieve certainty a priori, before the fact; in love, in fortunate circumstances, certainty comes a posteriori, after the fact. The truth of love is tested in time.

Stone feels that Langs views the frame as sacrosanct, as a bed of Procrustes, as too rigid. Certainly, an important difference in background surfaces in the dialogue: Stone speaks mainly of his own experiences with patients, Langs of his reactions to accounts of cases by students and residents, who, in Langs' view, are both prone to error and vulnerable to countertransference. Such facts are important to remember in order to understand the positions espoused. Langs also makes reference to his experience as an analytic candidate. Both Langs and Stone concur about the "conditions of training analysis [as] a disastrous fact of our training . . . a gross modification of the analytic situation. Gross!" (pp. 18–19). Langs also expresses the view that "all analytic research is an effort to complete the unfinished business of one's personal analysis. The gift is to do it in a creative way" (p. 17).

The unfinished business of men in analysis with men is often the father-son relationship, a problem for Freud and his followers and for many analysts and their analysands-students ever since. It is endemic to the profession. The father-son dilemma is in evidence here, too. Langs' efforts to educate Stone to see the unconscious implications of his consciously well-intentioned behavior are met with Stone's temperamental query, "Are you 'wild analyzing' me?" (p. 286).

Perhaps the most interesting exchange between Langs and Stone is about the relationship of reality to fantasy. Invoking the patient's true and valid unconscious perceptiveness as manifested by the patient's introduction of a modification in the frame, Langs proceeds to interpret—that is, to translate—the manifest as a derivative communication:

> I would argue that the patient has actually perceived, unconsciously, kernels of truth regarding unconscious motives within yourself for deviating. These would be communicated indirectly, as a rule, in what he is saying, and his response would not be totally distorted. Granted that the therapist is not consciously involved in homosexual fantasies about the patient, granted that he does not have conscious sexual wishes for his wife, nonetheless, I think the patient would be entitled to feel that there are some unresolved, unconscious, homosexual and seductive problems within the therapist and that they were expressed through the acceptance of the modification in the frame [pp. 284–285].

Trying such a formulation out for size on himself, Stone cannot hold back his sense of outrage: "I think you are absolutely wrong here, due to the fact that unconscious fantasy is given preeminence and predominance in life that is utterly unrealistic" (p. 285). Stone here and elsewhere feels that Langs is ignoring reality. Langs' surprise is just as poignant as Stone's outrage: "It is odd to hear you imply that I ignore reality when I am actually stressing it—realities of which the analyst may be unaware. You are addressing manifest reality; I acknowledge its presence and add latent reality, if I may use the phrase, as well" (p. 284).

This exchange amounts to a reversal of roles. The orthodox Freudian analyst professes a commonsense faith in the external, consensually validated reality of overt action as prior to an internal, intrapsychic reality of a hypostatized unconscious fantasy. Langs the innovator is ultra-orthodox in his faith in an intrapsychic reality as a valid criterion for judging external reality. This contradicts his other emphasis on day residues. The dream is a reaction to an event, not prior to an event. The dream or daydream is *not* an unconscious fantasy—it is an outcropping into consciousness of unconsciously transformed other thoughts, prior in time, which can be recalled.

But who is the proper judge of the validity of memory or of the validity of imputed motives—the person who remembers and who avows motives, or another person with a vested interest, who listens to the story? How can the debate between Langs and Stone be settled to satisfy the requirements of scientific, or other, proof?

From Freud on, analysts have been tempted to consider themselves experts in the unconscious, implying a special perceptiveness about other people's hidden motives. This expertise betrays a hidden authoritarianism stemming from the reality of social, economic, or other status. As authoritarian as Freud was in his politics, he was egalitarian about "the unconscious." In "the unconscious" we all covet, lust, and murder, but in real life a father can say to a son: "Do as I say, don't do as I do." Langs has again created a transvaluation. Whereas the traditional analyst is an expert on the analysand's unconscious, the innovation is to set up the patient as an expert adjudicating the analyst's unconscious, or hidden, motives. No wonder Stone was outraged at such a revolutionary turning of the tables.

This is also related to Langs' pervasive skepticism toward direct and truthful human communication. He will not take a straight yes or no for an answer. Yet, although the concept of encoded, derivative communication squares with the human capacity to conceal truth and practice duplicity through the use of language, it does not follow that direct communication does not exist. Langs has converted a potentiality into an actuality, a probability into a certainty—a consequence of taking the notion of "the unconscious" too literally. Furthermore, the suspicion of direct communication, if pushed too far, can be as disabling as the disregard for indirect, or derivative, communication. Both modes of communication need to be subjected to the test of truth.

The dialogue between Langs and Searles (1980) creates a different atmosphere. Two circumstances make for an immediate affinity between them: Searles' political status as a maverick in relation to the analytic establishment; and his ideological approach (inspired by the teachings of Sullivan) that psychopathology is an interactional product, that the patient cures the doctor, and that the doctor may himself be disturbed, or have a "psychotic core." Searles has been known for years as a therapist marked by originality, probity, courage, and bluntness in his dealings with some of the most severely disturbed patients at Chestnut Lodge, Maryland, and for his numerous imaginative contributions to the literature.

Searles is sympathetic to Langs' position on the frame, the concept of the adaptive context and derivative communication, and the approach of monitoring one's behavior toward the patient rather than chalking problems up to the patient's transference.

The two men also share many private sentiments about the injustices of the analytic establishment. Langs describes poignantly his dissatisfaction with his training analyst: "I think I will be forever ungrateful and angry about the modifications in the framework of my analysis and its lasting effects on me. And then I have to have a perspective. Such deviations have been and still are a reflection of a shared blind spot" (Langs & Searles, 1980, p. 93). He also described his break with his institute and society:

> One of the very positive things about my alienation from my colleagues and Institute is that it helped me to resolve a good piece of—I'll never resolve it entirely—but a good piece of my largely inappropriate need for their approval, for their sanction, for their love, which had been among the conscious motives for my work. . . . These needs are reflected in my technique books (Langs, 1973, 1974), which I wrote with my teachers at the Institute in mind. At the time, I believed that what I wrote was true, and I was already establishing my independence by working in ways regarding which they openly disapproved [p. 99].

The break between Langs and the group has been complete. (A number of Langs' former teachers and peers, whom I approached recently for reactions to his work, declined to get involved.) Langs' isolation has even led him to "keep asking myself, Am I trying to be a martyr? Am I inviting all of this condemnation? And I have absolutely decided that this is not martyrdom or masochism, but a love of truth—yes, a dedication to fathom the truth regardless of personal cost" (p. 86). But Langs still worries:

> . . . On one level, I really feel that I have freed myself in many ways, but I don't mean to imply that it's not still a great concern. In fact, one of the things that disturbs me most at this time—in all honesty—is that I am still

preoccupied with just that very area. How much is my work being accepted? When will I have my day? When will they regret it? When and how will it all be resolved? There is something I haven't worked through. I know it, I am working on it. Still, I think that in terms of what I am writing and creating now, I have become far more free of those shackles than I had been before, in a very positive sense. I didn't mean to imply, though, that it doesn't remain a kind of hurt and almost a damned obsession [p. 102].

These personal statements illustrate the ubiquitous connection between the man and his creation in matters belonging to the sphere of thought and action. The personal equation has even penetrated such a priori, impersonal disciplines as physics and astronomy. How much more important is the personal element in a profession like therapy or in a discipline like psychoanalysis.

Scientific consensus, doctrinal compliance, and group loyalty are forever a vexing problem for analysts. It is possible to be a lonely investigator in the laboratory, but a psychotherapist cannot survive in isolation. He needs a group and a public. Freud rightly described himself as the leader of the psychoanalytic *movement.* He also created the paradigm of the drama of the innovator and future leader – the initial experience of the revelation of truth, the revolt against an establishment, the gathering of faithful disciples and the appearance of schismatics, the spread of the message and the creation of a wide following, the institutionalization of the group as an organized body, and the conversion of revealed truth into dogma.

The story of Langs' "schism" has not been published. It was not a heresy but a manifestation of individuality and a quest for independence. The problem is with the group, which cannot accommodate an ideological variant in its midst, and with the individual, who craves the approval of the group but will not sell his originality short. The docile stay and the naughty go away. As Langs, inspired by Winnicott (1949), avows: "Whenever an analyst writes, it is an effort to complete his own analysis" (p. 48). And, he should have added, it is to resolve the business of relating to the group, to teachers, students, and patients as well.

Give a dog a bad name and hang him, as the saying goes; such namecalling is a strategy for maintaining group cohesion. The epithet "wild" (Chessick, 1981) is one of the mildest of those thrown at Langs in a number of reviews of his books. On the other hand, a follower of Langs qualified the absence of serious debate on the communicative approach in the psychoanalytic literature as narcissistic defensiveness (Raney, 1983). Cursing enemies, excommunicating heretics, and pinning psychopathological labels on opponents – the varieties of name-calling. In this case, the establishment chose silence. Obliteration is a fate worse than excommunication.

But we are dealing with careers, not curses. Langs has gone on to create a career, to win friends and influence people, in imitation of Freud's example. Freud's motto in *The Interpretation of Dreams* (1900b), "*Flectere si nequeo superos, Acheronta movebo*" (If I cannot bend the upper gods, I shall move the underworld) had a political correlate: Since he could not conquer the Viennese academic establishment, he went directly to the public and created a world movement. He understood the sociopolitics of groups and of ideologies (Lothane, 1983a). He chose to express it in the terminology of the sciences. Like Freud, Langs has shifted from the career of therapist to a career of teacher, author, lecturer, leader, and reformer. Freud and others published their cases; Langs has decided to refrain from writing about his cases. His clinical examples are from the caseloads of students in supervision. This sociopolitical fact deserves some consideration, because it has a bearing on the evolution of his theoretical emphases. What Einstein said about physicists applies even more so to analysts: "If you want to find out anything from theoretical physicists about the methods they use, I advise you to stick closely to one principle: Don't listen to their words, fix your attention on their deeds" (quoted in Szasz, 1961, p. 2).

In Langs' case, he has largely taught residents and young therapists. These are practitioners in institutional settings or beginning in private practice, therapists who are relatively inexperienced and insecure. People in institutional, as compared to entrepreneurial, settings often treat individuals who lack social or economic independence. Both therapist and patient are at the mercy of the system; they are not free to choose what they want or to decide policies. This situation is not unlike the fate of the training analyst and the candidate in an analytic institute. Only the most powerful training analysts in a system can call their own shots. Others, along with their trainees, are subject to scrutiny and pressure. The institutional frame is a compromised one from the word go.

It is thus understandable that Langs, dealing with interactions in such settings, should have placed such a great deal of stress on issues of frame and developed a method so heavily focused on the therapist. To be sure, increased self-awareness and responsibility is a moral duty of every practitioner, institutional or entrepreneurial. Free entrepreneurs are beholden only to their conscience and to society at large, whereas those within the system are beholden to their supervisors, an obligation that becomes a third-party infringement in the patient-therapist relationship. Ultimately, the patient bears the consequences of the supervisor-supervisee struggle. This struggle is often irrelevant to the patient in the system, it is relevant only to the needs of the other two players, and the patient is used as a pawn in their game. From the outset, furthermore, it has to be decided whose agent the supervisor is going to be, the patient's or the therapist's. Langs (1979) defines his position unequivocally: "The supervisor's commitment must be primarily to the patient in therapy and only secondary to the trainee; physicianly responsibilities precede all else in any type of therapeutic situation. Supervisory interventions for which the supervisee may be unprepared are thus at times indicated, in the interests of securing for the patient a sound therapy situation" (p. 324). Such an advocacy of the patient, a third party to the teacher-student relationship, can result in the interests of the student being sacrificed (see Lothane, 1984b).

Langs has commented in print on his analyst but not on his supervisors at the institute or how they affected him personally and the analyses of his patients. The amount of pressure to which he may have been subjected can only be surmised from its reverberations in the dialogue with Searles (Langs & Searles, 1980), where Searles expresses the following reaction:

> I feel you are going to destroy me. You are starting to put the squeeze on me. It is similar to what you did with some of those poor bastardly therapists in the *"Bipersonal Field"* (Langs, 1976a) and, my God, I dread it and I cringe and I can't supply those answers. . . . I have told many audiences that, in my work with nonschizophrenic patients, at one or another juncture, relatively infrequently, I express feelings with an explicitness which is relatively commonplace in my work with schizophrenic patients; but what determines my timing of my doing so I cannot, I can't possibly say (p. 124).

Searles juxtaposes his freely flowing, intuitive style with Langs', who says of himself: "I am a stickler on methodology" (p. 125). Searles is also critical of Langs' stance as teacher: ". . . I doubt very much that you realize how pulverizingly critical and condemnatory you are being, at least verbally, to the therapist. . . . Nonverbally you're much less unkind than your words would indicate" (p. 131). Speaking doctor to doctor, Searles offers the following advice: "I would recommend to you that, in your work with the therapists in your seminar, you utilize something of the same allusive subtlety that you recommend they utilize in their work with their patients, as regards any implied acknowledgement of the therapist's psychopathology as it becomes revealed by their work with the patients" (p. 138). Langs concedes the point and notes in self-defense: "And I do use discretion and modulation. . . . It's a dilemma. It is not me that disturbs the supervisee, but the patient; I am trying to be open and helpful" (p. 139).

Langs' teachers at the institute may have also sincerely felt that they were critical of their student for his own good, or for the good of the patients they thought they were protecting. It is easier to achieve consensus in medicine, where the target of treatment is the disease, not the patient. In the field of psychological treatment there is the perennial conflict of personal vested interests. There is also the inflated narcissism of minor differences. An interpretation may be brilliant, but also off by a hair's breadth; it is a matter of personal taste. But in medicine as elsewhere the dilemma has always been: whose interests come first, the patient's or the doctor's?

Can beggars be choosers? The wave of consumerism that has changed the nature of the practice of medicine and psychiatry may soon sweep through the schools that teach psychoanalysis and psychotherapy. Students will claim that the teacher should be their advocate primarily and the patient's secondarily. Physicians have traditionally stuck together. Psychoanalysts have persecuted peers and students in the interests of their own power and in the defense of their own orthodoxy. The principle of the adaptive context will have to be applied to the teacher-student relationship. What is the teacher's impact on the student? What is the teacher's hidden agenda? How truthful or deceitful is the teacher being with the student, how exploitative?

Coming from a different direction than Stone, Searles (Langs & Searles, 1980) disagreed with Langs' skepticism about the ability of patients consciously to "tell me when something is quite off the mark" (p. 98). He also found his own analyst's self-revelations "very helpful, very helpful. It would have been intolerably impersonal without them. A lot of it was pretty impersonal anyway; but there was enough leaven of a person there to make it reassuring. It was very useful" (p. 42). For Langs this is anathema. Yet, this "leaven of a person" is the leaven of love in human relation. Without it there is no relationship. Since psychological treatment is a personal relationship, since the person is the instrumentality of that treatment, it cannot be and grow without this leaven.

Thus posited, the problem of technique can be examined in a new perspective: what is the right technique, what is right love, and how do the two relate to each other in the enterprise called psychotherapy? Freud began with the phenomenon of hysteria, stumbled on the phenomenon of love, and invented transference in an attempt to bring law and order into love. The analysis of transference became his definitive conception of the right technique. He did not often treat of love, but did on occasion treat with love. Ferenczi, by contrast, emphasized love.

Freud's abandonment of the seduction theory had momentous consequences for the development of psychoanalytic theory and practice (Lothane, 1983b). What would have happened if he had not abjured the seduction theory? He would have been like Ferenczi, who remained true to the traumatic conception of neurosis and the neurosogenic effect of cruel parents on their children. Ferenczi also advocated, according to

Szasz (1965), the "abandoning of transference-analysis and, indeed, analysis of any kind in favor of dwelling sympathetically on the patient's past disappointments and making heroic efforts to undo them." Ferenczi is thus the father of the here-and-now wave: of Horney's and Sullivan's emphasis on the present over the past; of Wilhelm Reich's character analysis; of Franz Alexander's corrective emotional experience; of Merton Gill and Robert Langs.

Langs is between Freud and Ferenczi. He does not treat of love directly, except, in the manner of Freud, by default. Love comes to you indirectly when you do things right, when you apply the right technique, when you say the right words, when you express the right ideas. Direct love is as impossible as direct consciousness of it. In his stress on the ideogenic nature of the symptom versus its affective side, on the pathogenic nature of unconscious fantasy, on the negative value of failed communication, Langs is like Freud. Like Freud, he also stresses interpretation. But as Freud (1933) himself saw:

> The associations to the dream are not yet the latent dream thoughts. . . . An association often comes to a stop precisely before the genuine dream thought. At that point we intervene on our own; we fill in the hints, draw undeniable conclusions, and give explicit utterance to what the patient has only touched on in his associations. This sounds as though we allowed our ingenuity and caprice to play with the material put at our disposal by the dreamer and as though we misused it in order to interpret *into* his utterances what cannot be interpreted *from* them [p. 12; italics Freud's].

This is the perennial problem of interpretation: How do we know whether we are interpreting from or into? Are we not dignifying the analyst's thoughts, the *analyst's* associations, by the pretentious title of interpretations? How do we know whether patients are alluding to the analyst or talking about themselves? We do not know for sure. But if interpreting is nothing more than entertaining options, it is of service in making further discoveries, subject to the judgment of history. The danger lies in claiming premature validity for such interpretations. As the expert in the unconscious, rather than as an observer of reality, the analyst may be tempted to engage in a kind of imperialism toward the patient or student.

In Langs' primary focus on the interaction, in the short shrift he gives to the notion of the transference neurosis ("for me that is a denial-based myth" [Langs & Searles, 1980, p. 55]) pointing to the traumatogenic behavior of the therapist, in his views on the seduction theory, Langs is more like Ferenczi than Freud. Is it technique or love? Technology or personology? Idea or feeling? Content or form? The choices between these pseudopolarities make up the body and soul of psychoanalysis, past and present. Langs' effort is a challenging link in this historical chain.

REFERENCES

Chessick, P. (1981). Critique: The wild supervisor. *American Journal of Psychotherapy*, *35*, 445–448.

Feldman, S. S. (1958). Blanket interpretations. *Psychoanalytic Quarterly*, *27*, 205–216.

Freud, S. (1895). Studies on hysteria. *S.E.*, *2*, p. 12.

Freud, S. (1900a). The Interpretation of Dreams. *S.E.*, *4–5*.

Freud, S. (1900b). Die Traumdeutung. *Gesammelte Werke* (Vols. 2–3). London: Imago, 1942.

Freud, S. (1901). Über den Traum. *Gesammelte Werke* (Vols. 2–3). London: Imago, 1942.

Freud, S. (1912). Recommendations to physicians practising psycho-analysis. *S.E.*, *12*.

Freud, S. (1913). On beginning the treatment. *S.E.*, *12*.

Freud, S. (1914). Recollecting, repeating, and working through. *S.E.*, *12*.

Freud, S. (1915a). Observations on transference–love. *S.E.*, *12*.

Freud, S. (1915). Die Verdrangung. *Gesammelte Werke* (Vols. 2–3). London: Imago, 1942.

Freud, S. (1933). New Introductory Lectures on Psycho-Analysis. *S.E.*, *22*, 12.

Homans, P. (1970). *Theology after Freud*. New York: Irvington.

Isakower, O. (1968, 1971). Personal communications.

Klein, M., & Tribich, D. (1979). On Freud's blindness. *Colloquim*, *2*, 52–59.

Langs, R. (1971). Day residues, recall residues, and dreams: Reality and the psyche. *Journal of the American Psychoanalytic Association*, *19*, 499–523.

Langs, R. (1972). A psychoanalytic study of material from patients in psychotherapy. In R. Langs, *Technique in translation* (p. 71–111). New York: Jason Aronson, 1978.

Langs, R. (1973). *The technique of psychoanalytic psychotherapy* (Vol. 1). New York: Jason Aronson.

Langs, R. (1974). *The technique of psychoanalytic psychotherapy* (Vol. 2). New York: Jason Aronson.

Langs, R. (1976). *The bipersonal field*. New York: Jason Aronson.

Langs, R. (1978a). *The listening process*. New York: Jason Aronson.

Langs, R. (1978b). *Technique in transition*. New York: Jason Aronson.

Langs, R. (1979). *The supervisory experience*. New York: Jason Aronson.

Langs, R. (1980a). *Interactions: The realm of transference and countertransference*. New York: Jason Aronson.

Langs, R. (1980b). Truth therapy, lie therapy. *International Journal of Psychoanalytic Psychotherapy*, *8*, 3–34.

Langs, R. (1981). Modes of cure in psychoanalysis and psychoanalytic psychotherapy. *International Journal of Psycho-Analysis*, *62*, 199–214.

Langs, R. (1982). *Psychotherapy: A basic text*. New York: Jason Aronson.

Langs, R., & Searles, H. (1980). *Intrapsychic and interpersonal dimensions of treatment*. New York: Jason Aronson.

Langs, R., & Stone, L. (1980). *The therapeutic environment and its setting*. New York: Jason Aronson.

Lothane, Z. (1980). The art of listening: A critique of Robert Langs. [Review of *The Listening Process*.] *Psychoanalytic Review*, *67*, 353–364.

Lothane, Z. (1981a). A perspective on Freud and psychoanalysis. [Review of *Freud, Biologist of the Mind*, by F. J. Sulloway.] *Psychoanalytic Review, 68*, 348–361.

Lothane, Z. (1981b). Listening with the third ear as an instrument in psychoanalysis: The contributions of Reik and Isakower. *Psychoanalytic Review, 68*, 487–503.

Lothane, Z. (1982). The psychopathology of hallucinations: A methodological analysis. *British Journal of Medical Psychology, 55*, 335–348.

Lothane, Z. (1983a). Reality, dream, and trauma. *Contemporary Psychoanalysis, 19*, 423–443.

Lothane, Z. (1983b). Cultist phenomena in psychoanalysis. In D. Halpern (Ed.), *Psychodynamic perspectives on religion, cult and sect.* Boston: John Wright/PSG.

Lothane, Z. (1984). Teaching the psychoanalytic method: Procedure and process. In L. Caligor, P. M. Bromberg, & J. Meltzer (Eds.), *Clinical perspectives on the supervision of psychoanalysis and psychotherapy.* New York: Plenum.

Masson, J. M. (1984). The assault on truth. New York: Farrar, Straus & Giroux.

Raney, J. O. (1984). Narcissistic defensiveness and the communicative approach, pp. 465–490. In J. O. Raney (Ed.), *Listening and interpreting.* New York: Jason Aronson.

Rapaport, D. (1960). The structure of psychoanalytic theory. *Psychological Issues, 2*, (2, Monograph 6).

Reich, W. (1949). *Character analysis.* New York: Noonday Press.

Sulloway, F. J. (1979). *Freud: Biologist of the mind.* New York: Basic Books.

Swales, P. (1982). Freud, Johann Weier and the status of seduction: The role of the witch in the conception of fantasy. *The Sciences, 22*, 21–25.

Szasz, T. (1961). *The myth of mental illness.* New York: Harper.

Szasz, T. (1965). *The ethics of psychoanalysis.* New York: Basic Books.

Winnicott, D. W. (1949). Hate in the counter-transference. *International Journal of Psycho-Analysis, 30*, 69–75.

Heinz Kohut: Beyond the Pleasure Principle, Contributions to Psychoanalysis

8

Hyman L. Muslin, M.D.

Heinz Kohut, the founder of the psychology of the self, died on October 8, 1981. He had come a long way in developing a theory of the mind which, starting with a relatively modest addition to the psychoanalytic structural model of the mind, evolved into a totally unique approach to the problems of modern humanity. Kohut, like Freud was a conquistador in many areas of peoples reactions to their surrounds. In some areas, his contributions were well worked out, for example in his systematized work on the crucial developmental issues that lead to either a cohesive self or a self vulnerable to fragmentation. Kohut's contributions to psychopathology have also been neatly systematized. Perhaps his views on the theory of cure in analysis, including his systematization of the transferences and their role in analytic cure, represent the most compelling of his contributions.

Kohut's insistence on prolonged empathic immersion into the *experience* of the patient—away from external behaviors and preformed theories including theories of self psychology—is perhaps, of all his contributions the central one. Other aspects of the theory and practise of the psychology of the self are in need of further elaboration and research. It remains a truism, however, that Kohut's discoveries and formulations have been a major force in liberating the field of psychoanalysis from the shackles of insistence on attention to the vicissitudes of the drives and their defenses, especially the insistence on the oedipal complex as the inevitable pathogenic force for human beings.

Heinz Kohut came to the University of Chicago from Vienna as a neurologist after World War II. He then began his training in psychiatry and psychoanalysis, although he had been analyzed in Vienna with August Aichorn. Shortly after his graduation from the Chicago Institute for Psychoanalysis, he joined the staff at the institute and began his lifelong career in teaching and research in psychoanalysis. He also continued his affiliation with the University of Chicago as a professor of psychiatry and lectured there regularly. Kohut's active participation in the local and national psychoanalytic community culminated in his election to the presidency of the American Psychoanalytic Association in 1966.

Prior to his first formal paper on narcissistic issues, Kohut wrote on a broad range of psychoanalytic topics, including empathy and introspection (1959) and psychological reactions to music. In 1966, with the paper "Forms and Transformation of Narcissism," Kohut began his total involvement with the understanding of the self, its development, anatomy, and psychopathology, and the treatment of the disorders of the self. From 1966 to 1977, Kohut focused on the self as a structure within the ego—the self that can be recognized within the classical psychoanalytic structural model. He delineated special psychopathological disorders of the self, as differentiated from the so-called structural neuroses in which the etiologic variables deal with drives and their conflicts—the transference neuroses commonly based on the inadequate resolution of the oedipal complex. Kohut emphasized that the self and its charge of energy, narcissism, should be recognized without bias as an important entity, separate from the other aspects of the intrapsychic world. Thus, although object relationships are important, narcissistic interests are of special value in the psyche and, in fact, narcissism has its own line of development. The next stage in Kohut's thinking was to delineate the treatment issues of the disorders of the self, particularly the special transferences he discovered in people suffering with treatable self disorders.

In his 1977 work, *The Restoration of the Self*, Kohut delineated the self as the "center of the psychological universe" and the maintenance of its cohesion as the essential ingredient of mental health. What Kohut terms "Tragic Man"—the individual preoccupied with gaining succor for his or her depleted self—here replaces "Guilty Man"—the individual preoccupied with the avoidance of oedipal guilt—as the central problem in Western civilization. The search for esteem, from early life through death, through the medium of the self-selfobject dyad, replaces anxiety as the central feature of humankind. Adequate esteem leads to a life of joy, not a life based on the taming of drives. In fact, as Kohut teaches, drives and their vicissitudes emerge as a central feature of the individual only when the self breaks down and these drives are recognized as disintegration products.

Kohut's contributions to psychoanalysis were in the area of the self and its vicissitudes, what he referred to as ". . . the phenomena that lie within the area 'beyond the pleasure principle' " (Kohut in Ornstein, 1978 p. 752). Starting from his initial investigations pertaining to the empathic investigation of the self (Kohut, 1959), Kohut staked out his arena of concentration as being centered on what he called "Tragic

Man", the conceptualization of the individual as blocked in his attempt to achieve self-realization. This version of man is at great distance from Freud's version of the individual in conflict over his or her pleasure-seeking drives, the so-called Guilty Man (Kohut, 1971).

Kohut's investigations into the inner mental life of human beings ultimately encompassed a theory of the developing self. This became his model of the mind, a theory of psychopathology, a new approach to the therapies of self disorders and neuroses, and a new version of the essence of the outcome of psychoanalytic therapies. Although Kohut's contributions extended into every facet of psychology and offer new explanations for the distresses of the modern individual, Kohut repeatedly emphasized that he placed the psychology of the self in the mainstream of psychoanalysis and that he wished to maintain "the continuity of psychoanalysis" (Kohut 1977, p. 172). He certainly added a new emphasis, however, by insisting that ". . . psychoanalysis is a psychology of complex mental states which with the aid of the perservering introspective – empathic immersion of the observer into the inner mental life of man, gathers its data in order to explain them" (Kohut 1977, p. 302). For Kohut, then, it is not transference and resistance but empathy that defines the essence of psychoanalysis. Scientific empathy, as the indispensable tool of the investigator of the inner mental life of humanity at once defines the field of observations and allows for an adaptation of theories and explanations in accordance with the data obtained by empathic cognition.

Although an appreciation of Kohut's contributions to depth psychology must encompass his theories of the development of the self and his views on the pathologies of the self and the psychoanalytic treatment of these disorders, it is also important to recognize in Kohut's work his conviction that the psychology of the self had important relevance to fields outside of mental illness and health. As Kohut remarked in his exchange of letters with Erich Heller (Heller & Kohut, 1978):

Whatever their limitations and shortcomings, I know not only that the psychology of the self explains more meaningfully certain areas of man's psychological experiences in mental illness and health than previous scientific approaches but also that its formulations can be more relevantly applied outside the field of normal and abnormal psychology. The explanations of the psychology of the self are in particular able to encompass the significance of man's scientific, religious, philosophical and artistic activities [p. 449–450].

It is my intention in this essay to offer a view of Kohut's notions of the developing self, the pathogenesis of self disorders and the treatment of the developing self, emphases of self psychology. Readers must answer for themselves the question asked by some critics of self psychology: Can an approach be called "psychoanalytic" if it does not subscribe to the primacy of the drives and especially the Oedipus complex in neurogenesis? Can self psychology be regarded as offering a psychoanalytic view if it considers the outcome of psychoanalysis as essentially an impetus to the development of a stunted self rather than–as classical psychoanalysis would say–the resolution of transferences centered on the oedipal conflicts of incest and parricide?

If one accepts the Kohutian definition of psychoanalysis as a depth psychology whose areas are limited only by the limitations of empathic cognitions, self psychology is in the mainstream of psychoanalysis. On the other hand, if psychoanalysis is to be considered as a conflict psychology of drives versus the restraining and taming forces, self psychology is not an addition to the theory of psychoanalysis. Its views would then constitute a new school of psychology. The goals of self-psychology analyses are reached when patients are enabled to seek out and invest appropriate self objects for the sustenance of their now cohesive selves. This statement of the end point of an analysis conducted to rehabilitate the self focuses immediately on the significant differences between self psychology and classical psychoanalysis. Classical psychoanalysis is concerned with the resolution of conflicts that are purported to be the instigators of the symptoms of neurotic distress. Other end points of a classical analysis are reached when the consciousness of ego is expanded through insight, when the patiient's drives are tamed, and when the Oedipus complex is resolved, with its attendant features of castration anxiety and excess guilt diminished. Finally, the patient at the end of a classical analysis is understood to have moved from dependency to autonomy and from narcissism to object love. Thus, classical analysis holds that an analysis is complete when the symptoms of the pathogenic conflicts are ameliorated, especially the castration anxiety and the hypertrophied guilt, and when the pathogenic complexes have become conscious, especially the persisting conflicts centering on the Oedipus complex, which has been reenacted and become the central focus of the transference drama. The analyst and the patient, in their constant preoccupation with the manifestations of the archaic oedipal phenomena, work on bringing to consciousness the buried pathogenic fears (Freud 1917a).

Self psychology holds that an analysis is complete when the self, formerly underdeveloped through fixations on archaic self-selfobject relationships, is provided with a therapeutic atmosphere in order to complete its development. The patient will be cured when his or her self is cohesive, when he or she has achieved sufficient structure from the development-enhancing psychoanalysis to reveal the activities emanating from a firm self. As Kohut (1977) stated: "Within the framework of the psychology of the self, we define mental health not only as freedom from the neurotic symptoms and inhibitions that interfere with the functions of a mental apparatus involved in loving and working, but also as the capacity of a firm self to avail itself of the talents and skills at an individual's disposal, enabling him to love and work successfully" (p. 284).

Thus, from the outset, the classical position concerns itself with the fate of the drives—their conflicts, their resolutions through recreation in the transference and their subsequent working through, especially of oedipal conflicts and oedipal transferences. Self psychology is concerned with the integrity of the self. If the self is healthy, drives are not experienced as isolated phenomena and no pathological conflicts involving drives would then ensue. The analyst, in this view, is occupied with rehabilitating a self that has become fixated for its sustenance on archaic measures that are unsuccessful. The result is an enfeebled self, unable to engage in life with vigor in a goal-directed fashion. The analysis in this view is also concerned with the establishment of transferences and interpretation, but they are directed at promoting the development of the self. In self-psychology analysis, the essence of the cure lies in the establishment and resolution ("re-solution") of selfobject transferences, each of which replicates an archaic selfobject relationship that has resulted in a fixation of developmental strivings. The modal psychoanalytic regression reactivates the pathogenic selfobject transference at the point where the selfobject functions required for development of the self were deficient. As will be discussed later in detail, the patient's stunted self now resumes development of the particular functions that were inadequately internalized through the failures of the selfobjects in the surround. The transferences that are established reflect the analysand's fixations on the point in psychological time when development ceased, ushering in, for the patient, the never-ending search to resurrect that particular selfobject from whom the patient tries again and again to obtain the necessary mirroring or power merging and make it into his or her own. Once the pathognomonic transferences are established, the mirroring or other selfobject functions are initiated. The patient begins to resume the development of the missing or defective self functions through transmuting internalizations. The process of internalization is set in motion through the optimal frustration of analysis which ultimately intensifies the imagos of the analyst's selfobject functions to the point of causing a permanent addition of selfobject functioning to adhere to the patient's self, thus, for example, eventuating in a movement from admiration of the mirroring selfobject to self-admiration.

We now turn to the significant aspect of the development of the self and the development and maintenance of the self-selfobject relationships, which self psychology holds are at the core of psychological life.

THE DEVELOPMENT OF THE SELF

In Kohut's (1977) view, the self is the center of the psychological universe, by which he meant that people can only be understood in terms of their experiences—their inner mental life—not their behavior (Kohut, 1959). It follows from this that any genuine investigation of man must be through the medium of empathy—vicarious introspection—which therefore defines and restricts the observational field of psychological understanding. Kohut's last statement about empathy was that it is to be understood as the capacity to think oneself into the inner life of another person (personal communication, 1981).

As we will see in more detail, for Kohut (1979):

> The self is the core of our personality. It has various constituents which we acquire in the interplay with those persons in our earliest childhood environment whom we experience as selfobjects. A firm self, resulting from optimal interactions between the child and his selfobjects is made up of the three major constituents: (1) one pole from which emanates the basic strivings for power and success; (2) another pole that harbors the basic idealized goals; and (3) an intermediate area of basic talents and skills that are activated by the tension arc that establishes itself between ambitions and ideals [p. 11].

Moreover, the self experience has a line of development as separate from the experience of single body parts and single functions. As Kohut (1974) comments: "The child's self experience arises separately, increasing in importance as it develops next to and more and more above his experience of body parts and single functions. And finally, the child reaches a stage in which the progressively tamed experience of single parts and functions has become related to the total experience of a cohesive self—the parts in other words do not build up the self, they become built into it" (p. 749).

The complete self is a supraordinate structure, which functions not only as the receiver of impressions derived from the environment but as the center of action. It is experienced as continuous in space and time, as a cohesive entity. The so-called bipolar self can be further identified in terms of its major constituents; the poles of ideals and ambitions and the intermediate area of talents and skills. These poles of the self come into their final form through interaction with the significant persons in infancy and childhood who serve as the instigators of these self functions.

The development of the pole of ambitions is initiated as a result of special activities of the parent, who functions as an admirer, approver, or echoer of the unfolding self and thus offers to the child an experience of unquestioning confirmation of the child's worth. From the point of view of the child, this parent is experienced as an entity over whom the child has total control—much as one controls various parts of one's body—thus the designation "selfobject," or in this case, the "mirroring selfobject." These early relationships are experienced as fusions or mergers—or, psychologically speaking, immersions—into the body and mind of the caretaking selfobject. Establishing the archaic self-selfobject mirroring dyad is crucial for psychological life. For structure-building to take place, however, the self-aggrandizing mirror functions must be *interiorized* or *internalized*—actually added to the contents of the self—so that self-esteem, an intrapsychic function, replaces selfobject mirroring, an interpersonal activity. In Kohut's view, inter-nalization of selfobject mirroring functions takes place along the lines first articulated by Freud (1917b) in *Mourning and Melancholia,* in which the mourner's unique reaction to loss—internalization of signifi-cant aspects of the departed person—is seen as a ubiquitous reaction to separation.

At about the same time in an infant's development as the establish-ment of the mirroring self/selfobject, the second major influence on self development occurs—the establishment of the idealizing parental imago selfobject. Whereas the mirroring selfobjects respond to and con-firm the infant's grandiosity, the idealized parent imago are figures whom the child looks up to and merges with as an imago of calmness, soothing, perfection and thus a source of strength. One other early self-selfobject experience is ordinarily present in the child's ontogeny. This is the experience of what Kohut (1977) called the alter ego—a twinship merger in which the child experiences the parental self as essentially the same as the child's own. This essential sameness is instrumental in enhancing the child's skills and unfolding the child's talents.

The next phase of the child's development is significant in the forma-tion of the cohesive self. This is the internalization of the selfobjects' functions of initiating and promoting esteem, so that what was a feature of the self-selfobject relationship now becomes a set of self functions. Kohut describes the interiorization of these functions as occurring in two steps: (1) optimal frustration and (2) transmuting internalization. Optimal frustration refers to the unavoidable disappointments in child rearing, so that the child does not obtain the instant feedback that he or she may be demanding. These unavoidable delays, absences, and misappreciations are not protracted or in any way traumatic—thus they are *optimal* frustrations. They promote the internalization of the mir-roring or other selfobject functions, so that the mirroring selfobject's approval is attached, so to say, to the child's self as a permanent source of nurturance (Kohut, 1971). Over time, the sequence of optimal frustra-tions leading to transmuting internalization creates a cohesive self. This structure is bipolar in its psychological shape, the archaic grandiosity transformed into the pole of ambition, and the internalized archaic idealizations transformed into the pole of ideals. In this early self, which can now be labeled the nuclear self, the pole of ambitions strives to live up to the pole of ideals through the talents and skills of the self. In fact, in the adult, the cohesion of the self is maintained through the tension arc created by the pole of ambitions striving to live up to the ideals through the exertions of the talents and skills in what Kohut (1977) called a program of action: "With the term tension arc,...I am referring to the abiding flow of actual psychological activity that establishes itself between the two poles of the self; i.e., a person's basic pursuits towards which he is driven by his ambitions and led by his ideals" (p. 180).

The bipolar self now experienced by the child as continuous in time and discrete in space maintains its cohesiveness—its resistance to breakup (fragmentation)—through two sources of self cement. One is the pool of endogenous stores of self support derived from the internalized functions of selfobjects to maintain self-esteem. The other is the continuing need for selfobjects throughout life.

Kohut found that self-selfobject relationships form the essence of psychological life from birth to death. The nature of this relationship, however, changes over time and in functioning. The earliest self-selfobject contacts, as previously noted, are actually merging types of relationships. They instill in the child, after optimal frustration, the supplies of esteem. From the archaic selfobject relationships, there is a developmental line of self-selfobject encounters to what is called the mature selfobject relationships. These offer an experience of empathic resonance—the admiration of a colleague through which the adult self can experience a revival of the memory traces of the archaic selfobject's mirroring or calming and soothing, and in this manner restore disequilibrium due to a temporary flagging of one's esteem. Throughout the individual's development, the self requires selfobject refueling to maintain its integrity. At times, these selfobject encounters will approach the approving, admiring, calming, merging interactions of the archaic self-selfobject fusions.

Thus, in the so-called anal stage of development, the child's need for the mirroring responses of the selfobject parent are necessary for the child's toilet-training accomplishments to be given value. In the oedipal phase of development, the child's selfobject requirement of the parents are that they respond to his or her increased assertiveness in the sexual and other spheres with admiration and pride at the vigor and creativeness displayed. The selfobject encounters in these early stages of development, although not of the earlier, archaic types, still continue to provide supportive experiences that will be interiorized and serve to enhance the achievement of the youngster in his or her development. The adolescent's need for the mirroring selfobject parent to give credence to his or her creative activities is well known, as is the intensity of the adolescent's need for intimate contact with an idealized selfobject. In both these instances, internalization of selfobject functioning is again affected. In later life, necessary refueling of one's worth is provided through mature selfobject encounters and the phenomenon of empathic resonance. In the senium for example, mirroring of one's achievements, of one's courage in the face of death is necessary.

In sum, the self is maintained in a cohesive manner through the strength of its constituents, the firm sense of assertiveness, the intact sense of one's values serving as a compass through life, and the ability to exert one's skills and talents in the pursuit of one's programs of actions, from writing a speech to caring for the disabled. Selves differ considerably in the relative weakness or strengths of their constituents. There are selves that are firm or enfeebled, resistant to fragmentation (cohesive) or highly vulnerable to losses of worth and thus prone to fragmentation. Charismatic selves are firm in the pole of assertiveness, whereas messianic selves are extremely leadership oriented. Some selves are mirror hungry, while others are chronically searching for a leader (Kohut & Wolf, 1978).

PATHOLOGY OF SELF OR SELF-DISORDERS

The position of self psychology with regard to psychopathology is that all forms of psychopathology are ultimately derived from defects in the overall structure of the self or from distortions of the self. Both of these are due to disturbances of self-selfobject relationships in childhood. Self psychology further asserts, in contrast to classical analysis, that conflicts in the object-instinctual realm – the realm of object love and object hate, in particular the set of conflicts called the Oedipus complex – are not the cause of psychopathology, but its results.

As we previously have seen, in adult life as well as in childhood, the cohesiveness or harmony or fragmentation of the self – whether it is enfeebled, distorted, or firm – is a result of the success or failure of the archaic self-selfobject relationships. A failure in the self-selfobject relationships in childhood or adult life leads to the painful experience of fragmentation. Fragmentation, in the view of self psychology, is the central pathologic experience of breakdown of the self. It is ushered in by a massive loss of self-esteem, followed immediately by the advent of the global anxiety referred to as "disintegration anxiety." Directly after the advent of disintegration anxiety, the self is experienced as losing its cohesiveness, with the usual experience of splitting or fragmentation of the self functions and self perception, including reality testing, memory, and orientation in space and time. There is also loss of the intact experience of self observing; the various experiences of the different organs previously coalesced together in the intact experience of the total bodyself are now experienced as separate and become focuses for enhanced attention and even preoccupation (hypochondria). In addition, the patient is in the throes of a separation reaction, with its attendant features of loss of vigor, esteem, and meaning in life. Finally, a failure in a self-selfobject encounter will commonly lead to a unique rage reaction. This so-called narcissistic rage reaction represents the reaction to the loss of control of the selfobject. The individual will vent destructiveness on anyone in the immediate surround (Kohut, 1971).

A self-selfobject failure in childhood has different consequences from a self-selfobject failure in adult life. In adult life, the cohesive self has continuing mature selfobject encounters, which are of value in maintaining continuing support to the self through empathic resonance – that is, by supplying mirroring or firmness to add to the cohesiveness of the self. A failed selfobject encounter in an adult with a cohesive self will ordinarily lead to a transitory fragmentation, with hypochondria, loss of esteem, temporary interference in mentation, and so forth.

In childhood, a failed self-selfobject relationship is of a different order. A massive or chronic failure during the phases of childhood when the self is unfolding may result in a fragmentation that will eventually be resolved – that is, the self will reconstitute itself and the fragmentation will subside – but the self will now have permanent alterations. The overall experience of the self will be that of a self chronically low in energy, a self depleted of vigor without evidence of the experience of joy. This self will react strongly to criticism and failures by becoming more withdrawn or, at times, caught up in the explosion of a narcissistic rage reaction. Depending on the specific type of selfobject failures, the resultant self distortion may be that of a self weakened in the pole of assertiveness, in the pole of ideals, or in the area of talents and skills. These defects will of course lead to the absence of formulated programs of action in life, for example, of educational, athletic, or musical pursuits.

The overall result of such self-selfobject failures may be a self that experiences life as empty and that is constantly in the throes of loneliness. Despite this loneliness and a desire for human encounters, this self may be quite resistant to such encounters and may maintain a conscious attitude of haughtiness and isolation. At times, this self may attempt to gain support for self-esteem through a variety of activities designed to lessen the chronic emptiness such as compulsive homo- or heterosexuality, addiction to compounds to provide calming experiences, or compulsive episodes of stealing.

At other times, selfobject failures in childhood eventuate in what appears to be a syndrome of neurosis. These reactions occur when, after a failed selfobject encounter in a particular phase of childhood, the child becomes preoccupied with the drive or developmental task specific to the phase, ultimately leading to a *fixation* on that drive or developmental task and leaving the child permanently preoccupied with the fears of that phase in life, which were never allayed. Thus, an oedipal fixation or an anal fixation represents a failed self-selfobject relationship in the corresponding developmental era of childhood. The secondary elaborations of the breakdown of the self during those times in childhood when developmental tasks need to be mastered involve an exaggerated focus on the drive currently of concern and defenses elaborated in an attempt to ameliorate or repress the exaggerated drive fragments. When the cohesive self breaks down or becomes fragmented, in response to a self-selfobject rupture, it may take one of several pathways. The fragmented self may maintain a state of *chronic fragmentation* (protracted fragmentation disorders, borderline personalities); the fragmented self may repair itself without evidence of the previous state of breakdown (episodic fragmentation); the fragmented self may reequilibrate itself with newly developed defenses against selfobject bonds (narcissistic personality disorders); or the fragmented self may focus on the drives that are salient in the current developmental phase or have been activated as a manifestation of a regressive reaction (neurotic syndromes) and may secondarily develop defenses against the egress of the specifically elaborated drives (Kohut, 1971, 1977).

Episodic Fragmentation Disorders

Reactions to a breakdown in self-selfobject bonds are, of course, ubiquitous, since self-selfobject bonds and failures are ubiquitous. As has been described, selfobject involvements range from archaic self-selfobject ties that continue over time to so-called mature selfobject encounters. In adults, the need to enter into an archaic self-selfobject bond is limited to instances in which the self is subjected to psychological trauma requiring a temporary merging relationship. These are, of course, instances in which the self is suddenly devoid of narcissistic supplies and is in need of the experience of the fusion with a mirroring selfobject or a revered leader. Archaic self-selfobject bonds always serve to invest the self with the experience of worth, of strength, of calming and soothing. In childhood, these experiences give the self the requisite strength of cohesion; in adulthood, when entered into temporarily in reaction to the stress of dissolution, they effect a repair to a fragmenting self. Mature selfobject encounters are entered into when the self is in need of a temporary enhancement of esteem, that is, in a situation of esteem-deficiency such as is the innumerable states of self-doubt individuals experience. In the mature selfobject encounter, the self's experience of the selfobject is in actuality not that of an object fused with one's self and under one's control; rather the self has a reactivation of the early self-selfobject mergers and experiences a state of esteem enhancement, thus effecting a repair of the self's cohesion. Seen in this way, much of adult interactional life consists of mature selfobject encounters with others who function temporarily to repair a flagging self-esteem or symbolic encounters with music or literature in which the self is uplifted or invigorated.

Thus, episodic fragmentations or near fragmentations or simple instances of loss of esteem or threatened loss of worth are part of one's modal reactions to a complex world of victories, near misses, and failures. In a more or less cohesive self, the repair in most instances will be effected by entering into a mature self-selfobject encounter. In those instances where the demands for cohesion are intense, the previously cohesive self will fragment, albeit temporarily and seek out an archaic self-selfobject encounter in which a merger will be effected. For example, in the case of a person who has just been informed that his or her longstanding state of weakness is due to a malignancy in the colon, the psychological reactions are frequently the self experience of fragmentation. This distress, one hopes, will be followed by the self-selfobject merger effected with a trusted caretaker or relative. In such situations, if empathic caretakers recognize the manifestations of the fragmentation and respond appropriately with a dose of mirroring or allow themselves to become the target for idealization, the fragmentation experience will be short-lived.

Self-fragmentation Resulting in Neurotic Syndromes.   In the view of self psychology, drives come into focus when the self is fragmenting – thus the statement that drives are disintegration products of a fragmenting self (Kohut, 1977). In this light, consider the self of the oedipal-phase child and the selfobject needs of his or her emerging phase-specific assertiveness, including the child's sexual assertiveness of a homoerotic and heteroerotic nature (with hostility toward the parent of the opposite sex). If the selfobject supports are missing or inadequate and the child experiences the parents' withdrawal or rejection during this important phase in development, the self depletion will result in a fragmented self. Thus, in some instances, the result will be not an eruption of undirected narcissistic rage, but an egress of animus unleased when a selfobject has failed in its functions—a preoccupation with the drives derailed from the now-fragmented self. In the ordinary functions of the self, the drives are a vital part of the self, seeking and maintaining contact with the world, including the world of selfobjects. In a fragmented self, the drives are now in a free state and clearly visible since they are not bound up with the functions of the cohesive self.

The unleashed phase-specific drives of the oedipal child whose self is now in a fragmented condition will eventuate in repetitive experiences of anxiety, centering on tissue destruction—the so-called castration anxiety, with its attendant features of anxiety dreams of mutilation—and the buildup of irrational guilt. If, however, the child in the oedipal phase becomes the recipient of helpful selfobject supports, he or she will emerge from this normal phase of development with heteroerotic and homoerotic strivings and a minimum of guilt and castration anxiety.

Thus, in contradistinction to classical psychoanalysis, self psychology does not regard the oedipal phase as "the pivotal point regarding the fate of the self that it is with regard to the formation of the psychic apparatus" (Kohut 1977, p. 240). The so-called neurotic syndromes, which in classical psychoanalysis emerge from the predetermined unfolding of the drives coming into intense conflict with ego defenses and superego, are conceptualized in self psychology as only one of the possible outcomes of a self in fragmentation. Self psychology holds that if the self is intact, there will be no preoccupation with the drives in an isolated fashion. Thus, from the viewpoint of the self psychologist, although an oedipal phase of development is ubiquitous, if there is an adequate set of selfobjects, the child emerges with a firming up of assertiveness, now more adequately controlled, and a firming up of the gender experience. Conversely, if there has been a selfobject failure to the modal egress of assertiveness in an oedipal youngster, the derailed (unattached) instinctual drives will emerge as naked lust and hostility.

The Narcissistic Personality and Behavior Disorders. When self-selfobject failures during the phase of the early development of the self are protracted, they result in a variety of self disorders. These are the narcissistic personality disorders and their acting-out varieties, the narcissistic behavior disorders. They ordinarily result from the failure of the functioning of the mirroring selfobject and the inability of the idealized parent to compensate for the primary selfobject failure (Kohut 1977). The cohesiveness of the resultant total self is defective, and both poles of the self are inadequately filled. This self is vulnerable to fragmentation, especially in relation to further losses of esteem from its milieu. The self experience is commonly a reflection of the diminutive poles of assertiveness and ideals – that is, emptiness and/or loneliness. However, the needs of the self for mirroring or leadership are commonly defended against by attitudes of haughtiness and superciliousness, reflecting anxiety about allowing any further selfobject encounters to transpire. Another common experience in persons with these disorders is to become immersed in transitory relationships in which an archaic self-selfobject dyad is formed and then rejected, ordinarily out of a mixture of anticipated psychic pain and disappointment because the relationship cannot offer them the longed-for childhood gratification. Fragmentation states commonly lead to intense loss of esteem – the so-called empty depression, without prominent guilt.

Other common features of the fragmentation states are the experience of disintegration anxiety – an anxiety state marked by panicky feelings, dissociations, and end-of-the world sensations – followed by mentational dysfunctioning (memory loss, reality-testing deficits, loss of synthesizing, and derailing of associations), and hypochondriasis. Hypochondriasis in fragmentation states reflects the state of the "unglued" self. Although the ordinary experience of a single organ or anatomical part is minimal in a cohesive self, when the self is fragmentating, a particular organ percept in the self that is now functionally split off from the rest of the self may suddenly be experienced in a highly charged fashion. A patient in the middle of a fragmentation reaction may complain of unusual body feelings and localize it to an awareness that her or his face, nose, or abdomen is now experienced quite differently. It may seem too large or too prominent. These experiences reflect the body percepts becoming split off and, for the first time, prominent in the patient's awareness. Patients with narcissistic personality disorders at times exhibit behavior that expresses their reactions to insult or their needs for claiming and soothing or mirroring. These narcissistic behavior disorders encompass the behavior of the compulsive homosexual, the addict, and delinquents who steal as a symbolic expression of the self need for a gift from the selfobject. Those addicts who experience the compound and the effects of the compound as an aid to calming and soothing are clearly demonstrating and gratifying archaic self needs, as are those homosexuals who feel mirrored in frantically sought out episodes of fellatio. Patients who suffer with narcissistic personality disorders do not experience protracted fragmentation states. Their fragmentation is transitory, and they ordinarily seek relief in complaining of their experience of isolation and inability to form and maintain human relationships.

In sum, patients with these self disorders have had failures in their self-selfobject relationships early in life. In effect, their self development is fixated, and thus they continue – albeit, unconsciously – to effect repeated archaic self-selfobject bonds. This is to no avail, however, since they will shortly reject these relationships. The failure of adequate internalization of the self in these patients leads to their vulnerability to fragmentation states. This is resolved in these patients by the self's capacity to erect firm defenses against the egress of the its desires for empathic understanding and gratification.

Protracted Fragmentation States

Patients with borderline disorders and psychoses of all kinds, demonstrate not only a heightened vulnerability to self fragmentation but a protracted quality to their fragmentation. When a so-called borderline patient develops a fragmentation state, which is followed by reality-testing loss (psychosis), derailing, and other symptoms of an acute psychotic decompensation, these pathological states may persist for a long time. Moreover, these patients do not have an adequate capacity to form a therapeutic self-selfobject dyad based on an alliance of effort to appreciate their inner mental life. These patients commonly experience an absence of as-if transference phenomena. They commonly develop a transference psychosis, insisting that the therapist feels this or that and now wishes to cause the patient harm. To repeat, chronic, protracted fragmentation disorders represent the end point of a massive failure in the selfobjects in these people's lives. Due to the failed selfobject functioning, these people cannot form alliances to investigate themselves because they do not have adequately developed functions of self observation (Kohut, 1977).

In summary, the central teaching of Kohut on the psychopathological syndromes is that all forms of psychopathology are due to disturbances of self-selfobject relationships, which result in structural defects in the self and render that self vulnerable to fragmentation and its vicissitudes. Whereas Freud's model of the mind—the model of structural theory—led to erupting instinctual derivatives coming into conflict with the superego and ego and leading to new defenses (neurotic symptoms), Kohut teaches that one must empathize with a self that is fragmented due to a current deficit of cohesiveness brought about by loss of esteem from whatever source. The model of classical psychoanalysis holds that psychopathological syndromes begins with a psyche in conflict and therefore in a state of anxiety. Should this conflict become protracted, the initial signal anxiety will intensify to massive anxiety and there will be a neurotic breakdown. Directly after this event, the psyche develops new symptoms and the offending drive is re-repressed, the psyche becoming once again calm (Freud, 1926). The Kohutian model, in contrast, focuses on the self in fragmentation as the initial manifestation of psychic disequilibrium, which may lead to an episodic fragmentation; a chronic fragmentation; the syndrome of repression of the self's needs, defended by attitudes of haughtiness and superciliousness; or the neurosis that represents the psyche focused on the drives, which are disintegration products of the fragmenting self.

Classical psychoanalysis holds that the Oedipus complex and its resolution or lack of same are the central instigators of neurosis and character disorders. Kohut's view, as has been described, is that if the parents function as supporters of their children's assertiveness, there will be no castration anxiety over "malignant" drives. The oedipal phase will end without castration anxiety or guilt if the parents function as adequate caretakers.

HOW DOES SELF PSYCHOLOGY ANALYSIS CURE?

Self-psychology analysis cures by acquisition of structure in the patient's self. Since a major tenet of self psychology, (one could say "finding" rather than "tenet") is that psychopathology most often reflects deficits in the self, the major thrust of the curative process is to be of aid in reinitiating the development of the self that has been fixated and retarded in its growth. As we have discussed, deficits in the self are seen as outcome products of a failed self-selfobject relationship of childhood, amounting to a deficit in the self structure (self function) that was inadequately internalized. The cure in self-psychology analysis is to develop — that is, to acquire, additional structures within the self. In classical psychoanalysis, in contrast, the cure is to ultimately resolve the fixation of the oedipal complex through the medium of the unfolding of the transference neurosis (Freud, 1917a). In the work of classical analysis, the material of the sessions is focused on the myriad manifestations of the oedipal fixations directed to, for, and against the analyst. The result of the interpretative work is to make the patient aware—and thus free the patient—of the fixations emanating from the oedipal drama. The result will be the acquisition of an expanded conflict-free sphere, the expanding of consciousness ("Where id was ego shall be") and the reduction of castration anxiety and the symptoms (new defenses) evoked by anxiety (Freud, 1926).

Self-psychology analysis, like all psychoanalyses, involves the elaboration of transference phenomena in the analytic work focused on the selfobject transferences and the previously thwarted developmental needs of the self. Patients who are analyzable (those who, while possessing deficits in their selves, have the capacity to form and develop stable alliances with their therapists) will have a spontaneous unfolding of their strivings for structure in the form of a specific self-selfobject transference. These transferences, which reflect the stalled development of the self in relating to a selfobject, encompass the specific functions that have not been internalized in the self of the analysand. They represent the stalled developmental needs of the self for confirming, admiration, and echoing (mirror transference) or the self's needs for firm ideals, calming, and guidance (idealized parent imago transference). The spontaneously unfolding transferences represent needs for the development of structure – not, as in classical analysis, the reliving (in fantasy) of the ancient oedipal strivings that requires explication. The end point of self-psychology analysis is the internalization of the analyst and his or her functions. These become metabolized into self structures that perform the now internalized functions of mirroring and other functions of the selfobject prior to internalizing.

The analysis can be said to begin with the establishment of the basic self-selfobject transference in which the patient's self is sustained (Kohut, 1968). In the course of the analysis, the basic selfobject transference is disrupted time and again by optimal failures of the analyst, akin to the optimal frustrations of the archaic self-selfobject relationships of childhood. After suitable awareness and interpretations of the analysand's retreat and regression (with manifestation of the reinstitution of archaic selfobject relationships), the basic selfobject transference will be reestablished. However, the optimal frustration sets into motion the transmuting internalization of the imago of the selfobject analyst and his or her mirroring or idealized parent function, thus leading to the acquisition of self structure. The process of analysis can never proceed without experiences that the analysand perceives as empathic failures. In this category of events one can place unavoidable interruptions (weekends and vacations) and the analyst's incorrect interpretations. These frustrations, if nontraumatic, will lead to interiorizations of the analyst's essential or basic positively enhancing selfobject functions, especially if the analyst, after grasping the analysand's distress or retreat into archaic preanalytic object-related behaviors, attempts to focus on the experienced rebuff. This latter process, involving empathic understanding of the analysand's experience, amounts to a transference interpretation in which the analyst demonstrates that the patient's self is held in high regard in the analytic relationship, in sharp contrast to relationships with the unempathic archaic selfobjects of the patient's past. The optimal frustrations that the patient experiences extend to the analyst's interpretations, since these, too, are not mirroring actions but are only words. The analyst cannot perform mirroring actions as he or she interprets, an action that serves only to clarify and illuminate.

To summarize, in the normal flow of the analysis, the curative process is a matter of the analysand's previously stunted self acquiring selfobject functions through internalization of the analyst's selfobject functions. This comes about, as does any building of self structure, through a hiatus in the relationship (optimal failure), which serves to energize the imago of the selfobject analyst and his or her functions. These then become absorbed into the self as the self's mirroring or other functions. Another way of understanding the structure building that comes out of analysis is to remember that analysis implies regression, so that the analyst and analysand are locked into a regressive transference. In an archaic selfobject relationship such as is found in childhood, the archaic selfobject is the source of regard. In the analytic transferences, the patient enters into a reactivation of the previously thwarted needs for structure so as to infuse the self with esteem and vigor. The analysand's experience of the analyst, the new selfobject, is as if the patient is once again in contact with a giver of the gifts of worth and value to the self (Kohut, 1977).

The Course of Analysis

An overview of the course of a self-psychology analysis approximates the process found in a classical psychoanalysis. There are two phases of treatment to be considered.

1. The Defense Transference.   This is, of course, the unconscious position of adjustment the analysand takes in reexperiencing the analyst as a parent figure. The conforming experience of the analysand, in the service of maintaining the archaic self-selfobject ties, serves secondarily as resistance to the new selfobject bond in analysis. Its major purpose is to protect the analysand from the possibility of recurring disappointment at the hands of unempathic selfobjects. Thus, the genuine needs of the analysand are repudiated so as to avoid psychic pain.

The defense transference, in the view of classical analysis, is effective in maintaining the repressed instinctual derivatives of oedipal previously buried yearnings for self-structure—for example, the wish to experience self worth through the confirmatory, admiring attitudes and actions of the mirroring selfobject—the analyst is called on to express his or her understanding of what the analysand is experiencing. In this manner, the analysand's transference strivings are "accepted" by the analyst, indicating that the analyst is mindful that a period of time, sometimes a long period, must elapse to allow the transference to unfold without challenge. Premature challenges to these transference strivings may be taken by the analysand as rejections of these very strivings, thus repeating the actual childhood milieu in which these self needs went underground, resulting in a deficient self. Some patients require more or less protracted periods of understanding. In any case, the analyst must be mindful that to understand these selfobject strivings without interpretation is at times of crucial importance in the curative process of a self-psychology analysis. Understanding, which is not simply acceptance, emphasizes that the outcome of a self-psychology analysis is the eventual growth of the patient's self through internalization of the analyst's selfobject ministrations.

The next phase of the analysis centers on the explaining or interpreting function of the analyst. The analytic work done in this phase of treatment deals with interpretations of the repressed strivings that ultimately will bring the patient into investing the analyst with attributes of one or other of the parental roles. If the interpretations are successful, the transference neurosis will now emerge. In a self-psychology analysis, however, the defense transference is in the service of maintaining out of the patient's awareness, the strivings of the self for mirroring and/or the firm ideals, leadership, or calming of the idealized parent. The analytic work done in this phase is directed at providing an environment that the analysand experiences as safe and where the analyst, if necessary, can interpret the defense of haughtiness or isolation against the emergence of the feared wishes for selfobject support.

2. The Basic Selfobject Transference. Kohut (1978) stated: "The discovery of the selfobject transferences forms the basis of my whole work concerning narcissism and the self" (p. 20). This dyad of patient and analyst reactivates the self needs of the analysand that had remained, as a result of faulty interactions in early life, disavowed or in a state of repression. Once the analysand enters an idealizing or mirror transference, the self achieves a state of cohesiveness. The analyst's activity in this phase consists of two sets of attitudes and behaviors, *understanding* and *explaining* (Kohut, 1977).

Once the patient begins to establish the analyst as the selfobject to whom he or she can reveal the previously buried yearnings for self-structure—for example, the wish to experience self worth through the confirmatory, admiring attitudes and actions of the mirroring self-object—the analyst is called on to express his or her understanding of what the analysand is experiencing. In this manner, the analysand's transference strivings are "accepted" by the analyst, indicating that the analyst is mindful that a period of time, sometimes a long period, must elapse to allow the transference to unfold without challenge. Premature challenges to these transference strivings may be taken by the analysand as rejections of these very strivings, thus repeating the actual childhood milieu in which these self needs went underground, resulting in a deficient self. Some patients require more or less protracted periods of understanding. In any case, the analyst must be mindful that to understand these selfobject strivings without interpretation is at times of crucial importance in the curative process of a self-psychology analysis. Understanding, which is not simply acceptance, emphasizes that the outcome of a self psychology analysis is the eventual growth of the patient's self through internalization of the analyst's selfobject ministrations.

The next phase of the analysis centers on the explaining or interpreting unavoidable interruption of the steady state of the basic selfobject transference. As the analysis proceeds, with the analysand now revealing his or her specific self needs in the selfobject transference that has spontaneously unfolded, an equilibrium is reached, a cohesive self state. This equilibrium, of course, is dependent on the presence of the selfobject, in the same manner in which infants experience equilibrium in the presence of their selfobjects. Only after internalization of the necessary mirroring and other functions performed by the selfobject is the self complete. These functions, as already described, become interiorized in the self directly after a failure of the selfobject to either empathically appreciate or respond to a self need—the notion of optimal frustration. Similarly, the analysand immersed in a selfobject transference onto the analyst experiences absences or unavoidable empathic failures by the analyst as if he or she once again has not been responded to. The patient is once again with the archaic selfobjects of the past, whose failures were not optimal but fixating because they were too protracted, too intense—in short, traumatic failures. The analyst's task here is to help the analysand recognize his or her experience in temporarily identifying the analyst with the childhood disappointers. Thus, the explaining (the interpretations) of the analyst in a self psychology analysis is necessary to reveal what might be called the tranference distortions that have interfered with the structure building in analysis.

Explaining or interpreting is necessary to illuminate not just the dynamics of the transference interactions but also its genetic roots. As the analyst explains (interprets) to the patient the dynamic and genetic explanations of the patient's thwarted needs and the reconstruction of the failed self-selfobject dyads in childhood, the analyst is offering to the patient an appreciation of the patient's past. This will be of service to the patient's empathic grasp of himself or herself and will be of help both in the subsequent working-through phase of the analysis and later when the analysis is terminated. Moreover, when the analyst is explaining, he or she is becoming more objective with the patient, in a sense, replacing the experience of merger with the experience of resonance. This reflects progress in the development of the self, from reliance on merger to the use of the empathic closeness of the analyst selfobject.

After the transference distortion is made clear, the analysand is enabled to experience the unavoidable interruptions, empathic misunderstandings, and other mistakes of the analyst as frustration – but optimal frustration. This experience results in the phenomena of internalization of function, the so-called transmuting internalization. As has been previously explained, transmuting internalization refers to the intrapsychic process in which the functions such as mirroring that were previously performed by an outside agency (the selfobject) are now experienced as imbricated or intertwined in one's self. The imago of the selfobject's functions after an empathic failure takes on greater intensity. These functions now exert their specific action in response to a specific intrapsychic signal – loss of self-esteem. These signals of need, which formerly were communicated to the selfobject or were responded to by the selfobject without overt communication, now evoke the intrapsychic functioning, so that the self is now in a cohesive state without the minute-to-minute presence of a selfobject that was formerly required. When the entire self is filled out, so that the poles of ideals and ambitions and functioning skills and talents are operational, a nuclear self exists that can initiate what Kohut (1977) called "programs of action" (p. 180).

Finally, the termination stage of a self-psychology analysis is arrived at when the patient experiences sufficient cohesiveness of his or her self as that the patient and analyst believe that further analysis will not result in further additions to the patient's self structures and that further insights will not be beneficial. At the termination stage, the patient's self will, ideally, be sufficiently strengthened to have a greatly enhanced resistance to fragmentation as well as an overall decrease in the experience of the self as lacking assertiveness or firm ideals. Thus, whether the analysis focuses on the patient's *primary* self trauma and its subsequent imbalances or on the patient's *compensatory* attempts to gain self balance, the outcome of the analysis is that the patient has now developed a cohesive self that can now seek out and invest in mature selfobjects for the necessary support in times of need (Kohut, 1977). In sum, in Kohut's view, the aim of a psychoanalytic cure is to firmly establish the patient's capacity to form mature, empathically directed, self-selfobject bonds so that mature self-selfobject encounters take the place of the bondage that had previously enslaved the self to the archaic selfobjects.

APPLICATIONS OF SELF PSYCHOLOGY

Kohut hoped that self psychology would have applications in the field of history and social sciences and that the psychology of the self could contribute wider meanings than the views of classical psychoanalysis in literature and the arts. The central contribution of self psychology to an understanding of humanity, its history, arts, and place in the universe comes from the acceptance of the empathic outlook in life. As Kohut (1973) stated: "... it (the empathic outlook) constitutes the very matrix of man's psychological survival" (p. 360). Kohut's (1975) description of empathy was summarized in three propositions:

> (1) Empathy, the recognition of the self in the other, is an indispensable tool of observation, without which vast areas of human life, including man's behavior in the social field, remain unintelligible. (2) Empathy, the expansion of the self to include the other, constitutes a powerful psychological bond between individuals which–more perhaps than even love, the expression and sublimation of the sexual drive–counteracts man's destructiveness against his fellows. And (3) empathy, the accepting, confirming and understanding human echo evoked by the self is a psychological nutriment without which human life as we know and cherish it could not be sustained" [p. 361].

Thus, Kohut believed that the contribution of self psychology to the understanding of people through scientific empathy added to the values and ideals of humanity, indeed, served to support the very survival of humankind. Kohut (1971, 1973, 1977) stressed over and over again that the central problem of humanity in the Westen world is the child who is understimulated, not responded to, and lacking leaders, who becomes the empty, isolated adult, still in search of approval or a target for idealization–in short, Kohut's Tragic Man. Kohut pointed to a major change in the structure of families from Freud's time, when children had closer ties to their families and the environment was experienced as close and even sexually overstimulating, leading to the type of conflict and psychopathology that Freud described. In the families of today, in Kohut's (1977) view, understimulation is rampant, leading to attempts at "erotic stimulation in order to relieve loneliness, in order to fill an emotional void" (p. 271). Thus, Kohut as social critic, as humanist, striving to appreciate (i.e., diagnose) the essential difficulties in humanity's quest for survival in the modern era, discerned that our greatest need is to be in an environment in which we can be singled out, appreciated, uplifted by invigorating leaders, and not be lost as a note in the underground. In short, we need not to be relegated to the state of anomie.

Literature and the Psychology of the Self

Kohut often pointed out that the great modern artists were the first to respond to the shifting problems of the modern individual. Thus, in the works of Ezra Pound, Eugene O'Neill, and Franz Kafka in the literary field, the emphasis on the breakup of the self and the striving to restore the self of fragmentation documented and even anticipated the dominant psychological problem of this era. In Kohut's view, Kafka's K is the everyman of our time, as he tries to get close to the great ones in power (*The Castle*) or dies a death without meaning (*The Trial*) or, as Gregor Samsa in *The Metmorphosis*, lives like a cockroach without being responded to by his family. Kohut often quoted three lines from O'Neill's play, *The Great God Brown* as an example of man's longing to restore his self: "Man is born broken. He lives by mending. The grace of God is glue" (see Kohut, 1977, p. 287).

The findings of self psychology are of great value to the student of applied psychoanalysis in literature. Kohut's emphasis on the empathic immersion into the self experience of the other is especially important in the appreciation of the great figures in literature. One cannot begin to assess the tragic downfall of the Ajax of Sophocles without immersing oneself in the self of the great military hero who has become a ludicrous spectacle after destroying sheep whom he thought were his enemies', Menelaus and Agamemnon. Consider the self of the aging monarch, Shakespeare's King Lear, whose prized daughter has refused his request for self-sustenance as he is about to pass on the baton of command and retire. Lear's experience of outrage must be experienced through empathic immersion into his particular self needs. And again, to gain a heightened regard for the issues with which Hamlet struggles, one must be able to read empathically into the self of the prince recently separated from his dead father, confronted with his newly married mother, and denied his ascension to the throne of Denmark. Once readers have been enabled to sink empathically into the literary figures presented by the author, they are able to appreciate the self state of the protagonists.

Another set of ideas from self psychology of great service in literary appreciation, is notion of the self-selfobject bond and its disruptions, which may lead to the experience of fragmentation and its vicissitudes, including disintegration anxiety, depletion of self-esteem, hypochondriasis, narcissistic rage, and loss of mentational functions such as reality-testing, synthesizing, and memory. Armed with this methodological approach of empathy and the notions of self psychology, the reader can approach each of Shakespeare's tragedies, for example, and illuminate the concerns, and failures of each of the protagonists and the reparative selfobject functions that each is seeking. Thus, Hamlet can be seen as responding to the losses he incurred with the reactions stemming from a depleted self and the interaction congruent with that self state. Lear, as previously stated, has had to suffer the loss of his major selfobject, Cordelia, and reveals his tragic fragmentation in the tempest. Othello is understood from the outset, in the view of self psychology, as experiencing concern over the attractiveness of his black self to his young, Causasian wife, and thus is vulnerable to Iago's sadistic innuendoes over her loyalty. Macbeth can be recognized as a man who has lost his selfobject, without whom he falters, and is compelled to seek surrogate selfobjects, the witches. They too fail him in giving self-support, and he dies. Thus, the findings and views of self psychology added a needed dimension to the appreciation of literature that parallel its contribution to the study of the individual in the clinical encounter.

Self Psychology and Music. Kohut expressed the conviction that the great artists, including the great modern composers, reflected in their art the great psychological problem of our era—the situation emanating from the endangered self (Kohut, 1977). One gains a unique contribution to the appreciations of music from the application of self psychology. The experience of music in its function as a selfobject are part of almost everyone's life. We may recall the uniquely calming, soothing experiences of listening to music. For some, these experiences are provided by the *Missa Solemnis* of Beethoven or the Mass in B Minor of Bach. For others or at different times, it is a modern popular singer or instrumentalist or a popular musician of an earlier era. Music, in those who respond to it, can be felt as an invigorating experience that may cause a quickening of the self and lead to programs of action. It is, of course, common to seek out music in which one finds an essential likeness—"music to match one's mood," as the expression goes—a twinship type of phenomenon. When one needs company to share one's inner mental life, one seeks a particular type or form of music, and one may seek a certain type of music or performer to merge with in order to shore up a flagging or enfeebled self.

Music can be said to perform selfobject functions as a result of its being linked with memories of archaic selfobjects of childhood and their self-sustaining qualities. The sounds of an admiring mirroring selfobject are experienced in musical expressions by the individual self as recapturing the memories of that blissful union. Similarly, in those to whom music and the state of their selves coexist, music can be experienced as a phenomenon akin to a twinship merger. In its ability to calm or evoke action, music performs functions similar to those of the idealized parent imago. The experience of becoming immersed in robust musical expression is also part of the feeling of being with a leader. Along

the same lines, the experience of listening to music that is spontaneously creative, such as improvised jazz, or music that is systematically
creative, such as the compositions of Arnold Schoenberg or Alban Berg,
may allow the listener to identify with the musicians' or the composer's
assertiveness and thus enhance the listener's self state.

At times, the musical message or tenderness or vigor may be direct,
without complex orchestration, or it may have complex counterpoint or
harmony. It may be experienced as too direct in its impact—too
simplistic—or as totally acceptable. Thus, Tchaikovsky's Sixth Sym-
phony may be experienced as maudlin, not subtle or beautiful. Some lis-
teners, who lack resistance to direct communications of gentleness, may
appreciate without restraint the operas of Puccini, whereas others with
resistance to direct mirroring messages find it prosaic. Thus, music may
serve a variety of self-object functions in these who can respond to it.

The Self in History

Kohut (1974b) believed that "History and psychoanalysis should be the
most important sciences of the future. They are important because humanity has reached a point in which populations will sooner or later
have to become stabilized. . . . If humans are to survive in a way that has
any similarity to what we have prized up till now as being the essence of
human life, the narcissistic motivations, I believe, must come into the
ascendancy" (p. 775). Kohut believed that the insights of self psychology
would be helpful to historians in understanding the formation, maintenance, and disruptive processes of groups.

Kohut described the notion of the group self as analogous to the individual's self. Thus, a nuclear group self would include the central ambitions and the ideals that characterize the group in its ordinary operations. To appreciate a group in operation, one would study the economic
and social circmstances that influenced its formation and the specific
psychological conditions that evoke fragmentation or cohesion,
including the need for a particular type of leadership. Kohut observed
that groups are held together not only by their shared ego ideal as
Freud (1921) maintained, but also by a shared group self—that is, by
shared assertiveness (Kohut, 1972). The group's integrity may be disturbed by destruction of the group values or damage to the group out-
lets for maintaining its prestige—for example, by an economic depression or military losses. Such imbalances in the group's esteem—similar
to an individual's loss of self esteem—may lead to fragmentation of the
group. The ensuing manifestation of narcissistic rage (acute or chronic)
may involve the entire group in acts of vengeance against outside forces
who are structured as oppressors (Kohut, 1972).

An important source for maintaining the integrity of any particular group is the leader needed or chosen by the group in various situations, especially in situations of impending fragmentation. Kohut identified two types of leaders. In the first type, the messianic leader or personality, there has been a fusion between the self and the pole of ideals, so that messianic leaders experience themselves as being in possession of total rectitude. These personalities set themselves up as the perfect leader, a god, worthy of reverence. Such a leader was Adolf Hitler, who effected repair to the German group self in its experience of ineptitude after World War I. The second type, the charismatic leader, has become one with his or her pole of assertiveness and thus experiences and exudes certitude and omnipotence. Winston Churchill was such a charismatic leader, needed by the British people during the crisis of confidence of World War II and abandoned when the need for an omnipotent selfobject was at its end (Kohut, 1976). Thus, the messianic or charismatic leader, who steps in to effect repair to the group self experiencing a common defect in assertiveness or sharing a common need for an idealized leader, is then experienced as the selfobject of the group self.

SUMMARY

The centerpiece of Kohut's work is the self and the self-selfobject dyad in the study of historical characters and literature as well as in the study of the developing person and the distressed patient petitioning for relief of his or her loneliness. Kohut never lost sight of his central finding, his anagnorisis that it is the *experiences* of man – the self – that is crucial to appreciate, not the drives nor the conflicts of man. From his seminal paper on empathy and introspection (Kohut, 1959) to his final works on the curative processes in psychoanalysis, Kohut taught that man must be understood through empathy, the royal road to the appreciation of the inner life. Kohut's works on the development of the self, on the archaic and mature self-selfobject dyads, on the theory of psychopathology and on the theories of cure in psychoanalysis are significant contributions to psychoanalysis and in my view will continue to exert an impact on the field of psychoanalysis. Will Kohut's views and findings be amalgamated into the mainstream of psychoanalytic theory and practice? This is a question for the future generations of psychoanalysts and one that Kohut would have welcomed, as he stated: "A worshipful attitude toward established explanatory systems – toward the polished accuracy of their definitions and the flawless consistency of their theories – becomes confining in the history of science – as do, indeed, man's analogous commitments in all of human history. Ideals are guides, not gods. If they become gods, they stifle man's playful creativeness; they impede the activities of the sector of the human spirit that points most meaningfully into the future" (1977, p. 312).

And further: "My deepest wish, however, is that my work – in amplification or emendation, in acceptance and even in rejection – will contribute to motivate the rising generation of psychoanalysts to pursue the path opened by the pioneers of yesterday, a path that will lead us further into the immense territory of that aspect of reality that can be investigated through scientifically disciplined introspection and empathy" (p. 312).

In this I have a sense of certitude: Heinz Kohut as theoretician, as practitioner, as humanist and as a man will never be forgotten.

REFERENCES

Freud, S. (1917a). Introductory lectures on psychoanalysis. *Standard Edition, 16,* 243–496.

Freud, S. (1917b). Mourning and melanchoia. *Standard Edition, 14,* 237–259.

Freud, S. (1921). Group psychology and the analysis of the ego. *Standard Edition, 18,* 65–144.

Freud, S. (1926). Inhibitions, symptoms and anxiety. *Standard Edition, 20,* 75–174.

Heller, E., & Kohut, H. (1978). Psychoanalysis and literature. *Critical Inquiry, 4,* 449–450.

Kohut, H. (1959). Introspection, empathy and psychoanalysis. *Journal of the American Psychoanalytic Association, 7,* 459–483.

Kohut, H. (1966). Forms and transformations of narcissism. *Journal of the American Psychoanalytic Association, 14,* 243–273.

Kohut, H. (1968). The psychoanalytic treatment of narcissistic personality disorders: Outline of a systematic approach. *The Psychoanalytic Study of the Child, 23,* 86–114.

Kohut, H. (1971). *Analysis of the self.* New York: International Universities Press.

Kohut, H. (1972). Thoughts on narcissism and narcissistic rage. *The Psychoanalytic Study of the Child, 27,* 360–400.

Kohut, H. (1974a). Remarks about the formation of the self. In P. Ornstein (Ed.), *The search for the self* (pp. 737–771). New York: International Universities Press, 1978.

Kohut, H. (1974b). The self in history. In P. Ornstein (Ed.), *The search for the self* (pp. 771–783). New York: International Universities Press, 1978.

Kohut, H. (1976). Creativeness, charisma and group psychology. In J. E. Gedo & G. H. Pollock (Eds.), Freud: The fusion of science and humanism (pp. 379–425). *Psychological Issues, 9,* (2/3, Monograph 34/35).

Kohut, H. (1977). *The restoration of the self.* New York: International Universities Press.

Kohut, H. (1979, June). "Four basic definitions of self psychology." Paper presented to the Workshop on Self Psychology. Chicago, IL.

Kohut, H., & Levarie, S. (1950). On the enjoyment of listening to music. *Psychoanalytic Quarterly, 19,* 64–87.

Kohut, H., & Wolf, E. (1978). The disorders of the self and their treatment. *International Journal of Psychoanalysis, 59,* 413–425.

9 Margaret S. Mahler: Symbiosis and Separation-Individuation

Anni Bergman, Ph.D.
Steven Ellman, Ph.D.

In this chapter we will trace the development of Margaret Mahler's research, clinical works and theoretical conceptualizations. Although Mahler's concepts have always been firmly grounded in either clinical or naturalistic observations, it is interesting and in keeping with a book whose theme traces developments beyond Freud, to first look briefly at Freud's concepts of early development and to compare these concepts with Mahler's pioneering work. Although Freud did not do observational studies, he at times wrote about early development, and in our opinion this aspect of his work has been somewhat neglected.

It would also be of some importance and interest to compare the theoretical statements of various writers about early development. Certainly such a comparison might include Jacobson, Hartmann, Winnicott and perhaps other authors from the British object relations school. Mahler's work would make this comparison particularly interesting since she and her co-workers have provided both theoretical conceptions and empirical observations about early development.

Freud was frequently concerned with how the infant began to learn about the external world. In *The Interpretation of Dreams* (1900), he presents his well-known views of the infant, at first primarily or only concerned with pleasure and later, through deprivation, coming to know about the external world. This conception of how the infant turns from its primary concern (pleasure or tension reduction) to secondary concerns (the outside world) is based heavily on a tension-regulation model. Freud's later views, which are contained in large part in his papers on narcissism and his metapsychological papers (1914, 1915), are less centered on a tension-regulation or reduction model. In these and other papers, Freud put forth the guidelines of an interesting theory of early development, but in this chapter we can only sketch out some of his ideas. Freud sees the early mental development of the infant and child as taking place along three polarities – pleasure-pain, subject-object, and active-passive – an idea that has a developmental unfolding. In early life, pleasure and pain predominate, and Freud maintains that for the infant or child (we do not know the age range to which Freud referred), the external world is at first primarily a matter of indifference. This corresponds to Freud's notion of primary narcissism, in which satisfaction or pleasure, from the infant's perspective, is autoerotic. At this time, the external world is not cathected with interest (in a general sense) and is indifferent for purposes of satisfaction (Freud, 1914). Interestingly, although Mahler uses different terminology, her autistic phase bears striking resemblance to this Freudian phase.

At Freud's next step in development, we run into something of a paradox. Freud (1915) postulates that as the infant continues to experience the external world, "it acquires objects from the external world, and, in spite of everything, it cannot avoid feeling internal instinctual stimuli for a time as unpleasurable" (p. 135). As the infant builds up perceptions of (primarily internal) stimuli as unpleasurable and (primarily external) stimuli as pleasurable, it takes into itself (or introjects) the pleasurable stimuli and casts out (or projects) the unpleasurable stimuli. At this point, Freud (1915) maintains that "the *original* 'reality-ego' which distinguished internal and external by means of sound object criterion changes into a purified pleasure-ego" (p. 136). This pleasure ego has divided the world into all that is pleasurable, which is equated with itself ("ego subject," in Freud's terms), and all that is unpleasurable, which is equated with the external world. One can attempt to equate this idea of the purified pleasure ego with some of Mahler's findings and formulations, but for the purposes of this chapter we wish to make several related points about the concepts Freud puts forth.

First, Freud pointed out that development of certain reality-ego functions may be nonmonotic. Thus, the infant at an age prior to the purified pleasure ego is considered by Freud to be, in some ways, in better contact with reality than when the pleasure ego is formed. We believe this line of reasoning is consistent with several of Freud's concepts at this time (Freud, 1915), but the main point we wish to dwell on is that at a time when the infant, according to Freud, is indifferent to the external world, it can still develop a rudimentary reality ego. Thus, Freud saw nothing incompatible with postulating a stage of primary narcissism in which pleasure is seen as passive, internal, and autoerotic, and yet at the same time certain types of "learning" can take place. The question for Freud was not whether the infant could correctly perceive certain aspects of reality but, rather, whether or how the object was viewed in terms of the infant's pleasurable and unpleasurable experiences. This is quite a different question than whether the infant can learn to respond during its first weeks or days of life.

As a second general point, Freud (1914, 1915) begins at about this time to make use of what today are frequently called projective-introjective mechanisms. These concepts are, of course, used frequently by Mahler as well as many others, but it is of interest to see the way she has both expanded and particularized the use of these concepts.

As a third related point, we wish to emphasize how during this era Freud stresses both the gradual nature of being able to know the pleasure-giving object as a separate entity and, even more important, the very gradual nature of the development of object love. Freud (1915, 1917) discusses aspects of the development of object love, but of course Mahler is able to delineate with much greater precision concepts such as libidinal object constancy on the pathway to object love. As we will see, Mahler's concepts and observations in many ways begin to fulfill the promissory notes that Freud left us in his many brilliant papers.

In this brief introduction we have touched on a few of the concepts that Freud introduced that bear some relationship to Mahler's work. We could, of course, make a much fuller comparison, but our intention is only to point out the relationship and set the stage to show how Mahler has built on and yet gone beyond what Freud could have even anticipated. In a chapter devoted to a historical recounting of the theorists who bear some important relation to Mahler's work, one would also have to include at least aspects of the work of Hartmann, Kris, and Lowenstein and large parts of Jacobson's work. Both Mahler (1979) and Kernberg (1980) have emphasized in different ways the importance of Jacobson's developmental concepts. Many other influential authors could be named, of course, but in our opinion, Spitz and Anna Freud's pioneering empirical studies were, in general, an inspiration to psychoanalytic researchers in many ways, particularly in demonstrating that theoretical concepts could be shown to have important empirical consequences.

Although all the authors mentioned have a variety of similarities (and differences) with respect to Mahler's work, in Loewald's (1979) words: "Her clear emphasis on the fundamental importance in early development and continuing throughout life, of differentiation and separation from an encompassing psychical matrix . . . have had a remarkable impact on current analytic understanding of children and adults." Although Freud implied the "dual unit" or dyad, Mahler makes it the beginning and most important part of her observational and theoretical field.

We shall discuss the work of Margaret Mahler in three parts: (1) her early papers, including her work on infantile psychosis; (2) her research project on separation-individuation and her theory of subphases resulting in beginning self and object constancy; and (3) applications of separation-individuation theory to psychoanalytic theory and treatment.

EARLY PAPERS

Mahler began her career as a pediatrician and director of a well-baby clinic in Vienna. The interests she developed at the outset of her professional life have remained important throughout her career. Probably the most important of these has been her interest in the mother and baby as a dyad, or, as she later referred to it, as a dual unity within one common boundary, a symbiotic pair. Beginning with her first paper delivered in this country, entitled "Pseudoimbecility: A Magic Cap of Invisibility" (Mahler, 1942), presented in 1940 to the Psychoanalytic Institute of New York, she demonstrated her interest in the pre-oedipal era, in motility, and in the affecto-motor communication between mother and child.

> Between child and mother there exists from the beginning a close phylogenetic bond which is unique and much more exclusive than communication by words or thoughts; it is an interrelationship through the medium of affective expressions . . . The interrelation between the unconscious of the mother and the reception of stimulation of the sense organs of the baby is the prototype for a way of communication between child and adult which is not confined within the limited sphere of language. (p. 4)

In her psychoanalytic work, Mahler began to treat several children suffering from childhood psychosis. This culminated in her eventual formulation of the autistic and symbiotic types of childhood psychosis (Mahler, 1952). She also became interested in determining how normal infants attain a sense of separate identity in the caretaking presence of their mothers. Examination of Mahler's papers of that period (those that preceeded the beginning of observational research) reveals how closely connected in her thinking were the phases of early normal develoopment and the consideration of extreme pathology. Mahler is essentially a psychoanalyst and a clinician, and her early papers are filled with clinical vignettes from the many severely disturbed children whom she treated as a child analyst. Yet her thinking about pathology never overshadowed her interest in normal mental life and her conviction about the importance of the early mother-child relationship.

In an early paper (Mahler, Ross, & DeFries, 1949), Mahler was already dealing with the child's problem around the waning of omnipotence.

The child gradually realizes that its power is waning. It has not only to renounce essential gratification, but must in addition lose its sense of omnipotence. The language of violent affect is rendered useless as a means of communication with the parents, and the child has to renounce them in favor of speech . . . It seems as if these affective outbursts at the age of 2 to 3 years are struggling attempts in the child to maintain the archaic common ground so familiar to it: the intensely pleasurable affective rapport with the parents in the child's affective domination of them. This attempt is destined, like the Oedipal strivings, to fail from the danger of loss of love and fear of castration.

Direct affective attacks failing, the child searches for other means to regain entrance to the Garden of Eden. This coincides in time with beginning to walk and the process of taking in impressions of the outside world with all the senses, acquiring knowledge and testing reality. The chld utilizes these newly gained discoveries, to share them with mother and father, and thus restore a common ground with them. The expressions of enchantment and affection, which the parents give so abundantly at the first presentations of such fact finding, bring the child a temporary restoration of the old affective and a new intellectual co-experience with the parents.

This quotation already contains descriptions of behaviors that later, during the observational study of separation and individuation, become incorporated into the careful delineation of the subphases.

Mahler's papers on child psychosis contain many references to her view on normal development. In 1952 she stated:

The intrauterine, parasite-host relationship within the mother organism must be replaced in the postnatal period by the infant's being enveloped, as it were, in the extrauterine matrix of the mother's nursing care, a kind of social symbiosis....

The turning from predominantly proprioceptive awareness to increased sensory awareness of the outer world occurs through the medium of affective rapport with the mother. The baby's libido position thus proceeds from the stage of fetal narcissism to primary body narcissism, a stage in which representation of the mother's body plays a large part....

To understand the dynamics in infantile psychosis, observation and study of the most important transitory step in the adaption to reality is necessary; namely, that step in the development of the sense of reality in which the mother is gradually left outside the omnipotent orbit of the self. This step is preliminary to, and perhaps alternates with, the process of endowing the mother with object-libidinal cathexis. The toddler gradually delimits his own individual entity from the primal mother-infant symbiotic unit. He separates his own self (and his mental representation) from that of the mother. This stage in ego development is a very vulnerable one, particularly in children in whose early life the somatopsychic symbiosis has been pathological. (pp. 132–134)

Mahler's interest and views on childhood psychosis and normal development were still closely intertwined at this point in her work. These remarks on early development occur in the same paper in which she outlines her views of autistic and symbiotic childhood psychosis. She describes primary autistic psychosis as a syndrome in which the mother, as representative of the outside world, seems never to have been perceived emotionally by the infant. The mother, therefore, remains a part object, seemingly devoid of specific cathexis and not distinguished from inanimate objects. These, according to Mahler, are infants with an inherently defective tension-regulating apparatus, which probably cannot be adequately complemented by even the most competent mothers. The inherent ego deficiency of these infants predisposes them from the very beginning to remain alienated from reality. Mahler (1952) states:

It would seem that autism is the basic defense attitude of these infants, for whom the beacon of emotional orientation in the outer world – the mother as primary love object – is nonexistent. Early infantile autism develops, I believe, because the infantile personality, devoid of emotional ties to the person of the mother, is unable to cope with external stimuli and inner excitations, which threaten from both sides his very existence as an entity. (p. 145)

Mahler contrasts the autistic psychosis with the symbiotic infantile psychosis. Symbiotic psychosis often goes unnoticed during the first 2 or 3 years of the child's life. It becomes evident at a point in development when the phase-specific demands include realization of separateness.

The mechanisms which are characteristic in the *symbiotic* infantile psychosis are the introjective, projective mechanisms and their psychotic elaboration . . . These mechanisms aim at a restoration of the symbiotic parasitic delusion of oneness with the mother and thus are the diametric opposites of the function of autism. . . . It seems that the symbiotic psychosis candidates are characterized by an abnormally low tolerance for frustration, and later by a more or less evident lack of emotional separation or differentiation from the mother. Reactions set in...at those points of the physiological and psychological maturation process at which separateness from the mother must be perceived and faced...agitated, catatoniclike temper tantrums and panic-stricken behavior dominate the picture; these are followed by bizarrely distorted reality testing and hallucinatory attempts at restitution. The aim is restoration and perpetuation of the delusional omnipotence phase of the mother-infant fusion of earliest times—a period at which the mother was an ever-ready extension of the self, at the service and command of "His Majesty, the Baby." (pp. 145–6)

THE SEPARATION-INDIVIDUATION PROCESS

Mahler's observational research study of normal mother-child pairs began in 1959, the findings of which have been described in the second volume of *The Selected Papers of Margaret S. Mahler* (1979) and in *The Psychological Birth of the Human Infant* (Mahler, Pine, & Bergman, 1975). This research was prompted by the following questions: How do normal infants, during the first three years of life attain intrapsychic self and object representations? How do they move out of the state of dual unity or symbiosis, during which they are not aware of themselves as separate, and achieve awareness of self as separate from other? How do they attain a measure of libidinal self and object constancy? The hypothesis of the study was that the human infant begins life in a state of complete dependence on the mothering one and in a state of nondifferentiation, or dual unity. The infant then undergoes a gradual process of differentiation or hatching out, which results in intrapsychic structures of self and object. The goal of the study was to learn about the process by which the first level of identity is achieved.

A setting was created in which mothers could interact freely with their infants. This was a large playroom with many appropriate toys, divided by a low, fencelike partition from the mothers' section. There mothers could sit comfortably and chat while watching their children, who were in a stimulating and safe environment. Participant observers were present at all times, mingling freely with mothers and children while maintaining a friendly yet neutral atmosphere. The participant observers later wrote down their observations in detail, and discussions took place in staff and research meetings, where observers and investigators met at least once but more often twice a week. The research thus created did not take place in an experimental artificial setting but in a very natural one—an indoor playground, as Mahler called it, where mothers were in charge of their children.

The observations of the participant observers were checked by regular nonparticipant observations conducted through a one-way mirror. Nonparticipant observers wrote down what they saw at the time, and thus could obtain greater objectivity and detail than participant observers. Participant observers, however, knew the mothers and children; their observations were more impressionistic and subjective, but, it was thought, more in tune with the affective tone of the mother-child pairs. The mother-child pairs were observed 3 to 4 times a week for 2½ hour-long sessions over a period of 2½ years. The frequency and length of sessions provided a large data base from which it was possible to obtain an intimate and detailed knowledge of each mother-child pair and the development of their relationship.

In addition to participant and nonparticipant observations, mother-child pairs were regularly filmed. All mothers were interviewed by senior staff members once a week. These clinical interviews provided information about the family's life at home. They also gave the mothers the opportunity to talk about any aspect of themselves or their children that they chose to discuss. Fathers were interviewed several times a year, and home visits were conducted regularly, especially during vacation periods.

Several aspects of the study were of special importance. One, as noted, was the frequency with which observations were undertaken. This provided for a measure of objectivity, since a judgment made one day could be corrected the next. Another essential aspect of the research design was that it combined data from longitudinal and cross-sectional perspectives. Each mother-child pair was observed from the time the child was about 6 months old to 3 years. At the same time, there were always several mother-child pairs being observed simultaneously. Thus, children of any given age could be compared both with each other and with himself or herself over a time period.

Another essential aspect of the study was that, although observational in method, it was guided by psychoanalytic concepts. We believe that there was a good deal of carry-over from the way psychoanalysts make inferences in the psychoanalytic setting to the way the observers used inferences in these observational studies. As Mahler has put it, in these studies the psychoanalytic eye was guided by the observations themselves, as in the psychoanalytic situation the psychoanalytic ear is led by the analysand's free associations. Thus, this research study relied heavily on the psychoanalytic acumen and empathy of the observers and investigators, who were psychoanalysts. It rested on the meaning and coherence that emerged out of many multifaceted daily observations. In the psychoanalytic situation, analyst and analysand together create the psychoanalytic life history. In the study of separation-individuation, the observers created the life history of the unfolding mother-child relationship and the unfolding sense of self of the infant.

THE SUBPHASES

It was the comparative nature of the cross-sectional aspect of the study that eventually led to the delineation of the subphases of the separation-individuation process. For example, in the first group of children observed, a 1-year old girl was seen to explore the room freely, climbing a lot. At first it seemed surprising that her mother sat calmly, staying in contact with the girl over a distance and directing her to avoid dangerous situations. It was thought at first that perhaps this mother-child pair did not like physical contact. However, over time, after observing more mother-child pairs with infants around 1 year of age, it became clear that this kind of exploration with relatively limited physical contact between mother and child was characteristic of this particular age. This eventually came to be termed the "practicing subphase." In another example, a 16-month-old boy seemed to be anxiously clinging to his mother. It was not difficult to understand this in terms of the particular mother-child relationship, since the mother had shown considerable ambivalence about her baby after he was born. But, again, after watching more mother-child pairs with children of that age, it became clear that greater concern about mother's whereabouts was a typical phenomenon of the toddler.

The subphases were delineated quite early in the study. However, the intensive study of each mother-child pair made it possible to observe and study the individual variations within the regularity of subphase specificity. Such variations involved the timing, intensity, quality, and mood that characterized each particular mother-child pair. The subphases will be described in the following pages. This description takes into account some of the more recent findings of infant researchers which have contributed to and enriched Mahler's original conceptualizations.

From 0–6 Months

Since Mahler undertook her research project on the normal separation-individuation process, a great deal of research has been done with infants and their caretakers for example that of Brazelton (1974, 1981); Sander (1976); and Stern (1971, 1974, 1982). This research has shown that neonates are more active and discriminating, more responsive to outside stimuli, than had ever been thought. It has even been shown that they are capable of performing complex tasks. In other words, our view of the infant has been revolutionized. Mahler (personal communication) has reconsidered and rethought her earlier formulations and has agreed that the word "autistic" does not well describe what we now know about the neonate.

A more recent formulation of what Mahler originally called the autistic phase is that it is the time during which newborns have the task of adjusting to extrauterine existence, of finding their own niche in the external world. They have to achieve physiological homeostasis, that is, adequate inner regulation in synchrony with the vocal and gestural rhythms of their caregiver. Each infant elicits his or her own mother's caregiving, and the mother responds with coenesthetic empathy to the needs of a particular infant. She is enabled to do so by reaching the state described by Winnicott (1956) as primary maternal preoccupation. Bergman (1982) has attempted to show from the mother's side how this particular empathic state is at times reached easily and smoothly and at other times with great difficulty.

The symbiotic phase, which is reached at around 2 months of age, is of great importance for separation-individuation theory, since on it rests the idea of a gradual hatching out, a psychological birth. The findings of contemporary infant research here pointed to the importance of distinguishing the regressed merger experience of pathology from the attunement and reciprocity of the normal symbiotic phase. Pine (1981) has hypothesized that what could be referred to as normal merging occurs during certain brief periods of high drive arousal. Bergman and Chernack (1982), in a paper dealing with preverbal communication, have shown how, during the symbiotic phase, differentiation and merging go hand in hand.

Observers agree that attunement, mutual empathy, or communion between mother and infant are at their height in the period from 2 to 5 months of age. Empathy is not possible without the ability to freely evoke states of loss of self, while maintaining the ability to regain a state of full awareness. The same happens in the creative process. Where does such ability come from? We believe that the blissfulness of the symbiotic stage, which is still longed for in later life, provides us with a reservoir of self-other experiences, which in normal development are pleasurable and creative.

McDevitt (1981) has elucidated the symbiotic phase from a more cognitive perspective. He states that by age 2 to 3 months, the infant (1) both anticipates and initiates the pleasure provided by interaction with the mother; (2) develops a sense of confidence and basic trust in the caregiver and in his or her own initiative; and (3) responds by smiling and direct eye contact. The work of infant researchers has made us more aware of the capacity of the infant not only to initiate contact but also to control it through gaze and gaze aversion. Thus, the infant's sense of self during the symbiotic phase is fed by experiences that, even at that early period, may be experienced as "his or her own," especially if the caregiving environment is responsive to the infant's more subtle signals and signs. The sense of self also receives important nutrients from the pleasure and attunement the infant experiences with the mother. Thus, from early on, there may be two strands to the infant's experience of self: self-alone and self-with-other. These should then be the forerunners or beginnings of separation-individuation. To separate, there must first be self-other and separate-self experiences. Sander (1976) has described these early experiences of self as being alone in the presence of someone, in Winnicott's sense. Thus, the symbiotic phase is the bedrock of libidinal attachment and intimacy on the one hand, and beginnings of self-alone experiences on the other. Even during the early months, for example, infants show individual preferences for color, for certain tunes, and for varying amounts of stimulation.

Subphase I – Differentiation

The subphase of differentiation begins at the height of symbiosis, when the baby begins more active and persistent visual and tactile exploration of the surroundings. The baby begins to perceive things at a greater distance and typically scans the environment, checking back to the mother regularly. This eminently important process of shifting attention cathexis to the outside is what has also been called the hatching process. The fully hatched baby, around the age of 9 to 10 months, is alert, can easily grasp what he or she wants, sits up freely (Resch, 1979), and is characterized by a general brightening of mood. The differentiation subphase is also the time when unpleasure at the stranger and even anxiety can begin (Emde, Gaensbauer, & Harmon, 1976). The baby also shows unpleasure and sometimes cries when left by the mother, but is usually comforted fairly easily by a nonintrusive mother substitute.

Pushing away from mother and exploration of the environment are quite characteristic of the differentiation subphase. During this time, the child explores, both visually and tactilely, the faces of individuals other than the mother. The infant is also particularly attracted by appendages that can be removed, such as eyeglasses, beads, or a pencil in the pocket. All these explorations of both the animate and the inanimate, of that which can be removed and held by the infant and that which clearly is part of the other, are important ingredients of the ongoing process of self-object differentiation.

The Practicing Subphase

The practicing subphase begins when the now hatched baby begins to be capable of independent locomotion. The early practicing period comprises the time of crawling, standing up, and coasting, whereas the practicing period proper begins with the mastery of upright locomotion. If we can think of symbiosis as the first blissful stage in human development, the stage of pleasure in mutuality and recognition and exploration of the mother, we can think of the practicing subphase as the second blissful period. The mastery of locomotion, at first crawling and then walking, brings with it an enormous increment of energy and pleasure. The ability to go after and get what one wants by one's own efforts, is an immense source of pleasure and satisfaction. Whereas, during differentiation, babies often cry when their mother or even others walk away from them, beginning locomotion counteracts the sense of helplessness. This is a period of rapid development, especially of locomotor and manipulative abilities. The narcissistic investment in the body and in mastery and exploration brings about a temporary lessening in the investment in the mother, who can now be taken for granted. This slight lessening of investment in the mother also protects the baby from a full realization of his or her separateness. The mother is simply assumed to be there unless she is absent for any length of time. More protracted separation changes the practicing infant's mood of elation to one of low-keyedness, a temporary lowering of mood which is understood to be caused by the need to hold on to the image of the mother.

Toddlers' expanding locomotor capacities widen their world; there is more to see, more to hear, and more to touch. Along with increasing awareness of the outside world goes the more highly integrated and differentiated knowledge of the body self, as the infant gains increasing mastery over body functions which become more and more intentional and goal directed. Finally, standing and eventually walking provide a whole new perspective of the world and add further to the small toddler's sense of elation and exuberance. Another important characteristic of this period is the relative hardiness of the infant, who is quite oblivious to the knocks and falls that are, of course, daily occurrences.

The Rapprochement Subphase

The expansiveness and omnipotence characteristic of the practicing subphase wane as the toddler increasingly comes face to face with the feeling of separateness caused by frustrations that occur as explorations are curtailed by obstacles in the real world. The child also has to face the fact that mother is not always automatically at hand to smooth the way for his explorations. Indeed, there are times when she curtails them in the interest of protecting the child's safety. The infant's former relative obliviousness of the mother is now replaced by active approaches to her.

This rapprochement subphase is again conceptualized in two parts – early rapprochement and the rapprochement crisis. During early rapprochement, the generally good mood of the practicing period still prevails as the toddlers attempt to bridge the gap that they are now beginning to perceive between themselves and their mother. Toddlers begin to want to share everything with their mother; most characteristically, they will bring things and put them in their mother's lap, but they will also seek out her active participation in their activities. The availability of the mother during this particular period is of great importance, but even under the most optimal conditions, the maturational spurt of toddlers' cognitive development makes them realize their separateness and relative helplessness. Toddlers, during rapprochement, wish to be autonomous and find all hindrances to their autonomy extremely disturbing, whether emanating from their own activities, from curtailment by adults, or from their inability to do what they would like.

The child's recognition of his or her separateness and limitation threatens his or her sense of omnipotence, which is still very closely connected with the child's self-esteem. In addition, toddlers have to come to terms with the fact that their mother's wishes and their own by no means always coincide. Toddlers still believe in the omnipotence of their parents and become very angry and sometimes desperate if the parents cannot do for them what they want. "He thinks we can do everything," a mother of a rapprochement-age toddler said recently. Some weeks later, the same mother said, with great relief: "He's beginning to accept that somebody or something can be gone and that I cannot do anything about it." For example, that morning, when the cereal he had wanted was gone, her son agreed to eat a piece of bread and butter rather than insisting or crying for more cereal.

While wanting to be independent and autonomous, rapprochement toddlers also often want to control the whereabouts of their mother and want her to partake in all their activities. Anxious clinging or daring darting away, hoping to be caught up and brought back by the mother, are typical behaviors. The toddler at this age does not easily tolerate the mother's attention being elsewhere and is typially quite demanding.

In the course of the rapprochement subphase, the child begins to have a separate mental self. Beginning language and symbolic functioning are very important in bringing a resolution of the rapprochement crisis. Being able to know and name others and eventually being able to know and name oneself are important indicators of internal processes that take place at that time. The child begins to know "mine" (Bergman, 1980), but "mine" at that time can express a wish or demand as well as a fact. "Mine" is a precursor to naming oneself or using the personal pronoun.

If development goes reasonably well and the mother is reasonably available to the toddler, the rapproachement crisis is eventually resolved by way of identification and internalizatin. Successful resolution of the rapprochement crisis by no means always takes place, however. A badly resolved rapprochement crisis leads to intense ambivalence and splitting of the object world into good and bad. The maternal representation may be internalized as an unassimilated bad introject. McDevitt and Mahler (1980) cite four conditions that would lead to poor resolution of the rapproachement crisis: (1) the love object is disappointing and unavailable or excessively unreliable and intrusive; (2) the child experiences the realization of his or her helplessness too abruptly and too painfully, resulting in a too sudden deflation of the child's sense of omnipotence; (3) there has been an excess of trauma; and (4) the child experiences to an unusual degree the nacissistic hurt of the preoedipal castration reaction which accompanies the discovery of the anatomical difference. Under such conditions, rapprochement-type behaviors persist rather than giving way. Such behaviors include excessive separation anxiety, depressive mood, passivity or demandingness, coercivenesss, possessiveness, envy, and temper tanrums.

On the Way to Object Constancy

The fourth and final subphase of separation-individuation is called "on the way to self and object constancy" and is recognized as being open-ended. In the context of separation-individuation theory, self and libidinal object constancy (the achievement of this final subphase) is not seen as a fixed fact, but rather as an ongoing, lifelong process. Nevertheless, a child who has successfully resolved the rapprochement crisis has made an important qualitative change that is quite unmistakable to observers.

Self-constancy develops along with object constancy. In the fourth subphase, the toddler's sense of self includes actions as well as perceptions and feelings. The toddler beings to like to be admired for what he or she can do. Earlier, doing and achieving mastery were enough. Now, the participation of the "other" is an important ingredient in the pleasure of mastery. The qualitative change that comes with the resolution of the rapprochement crisis is comparable to the qualitative change that comes when hatching is accomplished.

Hatching, which means living in the outside world while taking the mother for granted, resolves the crisis of differentiation when the infant, for the first time, becomes exceedingly sensitive to separation from the mother. The infant needs to take the mother for granted—that is, to stay omnipotently at one with her, while at the same time, turning to the outside world with curiosity, pleasure, and eagerness. The rapprochement crisis is the second crisis of separation. To bring it to a satisfactory resolution, the child has to achieve a degree of internalization, which allows the lessening and eventual relinquishment of omnipotent control. The development of the symbolic function is intimately connected with the lessening of omnipotent control, as it allows the senior toddler to live out and practice in play some of the wishes and fears that arise from the conflict over autonomy and the need or wish to still be "at one" with the powerful, good mother.

Summary

The delineation of the subphases of the separation-individuation process describes the psychological birth of the human infant. Out of the union or attunement of symbiosis with the mother, the infant grows to an increasing awareness of separateness and develops his or her own unique characteristics, in part inborn, in part the result of the intimate interaction between the infant and his or her love objects, the parents. The infant also grows from a stage in which the object is only dimly perceived as outside and separate, toward the attainment of a unique attachment to the love object; the infant grows further, toward the stage of loving in which a positive image can be maintained even in the face of anger and frustration and in which the capacity for concern for the other takes the place of the demand for omnipotent control.

Each overlapping stage paves the way for the next. Thus, the solid and pleasurable period of symbiosis means that the child will be more prepared for the stage of differentiation to follow and will meet the stranger or strangeness of the outside world with greater confidence and less anxiety. Similarly, a rich practicing subphase which affords ample opportunity for exploring the outside world while remaining in contact over distance with a supportive and admiring caregiver will provide the child with a reservoir of resources with which to withstand the onslaughts of the crisis of rapprochement.

The task for the parent changes as the separation-individuation process progresses. During practicing, the parent has to be able to follow the cue of the child who now requires more space in which to try out his or her burgeoning abilities. It is during the period of rapprochement that it becomes more difficult for the mother to remain emotionally available, as the child who has appeared more autonomous during practicing now returns to the mother often with conflicting and unfulfillable demands. Nevertheless, parents who can be playful and patient during the rapprochement period will help the child toward more favorable resolutions during the period on the way to object constancy.

While each subphase paves the way for the next, each subphase also contains a potential for repair if optimal conditions have not prevailed in the preceding period. Each subphase is also separate and discrete (Mahler, Pine, & Bergman, 1975), with its own rewards as well as its own tasks. The little child's personality is pliable and patterns are not fixed, leaving a great deal of room for adaptation. For example, a particular child whose symbiotic phase had been colored by his mother's depression during that period seemed to differentiate rather late. It seemed at first like a possible danger signal. It later seemed, however, that this child had found a way of making up for what he had missed by remaining in the symbiotic orbit for a longer time by emerging into the outside world only slowly, as he became ready to do so. Since this particular mother could respond much better to the active child of separation-individuation, he began to catch up and developed well as time went on.

The theory of separation-individuation is a dynamic developmental theory. It leaves room for progression and regression as well as for the back-and-forth movement between needs for closeness and attachment and needs for exploration and disengagement.

An important result of the study of separation-individuation is the enrichment of knowledge on several topics which, although already familiar to psychoanalysts and developmentalists, were further illuminated during the years of the research. We would like to mention a few contributions that have dealt with psychoanalytic concepts from a developmental perspective. In an important paper on the "Development of Basic Moods," Mahler (1966) considers the tendency to depressive moods in women and ties it to conflicts arising during the rapprochment subphase. Furer (1967) writes about developmental aspects of the superego. He considers "identification with the comforter" as a forerunner of the superego and feels that this identification with the active mother "increases the child's capacity to bind its aggression and thus helps bring about the required reaction formation." In an examination of the relationship between adaptation and defense, Mahler and McDevitt (1968) say:

> The child's experiences over the course of time, on the basis of his drive and ego endowment, lead to more or less successful adaptation. His adaptive style contributes to his character traits, as do his defense behaviors.

We have observed in our research the process by which these behaviors gradually become internalized as more or less successful defense mechanisms. (p. 100)

McDevitt (1982) traces the emergence of hostile aggression in the course of the separation-individuation process. Bergman (1982) describes the development of the girl during separation-individuation, with implications for later development.

We would like to mention some other important issues that have been elucidated by the developmental point of view and by the detailed scrutiny of our day-to-day observations in the study of separation-individuation. The first of these is stranger anxiety.

It was Spitz (1957) who first drew attention to stranger anxiety and considered it the second organizer at the age of 7 months. This phenomenon has attracted a great deal of attention since Spitz first discribed it, and the separation-individuation study has contributed to a more detailed understanding of a variety of phenomena subsumed under the concept of stranger reactions. Stranger anxiety is the most visible of a large array of phenomena with which an infant indicates increasing recognition of mother as unique as well as interest and curiosity in the world beyond mother. Thus, we prefer the term "stranger reactions" rather than "stranger anxiety." Stranger reactions can include a variety of affects, ranging from interest and curiosity to wariness and finally anxiety and distress. Stranger reactions can even be directed, at a certain age, to the mother or father if they look different from the way they usually do. Early in the study, we heard about a little boy who, at the age of 4 months, cried when he saw his mother wearing a shower cap. We recently heard of a little girl, age 5 months, who was quite concerned when she saw her father after he had shaved his beard and mustache. These are early indications that the child is beginning to form an inner image, which is disturbed if what the child sees is suddenly very different from what she or he expects. It seems to us that the timing, the kind, and intensity of the stranger reaction is intimately connected with the mother-child relationship. For example, we recently saw a little girl who showed a marked stranger reaction, even anxiety, at the unusually early age of 3 to 4 months. She was the daughter of a young mother from a foreign country who had not yet learned the language very well. This young woman had been quite depressed after she married an American man and came to live in this country. After the birth of her daughter, her mood improved and she developed an extremely close symbiotic relationship with the girl. Mother and daughter seemed rather insulated from the rest of the world in which they lived. Thus, it seemed very interesting that this particular little girl showed such early stranger reaction and reacted to outsiders not with curiosity or interest, but with displeasure. When she was seen again at the age of 6 months, she was still rather wary but willing to engage in play with a stranger as long as her mother stayed close by.

"Customs inspection" is a term that was coined during the separation-individuation study to describe another type of stranger reaction. This is the way in which the child in the period of differentiation, around 7 to 10 months, will examine the faces of strangers, both visually and tactilely, with great interest and absorption. Not all children feel free to engage in this activity with the same amount of intensity and interest, but most will show some interest in the stranger and wish to touch and explore parts of the stranger's face or at least such appendages as beads or eyeglasses.

Yet another kind of stranger reaction was recently observed in a little boy during the differentiation subphase. This little boy seemed to enjoy attracting the interest of strangers, and he had learned that when he shouted, most people would look around and smile at him. Thus, in strange places, he would often shout at strangers and then show great pleasure when they paid attention to him. Separation-individuation studies have shown us that the outside world is not just a threat to the unique mother-child relationship, but it is also often a source of great excitement and pleasure.

It has long been known that separation from their mother is often painful to children during the first 2 to 3 years of life. Once again, the study of separation-individuation has given us a developmental view of such separation reactions. It has shown us that sensitivity to separation is very different during the different subphases of the separation-individuation process. Of course, each child's sensitivity to separations will also be determined by the mother-child relationship and by the way the mother handles such separations. Regardless of these individual differences, however, we were able to see a developmental line of separation reactions (McDevitt, 1980b). The period of the differentiation subphase is a time when most infants first show active protest or distress at separation. This seems to be when they are on the verge of being able to move independently themselves and are trying to do so, but cannot do so yet. It is at this time that they seem to perceive their mother walking away from them and often cry. Most infants at that time accept substitutes without too much difficulty, but the period of differentiation is a sensitive one. It is as if the infant's capacities of discrimination area head of the his or her capacity to act. The infant is acutely aware that when mother walks away he or she is not yet able to follow her or call to her. However, the infant has a beginning image of the mother and begins to look at the door through which she might have left. It is also often comforting to the infant to be taken to a window. The child seems, at this time, to have a vague feeling that mother is out there. Thus, going to the window and observing the world in which she is somehow known to be seems to ameliorate the feeling of helplessness or entrapment that might othewise be present. One mother who was especially sensitive observed that her little boy, at a somewhat older age, would wait by the door in the late afternoon, thereby indicating to her that he was waiting for his father to come home.

By the time they reach the practicing period from about 8 to 16 months, children are quite aware that their mother might leave and may protest her leaving as soon as she prepares to do so. On the other hand, their newly found ability to crawl, and later to walk, seems to compensate to some extent. No longer are they so dependent on a mother substitute for comfort. Children are now more able to do things for and by themselves that are enjoyable and exciting. They can also attempt to follow the mother. They can go to the door through which she left. They can be more actively engaged with substitute caretakers in the mother's absence.

Nevertheless, during the early practicing period, from about 8 to 13 months, it was observed that infants tended to become much less active when their mother was out of the room. Pleasure and cathexis in the outside world was definitely reduced, and infants began to withdraw into a state called "low-keyedness" (Mahler & McDevitt, 1968). Low-keyedness was conceptualized as a state of holding on to the image of the absent mother by reducing activity and stimulation from the outside. This withdrawal and low-keyedness can be quite dramatic. Equally dramatic is the way in which the child at this age will immediately come back to life as soon as he or she is reunited with mother.

It is during the period of practicing that the invisible bond with mother is at its height, and the infant seems to feel as if she were at one with him or her, even while at a distance. Infants at this age characteristically will play at a distance from their mother but periodically look at her and check back, apparently receiving sustenance from the visual contact. Absence of the mother at this age, if it is too prolonged, and if no adequate substitute caretaker is available, disrupts too suddenly the illusion of oneness with the mother and thus disrupts the elation that is so characteristic of the practicing subphase. It may also lead the child to become restless and search for the mother or to get into dangerous or precipitous situations, probably with the hope of being rescued by her.

The increased sense of separateness during the period of rapproachement brings with it a sense of vulnerability, loneliness, and often helplessness. Thus, most children become much more sensitive to separation. Toddlers of the rapprochement subphase are often constantly preoccupied with their mother's whereabouts. They insist on following her through the door and will protest vigorously when separated. Phenomena such as shadowing and darting away have been described as characteristic of toddlers during this period. They can be quite insistent on their mother's exclusive attention and, if it is not easily available, attempt to get this attention by clinging and coercion. Substitutes are no longer as easily accepted, and often familiar substitute caretakers, even fathers, are angrily rejected when the mother is desired. A kind of splitting often occurs in which the absent mother is longed for and the present caretaker is rejected. Beginning feelings of ambivalence are directed toward the mother, who is often seen as interfering with the child's budding autonomy. Thus, the mother is split into the good absent mother who is longed for and the bad present one who is rejected. At the time of reunion, the mother who returns is no longer necessarily experienced as the pleasurable, life-giving force that she was during practicing. Instead, when she returns she is sometimes avoided. The child veers away and seems angry instead of smiling at the mother's return, and it takes considerable time for a pleasurable reunion to be effected.

The beginning abilities for symbolic play and language help the toddler withstand separation from the mother. It is only with the advent of the fourth subphase however, on the way to object constancy, that mother's absence can truly be accepted and the child can be content for longer periods of time without her. By then, the child can understand quite well where mother or father is when they are not with him or her and can pleasurably anticipate their return. Symbolic play and imitation are important tools for the mastery of separations. These can be played out endlessly by children of different ages, beginning with the simple peek-a-boo of the young infant.

It is important to remember that Mahler's study of separation-individuation was designed to study the emergence of separateness, not the reaction to separation. Children were studied in the caretaking presence of their mothers. Yet, even in this setting, mothers would leave the room for brief periods for their interviews, providing some insight into the developmental reactions to separation from mother.

DISCUSSION

In the beginning of this essay, we briefly mentioned some of Freud's ideas about early development. His ideas about introjective and projective mechanisms were an early attempt to conceptualize how the infant starts to distinguish self and nonself on the basis of other than "reality-ego" considerations. We have attempted to convey a number of the pathways that Mahler and her co-workers have taken to elucidate this and many other related issues. Clearly, Mahler agrees with Freud's contention that the infant and child can normally develop structures on the basis of factors other than those that Freud referred to as reality-ego related. Mahler's conceptualization of libidinal object constancy and the phases of development that lead up to libidinal object constancy are clearly instances of factors that are not simply based on the reality ego.

We deliberately have not used the term "cognitive" in contrast to "emotional" factors, since we believe this type of dichotomy is, for the most part, not a useful one in early development. One might say, for example, that Mahler and Piaget both refer to a series of cognitive structures developed by the infant or child, but to some extent they are talking about different types of cognitive structures. Moreover, for Mahler the intermesh of the infant's and mother's affective states is often a reliable indicator or predictor of how the infant's structures will develop. Thus, Mahler maintains (as did Freud) that cognitive structures that develop in relation to the self (selves) and important object representations follow different developmental lines than other cognitive structures such as these described by Piaget. If this is the case, it raises questions about the relationship between observations and theoretical concepts from a psychoanalytic perspective, on the one hand, and infant experiments, observations, and theoretical concepts of researchers from other perspectives (such as those of cognitive and learning theorists), on the other.

To be more concrete, let us take the example, cited earlier, in which Mahler recently altered her concept of the autistic phase because of current infant research. Clearly, contemporary studies have been striking in pointing out the early perceptual and response capabilities of the infant. Moreover, a number of psychoanalysts, such as Stern, have pointed out that these studies contradict aspects of Mahler's and Freud's thought. Even though the autistic phase is not a central concept to Freud (nor, for that matter is primary narcissism), the examination of this issue might elucidate some of the difficulties in comparing findings that are couched in psychoanalytic terms with findings from other theoretical points of view. This examination might also touch on some of the difficulties of formulating psychoanalytic concepts.

Freud's notion of primary narcissism can be interpreted in several ways, but one narrow interpretation of Freud (or Mahler) is that he was referring primarily to the building of rudimentary representations of self and object by the infant. During primary narcissism, the infant is not concerned with the object as object—not because the infant cannot discriminate the object, but rather because no accumulation of experi-

ence (in normal development) has occurred that leads the infant to anticipate a consistent or long period of frustration of primary gratification.
If such an accumulation of experience occurs very early, Freud implicitly predicts traumatic results. Freud (1915) states that even though
"the ego is autoerotic [and] it has no need of the external world, in consequences of experience, . . . it acquires objects from that world and, in
spite of everything, it cannot avoid feeling internal instinctual stimuli
. . . as unpleasurable." The purified pleasure ego, then, develops as a response to unpleasurable stimuli, and although it brings the infant closer
to the object, it also causes some distortion in the infant's rudimentary
sense of reality.

Freud is here making a unique type of prediction, a prediction that
should differentiate to some extent his theoretical position from other
positions. There are, of course, difficulties in testing these ideas. We
have little idea of the time periods that Freud is postulating. It may be
difficult to find ways to measure the infant's postulated split of the world
into all good (inside) and all bad (outside). Freud is silent about factors
that might influence (retard or advance) the development of the
purified pleasure ego, nor does he tell us in detail about factors that
might continue the purified pleasure ego longer than developmentally
appropriate or that might lead to the dissipation of the structure earlier
than might be desirable. In short, Freud tells us very little that would
enable us to develop a testable theory from his writings. It is obviously
difficult, therefore, to compare his account of development with other
accounts. We believe, however, that even in Freud's sparse writings on
early development, there are ideas rich enough that if one rigorously applied his assumptions and tried several time sequences, it might be possible to empirically test his conceptualizations.

Why, one might ask, have we in our summary of Mahler's contributions reviewed some relatively obscure sections of Freud's writings?
We have done so in part because Freud's writings are finalized and in
some ways are a simpler version of an early developmental schema than
are other psychoanalytic theories. In the main, however, we wish to
give a brief illustration of both the difficulties and the potential of even
such a seemingly "discarded" (Lichtenberg, 1982) part of Freud's writings as his metapsychological papers. In our opinion, Mahler's pioneering work has some of the same difficulties but clearly much more
potential because of the richness of the observations and concepts of her
work.

Let us go, therefore, to Mahler's conceptualization of the autistic
phase, which we roughly equated with Freud's ideas of primary narcissism and autoeroticism. This concept is one of the few aspects of
Mahler's writngs that has been actively disputed. In addition, it is

clearly not a central concept for her (her research has not included this phase of development), and therefore might prove useful as an illustration of the richness of her ideas.

In our opinion, the concept of the autistic phase has been translated as a phase without stable representations, or an "objectless" period. This, of course, is one possible translation, but one not necessarily in keeping with Mahler's ideas or with Jacobson's notion of the psychophysiological self, which Mahler has utilized. The key to this notion is the definition of an "objectless" period. If one means a period where no stable perceptions or memories are retained, then the first month of life is probably not an objectless state. However, Mahler, Freud, and Jacobson all describe the state of the infant in this period with respect to gratifying and aversive experiences. They maintain that the infant is interested not in the object, but in the gratification or maintenance of homeostatis or in something other than the object itself. The fact that the infant possesses aspects of the rudimentary ego does not alter this concept. What, then, is the contradiction with other research? For if one means by "objectless" state an infant whose main interest is in gratification and who is not motivated or interested in the object, (we are of course simplifying), then there is no contradiction.

Part of the difficulty, then, may lie in the manner in which the concepts are stated. Or perhaps it is more accurate to say that the difficulty lies in the fact that the concepts are incompletely stated. Here Mahler has not gone beyond Freud, and all the questions we previously asked about Freud's ideas can be appropriately applied to Mahler. We believe, however, that all the conditions are present for separation-individuation concepts to be put in the form of a theory that can both do justice to the richness of psychoanalytic concepts and at the same time be empirically rigorous.

The line of thought and research that Mahler has pursued in her separation-individuation research is probably the outstanding example in psychoanalysis of how concepts have guided research and, in turn, have themselves been enriched and expanded by the research. Given the outstanding quality and amount of this work, however, we might briefly summarize what we believe are some of the difficulties in this conceptual field. Difficulty in knowing how to conceptually coordinate separation-individuation and other aspects of psychoanalysis may in part be an empirical question. At this point, however, it is hard to know how to coordinate concepts such as psychosexual stages, drives, or other aspects of psychological structure in ego psychology. For example, one might ask if drive is a concept that is compatible with the separation-individuation theoretical framework and if so, does a concept like drive add to this framework? How does one think of psychosexual factors in relationship to processes of differentiation or individuation? Many questions such as these can be asked, and it is not a criticism but rather a comment about psychoanalytic thought that there are few substantive attempts to logically order and coordinate these concepts. Only if this is done can firm empirical consequences be derived from a theoretical position.

A similar point can be made about separation-individuation concepts even outside the context of the more general psychoanalytic concepts. It is difficult to know the logical status of certain concepts. That is, it is hard to know which concepts are absolutely essential and which are more peripheral. It is also difficult to know how to translate certain concepts into ideas that have firm empirical consequences. For example, there are many examples in the research of children who deviated from what would seem to be expected theoretical norms, but the delimiting conditions were not often given in generalizable statements. A substantial elucidation of these difficulties is beyond the scope of this chapter, however.

We have attempted to give one example of how some of Mahler's and Freud's less-developed ideas and psychoanalytic explanations may be powerful if stated in more specific terms. When that occurs, we may see that even the concept of the autistic phase has a good deal of explanatory power.

ACKNOWLEDGMENTS

The authors wish to thank David Pollens for his assistance in the preparation of this article.

REFERENCES

Bergman, A. (1980). Ours, yours, mine. In R. F. Lax, S. Bach, & J. A. Burland (Eds.), *Rapprochement: The critical subphase of separation-individuation* (pp. 199–216). New York: Aronson.

Bergman, A. (1982). Considerations about the development of the girl during the separation-individuation process. In D. Mendell (Ed.), *Early female development: Current psychoanalytic views* (pp. 61–80). New York: Spectrum Publications.

Bergman, A., & Chernack, M. (1982). From command to request: The development of language in the treatment of symbiotic psychotic child. *International Journal of Psychoanalytic Psychotherapy, 9,* 583–602.

Brazelton, T. B. (1974). The origins of reciprocity: The early mother-infant interaction. In M. Lewis & L. A. Rosenblum (Eds.), *The effect of the infant on its caregiver* (pp. 49–76). New York: Wiley.

Brazelton, T. B. (1981). Neonatal assessment. In S. I. Greenspan & G. H. Pollock (Eds.), *The course of life: Psychoanalytic contributions toward understanding human development* (Vol. 1) (pp. 203–233). Washington, D.C.: U.S. Government Printing Office.

Emde, R., Gaensbauer, T., & Harmon, R. (1976). Emotional expression in infancy: A biobehavioral study. *Psychological Issues, 10* (1 Monograph 37).

Freud, S. (1900). The interpretation of dreams. *Standard Edition, 5,* 339–621.

Freud, S. (1914). On narcissism: An introduction. *Standard Edition, 14,* 73–102.

Freud, S. (1915). Instincts and their vicissitudes. *Standard Edition, 14,* 117–140.

Freud, S. (1917). Mourning and melancholia. *Standard Edition, 14,* 243–258.

Furer, M. (1967). Some developmental aspects of the superego. *International Journal of Psycho-Analysis, 48,* 277–280.

Kernberg, O. (1980). *Internal world and external reality.* New York: Aronson.

Lichtenberg, J. D. (1982). Reflections of the first year of life. *Psychoanalytic Inquiry, 1,* 695–729.

Loewald, H. W. (1984). Review of *The selected papers of Margaret S. Mahler. Journal of the American Psychoanalytic Association, 32,* 165–175.

Mahler, M. S. (1942). Pseudoimbecility: A magic cap of invisibility. In *The selected papers of Margaret S. Mahler, vol. 1* (pp. 3–16). New York: Jason Aronson.

Mahler, M. S. (1952). On child psychosis and schizophrenia: Autistic and symbiotic infantile psychoses. In *The selected papers of Margaret S. Mahler, vol. 1* (pp. 131–153). New York: Jason Aronson.

Mahler, M. S. (1961). On sadness and grief in infancy and childhood: Loss and restoration of the symbiotic love object. In *The selected papers of Margaret S. Mahler, vol. 1* (pp. 261–279). New York: Jason Aronson.

Mahler, M. S. (1966). Notes on the development of basic moods: The depressive affect. In *The selected papers of Margaret S. Mahler, vol. 2* (pp. 59–75). New York: Jason Aronson.

Mahler, M. S. (1975). On the current status of the infantile neurosis. In *The selected papers of Margaret S. Mahler, vol. 2* (pp. 189–193). New York: Jason Aronson.

Mahler, M. S. (1979). *The selected papers of Margaret S. Mahler* (Vols. 1, 2, & 3). New York: Jason Aronson.

Mahler, M. S. (1981). Aggression in the service of separation-individuation: Case study of a mother-daughter relationship. *Psychoanalytic Quarterly, 50,* 625–638.

Mahler, M. S., & McDevitt, J. B. (1968). Observations on adaptation and defense *in statu nascendi.* In *The selected papers of Margaret S. Mahler* (Vol. 2) (pp. 99–112). New York: Jason Aronson, 1979.

Mahler, M. S., Pine, F., & Bergman, A. (1975). *The psychological birth of the human infant.* New York: Basic Books.

Mahler, M. S., Ross, J. R. & DeFries, Z. (1949). Clinical studies in benign and malignant cases of childhood psychosis (schizophrenia-like). *American Journal of Orthopsychiatry, 19,* 295–305.

McDevitt, J. B. (1980a). *The emergence of hostile aggression and its defensive and adaptive modifications during the separation-individuation process.* Brill Memorial Lecture, prescribed at the New York Psychoanalytic Society, New York.

McDevitt, J. B. (1980b). The role of internalization in the development of object relations during the separation-individuation phase. In R. L. Lax, S. Bach, & J. A. Burland (Eds.), *Rapprochement: The critical subphase of separation-individuation* (pp. 135–149). New York: Aronson.

McDevitt, J. B. and Mahler, M. S. (1980). Object constancy, individuality and internalization. In S. I. Greenspan and G. H. Pollock (Eds.), *The course of life: Vol. 1. Infancy and early childhood* (pp. 407–424). Washington, D.C.: U.S. Government Printing Office.

Pine, F. (1978). On the expansion of the affect array: A developmental description. In R. F. Lax, S. Bach, and J. A. Burland (Eds.), *Rapprochement* (pp. 217–233). New York: Aronson, 1980.

Pine, F. (1981). In the beginning: Contributions to a psychoanalytic developmental psychology. *International Review of Psychoanalysis, 8,* 15–33.

Resch, R. C. (1979). Hatching in the human infant as the beginning of separation-individuation: What it is and what it looks like. *The Psychoanalytic Study of the Child, 34,* 421–441.

Sander, L. W. (1976). Issues in early mother-child interactions. In E. N. Rexford, L. W. Sander, & T. Shapiro (Eds.), *Infant psychiatry: A new synthesis* (pp. 127–147). New Haven: Yale University Press.

Settlage, C. F. (1974). Danger signals in the separation-individuation process. In D. Bergsma (Ed.), *The infant at risk.* (March of Dimes National Florida Symposium, Vol. 10). unpaginated

Spitz, R. (1957). *No and yes: On the genesis of human communication.* New York: International Universities Press.

Stern, D. (1971). A micro-analysis of mother-infant interaction. *Journal of the American Academy of Child Psychiatry, 13,* 501–517.

Stern, D. (1974). The goal and structure of mother-infant play. *Journal of American Academy of Child Psychiatry, 13,* 402–421.

Stern, D. (1982). Implications of infancy research for clinical theory and practice. Paper presented at the 13th Annual Margaret S. Mahler Symposium, Philadelphia.

Winnicott, D. (1956). Primary maternal preoccupation. In *Collected papers: Through Pediatrics to Psycho-analysis* (1958, pp. 300–305). London: Tavistock Publications.

Otto Kernberg: Psychoanalysis and Object Relations Theory; The Beginnings of an Integrative Approach

10

Monica Carsky, Ph.D.
Steven Ellman, Ph.D.

It is a difficult task to attempt to summarize and critique Otto Kernberg's psychoanalytic contributions, for he has presented the most systematic and wide-sweeping clinical and theoretical statements of the last decade, perhaps even since Freud. His work touches on many if not most of the topics that have been of interest to contemporary analysts. In addition, he has been instrumental in introducing many topics to the American psychoanalytic community. Even reviewers who have been sharply critical of Kernberg, such as Calef and Weinshel (1979), have stated that "no other single colleague has been so instrumental in confronting American psychoanalysts with Kleinian concepts and theories" (pp. 470–471). Clearly, this is damning Kernberg with faint praise, since much of the American psychoanalytic community is in opposition to many aspects of Melanie Klein's theoretical contributions. Although there is no question that Kernberg has been strongly influenced by Kleinian concepts, however, there is also no question that he is attempting to integrate many different parts of what is called the British object relations school, as well as aspects of Freudian thought, ego psychology, and different strands of research in neurophysiology and physiological psychology. This list is by no means complete. Kernberg is strongly interested in research in affect, for example, whether from psychoanalysis, physiology, or academic psychology.

Given that we are dealing with a theoretical integration of such large proportions, one that blends the familiar and unfamiliar, it is not surprising that a number of critics have pointed out various difficulties in Kernberg's theoretical attempts. Before we try to evaluate Kernberg's writings, it is important to put our critical stance into an appropriate historical perspective. In our opinion, there is no psychoanalytic theorist whose theory would stand up to some of the criticism that has been directed at Kernberg. Psychoanalysis has yet to produce a full theory as defined by philosophers of science such as Nagel (1961) or Popper (1962). Leaving aside philosophical conceptions of theory, it is clear to most students of Freud's or Hartmann's writings that many concepts remain without clear definition and are not well integrated into a theoretical structure. If we are to evaluate Kernberg reasonably, it must be within contemporary psychoanalytic standards. In addition, much of contemporary criticism in psychoanalysis is not based on either logical or empirical grounds but rather is often simply or mostly a reflection of the critics' values. We will attempt to evaluate Kernberg's contributions in terms of both his stated aims and our view of the state of contemporary psychoanalytic theory.

Some of our views of contemporary theory have been stated elsewhere (Ellman & Moskowitz, 1980; Moskowitz & Ellman, unpublished manuscript), but for this introduction we will briefly restate them. We believe that in many of the social sciences it is difficult to state clearly how the different aspects of a theory are organized. Thus, at times, it may not be clear what are the central assumptions of a given theory, as opposed to assumptions or statements that are more peripheral. Frequently, the coordinating logic (see Nagel, 1961) of a theory is also unclear, so that it is hard to know what assumptions should be combined to predict or to explain a given event. Most often, however, the phenomena to be explained are relatively clear and are at least somewhat separated from the theory itself. Psychoanalytic theory shares some of these difficulties, and it is not clear at times what phenomena some psychoanalytic theories are addressing.

Fortunately, Kernberg usually indicates clearly what phenomena he is trying to explain. In our discussion, we will initially introduce the clinical phenomena that have been the main impetus for Kernberg's theorizing, and from that point on will go back and forth between Kernberg's theorizing and the clinical phenomena or observations he wishes to explain. It will be clear as we proceed that the observations and the theory become more and more intertwined. Nevertheless, we think that Kernberg is attempting to explain important clinical phenomena. In fact, this is a major reason for his present importance in psychoanalysis. We do not believe that Kernberg's clinical observations are simply or mainly an artifact of his theorizing.

It may be hard to see in the present context why it would be necessary to mention any of Freud's writings. From our point of view, however, there is a somewhat neglected aspect of Freud's work that is particularly germane to most object relations theorists. (We are obviously including Kernberg as an object relations theorist.) This is most clearly seen in Frued's metapsychological papers, where he frequently presents his views on early development. Certainly Freud's (1915) view of the developmental phase that he termed the purified pleasure ego has been included in one form or another in the work of a number of contemporary authors (Kohut, 1966, 1971; Mahler, 1968; Mahler, Pine, & Bergman, 1975). In these writings, Freud deals with what he termed the origins of the three polarities of the mind and sets the stage for the differentiation of types of identification processes. That is, Freud (1914, 1917) began to conceptualize the process of introjection or early identifications with more specific and developmentally later types of identifications. Melanie Klein, in many ways, expanded on this phase of Freud's work, as well as Freud's theory of instinct[1] as stated in *Beyond the Pleasure Principle* (1920). To greatly oversimplify Klein's work, one may say that she was the first psychoanalytic theorist to attempt to integrate object relations and instinctual points of view. Kernberg has clearly stated that he is also attempting to unite drive and object relations points of view. In addition, he is attempting to stay within a general ego psychological framework, so that the psychoanalytic conception of drive that Kernberg is utilizing arises from Hartmann's emendations and clarifications of Freudian theory. Thus, in a later era, Kernberg is attempting to integrate important aspects of the British object relations and ego psychological points of view. Given this broad statement, we should point out that many different and at times divergent points of view are encompassed both between and within these two so-called points of view. Kernberg is both eclectic and selective, but he is trying to utilize the concepts that he regards as essential to each position.

Kernberg has attempted to combine at least four elements from either an ego psychological or object relations perspective. These are the following:

1. *Structure.* Although Kernberg has moved the concepts such as self-representation, self-image, and so forth into a more central focus, he has retained Freud's tripartite structure of ego, id, and superego. As we will see, with most of these concepts Kernberg utilizes object relations theorizing to a greater extent when dealing with questions of struc-

---

[1]In this chapter, we will use the terms "instinct" and "drive" interchangeably. Either term refers to Freud's more flexible use of the term *trieb*, as opposed to the ethologist's use of "instinct" as equivalent to a physiological process resulting in a fixed action pattern or a stereotyped behavior pattern.

turalization early in childhood development and utilizes the tripartite model in later childhood development, particularly in the oedipal period.

2. *Defense*. Although defense is certainly a part of structure, the concept of defense is important enough in Kernberg's writings to warrant special notice. By and large, what Kernberg calls low-level defenses are those that have been discussed by object relation theorists (such as splitting and projective identification), whereas most of Kernberg's high-level defenses (such as repression and isolation) stem from Freudian and ego psychological theorists. In Kernberg's conceptualizations, the main defenses utilized are thus an important indication of the general state of an individual's psychological structure.

3. *Development*. Kernberg has attempted to integrate the concept of object relations phases (schizoid, depressive phase) with the concept of psychosexual development and Mahler's (1968; Mahler, Pine, & Bergman, 1975) developmental findings. Here again, one may see the viewpoint of Mahler and object relations being used more extensively in considering preoedipal development, while Kernberg utilizes ego psychological concepts in considering oedipal development.

4. *Instinct or drive*. This is a concept that Kernberg has consistently maintained in his theorizing. Since some object relations theorists, such as Fairbairn or Guntrip, have explicitly rejected Freud's, Hartmann's, or Klein's concept of drive, Kernberg is not combining two points of view but rather including this aspect of Freudian ego psychological theorizing in his theoretical framework. In fact, with respect to the concept of drive, Kernberg attempts to integrate segments of modern neurophysiology and neuropsychology with a psychoanalytic concept of drive. It should be pointed out that Kernberg's conceptualization of emotion and affect are particularly important in his theorizing, and for Kernberg (1976, 1980c, 1982h) these concepts to some extent replace drive as a motivational concept.

The main focus of Kernberg's theorizing is the type of patients that the British school (Balint, 1968; Fairbairn, 1952; Guntrip, 1968, 1971; Winnicott, 1965, 1975; and others) has been describing for the last 30 to 40 years. Kernberg has grouped these patients and maintains that many of these other theorists wrote about people who manifest borderline pathology.

In describing Kernberg's work, we will first note the clinical observations which Kernberg's theory seeks to explain. Then we will present summaries of his contributions in five areas: (1) development; (2) psychoanalytic classification of character pathology, including the borderline diagnosis; (3) treatment implications, derived from the developmental theory and diagnostic system, including the rationale for various treatment recommendations as well as Kernberg's view of countertransference and the therapeutic stance; (4) groups and institutions, including issues in hospital treatment; and (5) a theory of drives and affects. Finally, we will comment on Kernberg's critics and will ourselves critically review what we consider to be major elements in Kernberg's contributions to psychoanalytic theory.

SUMMARY OF KERNBERG'S WORK

The Clinical Observations

Kernberg's clinical observation of "borderline adults" has been one of the factors that has led him to expand "traditional" psychoanalytic theory. He observes that this type of person can often maintain rapidly fluctuating, contradictory ego states. These ego states can be manifested as rapidly changing, intense transference reactions (from idealization and love to intense hatred and rage) and can also be seen in initial clinical contacts. Kernberg (1967, 1975a, 1980c) has inferred that these contradictory ego states are actively separated or split and that a person who shows splitting cannot reconcile these contradictory states. In fact, if someone else points out the person's contradictory attitudes, states, or actions, the person would always manifest anxiety. A person's reaction to such an intervention is an important diagnostic indicator to Kernberg (1976, 1981f).

Kernberg feels that when analysts and therapists do not recognize that splitting is taking place they may fail to understand what is happening in a therapeutic situation. He notes a tendency for alternating transference states to remain static when therapy is viewed over a long period of time. The analyst sometimes takes one of the positive states to be the manifestation of a good working alliance or, alternately, might feel that a patient's rageful attacks may represent an important breakthrough, in which the patient may become aware of and begin to understand these "primitive impulses." Kernberg believes that often no intrapsychic change is taking place. Instead, the patient simply alternates presentation of these states. Often, the patient uses the tolerant atmosphere of therapy to derive greater gratification of (in particular) his or her aggressive impulses than would be allowed elsewhere. Or, as in the Menninger study of the effects of supportive psychotherapy (where there was little transference interpretation, and signs of latent negative transference, especially, were unacknowledged), the patient-therapist relationship is shallow or mechanical (Kernberg et al, 1972).

Kernberg points out that according to traditional observations of this patient population (Federn, 1947; Frosch, 1960; Knight, 1954; Schmideberg, 1947; Zetzel, 1971) they tend to lose the ability to test reality adequately in the context of the psychotherapy (transference psychoses), to act out severely, and to consciously experience primary process material while apparently lacking a capacity for introspection and insight.

The primitive, early reactions of borderline patients to their therapists seem to be not only preoedipal in content, but also less organized than neurotic transference. Kernberg (1976) concludes that the work of various object relations theorists (Klein, Fairbairn, Guntrip, etc.) described these reactions most accurately as recreations of early actual or fantasied object relationships – as "the pathologically fixed remnants of the normal processes of early introjection" (p. 25).

These observations and conclusions led Kernberg to propose both a developmental model to account for borderline pathology and technical innovations for the psychotherapy of borderline conditions.

The Developmental Model

Kernberg's (1966, 1975a, 1976) developmental model is organized around the internalization of object relations, a process he takes to be crucial in the formation of psychic structures. He posits three types of internalization or, in his terms, three different identification systems. Each process results in a psychic structure, which is named accordingly (introjects, identifications, and ego identity). Thus, the process of introjection results in an introject, and so forth. As Kernberg (1976) described it: "All processes of internalization consist of three basic components: (a) object-images or object-representations; (b) self-images or self-representations; and (c) drive derivatives or dispositions to specific affective states" (p. 26). Psychic organization takes place at two levels. In the earlier and more basic organization, splitting is the main defense mechanism; during these periods, self-object-affect (S-O-A) units with opposite affective tones are unintegrated, either as a passive consequence of lack of maturity or as active process (splitting). In the more advanced level of organization, repression is the main defense utilized. Ego and superego development and integration can be assessed by the degree to which repression and its associated higher-level defenses have succeeded the more primitive condition (Kernberg, 1976).

Kernberg follows Melanie Klein (1946) in taking introjection to play an important role in the early development of the ego. However, he suggests that it is a mechanism based on primary autonomous functions of perception and memory, rejecting Klein's views of the importance of very early oral incorporative *fantasies* . We will, at a later point, describe Kernberg's more detailed account of the relationship between his model and findings in cognition, perception, and neurophysiological processes.

Kernberg (1976) defines introjection as "the reproduction and fixation of an interaction with the environment by means of an organized cluster of memory traces" (p. 29) with the S-O-A components. For him those components are "(i) the image of an object, (ii) the image of the self in interaction with the object, and (iii) the affective coloring of both the object-image and the self-image under the influence of the drive representative present at the time of the interaction" (p. 29). Introjection goes beyond the primary apparatuses because it entails complex organization of the results of perception and of memory traces, in which perception of the external world is linked to perception of subjective experience. Although the earliest introjections do not clearly differentiate self and object images, a dyadic element is present.

The affective tone of the introjection is important because the various S-O-A introjections are gradually sorted and organized by affective valence. Kernberg (1976) writes "Introjections taking place under the *positive valence* of libidinal instinctual gratification, as in loving mother-child contact, tend to fuse and become organized in what has been frequently called 'the good internal object.' Introjections taking place under the *negative valence* of aggressive drive derivatives tend to fuse with similar negative valence introjections and become organized in 'the bad internal objects" (p. 30).

Kernberg sees affect in the first months of life as particlarly important. Its "irradiating" effect on introjects (which may include perceived self and object representations) is such that the resulting perceptual constellations differ most according to their associated affective states. Affect states, then, are the manner in which introjects of opposite valence are kept apart, since the immature psyche is unable to integrate different temporal experiences and opposite affective experiences.

Although Kernberg stresses the importance of affect in building up separated S-O-A units, his account of developmental stages parallels that of Mahler (1968; Mahler, Pine, & Bergman, 1975). His stages may be summarized as follows:

Stage 1. This is the stage of normal autism, or primary undifferentiation in the first month of life, before the "good," combined self-object constellation develops through positive experiences. Pathology at this stage would mean that this undifferentiated image would not develop, and a normal symbiotic relationship with the mother would not take place, being replaced by autistic psychosis.

Stage 2. This stage, normal "symbiosis," from the third or fourth to the sixth or ninth month, consists of the consolidation of an undifferentiated, "good" self-object representation, and corresponds to the periods of Mahler's symbiotic phase and differentiation subphase. Even when self- and object images begin to be separated—still within the umbrella of libidinally organized S-O-A units—they are weakly delineated, and, Kernberg (1976) says, there is a "persisting tendency for defensive regressive refusion of 'good' self and object images when severe trauma or frustration determine pathological development of this stage" (p. 60). Fixation at, or regression to, this self-object dedifferentiation and loss of ego boundaries is typical of childhood symbiotic psychosis (Mahler, 1968), most types of adult schizophrenia (Jacobson, 1954), and depressive psychoses (Jacobson, 1966).

Stage 3. In this stage, self- and object representations are clearly differentiated, within both the core "good" self-object and core "bad" self-object. Self-images from one positively experienced S-O-A unit are linked with those from other positively valenced S-O-A units, with parallel joining of object representations. With the increasing complexity of the resulting representations, this process "contributes to the differentiation of self and other and to definition of ego boundaries" (Kernberg, 1976, p. 30). This stage corresponds to Mahler's separation-individuation phase (excluding the differentiation subphase), and lasts from 6 to 9 months of age through 18 to 36 months. Object constancy (Hartmann, 1964) and stable ego boundaries should be achieved, but relationships are still with part objects. Integration of self- and object representations occurs only at the close of this stage. Kernberg follows Mahler in suggesting that borderline pathology follows from fixation and/or regression to this phase of internalized object relationships.

This is the stage in which active separation (the defense of splitting) between good self-images and bad self-images and between good object and bad object images occurs. In patients with borderline pathology, the combined S-O-A units of opposing valence persist in an unintegrated fashion, and are not replaced or accompanied by higher-level developments. Kernberg (1976) maintains that when opposing S-O-A units are initially introjected, they are kept apart to avoid the anxiety associated with the negative valences "from being generalized throughout the ego," and to "protect the integration of positive introjections into a positive ego core" (p. 36). However, defensive splitting represents a later development, in which the opposing S-O-A units are actively separated.

Kernberg suggests that the ego comes into being at the point when introjections are used defensively. This is a state in which the "good internal objects" (mostly undifferentiated self- and object representations with a positive valence) along with the "good external objects" (positively experienced aspects of reality), form the purified pleasure ego, while the negative S-O-A units are viewed as outside. "Good" self-images and "good" object images begin to be separated. Slightly later, all these "units" become more elaborate, and the differentiation between "good internal objects" and "good external objects" occurs. Now the defense of projection can be utilized across a relatively clear boundary, so that the array of "bad external objects" includes some that are "bad" via projection of introjections that had a negative valence. This clear utilization of projection is an important development of Stage 3. Correspondingly, the defensive use of active splitting decreases over time, and the individual successfully traverses to Stage 4.

Although we have been focusing on the building up of S-O-A units and the unfolding of defensive processes, the second internalization process, identification, also begins to be used in Stage 3. This is a higher-level form of introjection, which includes the role aspects of the interpersonal interactions and hence requires some development of perceptual and cognitive abilities so that socially recognized functions can be conceptualized by the child (Kernberg, 1976, p. 31). The affective components of such internalizations are also more advanced and differentiated than those associated with introjections. The view of the self is likewise more differentiated, so that it is possible to view the object taking a role with respect to the self. Identifications, like introjection, contribute to the formation of psychic structure and yet may also be used for defensive purposes. Identification continues as a process throughout life at different levels of ego integration, and its results are more subtle and better integrated when the ego is more integrated and splitting mechanisms are not used (Kernberg, 1976, p. 77). In psychotic identifications, where self- and object images are pathologically refused,[2] identifications are distorted by the projection of primitive superego forerunners or repressed drive derivatives onto the object, so that the internalized object relation is altered in the direction of "all good" or "all bad" introjections. When pathological identifications occur at a more integrated level, they result in pathological character traits.

Stage 4. In Stage 4, contradictory self- and other representations are integrated into percepts of the self and others that more accurately reflect complex experiences of the self and other persons. Failure to achieve this integration results in "identity diffusion." In this stage, repression appears as a defense, and ego, superego, and id are also differentiated. This period begins toward the end of the third year of life and continues through the oedipal period. Pathology from this stage is that of patients with neuroses or "higher-level" character pathology (hysterical, obsessive-compulsive, and depressive-masochistic characters).

Narcissistic personality disorders may also result from abnormal development during this stage, when instead of integration of self and ob-

---

[2]Kernberg adopts Jacobson's (1954) definition of refusion, as attempts to maintain absolute gratification through fantasies that the self and object are merged, fantasies that ignore realistic differences.

ject, there is, in Kernberg's (1976) words, "(1) a pathological condensation of real self, ideal self, and ideal object structures; (2) repression and/or dissociation of 'bad' self-representations; (3) generalized devaluation of object representations; and (4) blurring of normal ego-superego boundaries" (p. 68; see also Kernberg, 1982f). This results in a grandiose self, which is separated from negatively valenced S-O-A experiences in a splitting process more typical of Stage 3.

Kernberg interprets Stage 4 as representing the achievement of what Klein (1948a,b) termed the "depressive position," in which, because of the new, more complex view of others as the objects of both hatred and love, both guilt and concern begin to appear. Representations of an ideal self and ideal object develop as wishes to counteract the increasingly accurate awareness of reality. Repression, which prevents the irruption into consciousness of various drive derivatives, separates id from ego during this stage, and the id becomes more organized. Hence, in neurotic or other higher-level psychopathology, one does not readily see primary process or direct expression of drives.

Integration of the superego as an independent intrapsychic structure takes place in Stage 4. This has two aspects: the condensation of ideal self- and object images into the basis of the ego ideal, and the integration of this with the sadistically determined superego forerunners. These superego forerunners are what Kernberg (1976) terms the "fantastically hostile, highly unrealistic object images reflecting 'expelled,' projected and reintrojected 'bad' self-object representations . . . and reflecting primitive efforts of the infant to protect the good relationship with the idealized mother by turning the aggressively invested images of her (fused with the respective self-images) against himself" (p. 71). With integration come decreases in projection and in the fantastically hostile and unreal nature of the superego elements.

Ego identity, the third process in the internalization of object relations, begins to occur in Stage 4. Ego identity is "the overall organization of identifications and introjections under the guiding principle of the synthetic function of the ego" (Kernberg, 1976, p. 72). This refers to the organization of a self-concept and of deeper, more realistic concepts of others.

Stage 5. Consolidation of superego and ego integration takes place in Stage 5, and ego identity continues to evolve. The individual is able to learn from experience, and "an integrated self, a stable world of integrated, internalized object representations, and a realistic self-knowledge reinforce one another" (Kernberg, 1976, p. 73). Representations of a social and cultural world are included. The internal world gives increasing meaning to present interactions and provides support for the individual in times of crisis. The individual has the capacity to discriminate subtle aspects of him- or herself and of others and develops "depersonified" attitudes and values with increasing capacity to communicate views and experiences in a way that others can understand. These capacities are absent in pathological conditions organized at earlier stages; the most striking example is the narcissistic personality, who cannot convey more than a shallow sense of who he or she is or who the other is in an interaction (Kernberg, 1976, p. 73). Although intimate connections among drives, affects, object relations, and cognitive and other ego functions are implied throughout Kernberg's model, these form a particularly complex and dense matrix in the successful outcome of Stage 5 – the healthy personality.

THE PSYCHOANALYTIC CLASSIFICATION OF CHARACTER PATHOLOGY

Kernberg's (1980a) model of psychopathology is primarily a conflict model; constitutional deficits may contribute to the intensity of certain conflicts and hence render the development of pathological ego structures or character traits more likely. For example, an infant constitutionally endowed with an intense aggressive drive may project more aggressively tinged S-O-A units onto external figures and may develop pathologically intense fears of castration directed at abnormal images of dangerous parents (Kernberg, 1975a). Or, children with organically based perceptual or other learning problems may have introjections and identifications distorted by their faulty apparatuses of primary autonomy. However, when considering adolescent and adult patients, Kernberg's position is that character pathology is best understood and interpreted as the result of dynamic conflicts. Even if a learning disability is present in a borderline patient, only after considerable treatment can its effect be differentiated from the results of pathological splitting and associated primitive defenses (Kernberg, personal communication).

Levels of Character Pathology

The developmental model previously outlined is the basis for a highly specific classification of higher-level, intermediate, and lower-level (borderline) character pathology. This classification is based on determining the level of instinctual development, superego development, defensive operations, and internalized object relations (Kernberg, 1976). Kernberg (1980, 1981c) has been a vocal critic of the DSM-III (American Psychiatric Association, 1980) categorization of personality disorders, because it fails to consider these psychoanalytic perspectives and thereby omits certain important diagnostic entities. In Kernberg's system, higher-level character pathology is marked by the achievement of genital primacy in the instinctual sphere; a well-integrated but excessively severe superego; defense mechanisms organized around repression (including intellectualization, rationalization, undoing, and higher forms of projection); and a stable, well-integrated concept of self and others. Most hysterical, obsessive-compulsive, and depressive-masochistic personalities are in this group—the classical neurotic patients.

At the intermediate level, pregenital fixation points are present, the superego is less well integrated than in higher-level pathology, and sadistic superego precursors play an important role. Defenses are organized around repression, but some more primitive defenses are present, with more infiltration of instinctual impulses than is present in the more sublimatory or reactive traits characteristic of higher-level pathology. Ego identity is established, and there is a stable concept of self and others, but object relations are quite conflicted. Many oral, passive-aggressive, sadomasochistic, and better-functioning infantile personalities and some narcissistic personalities are at this level.

Lower-level character pathology is characterized by borderline personality organization with, in the instinctual realm, "pathological condensation of genital and pregenital instinctual strivings . . . with a predominance of pregenital aggression" (Kernberg, 1976, p. 141). Lack of superego integration and the continuing influence of sadistic superego forerunners are more marked than in the intermediate group. Defenses are organized around splitting, with primitive forms of projection, denial, and other mechanisms, which allow partial expression of the rejected impulse to a greater degree than in the other levels of pathology. Object constancy is not firmly established, identity diffusion is present, and object relationships are conceptualized in terms of part objects.

The Borderline Concept

Kernberg is one of a very small number of investigators who have actually given a detailed definition of the term "borderline personality." He provides a description of the intrapsychic structures and other concepts he considers relevant to this diagnosis along with a sophisticated phenomenological description of the patients. Kernberg prefers the term "borderline personality organization" to "borderline state" or "borderline personality disorder," underlining his belief that such patients have a specific and stable personality organization characterized by ego pathology, which differs from neuroses and less severe character disorders on the one hand, and the psychoses on the other. These patients suffer from a particular type of psychic organization, which has a certain type of history and resistance to rapid change. They are not in a transitory "state," fluctuating between neurosis and psychosis, nor are they defined solely by their obvious symptoms, as in psychiatric use of the term "disorder." Kernberg (1967, 1975a) stresses that similar symptomatology may occur as a result of different intrapsychic configurations and conflicts, so that very detailed diagnostic study is necessary.

Kernberg's delineations of borderline and narcissistic patient groups rely on description of symptoms and complaints presented by these patients, but also, just as important, on inferences about types of psychic structure, defenses, and predominant conflicts. In his concern with "internalized object relations," he has devoted considerable work to explicating the method by which one makes inferences about this and other hypothetical constructs, such as defenses or structures, on the basis of a patient's interview behavior, for example.

On a descriptive level, patients suffering from borderline personality organization present symptoms that, if occurring in combination, suggest pathological ego structure: chronic, diffuse anxiety; polysymptomatic neuroses (severe phobias, rationalized obsessive-compulsive symptoms, multiple, elaborate, or bizarre conversion symptoms, dissociative reactions, hypochondriasis with chronic rituals and withdrawal, and paranoid trends with other symptoms); polymorphous perverse sexual trends; impulse neurosis; and addictions (Kernberg, 1975a). Certain lower-level character disorders (infantile, narcissistic, antisocial, and "as-if" personalities) and paranoid, schizoid, hypomanic, or cyclothymic personalities also usually have borderline structure.

Inferences about the patient's psychological organization are based on other observations. "Nonspecific manifestations of ego weakness" are noted by assessing lack of anxiety tolerance, as when additional anxiety results in further symptom formation or regressive behavior; lack of impulse control, where any increase in anxiety or drive pressure results in unpredictable impulsivity; the lack of developed sublimatory channels (here the patient's talents and opportunities must be considered). A second sign is the appearance of primary process thinking, particularly in unstructured situations such as projective psychological testing (Carr, Goldstein, Hunt, & Kernberg, 1979; Kernberg, 1975a). The presence of the primitive defensive operations of splitting, projective identification, denial, primitive idealization, and devaluation are important signs of borderline pathology. These may require subtle inferences from interview behavior or interactions with the interviewer over a period of time to establish their presence.

The Structural Interview

Aside from the presumptive diagnostic elements that may be indicated by a patient's history or presenting complaints, evidence for structural organization is found in the patient's reactions to being interviewed in a way that focuses on the ego functions and features characterizing neurotic, borderline, and psychotic structures (Kernberg, 1981f).

In particular, the interviewer wishes to understand (1) the degree of identity integration, (2) types of defenses, and (3) the capacity to test reality, including the subtle ability to "evaluate the self and others realistically and in depth" (Kernberg, 1981f, p. 171). Borderline disorders may be differentiated from psychoses by the borderline patient's ability to test reality in the sense that distinctions between internal and external and self and object representations remain. In contrast to neurotic patients, however, persons with borderline structure will show identity diffusion, lower-level defenses similar to those used by psychotic patients, and subtle alterations in the relationship to reality and feelings of reality. Because their capacity to appreciate ordinary social reality is intact, however, and because their defenses protect against the anxiety of intrapsychic conflict (rather than the anxiety of dedifferentiation, as in the psychoses), they respond to interpretations in the interview with better functioning or, at least, without regression.

Thus, the interviewer seeks to assess the patient's view of his or her problems, understanding of self and others, and ability to make use of the interviewer's questions and tentative interpretations. The interviewer focuses on areas that seem odd, contradictory, or unclear to see if the patient can also observe such contradictions and appreciate the possible explanations for these offered by the interviewer.

The "pathology of internalized object relationships," which contributes to the borderline diagnosis, also relies on complex inferences from character traits and the patient's behavior with the interviewer. Kernberg (1976) states: "These patients have little capacity for a realistic evaluation of others and for realistic empathy with others; they experience other people as distant objects, to whom they adapt 'realistically' only as long as there is no emotional involvement with them" (pp. 36–37). They do not empathize well with others, and are "ignorant of the higher, more mature and differentiated aspects of other people's personalities" (p. 37). Hence their relationships are shallow, they are unable to experience guilt and concern, and they give evidence of exploitiveness and unreasonable demands without signs of tact or consideration. In trying to control his or her environment, the patient manipulates others. When they begin psychotherapy, these patients immediately present chaotic and primitive object relations in the transference, as opposed to the gradual unfolding of more mature and then less mature transferences found in neurotic patients (Kernberg, 1976).

Special Diagnostic Issues

Several examples exemplify Kernberg's contention that similar symptomatology may stem from different types of underlying pathology and structure.

Hysterical versus Infantile Personality. Hysterical patients, while showing superficial similarities to infantile patients, have some conflict-free areas where their functioning is stable and appropriate. They are impulsive or clinging only in certain relationships or areas of conflict. Their need to be loved and admired, although it has oral, dependent components, is closer to an expression of genital needs. Oedipal dynamics contribute to differential relationships with men and women, and the provocativeness of these patients is usually not accompanied by promiscuity. Stable, if neurotic, heterosexual relationships are present.

In contrast, infantile patients are more socially inappropriate and impulsive across all areas of life. Oral, demanding elements are more prominent, so that the need to be loved is "more helpless" in quality, and exhibitionistic trends have a primitive, narcissistic, exploitive quality. Promiscuity may be present in conjunction with unstable, changing relationships (Kernberg, 1975a). Such patients frequently are organized at a borderline level (Kernberg, 1981c).

Depression. Kernberg stresses the importance of differentiating depression as a symptom from depressive-masochistic character traits. The higher-level depressive personality, for example, may experience depression in connection with guilt over oedipal strivings or with true concern for the self and others, because of the presence of superego integration. Depression that represents helpless rage or disappointment in an ideal suggests less superego integration. Severe depression that causes breakdown in ego functioning also suggests the presence of a sadistic superego, probably associated with borderline organization. However, both the quantity and quality of depression must be considered when making a structural diagnosis, as the absence of any depressive concern or guilt for others may also be a sign of borderline organization in narcissistic and antisocial personalities (Kernberg, 1975a, 1977a).

Adolescence. The stresses of identity consolidation in adolescence may, in conjunction with environmental pressures (such as gang membership or cultural norms), suggest the presence of severe personality disturbance. Kernberg recommends assessment of the presence or absence of whole-object relationships, ideals, and the capacity for sublimation and work. Adolescents with borderline personality structure will be far less able to describe themselves or their friends in depth and do not show evidence that they can invest themselves in ideals or goals that have meaning to them (Kernberg, 1978, 1979b, 1982e).

Borderline versus Schizophrenic Conditions. In the absence of clear signs of formal thought disorder, hallucinations, or delusions, the primitive defenses present in both borderline and schizophrenic conditions serve different functions, which can be used in interviewing to make this distinction. In patients with borderline structure, these defenses protect the patients from the experience of ambivalence, and "a feared contamination and deterioration of all love relationshps by hatred" (Kernberg, 1975a, p. 179). Schizophrenic patients use splitting and allied mechanisms to prevent "total loss of ego boundaries and dreaded fusion experiences with others" (p. 179), particularly under the stress of strong affects. This is because persons with psychotic structure do not have clearly differentiated self- and object images. Since primitive defense mechanisms cause ego weakness in patients with borderline structure, interpretations should strengthen the ego and lead to better functioning in the interview—more reflectiveness and attempts at integration and better reality testing. Interpretation of the same primitive defenses in schizophrenic patients reveals difficulty with self-object differentiation and hence leads to regression—more overt primary process or delusional thought, loosening of associations, or paranoid distortions of the interviewer—in response to the interpretations given during the interview. Hence, the interview should be conducted with inquiry into responses which are unusual or subtly inappropriate, to test the patient's defensive functioning.

Transference psychosis, which may be present in both borderline and schizophrenic conditions, is different in each group because of the different mechanisms involved. With borderline patients, the transference psychosis is limited to the treatment hours and responds to Kernberg's recommendations for structuring the treatment. With psychotic patients, their psychotic behavior and lack of reality testing in treatment is for a long time no different from that outside the treatment. Later on, they may feel convinced that they and the therapist are one. This is in contrast to the transference psychosis of borderline patients, who always maintain some sort of boundary, even if they feel themselves to be interchanging aspects of identity with the therapist (Kernberg, 1975a, 1980c).

TREATMENT IMPLICATIONS

Kernberg goes into considerable detail in his diagnostic system because he believes that borderline structure, as well as certain other
characterological features of diagnosis, have specific implications for
treatment and prognosis. For example, he views dishonesty by the patient as a particularly unfavorable prognostic sign, which might lead to a
recommendation for the use of major environmental supports or other
modifications in psychotherapy (Kernberg, 1975a). On the other hand,
he warns against supportive psychotherapy for schizoid patients. Narcissistic patients with different types of functioning warrant different
types of treatment.

Recommendations for Patient Subgroups

Kernberg recommends expressive psychoanalytic psychotherapy,
incorporating his modifications, for patients with borderline personality
organization, including patients with narcissistic personality disorder
who function on an overt borderline level. That is, the pathological self-
structure in some narcissistic patients is sufficiently stable to allow the
patient to function without the impulsiveness, chaotic relationships and
general manifestations of ego weakness that characterize borderline
functioning. Others, especially those who present with narcissistic rage,
function in a manner similar to borderline patients (Kernberg, 1975a,
1980a,c).

For patients with narcissistic personality disorders, Kernberg recommends unmodified psychoanalysis if at all possible. Without the analytic
setting, such patients tend to remain shallow, empty, and uninvested in
the treatment and do not develop very meaningful transference reactions. Even if they do undertake analysis, however, they may wish to
stop the treatment after amelioration of some of their more painful experiences of envy or disruptive impulsiveness, feeling content to remain
somewhat shallow and unempathic. At such times, the analyst may need
to shift to a partially supportive technique to help the patient maintain a
better adaptation by protecting some of the narcissistic defenses when
these cannot all be worked through (Kernberg, 1975a, 1979a).

Some cases present the following contraindications for expressive
psychotherapy: (1) inability to work verbally with symbolic material; (2)
a combination of low motivation and high secondary gain; (3) severe negative therapeutic reaction; (4) severe cases of antisocial personality, so
that the therapist cannot assume the patient will be honest even most of
the time; and (5) life circumstances that prevent the patient from the frequency of sessions required for expressive treatment (usually two or

three times a week). These contraindications can include patients from across the diagnostic spectrum, although the more disturbed borderline, narcissistic, and psychotic patients will fall into the first four categories more often. Such patients should be treated with a frankly supportive treatment, with rational, concrete treatment goals. The therapist should represent a commonsense point of view, making suggestions, consulting with family members if necessary, and should interpret primitive defenses and conscious negative transference only in the context of showing how these create difficulties in the patient's life. Idealization of the therapist should be discussed only if it interferes with the work, for example, by inhibiting the patient's questions or disagreements. The major focus is on clear life goals. There are some patients who simply need a lifelong supportive relationship, but this alternative should be chosen only after other treatments have been ruled out (Kernberg, 1980e, 1982i, g). Kernberg (1977b) has also discussed indications and technique for brief psychotherapies.

There are two groups of patients who do not do well with supportive treatment, according to Kernberg. These are well-functioning schizoid individuals, who would enter and leave a supportive therapy untouched by the human interaction, and certain narcissistic patients who are lonely, isolated, and empty. These characteristics are unlikely to change without exploration in detail of the primitive defenses and representations of self and others that contribute to the shadowy quality of personality conveyed by these patients. Patients who cannot experience much empathy for others cannot learn to do so without the development of higher-order, more complex representations of self and others interacting. For these patients—narcissistic patients functioning on a borderline level and most patients with borderline personality organization—Kernberg (1980e, 1982d, i, g) recommends his modified, expressive psychotherapy.

Rationale for Technical Recommendations

Kernberg proposes that the model of development and psychopathology summarized earlier explains the behavior of severely disturbed patients in various types of treatment as well as processes in the traditional psychoanalysis of healthier, neurotic patients. The structural differences between borderline and neurotic patients cause them to respond differently to classical psychoanalytic technique. Neurotic patients, who have a well-formed tripartite structure, suffer from intrapsychic conflict usually conceptualized as conflict among id, ego, and superego or between conflicting, higher-order, relatively well-integrated identifications that represent various compromise solutions to the basic conflicts. Kernberg (1980b) lays particular stress on this last point, insisting that there is no impulse-defense configuration without an implied object relationship within which these defenses and impulses are expressed. Borderline patients have primitive intrapsychic structures, which have not been consolidated into the tripartite structure but instead have various split-off self-object-affect units, so that these patients have little awareness that the loved and hated object is one and the same. Their defenses are primitive and tend to weaken, rather than protect, the ego; and the superego is close to being an internal persecutor, rather than a depersonified source of values and self-esteem. Id material may be conscious.

In the psychoanalysis of neurotic patients, defenses are interpreted as they are manifested as resistances, with a gradual unfolding of a regressive transference neurosis, which reveals the conflicts that create the patients' problems. Such patients' defenses may be less than optimally adaptive, but they do protect the ego; hence, their interpretation and undoing represents a stress that only patients with intact ego functions can withstand. Id material becomes available only after considerable work, and impulsive action is brief. As infantile conflicts are resolved, more flexible and efficient defenses come into being.

When borderline patients are treated with standard psychoanalytic technique, the absence of external structure to support reality-testing functions tends to lead to rapid emergence of primary process material, transference psychosis, or, at least, intense early transference reactions prior to the development of any kind of working alliance. Thus, Kernberg (1982d, 1983) feels a need for a clear distinction between psychoanalysis proper and modifications of technique that might be termed "psychoanalytic psychotherapy."

When patients with good ego strength are treated with one of the psychoanalytic psychotherapies, the results are good in terms of behavioral change and alteration in character traits (although not character structure). Kernberg believes this is a direct result of these patients' greater ego strength and capacity to develop a relationship in which they can accept help. However, when borderline patients are treated with a type of psychotherapy that seeks to interpret only certain defenses or to avoid interpretation of the negative transference, the patients' severe psychological problems persist, and a chronically shallow treatment relationship often develops, with acting out elsewhere in the patient's life.

In severe psychopathologies, in Kernberg's (1980b) view, "what appear to be inappropriate, primitive, chaotic character traits and interpersonal interactions, impulsive behavior, and affect storms are actually reflections of the fantastic early object-relations-derived structures that are the building blocks of the later tripartite system" (p.

187). These are not reflections of actual early relationships, in most cases, but of their distorted internalization and continuation in the intrapsychic world without integration into more accurate, complex representations and more mature intrapsychic structures. Ego weakness results from the persistence of the defenses of splitting and of primitive forms of projection, denial, idealization, and devaluation. Thus, pathology is seen as resulting from conflicts and defenses rather than from a deficit.

Kernberg believes that the poor results when borderline patients are treated with psychotherapy are due to the interaction of their pathological structures with the therapeutic techniques. He makes the following argument:

1. Since patients with borderline pathology suffer from ego weakness as a result of their primitive defenses, systematic interpretation of defenses is indicated to strengthen the ego. Interpretation of defenses will not lead to regression, but will aid the patient's capacity to observe and begin to integrate the defensively split S-O-A units.

2. Emphasis on developing a positive transference or providing the patient with a benign model for identification does not accomplish its goal with seriously disturbed patients. Borderline patients typically present strong negative, often paranoid, transferences at some point in the treatment as the negatively experienced S-O-A units are activated in the therapeutic relationship. More often than not, they will be unable to identify with the therapist's healthy ego without some interpretation and resolution of their negative transferences. Without this, or with avoidance of negative transference material, the therapist-patient dyad may simply come to be a reenactment of one of the positively experienced S-O-A units, while other parts of the patient's personality are expressed outside the treatment. The treatment is rendered shallow and meaningless and has little effect on the patient's life.

3. Interventions that would gratify some of the patient's transference demands, made with the idea of lessening pressure on the weak ego, fail to help the patient, but rather tend to support the enactment of one side of the patient's conflicts as a defense against a perception of the therapist as evil or devalued. Hence, such interventions contribute to the patient's distortions of the treatment situation. With healthier patients, gratification of transference wishes is likely to have a more benign effect, as the patient's capacity to use what is good and to identify with a good parental figure is not so distorted (Kernberg, 1980b, p. 194).

4. Since borderline patients present conscious conflicts that may involve primitive drive content, efforts to avoid "deep" material are misguided. The therapist's avoidance of impulses that are conscious and

troubling to the patient would tend to reinforce the patient's fear of these impulses and tendency to express them outside the treatment.

Kernberg therefore recommends a modified form of expressive psychotherapy, not psychoanalysis proper, for most borderline patients. Kernberg's suggestions may be summarized as follows:

Interpretation. Interpretation and clarification, rather than suggestion and manipulation, are the major technical tools to be used. Very often, however, the patient's interpretation of the interpretations or other remarks must be explored, and this may often require the therapist to clarify what he or she meant, as opposed to the patient's distorted perception of what was said. Kernberg (1980b, p. 196; 1982g) believes that with these patients, such clarifications will be more frequent than interpretations, thereby giving a different emphasis to the treatment.

Maintenance of Technical Neutrality. To be able to use interpretation, suggestion and manipulation are contraindicated, and technical neutrality should be maintained as far as possible. However, severely disturbed patients are often unable to observe the inappropriateness of their behavior (for example, repeated verbal attacks on the therapist) or may act in such a way as to endanger their lives or the treatment. It may be necessary to structure the treatment or the patient's life. For example, one might forbid shouting at the therapist, beyond a certain point, in a patient who does not seem to be able to reflect in any way on the meaning of this behavior and who, on the contrary, experiences some drive discharge and then seems unconcerned about this aggression. Limiting this behavior would tend to make the patient anxious and might advance the treatment. Or patients may be asked to live in a halfway house or to meet with another professional who would monitor the patient's activities and give advice, freeing the therapist from the need to "take over" in this way so that an interpretive approach could still be maintained. These interventions would be introduced, ideally, as parameters (Eissler, 1953), gradually eliminated, and their effect interpreted as the therapist seeks to return to a position of technical neutrality. Less dramatic deviations will occur in every session, when the therapist has to clarify the patient's distortions of reality and, in so doing, momentarily takes over an ego function and moves away from a neutral position.

Transference Analysis. Transference analysis will be partial because of the need for simultaneous consideration of the patient's life situation and treatment goals. In addition, genetic reconstructions are possible only very late in the treatment, if at all; earlier transference interpretations should have a hypothetical quality ("You are acting as if you feel I am a cruel father figure whom you anxiously need to placate"), to avoid premature assumptions about the reality of the patient's childhood experience. This is necessary to deal with the many shifting and fantastic S-O-A units activated in the transference, not all of which will represent actual parent-child interactions. This interferes with actual reconstruction; however, over the course of treatment, as these structures become more integrated, part-object relations and part-object transferences should be transformed into more mature relationships and transferences.

Kernberg suggests a face-to-face therapy that adheres as closely as possible to classical analytic technique, within the constraints imposed by the differences that have been noted between psychoanalysis and this type of psychoanalytic psychotherapy. In addition, the therapist should try to clarify the use of splitting and the nature of the various S-O-A units that will be reenacted recurringly in the treatment. When doing this, it is important to focus on both the current reactivation and the one against which it functions as a defense. Thus, even in the course of discussing a patient's hostile transference attitude, the therapist should note other signs of positive feeling (for example, the patient abuses the therapist, but comes faithfully on time to do so) — the more so because such positive attitudes may form the basis for a working alliance. The cognitive aspect of such interpretations is directed at the patient's capacity to develop an observing ego and does not contribute to intellectualization or rationalization, according to Kernberg. Rather, in primitively organized patients, cognition is close to affect and psychic structures and helps to organize the patient's chaotic experience. In addition, such comments occur in the context of the therapist's attempt to render a confused, distant, or fragmentary patient-therapist interaction a meaningful human experience, even though it may be based on bizarre fantasies in the patient's mind (Kernberg, 1975a, 1979b, 1980b, c, 1982g).

The Therapeutic Stance

In psychotherapeutic treatment of seriously disturbed patients, Kernberg suggests, nonverbal aspects of the patient's communication play a larger role than they do in the treatment of healthier patients. Patients with borderline or schizophrenic conditions may manifest nonverbal behavior that is at odds with their remarks as a result of the use of splitting. Or they may express an S-O-A unit through attempts to induce the therapist to play one of the roles in this unit, attempts that may be conveyed through nonverbal means or through the use of words for their emotional effect. Kernberg (1975a, 1977c) recommends that the therapist follow Bion's (1965, 1967, 1970) idea of the analyst as a "container," to try to integrate within himself or herself the disparate elements the patient presents, in order to articulate the patient's current experience and defenses in the transference. The analyst's willingness to tolerate great confusion, fragmentation, and aggression in the patient, while actively seeking to explore it—thereby conveying an attitude of hope and acceptance—makes possible the treatment of very seriously disturbed patients.

In a similar vein, Kernberg (1976a, 1981a) is a major proponent of what he terms the "totalistic" view of countertransference, in which countertransference is defined as "the total emotional reaction of the psychoanalyst to the patient in the treatment situation" (1975a, p. 49). While advocating the resolution of countertransference reactions, Kernberg stresses the importance of examining one's reactions for information about the patient, a view characteristic of Kleinian and interpersonalist theories. Kernberg claims that with more seriously disturbed patients, the therapist's reactions have more to do with his or her general capacity to tolerate stress and anxiety than with the therapist's neurotic needs. Since the patient often presents a very chaotic picture, the therapist's attempt to maintain empathic contact with the patient through partial identifications may lead to some regression in the therapist's ability to function (Kernberg, 1975a, 1977c). Kernberg (1977c, 1981a) also describes very meaningfully the experience of a therapist in a stalemated treatment effort, and offers suggestions for the resolution of chronic impasses.

GROUPS AND INSTITUTIONS

Kernberg's ideas about hospital treatment and psychotherapy and his creative application of psychoanalytic thinking to psychiatric settings are based on his views about group and institutional processes. Although less well known, his papers on these topics reflect a deep awareness of the complexities of group life.

Analysis of Group and Institutional Processes

Following in the tradition of Miller and Rice (1967; Rice, 1965, 1967) and building on the contributions of Freud and the British object relations group theorists such as Bion (1959), Kernberg has sought to apply a psychoanalytically sophisticated open-systems theory to group and institutional processes. He proposes that the tendency for normal individuals to behave and think regressively in unstructured or large groups is due to the threat to personal identity posed by such groups. This threat arises because such groups activate primitive internalized object relations in their members, with associated primitive defenses and intense, pregenital, aggressive and sexual impulses (Kernberg, 1980b).

In order to understand institutional functioning, it is necessary to examine the institution's task, the resources available to it for this task, and the structure of authority and responsibility in the institution. Kernberg (1973, 1975b, 1980c) discusses, for example, three types of problems that prevent the accomplishment of an institution's task: (1) the nature of the task may be unclear or contradictory, or the task may be seen to be impossible when it is clearly defined; (2) the administrative structure, that is, the structure that controls and maintains the institution's internal and external boundaries, may be unsuitable for the institution's task, or the organization may be structured to meet the emotional needs of administrators or staff, not to perform the task; and (3) psychopathology in the leader or leaders within the institution may hinder the accomplishment of the organization's task.

Kernberg's contributions in this area have focused particularly on the dilemmas of leadership and the interaction between leaders and groups or institutions. The leader is the individual who manages the boundaries of the group—its time, membership, agenda, and utilization of resources—so it can carry out its task. Because groups exist within organizations and consist of individuals who themselves contain intrapsychic structures at different levels of organization, leaders must be aware of boundary issues throughout these levels. In contrast to Miller's (1969) view of systems as hierarchically arranged in, as it were, concentric circles (society, institution, division of the institution, individual, intrapsychic structures, and internalized object relations), Kernberg takes the position that hierarchies in most group situations, cannot be reduced to this one-dimensional model. Usually the leader must control the group's contact with nonconcentric sets of systems that impinge on the group in different ways. In therapeutic settings, in addition to administrative and political pressures on task definition and resources, professional, personal and technical value systems are influential (Kernberg, 1975b). Kernberg suggests that the best way for a leader—particularly the leader of a therapy group or hospital community—to understand the effect of these pressures and responsibilities on the group, is to observe his or her own emotional and cognitive experience in the group. This view is similar to Kernberg's espousal of the usefulness of countertransference (defined broadly) in individual psychotherapy.

Regressive pressures on staff members in organizations lead to a tendency to attribute the causes of institutional problems to the leader's incompetence or personality, so that the individual may defend against awareness of problems with the institution's task or structure. Organizational pressures can affect the leader's personality functioning, however, and some institutional problems are created by individuals with particular types of psychopathology who actively seek positions of authority. Hence, organizational consultants must combine the ability to define tasks and assess institutional structures with the capacity to assess the personal qualities of leaders from a psychoanalytic perspective (Kernberg, 1980b).

Hospital Treatment

Kernberg recommends hospitalization to protect the patient who might otherwise irreparably damage his or her life, career, or relationships and to protect psychoanalytic psychotherapy by allowing the therapist to maintain a position of technical neutrality, aside from the recommendation for hospitalization. This might be necessary with a patient who had the capacity to benefit from an expressive psychotherapy but who also needed external guidance and support. Hospitalization or a period of residence in a halfway house would then serve to prepare the patient for outpatient treatment in which the patient will take responsibility for his or her own life and would in other respects maintain a therapeutic alliance. Some patients immediately threaten the continuation of their psychotherapy with impulsive behavior, attempts to control the therapist, or attempts to force the therapist to take responsibility for the patient's life. In some such cases, an initial period of hospitalization may help to clarify the patient's psychological strengths and weaknesses (Kernberg, 1975a, 1976, 1981d, 1982b).

The group activities, rules, and regulations and the multiple, new interactions in which the patient must engage in the hospital provide a way to diagnose the patient's pathological internal object relations. The combination of psychopathology in the patient and the many group situations in the hospital allows the patient to replicate his or her internal conflicts in the social field (Kernberg, 1973, 1976). Kernberg (1973, 1975b, 1981d, e, 1982a) gives an outline for hospital administration which provides a structure that maximizes the staff's ability to gather and utilize such data therapeutically. The hospital psychotherapist might then use such data to help patients explore the internal conflicts that are causing them to act a certain way in the hospital. For example, borderline or schizophrenic patients may quickly develop opposite relationships with different subgroups of staff, based on their defensive use of splitting, with the tendency to create in the external world the "good" and "bad" internalized object relationships that comprise their psychic worlds. Kernberg (1973, 1976) has also provided detailed, sophisticated suggestions on the role of the various modalities of treatment (the milieu, groups, nursing and medical management, activities, and hospital psychotherapy of various kinds, with or without a separation between the therapist and administrator) in the psychoanalytic hospital. Underlying his recommendations is the assumption that unmistakable evidence of the staff's respect and concern for the patient is a crucial element in hospitalization, since patients who are hospitalized are those who do not have sufficient respect or concern for themselves to manage their lives. Ideally, through the hospitalization, the patient will develop a therapeutic alliance that will sustain outpatient psychotherapy. This change occurs, in part, because so many aspects of hospitalization are clearly and realistically helpful, in contrast to the patient's fantasied, transference distortions (Kernberg, 1973).

THE THEORY OF AFFECTS AND DRIVES

We will conclude this summary of Kernberg's contributions with his theory of drives and affects, which in many ways is his most carefully considered theoretical statement. We have already summarized Kernberg's model of the developmental stages of internalized object relations, the final phase of which is the integration of contradictory S-O-A units into complex perceptions of self and other, and the maturation of ego and superego into adaptive structures. We consider Kernberg's theory of drives and affects separately, even though it is intended to fit into the developmental model, because it represents an additional focus in his work in which he interprets neurophysiological data and reexamines the dual instinct theory (Kernberg, 1976, 1980d, 1982d, h).

Kernberg proposes that

> the units of internalized object relations (the S-O-A units) constitute subsystems on the basis of which both drives and the overall psychic structures of ego, superego and id are organized as integrating systems. Instincts (represented by psychologically organized drive systems) and the overall psychic structures (id, ego, superego) then become component systems of the personality at large, which constitutes the suprasystem. In turn, the units of internalized object relations themselves constitute an integrating system for subsystems represented by inborn perceptive and behavior patterns, affect dispositions, neurovegetative discharge patterns, and nonspecific arousal mechanisms [p. 85].

Kernberg (1976) states that by conceptualizing the elements of this theory as subsystems and suprasystems, he avoids proposing "a neurophysiological model of the mind or a mechanical model of body-mind equivalence" (p. 86). Thus, he speaks of hierarchies of organized systems. At some point, however, there is a shift from "neurophysiologically based functions" and "physiological units," (which would refer to changes in electrical patterns or neurotransmitters) to the integration of these units into a "higher system represented by purely intrapsychic structures, namely, the primitive units of internalized object relations (self-object-affect units)" (p. 86). These units are themselves eventually integrated into id, ego, and superego.

"Affect dispositions," which are inborn and determined by brain functioning, constitute primary motivational systems, in that they represent dispositions to the subjective experience of pleasure and unpleasure. These affect dispositions "integrate the perception of (1) central (pleasurable or unpleasurable) states [that is, perception in the central nervous system], (2) physiological discharge phenomena, (3) inborn perceptive and behavior patterns, and (4) environmental responses" (Kernberg, 1976, p. 87). The Freudian concept of instinct may be included here. Affective patterns communicate the infant's needs to the mother and thereby initiate interactions, which are stored as memory traces with affective and cognitive components. "Affects are the primary motivational system, in the sense that they are at the center of each of the infinite number of gratifying and frustrating events the infant experiences with his environment" (Kernberg, 1982h, p. 907), each of which leads to an internalized object relation, fixed by memory.

Affect and cognition evolve together at first because their respective memory traces are integrated in affective memory (Kernberg, 1976), but eventually differentiation of pleasurable and unpleasurable experiences and of components of self and other takes place. At this point, Kernberg (1982h) asserts, the "good" and "bad" experiences generate the overall organization of motivational systems, which we term love and hate.

Kernberg (1982h) then suggests that love and hate become stable intrapsychic structures, "in genetic continuity through various developmental stages" (p. 908), which can be equated with the psychoanalytic concepts of the two drive systems, libido and aggression. At this stage of organization, affects serve a signal function for the two drives, and increasingly complex subjective, behavioral, and cognitive elaborations of affects and drives develop. Drives will always be manifested by specific wishes in the context of particular object relations, a phenomenon that is more precisely articulated than an affect state.

Kernberg's (1976) theory deals with economic issues as follows: Variations in the intensity of drives or affects can be attributed to either constitutional variations in the innate components of the system (the hypothalamus, genetically determined behavioral patterns, etc.), or to variations in the environment (the responses of the mother and so forth). Neutralization (Hartmann, 1955) takes place when positively and negatively valenced self-object-affect units are combined to form more complex and realistic self- and object representations with the achievement of the depressive position. Kernberg (1976) writes: "*The synthesis of identification systems neutralizes aggression and possibly provides the most important single energy source for the higher level of repressive mechanisms to come*, and implicitly, for the development of secondary autonomy in general" (pp. 45–46, italics in original). What Hartmann termed fusion of drives is also included, according to Kernberg, in the combination or integration of opposing affects as part of the integration of contradictory S-O-A units. Similarly, sublimation is not simply a change in the use of drive derivatives in an economic sense; it, too, has an object relations component: Sublimatory activity requires the capacity for some whole, integrated object relationships, some genuine concern for oneself and others (Kernberg, 1975a, p. 134). Nonetheless, despite the importance Kernberg assigns object relations in his theory of affects and drives, he also argues for the importance of aggressive drive manifestations and the biologically based changes in drives, which influence object relations (as in the genital strivings of the oedipal period). Thus, he claims to support the proposition that drives, rather than object relations, constitute the primary motivational system of the organism.

DISCUSSION

We will now offer commentary on the contributions of Kernberg that we have attempted to summarize. Since we are not here comparing Kernberg's positions with those of other analysts, such as Kohut or Brenner, we will restrict ourselves to a critical discussion of Kernberg's clinical and theoretical work.

At the very least, Kernberg has synthesized a good deal of the clinical observations of the object relations school and helped to develop a nosology that orders these observations. Thus, for example, Guntrip's (1968, 1971) or Fairbairn's (1952) observations of the schizoid person fit nicely into Kernberg's conceptualization of one type of patient with borderline personality structure. Kernberg is able to show how some of the writings of Winnicott (1965, 1975), Melanie Klein (1946), Balint (1968), and even Greenson (1954) can be understood within his concept of the borderline personality. His way of thinking about the levels of severity of character pathology, based in part on object relations concepts, may prove to be extremely useful. In addition, he has integrated the British object relations school's stress on aggression into his clinical and technical writings in a way that helpfully underscores the importance of dealing with aggression, both in clinical situations and in theory development.

We consider it a strength of Kernberg's writings that he frequently relates his theoretical points to observable clinical phenomena. For example, he has not only shown in his attempts at theoretical integration how a variety of authors (Balint, 1968; Fairbairn, 1952; Frosch, 1960; Greenson, 1954; Guntrip, 1968, 1971; M. Klein, 1946; Schmideberg, 1947; Winnicott, 1965, 1975) refer to the use of primitive defenses such as splitting and projective identification by borderline patients (using Kernberg's definition of borderline, not necessarily those authors' own), but he has also sought to describe how one might infer the use of splitting or projective identification by a patient in a clinical interview. Similarly, he is willing to claim that practical consequences follow from his theoretical assumptions about diagnosis and particularly from assessment of level of defensive functioning. This willingness to make predictions makes it easier for other investigators to test his inferences and conclusions. As an example, Kernberg is remarkably specific and detailed in relating prognosis and choice of psychological treatment method to diagnosis based on his nosology. A patient suffering from a narcissistic personality disorder, without overt borderline-level functioning, should be treated with unmodified psychoanalysis; a patient with narcissistic personality disorder who functions overtly on a borderline level should be treated with Kernberg's modified psychoanalytic psychotherapy. The same types of patients might require a shift to a supportive type of psychotherapy at some point in the analysis or psychotherapy, but this would not result in the type of change to be expected from psychoanalysis or from Kernberg's modified form of psychoanalytic psychotherapy. Some narcissistic patients present negative prognostic features (severe antisocial features, conscious enjoyment of others' suffering, chronic absence of human involvement, etc.), which indicate a need for supportive psychotherapy from the onset (Kernberg, 1975a, 1979a, 1980c, 1982g, i).

To summarize at this point, Kernberg's achievements in the areas of clinical writing and observations seem particularly impressive:

1. He has synthesized the writings of a number of authors, particularly those of the British object relations school but also including Jacobson and Mahler, and shown how their clinical observations can be conceptualized in the context of his definition of the borderline personality organization.

2. He has added a number of his own clinical observations and worked out a detailed classificatory system, particularly for character

pathology and the borderline personality, within a five-level structure for describing the full range of psychopathology.

3. He has specified a method of interviewing with stated criteria derived from the interview, through which one can reach complex diagnostic determinations.

4. He has related his diagnostic categories to choice of treatment and to prognostic statements about therapy outcomes.

Kernberg has covered a vast territory in his clinical writings, and he covers it in a systematic fashion. We must join other writers (Calef & Weinshel, 1979), however, in wondering how he is able to make so many prognostic statements with such assurance.[3] His level of specificity is rare in our field and it would be virtually impossible for Kernberg to have personally diagnosed and treated (and treated to the point of termination, in order to substantiate prognostic claims) all the different types and subtypes of patients that are the subjects of his classification system, treatment recommendations, and prognostic statements. Thus, his prognostic statements, for example, must come from a combination of research findings, consultations, supervision, and his experience of being involved in and directing a variety of clinical facilities.

Does Kernberg base his prognostic statements on research findings (Kernberg et al, 1972) from the Menninger outcome studies or on his impressive clinical experience? It is often difficult to tell, but most often he writes with the assurance and precision of someone who has a great deal of empirical research to buttress his points. He understandably does not give extensive clinical examples, that is, complete case studies, for if he did, given the range of categories and subcategories he discusses, he would literally fill our journals with clinical examples. Though it is beyond the scope of our chapter to evaluate the major outcome research with which he has been involved, we believe that Kernberg would acknowledge that his assurance about all his prognostic statements could not reasonably be based on this research. Moreover, although this research is of great interest, it is by no means free from serious methodological criticisms, which affect the types of prognostic statements Kernberg has made. It is our assumption, then, that a number of Kernberg's statements and recommendations are based on his clinical experience.

Given that this is the case, it is understandable that Kernberg has been criticized (Calef & Weinshel, 1979) for his tone in his clinical writings. He writes as if he has sound evidence for his assertions, but, at

---

[3]Although in one recent paper Kernberg (1982i) notes the necessity for caution in such statements and urges further research, the preponderance of his writings imply greater surety about these matters.

least up to this point, he has not fully indicated the nature and extent of his evidence. We join in the criticism that has been leveled at Kernberg in this area, but we wish to note what we believe are two mitigating considerations. First, one can criticize any number of psychoanalytic authors for writing as if something had been "demonstrated," when they were really stating their views based on, perhaps very interesting, but nevertheless limited, clinical observations. Second, unlike the types of statements made by many other psychoanalytic authors, Kernberg's statements are in a form that makes them potentially testable (although to test his assertions would require a very elaborate and difficult research undertaking).

A number of analysts have criticized Kernberg's clinical concepts on other grounds than those we have noted. Although it is beyond the scope of this exposition to enter into the type of detailed criticism leveled by, for example, Calef and Weinshel (1979) or implied by the type of reconciliation between Kohut and Kernberg attempted by Stolorow and Lachman (1980), we will comment briefly on Calef and Weinshel's critique.

We believe that Calef and Weinshel have brought up interesting and potentially devastating criticisms. They include the ones we have previously discussed, and, most seriously, they cast doubt on the validity of Kernberg's contention that there are people with a *stable* personality organization which he has labeled borderline. (A related criticism, that Kernberg claims premature diagnostic closure in a very complex area, which still needs further exploration, is offered by Sugarman and Lerner (1980). Calef and Weinshel also feel that Kernberg's concepts tend to dilute basic psychoanalytic concepts such as regression, and the very idea of intrapsychic conflict. However, a central point in their critique is their attempt to question the borderline concept itself. They criticize Kernberg for discarding the idea of a continuum that would include borderline and psychotic conditions and for maintaining that conventional reality testing is either present or absent. Instead, Calef and Weinshel (1979) conclude that "the relativity of reality testing . . . makes it a difficult area to establish hard and fast, categorical, isolated criteria for the diagnosis of a psychosis" (p. 485) and, by extension, makes it difficult to delineate people with borderline personality organization from people who are psychotic.

With respect to Calef and Weinshel's criticisms, we would comment that many of their points could be framed and tested or could at least be subject to empirical observation. We would hope that if they are serious critics, they would endeavor to spell out the empirical justification for some of their criticism. It hardly seems enough to doubt Kernberg's observations. We are not asserting that they are necessarily mistaken about some of their points, but that, they should attempt, as Stone

(1980), for instance, has done, a more clinically and empirically oriented approach to some of their criticism. To criticize Kernberg's categorical formulation of the concept of reality testing, they might offer data that support a continuum approach. Stone (1980) has provided examples of interviews in which assessment of structure according to Kernberg's criteria was extremely problematic, particularly in patients with unusual types of affective illness or in recovering schizophrenic patients, leading him to suggest that reality testing is not dichotomous in all situations. Our criticism of Calef and Weinshel is that at times they seem to come close to simply saying Kernberg is wrong because he is not "psychoanalytic."

This brings us to consideration of criticisms of Kernberg's theoretical endeavors. Calef and Weinshel state that Kernberg's theoretical position is close to, if not actually, a paradigm shift from classical Freudian and ego psychoanalytic theories.[4] Within the limits of their article, however, they do not present convincing logical arguments for their assertion.

The question of Kernberg's theoretical position is taken up more centrally in a paper by Klein and Tribich (1981). In this article, Klein and Tribich are not specifically concerned with the idea of a paradigm shift, but they state that from their point of view, "Kernberg's raprochement between Freudian instinct theory and object-relations theory obscures the differences between these two competing theories without taking any recognition of their differences" (p. 41). As is the case with Calef and Weinshel (who criticize Kernberg's more clinical positions), Klein and Tribich raise fundamental questions concerning Kernberg's theoretical positions. For example, they maintain that Kernberg's dismissal of "Bowlby, Fairbairn, Guntrip, and Winnicott is not based on any scientific discussion of their theories but on the fact that these theories reject Freudian motivational theory" (p. 41). We will not fully explore Klein and Tribich's criticisms here, but we can comment that we find it strange to maintain that Kernberg rejects all these theories. This in fact is not the case; Kernberg does attempt to integrate aspects of Fairbairn, Guntrip, and Winnicott into his theoretical and clinical writings.

Before discussing more substantive criticisms of Kernberg's theoretical work, however, we would like to expand our introductory comments on the state of psychoanalytic theory and theoretical criticism. As we implied, we believe that much of the work in both areas leaves something to be desired, when considered from the point of view of philosophy of science. Because the standards for criticism typically seem to be

_____

[4]We are considering the psychoanalytic version of ego psychology or the structural view as part of the classical theory.

so subjective (Ellman & Moskowitz, 1980; Moskowitz & Ellman, 1983), any new psychoanalytic theoretical proposal or integration is vulnerable. We believe this statement applies as we have noted, to some of Calef and Weinshel's comments, and we would suggest that it applies also to some, although not all, of Klein and Tribich's remarks. It can be useful to discuss how one theorist's use of a concept differs from another theorist's, but this does not constitute a criticism, unless one discovers logical fallacies within the system or data that contradict the theory. To criticize Kernberg for differing with Freud, for example, is not a theoretical criticism, but a value judgment.

However, we must also tender this and some other general criticisms in consideration of some of Kernberg's writings. We think that his points would be clearer if he would place greater emphasis on stating his definitions, assumptions, and positions and less on cataloging theorists with whom he agrees or disagrees. The clarity of the presentation of Kernberg's theoretical propositions sometimes suffers from his tendency to give such qualified and complex statements that it becomes difficult to use his theoretical assertions to make definite predictions. In addition, the "catalogs" of theorists give Kernberg's theoretical work somewhat of an arbitrary feeling, akin to what we believe is an arbitrariness in the writings of some of his critics, which seems to imply, "If you disagree with so and so, then you are not psychoanalytic and, therefore, you are wrong." This type of comment, although all too prevalent in psychoanalytic writings, is not up to Kernberg's standards. We would thus have to agree with Klein and Tribich (1981, p. 39) when they criticize Kernberg's rejection of Guntrip for his "emotionally charged" attacks on instinct theory. Furthermore, we feel that Kernberg does not have a strong position from which to censure another theorist for deviating from classical psychoanalytic instinct theory.

A philosophical approach to the critical review of Kernberg's theoretical contributions would deal with different types of issues. We would wish to examine questions such as the following: How well does Kernberg integrate object relations theory with Freudian theory? Aside from consideration of various psychoanalytic traditions, does Kernberg have a well-integrated theoretical position? And, in a more general sense, is Kernberg's theory a good theory, according to the requirements of theory making such as logical structure, rules of inference, and so forth (Nagel, 1961; Popper, 1962)? We would submit that no psychoanalytic theorist's work could withstand this type of scrutiny. Hence, again, the harsh tone of some of the criticism directed at Kernberg seems unwarranted.

It would be useful, however, to discuss briefly some of Kernberg's contributions from the standpoint of these questions to suggest directions for further work. We will comment on Kernberg's instinct theory, since he claims that in this work he integrates classical drive theory and object relations concepts as well as newer data from neurophysiological studies. It is thus appropriate to ask how well he succeeds in this theoretical integration. This question is separate from comments about the validity, elegance, or heuristic value of Kernberg's theory and from questions about whether or not it is "psychoanalytic."

In his discussion of instinct theory, Kernberg (1982h) goes over a familiar but nevertheless important point: Freud's term *trieb*, which is usually rendered as "instinct," may more reasonably be translated as "drive." Kernberg is pointing out, as have others (Bibring, 1969; Hartmann, 1964; Holder, 1970; Schur, 1966), that by instinct Freud did not mean a fixed, prewired, behavioral pattern (which is more of an ethological idea). Rather, in his concept of instinct or drive, a variety of behaviors or mental events might emerge as a result of internal stimuli or excitation. Kernberg's substantive attempt is to link or translate Freud's ideas into modern neurophysiological and neurobehavioral concepts. It is, again, beyond the scope of this chapter to discuss fully this aspect of Kernberg's writings, but in summarizing Kernberg's ideas we hope to give a sense of his position and our evaluation of this position.

Kernberg (1976) places affect dispositions at the center of his statements on motivation. He concludes:

> Affect dispositions constitute the primary motivational systems which integrate the perception of (1) central (pleasurable or unpleasurable) states, (2) physiological discharge phenomena, (3) inborn perceptive and behavior patterns, and (4) environmental responses as they impinge on specialized and general extroceptive and introceptive perceptions. The earliest "self-object-affect" units are, I suggest, constellations of affectively integrated and cognitively stored perceptions of affective, physiological, behavioral, and environmental changes—perceptions within which the "self" and "nonself" components are as yet undifferentiated [p. 87].

In this passage, Kernberg is attempting to link what he considers to be Freudian psychoanalytic theoretical statements with neurophysiological statements through the use of an object relations perspective. He goes on to specifically include MacLean's (1967, 1972) model of three concentric brains as being relevant to the way he conceives of instinct as developing in the human being

> gradually out of the assembly of these "building blocks," so that the series of pleasurable affect-determined units and the series of unpleasurable affect-determined units gradually evolve into the libidinally invested and aggressively invested constellations of psychic drive systems—that is, into libido and aggression, respectively, as the two major psychological drives. In other words, affects are at first primary organizers of instinc-

tive components such as specialized extroceptive perception and innate behavior patterns and, later on, constitute the "signal" activator of the organized hierarchy of "instinctually" determined behavior [pp. 87–88].

These two quotes give a reasonable flavor of the complexity and direction of Kernberg's ideas on instinct. We believe that, in fact, his theoretical compilation places him substantively closer to Bowlby (1969, 1973, 1980) and perhaps even Fairbairn and Guntrip than to Freud. Central to Freud's (1915) ideas about instinct is the formulation that it is generated internally and that the instincts appear "as a constant force" (p. 119). Nowhere in Kernberg's writings do we see this essential aspect of Freud's concept that instincts provide a form of constant internal stimulation that makes substantial demands on the nervous system. To quote Freud (1915):

Instinctual stimuli, which orginate from within the organism, cannot be dealt with by this mechanism. Thus they make far higher demands on the nervous system and cause it to undertake involved and interconnected activities by which the external world is so changed as to afford satisfaction to the internal source of stimulation. Above all, they oblige the nervous system to renounce its ideal intention of keeping off stimuli, for they maintain an incessant and unavoidable afflux of stimulation. We may therefore well conclude that instincts and not external stimuli are the true motive forces behind the advances that have led the nervous system, with its unlimited capacities, to its present high level of development. There is naturally nothing to prevent our supposing that the instincts themselves are, at least in part, precipitates of the effects of external stimulation, which in the course of phylogenesis have brought about modifications in the living substance [p. 120].

We have included this long quote from Freud in an attempt to capture what we believe is a subtle but nevertheless important difference between Freud and Kernberg's concept of instincts. Certainly from at least 1915 on, Freud stressed the internal or endogenous nature of the instincts, not only as a motivational concept but also, in higher-level organisms (particularly primates), as a system that stimulated the development of the central nervous itself. Thus, the infant's and child's task of "mastering" internal or endogenous stimulation is in fact a central task. Clearly, environmental factors can make this task easier or harder, and clearly the environment is important in development, but the "constant pressure" of endogenous stimuli will be there regardless of the type of "instinctual building blocks" that are present in the infant's environment. If we take Kernberg seriously in his attempted neurophysiological integration, then he is moving toward more of an environmentalist position than Freud held. By and large, Kernberg does not see endogenous stimulation as a central concern. Hence, in this area of his theorizing, he has not really integrated Freud's position into his own.

We would say that, in general, Kernberg has not fully integrated the various positions he uses; that critics (Calef and Weinshel, Klein and Tribich) appear from both sides of the controversy between Freudian and object relations theories is consistent with this view. At times, Kernberg merely places together different theoretical positions rather than integrating these positions, for example, by showing how a particular definition of a concept adds to the power of the theory. Similarly, he often presents his selections among possible points of view without giving the clinical or logical justification as to why he has chosen certain positions and not others. It is never really clear that additional explanatory power is gained by combining object relations and Freudian (or ego psychological) concepts.

This brings us to a related logical criticism. Given that he has selected and defined certain concepts in the formation of his theory, Kernberg provides little in the way of theoretical or logical structures (rules of inference) to show how his theoretical positions link together in an overall theoretical system. For example, he might begin to provide rules that would predict under what circumstances active splitting replaces passive splitting and develop criteria independent of the theoretical concepts to test the predictions implied by such rules. At this stage, he does not clarify the explanatory power of his theory. To put this in another way, he does not show what the developmental, affect, or instinctual aspects of his theory really add to our understanding of his clinical and nosological observations and conceptions. In a sense, to use Rubinstein's (1967) term, his theory often seems to be "merely descriptive." Although this is not necessarily a criticism, Kernberg obviously aspires to something more. Yet often he does not show how this theory is more than a plausible restatement of his clinical points.

We have been critical of Kernberg in the latter part of this review, but we reiterate that these criticisms follow from the application of standards that, in our opinion, no psychoanalytic theorists could meet. We have expected Kernberg to present a full-blown theory of the kind that not even Freud managed to produce. Moreover, if Kernberg has not carried out the type of theory building or logical analysis that would enable him to present more convincing arguments, neither have his critics. One must sympathize with Kernberg to some extent, since his task is the harder one and since he has, at times, attempted to alter or clarify his positions in response to points raised by critics.

In conclusion, we would say that Kernberg has raised fundamental issues and, more than any other contemporary writer, he has pursued these questions with vigor and insight. The answers he proposes are among the most interesting presented by today's psychoanalytic theorists. He is also one of a relatively small number of psychoanalytic thinkers who devote considerable attention to research issues and findings (Carr, Goldstein, Hunt, & Kernberg, 1979; Kernberg, 1981b; Kernberg et al., 1972). Despite our critique, we are impressed with Kernberg's attempts to develop a comprehensive and systematic theory of development, psychopathology, and treatment, and he must be considered a major psychoanalytic theorist. In many areas, one cannot begin to formulate appropriately a problem without referring to Kernberg's work. That is, by itself, no small achievement.

REFERENCES

American Psychiatric Association. (1980). *Diagnostic and statistical manual of mental disorders* (3rd ed.). Washington, D.C.: Author.

Balint, M. (1968). *The basic fault*. New York: Basic Books.

Bibring, E. (1969). The development and problems of the theory of the instincts. *International Journal of Psycho-Analysis, 50*, 293–308.

Bion, W. R. (1959). *Experiences in groups*. New York: Basic Books.

Bion, W. R. (1965). *Transformations*. London: Heinemann.

Bion, W. R. (1967). *Second thoughts: Selected papers on psychoanalysis*. London: Heinemann.

Bion, W. R. (1970). *Attention and interpretation*. London: Heinemann.

Bowlby, J. (1969). *Attachment and loss: Vol. 1. Attachment*. New York: Basic Books.

Bowlby, J. (1973). *Attachment and loss: Vol. 2. Separation*. New York: Basic Books.

Bowlby, J. (1980). *Loss: Sadness and depression*. London: Hogarth.

Calef, V., & Weinshel, E. M. (1979). The new psychoanalysis and psychoanalytic revisionism. *Psychoanalytic Quarterly, 48*, 470–491.

Carr, A. C., Goldstein, E. G., Hunt, H. F., & Kernberg, O. F. (1979). Psychological tests and borderline patients. *Journal of Personality Assessment, 43*, 582–590.

Eissler, K. R. (1953). The effect of the structure of the ego on psychoanalytic technique. *Journal of the American Psychoanalytic Association, 1*, 104–143.

Ellman, S. J., & Moskowitz, M. (1980). An examination of some recent criticisms of psychoanalytic "metapsychology." *Psychoanalytic Quarterly, 49*, 631–662.

Fairbairn, W. R. D. (1952). *An object-relations theory of the personality*. New York: Basic Books.

Federn, P. (1947). Principles of psychotherapy in latent schizophrenia. *American Journal of Psychotherapy, 1*, 129–139.

Frosch, J. (1960). Psychotic character. *Journal of the American Psychoanalytic Association, 8*, 544–551.

Freud, S. (1914). On narcissism: An introduction. *Standard Edition, 14*, 73–102.

Freud, S. (1915). Instincts and their vicissitudes. *Standard Edition, 14*, 117–140.

Freud, S. (1917). Mourning and melancholia. *Standard Edition, 14*, 243–258.

Freud, S. (1920). Beyond the pleasure principle. *Standard Edition, 18*, 7–64.

Greenson, R. (1954). The struggle against identification. *Journal of the American Psychoanalytic Association, 2*, 200–217.

Guntrip, H. (1968). *Schizoid phenomena, object relations, and the self*. New York: International Universities Press.

Guntrip, H. (1971). *Psychoanalytic theory, therapy, and the self*. New York: Basic Books.

Hartmann, H. (1955). Notes on the theory of sublimation. In H. Hartmann, *Essays on ego psychology: Selected problems in psychoanalytic theory* (pp. 215-240). New York: International Universities Press, 1964.

Holder, A. (1970). Instinct and drive. In H. Nagera (Ed.), *Basic psychoanalytic concepts of the theory of instincts* (Vol. 3, pp. 19-22). New York: Basic Books.

Jacobson, E. (1954). Contribution to the metapsychology of psychotic identifications. *Journal of the American Psychoanalytic Association, 2,* 239-262.

Jacobson, E. (1971). Differences between schizophrenic and melancholic states of depression. In E. Jacobson, *Depression* (pp. 264-283). New York: International Universities Press. (original work published 1966)

Kernberg, O. F. (1966). Structural derivatives of object relationships. *International Journal of Psycho-Analysis, 47,* 236-253.

Kernberg, O. F. (1967). Borderline personality organization. *Journal of the American Psychoanalytic Association, 15,* 641-685.

Kernberg, O. F. (1973). Psychoanalytic object-relations theory, group processes, and administration: Toward an integrative theory of hospital treatment. *Annual of Psychoanalysis, 1,* 363-388.

Kernberg, O. F. (1975a). *Borderline conditions and pathological narcissism.* New York: Jason Aronson.

Kernberg, O. F. (1975b). A systems approach to priority setting of interventions in groups. *International Journal of Group Psychotherapy, 25,* 251-275.

Kernberg, O. F. (1976). *Object relations theory and clinical psychoanalysis.* New York: Jason Aronson.

Kernberg, O. F. (1977a, May). *Characterological determinants of depression.* Paper presented at the annual meeting of the American Psychiatric Association, Toronto, Ontario, Canada.

Kernberg, O. F. (1977b, December). *Some objectives and technique in brief psychotherapy.* Paper presented at the symposium on Brief Psychotherapy, sponsored by the American Psychoanalytic Association, New York.

Kernberg, O. F. (1977c). Structural change and its impediments. In P. Hartocollis (Ed.), *Borderline personality disorders* (pp. 275-306). New York: International Universities Press.

Kernberg, O. F. (1978). The diagnosis of borderline conditions in adolescence. *Adolescent Psychiatry, 6,* 298-319.

Kernberg, O. F. (1979a, November 6). Character structure and analyzability. In *Character structure and analyzability,* panel at a scientific meeting of the Association for Psychoanalytic Medicine, New York.

Kernberg, O. F. (1979b). Psychoanalytic psychotherapy with borderline adolescents. In S. C. Feinstein & P. L. Giovacchini (Eds.), *Adolescent psychiatry* (Vol. 7, pp. 294-321). Chicago: University of Chicago Press.

Kernberg, O. F. (1980a). *Contemporary psychoanalytic theories of narcissism.* Unpublished manuscript.

Kernberg, O. F. (1980b). *Internal world and external reality.* New York: Jason Aronson.

Kernberg, O. F. (1980c). Neurosis, psychosis, and the borderline states. In H. I. Kaplan, A. M. Freedman, & B. J. Sadock (Eds.), *Comprehensive textbook of psychiatry* (Vol. 3, pp. 1079-1092). Baltimore: Williams & Wilkins.

Kernberg, O. F. (1980d, May 4). The place of affects in psychoanalytic theory. In *New directions in affect theory,* panel at the Annual Meeting of the American Psychoanalytic Association, San Francisco.

Kernberg, O. F. (1980, September 5). *Supportive psychotherapy.* Presentation at clinical grand rounds, The New York Hospital–Cornell Medical Center, Westchester Division.

Kernberg, O. F. (1981a, March). Countertransference, transference regression, and the incapacity to depend. In *Current concepts of transference and countertransference*, symposium organized by the Association for Psychoanalytic Medicine, New York.

Kernberg, O. F. (1981b, June). *Dilemmas in research on long-term psychotherapy*. Paper presented at the Annual Meeting of the Society for Psychotherapy Research, Aspen, Colorado.

Kernberg, O. F. (1981c, September 11). *Problems in the classification of personality disorders*. Presentation at clinical grand rounds, The New York Hospital–Cornell Medical College, Westchester Division.

Kernberg, O. F. (1981d). Psychiatric hospital treatment in the United States. *Nordisk Psykiatrisk Tidsskrift, 5,* 283–298.

Kernberg, O. F. (1981e). Some issues in the theory of hospital treatment. *Tidsskrift for Den Norske Loegeforening, 14,* 837–843.

Kernberg, O. F. (1981f). Structural interviewing. *Psychiatric Clinics of North America, 4,* 169–196.

Kernberg, O. F. (1982a). Advantages and liabilities of the therapeutic community. In M. Pines & L. Rafaelsen (Eds.), *The individual and the group, Vol. 1.* New York: Plenum.

Kernberg, O. F. (1982b, April 18). Clinical management of suicidal potential in borderline patients. In *Borderline personality disorders and suicidal behavior*, panel at the 15th Annual Meeting of the American Association of Suicidology, New York.

Kernberg, O. F. (1982c, May 8). *The dynamic unconscious and the self.* Presentation at a meeting of the Association for Philosophy of Science, Psychotherapy and Ethics, New York.

Kernberg, O. F. (1982d). *An ego psychology-object relations model of psychoanalytic psychotherapy*. Unpublished manuscript.

Kernberg, O. F. (1982e, May 16). *Identity, alienation, and ideology in adolescence*. Presentation at the Annual Meeting of the American Society for Adolescent Psychiatry, Toronto, Ontario, Canada.

Kernberg, O. F. (1982f). Narcissism. In S. Gilman (Ed.), *Introducing psychoanalytic theory* (pp. 126–136). New York: Brunner/Mazel.

Kernberg, O. F. (1982g, May). *The psychotherapeutic treatment of borderline personalities*. Presentation at the review-update program on narcissistic and borderline personalities at the American Psychiatric Association, Toronto.

Kernberg, O. F. (1982h). Self, ego, affects and drives. *Journal of the American Psychoanalytic Association, 30,* 893–918.

Kernberg, O. F. (1982i). Supportive psychotherapy with borderline conditions. In J. O. Cavenar & H. K. Brodie (Eds.), *Critical problems in psychiatry* (pp. 180–202). Philadelphia: Lippincott.

Kernberg, O. F. (1983). To teach or not to teach. In E. Joseph & R. S. Wallerstein (Eds.), *The influence of the practice and theory of psychotherapy on education in psychoanalysis* (Vol. 1). International Psycho-Analytic Association Monograph Series, pp. 1–37.

Kernberg, O. F., Burstein, E. D., Coyne, L. Appelbaum, A., Horwitz, L., & Voth, H. (1972). Psychotherapy and psychoanalysis: Final report of the Menninger Foundation's psychotherapy research project. *Bulletin of the Menninger Clinic, 36,* (1 & 2).

Klein, M. (1946). Notes on some schizoid mechanisms. *International Journal of Psycho-Analysis, 27,* 99–110.

Klein, M. (1948a). A contribution to the psychogenesis of manic-depressive states. In M. Klein, *Contributions to psycho-analysis, 1921–1945* (pp. 282–310). London: Hogarth. (Original work published 1935)

Klein, M. (1948b). Mourning and its relation to manic-depressive states. In M. Klein, *Contributions to psycho-analysis, 1921–1945* (pp. 311–338). London: Hogarth. (Original work published 1940)

Klein, M., & Tribich, D. (1981). Kernberg's object-relations theory: A critical evaluation. *International Journal of Psycho-Analysis, 62*, 27–43.

Knight, R. P. (1954). Borderline states. In R. P. Knight & C. R. Friedman (Eds.), *Psychoanalytic psychiatry and psychology* (pp. 97–109). New York: International Universities Press.

Kohut, H. (1966). Forms and transformations of narcissism. *Journal of the American Psychoanalytic Association, 14*, 243–272.

Kohut, H. (1971). *The analysis of the self.* New York: International Universities Press.

MacLean, P. D. (1967). The brain in relation to empathy and medical education. *Journal of Nervous and Mental Disease, 144*, 374–382.

MacLean, P. D. (1972). Cerebral evolution and emotional processes: New findings on the striatal complex. *Annals of the New York Academy of Science, 193*, 137–149.

Mahler, M. S. (1968). *On human symbiosis and the vicissitudes of individuation: Infantile psychosis.* New York: International Universities Press.

Mahler, M. S., & Pine, F., & Bergman, A. (1975). *The psychological birth of the human infant.* New York: Basic Books.

Miller, G. A., & Rice, A. K. (1967). *Systems of organization.* London: Tavistock.

Miller, J. G. (1969). Living systems: Basic concepts. In W. Gray, F. J. Duhl, & N. D. Rizzo (Eds.), *General systems theory and psychiatry* (pp. 51–133). Boston: Little, Brown.

Moskowitz, M., & Ellman, S. J. (1983). A critical analysis of the concept of metapsychology in psychoanalysis. Unpublished manuscript.

Nagel, E. (1961). *The structure of science.* New York: Harcourt, Brace & World.

Popper, K. (1962). *Conjectures and refutations: The growth of scientific knowledge.* New York: Basic Books.

Rice, A. K. (1965). *Learning for leadership.* London: Tavistock.

Rice, A. K. (1969). Individual, group and intergroup processes. *Human Relations, 22*, 565–584.

Rubinstein, B. B. (1967). *Explanation and mere description: A metascientific examination of certain aspects of the psychoanalytic theory of motivation.* New York: International Universities Press.

Schmideberg, M. (1947). The treatment of psychopaths and borderline patients. *American Journal of Psychotherapy, 1*, 45–55.

Schur, M. (1966). *The id and the principles of regulatory functioning.* New York: International Universities Press.

Stolorow, R. D., & Lachman, F. M. (1980). *Psychoanalysis of developmental arrests.* New York: International Universities Press.

Stone, M. H. (1980). *The borderline syndromes.* New York: McGraw Hill.

Sugarman, A., & Lerner, H. (1980). Reflections on the current state of the borderline concept. In J. Kwawer, H. Lerner, P. Lerner, & A. Sugarman (Eds.), *Borderline phenomena and the Rorschach* (pp. 11–37). New York: International Universities Press.

Winnicott, D. W. (1965). *The maturational processes and the facilitating environment.* New York: International Universities Press.

Winnicott, D. W. (1975). *Through paediatrics to psychoanalysis.* New York: Basic Books.

Zetzel, E. (1971). A developmental approach to the borderline patient. *American Journal of Psychiatry, 127*, 867–871.

Wilfred R. Bion: An Odyssey into the Deep and Formless Infinite

11

James S. Grotstein, M.D.

Bion wrote less extensively than many of the other subjects of this volume or than many other significant contributors to psychoanalysis. Yet, what he did write seems to have stirred profound respect, much antipathy, considerable confusion, and even astonishment in his audiences. Most who read him do not understand him. Many idealize him because of the experience his writing gave them, to say nothing of his presence when he was alive – "an odyssey through the deep and formless infinite void," as I once heard it described. Having had an analysis with Bion, I can well empathize with this extensive spectrum of feelings he inspired. Bion's influence and reputation owe much to his capacity for indirectly evoking experiences in his audience. As a particular instance of this "telescoped effect," some time after I finished my analysis with Bion I heard him deliver a lecture at the Los Angeles Psychoanalytic Institute. I recall having been unimpressed, somewhat bored, and a little restless. When I went home that evening, I found that my mind was in a whirl, and I could not sleep. I then felt constrained to complete the outlines of three papers before I could lie down to rest.

Who was Wilfred Bion? Why and how did he evoke such disparate emotions in people? He was first of all an Englishman (actually Anglo-Indian) who seems to have been able to harmonize his Indian childhood with a magnificent education at an English public school and at Oxford, to mix them further with his capacity for wonderment and surprise, and to bring them all to psychoanalysis in a unique way. Specifically, he was able to bring to psychoanalytic theory and practice the perspectives of Plato's theory of forms and Immanuel Kant's *Critique of Pure Reason,*

and he expanded the Freudian theory of the unconsciouus from the nar-
rower limitations of its biological foundations into a broader scope con-
sonant with the long tradition of Western—and even Eastern—
epistemology.

Among the concepts that formed his work, Bion appreciated the concept of inherent preconception from Plato's theory of forms and formulated that they, under the impact of sensory-emotional experience, link
up with its external counterpart, its *realization*, to become a *conception*
the continuing affirmation and abstraction of this conception allow it to
become a concept—like the concept of a breast, for instance. Bion also
called these inherent preconceptions "thoughts without a thinker," in
the sense that they are thoughts that are older than the human race that
now thinks them. The mind had to be created, according to Bion, in order to think these primordial "thoughts." He invokes Kant in this way:
Intuition without concept is blind; concept without intuition is empty.
The infant has the intuition of his or her experience but is as yet empty
of the power to conceive of these experiences by a notational system—to
make sense of them. The task of analysis, Bion believed, is to allow
preceonceptual experiences to be conceived so as to *realize* one's intuition. Bion (1980) states: "A 'marriage' is taking place between you and
you; a marriage between your thoughts and your feelings. The intuition
which is blind and the concept which is empty can get together in a way
which makes a complete mature thought" (p. 27).

Bion felt that, although language is one of the supreme accomplishments of human beings and is essential for communication, it is also a vehicle for deception and inaccuracies. Language is static and belongs to
the sensual aspects of our development. It is therefore personal and ultimately misleading or even suspect. Bion's conception of the "suspension
of memory and desire" reflects this belief on his part that language in
general and *understanding* in particular are vehicles of desire and
therefore obtrude the ultimate experience of pure Truth. Language,
and even knowledge (which he mathematically symbolized as K), are
only transient approximations to Truth (O), and we should not confuse
one with the other. This was one of the reasons, I believe, that Bion used
mathematical analogies and even spent a considerable amount of time
trying to develop a mathematical grid on polar-coordinated space with
the aim of giving exact definition to psychoanalytic elements. Mathematics are free of the sensuousness of memory and desire, he believed,
and therefore are more suitable in their unsaturation to describe phenomena from the internal world that are not describable by a language,
such as verbal language, that belongs to the sensory matrix.

Although this point may seem obscure to many, its merit lies in Bion's
attempt to help us get beyond (behind, below) the language barrier so as

to approximate pure experience before language. In this regard, is closely in tune with the current work of Lacan and Derrida, the French deconstructionists. Lacan in particular has called attention to the alteration of subjectivity, as "I" descends into the "symbolic order of language." Bion and Lacan seem to agree that words, like idols, become static reifications of experience and progressively alienate oneself from it. Words seem to grasp and enclose the experience so as to squeeze the life out of it and rob it of meaning. In addition to mathematics, Bion also cited music, poetry, and art as generally superior ways of presenting the domain of intuition.

Bion is perhaps best known to the mental health public for his *Experiences in Groups* (1961), in which he revealed some of the most far-reaching innovations in the psychoanalysis of group process since Freud. Like Freud before him, Bion viewed the group as a single entity, with a psychology that is superordinate to the individuals who comprise it. By applying the principles of individual psychoanalysis, however, he localized unique transferences to the group leader and special forms of resistance unique to the group situation.

Bion's vast experience with the psychoanalysis of psychotic patients allowed him to make fascinating forays into psychotic thinking, and his metapsychological concepts owe much to these experiences. One key concept he obtained from analyzing psychotics is the notion of the *container and the contained*, which designated a mother who was able to contain her infant's projective identifications. Her ability to do so (her reverie) allows the infant to internalize her as a mother who can, through her reverie, contain the infant's anguish and can thus form the basis of a "thinking couple." Bion's theory of thinking distinguishes between thoughts and the mind that had to be created to think them. Thinking in the normal individual comprises projective identifications of "thoughts without a thinker" and sensory-emotional impressions onto an internalized object surface, which endures the impact of these "thoughts" and then "thinks" them.

The concept of the container and the contained is often associated with the more passive aspect of its action – that is, the passive absorption of the infant's or patient's mental pain. Bion meant far more than that. The mother (or the analyst) must not only absorb the infant's (or patient's) pain without being *transformed* by it – that is, yielding to the infant's projections, identifying with them, and responding reactively in turn – but must also delay them, sort them out as a prism does with a beam of intense light, refracting them into a color spectrum of hierarchic meanings, and then, finally, act upon them by relating to the infant's specific needs. By doing this, mother turns the infant's screams into meaning, and, rather than thoughtlessly resorting to reflex action because of her hurt, uses the countainment experience for purposes of thoughtful *translation*. Not only does this become internalized by the infant as a model for thinking, but it also becomes a model for permitting the experiencing of the experience so as to "learn from experience," which Bion believed to be the sine qua non of normal development.

Before elaborating some of the concepts that are of importance in a survey of Bion's work, I will digress for a moment to give a few facts of Bion's life. I must caution the reader, however, that these facts are an "exercise in *K*," and Bion would not for a moment want them to be confused with the truth (*O*). He was born in Muttra, in the remote United Provinces of British India, on September 8, 1897. His father belonged to the British Civil Service and was an engineer. His mother was from a lower social caste than his father. Bion was raised by two native women who read him stories from the Mahabharata[1], which made an everlasting impression on him. As was the custom with children whose parents were employed by the British Civil Service, he was sent back to England at age 8 to study at a public school, Bishops Stortford, which he attended from 1906 to 1915. Shortly after World War I broke out, he gained a commission in the Royal Tank Regiment, took part in the Battle of Cambrai (the first major engagement in which tanks were deployed against the Germans), and was awarded the Distinguished Service Order by King George V. He fought in every subsequent major battle on the Western Front, poignant pictures of which can be read in his posthumously published autobiography, *The Long Week-End: 1897–1919* (1982).

Bion was demobilized late in 1918 and then went to Queens College, Oxford, in January of 1919, where he studied modern history. It was there that he met H. J. Paton, a tutor of philosophy who introduced him to the works of Kant and other philosophers. Following graduation, he returned to Bishops Stortford College to teach history and French. He also had an active amateur career as a rugby football player and coach for the swimming team.

In 1923 or 1924 he left to study medicine at University College Hospital in London and qualified in 1929. While there, he came under the influence of Wilfred Trotter, the distinguished surgeon, who was interested in the psychology of groups. This association was to be of great importance in Bion's future years when he made his important contributions to the theory of groups. After a short stint as a medical officer in the Royal Air Force, he went to London in 1932 and began to practice psychiatry. He entered analysis with John Rickman and began his training as a candidate in the British Institute for Psycho-Analysis, but was

---

[1]Sacred Indian epic poem dealing with the ideas of goodness and evil.

interrupted by the outbreak of World War II in 1939. While Officer-in-Charge of the Military Training Wing at Northfield Military Hospital, Bion seems to have arrived at the first inklings of his conception of group psychology.

After the war Bion returned to the Tavistock Clinic and was appointed chairman of the Executive Committee. After finishing his analysis with John Rickman, he was introduced by the latter to Melanie Klein, with whom he began a second analysis.

He married in 1940, but the marriage ended with his wife's tragic death after the birth of their only child, Parthenope, in 1945. Some years later he married Francesca, whom he met at the Tavistock Institute of Human Relations and with whom he had two additional children, Julian, now a practicing physician, and Nichola, a linguist who is currently working in publishing. Bion developed an excellent reputation as an analyst in London and became president of the British Society for Psycho-Analysis. He disliked this prominence, however, and often quipped "I was so loaded down with honors that I almost sank without a trace!"

In 1966 he made a lecture tour of Los Angeles and returned the following year to remain for 12 years. During that time he exercised a profound and extensive impact on the psychoanalytic community of that city. He also frequently traveled to Rio de Janeiro and Sao Paulo. It is interesting that Bion seems to be more popular and his works are better known in the psychoanalytic community of South America than in any other area.

Bion retired in 1979 and returned to England to be with his children. He died suddenly of leukemia on November 8 of that year.

BION'S WORK

Experiences in Groups

It is interesting to note that the mental health public knows more about Bion's (1961) concepts of group psychology than they do about him as a psychoanalytic theorist. What is now known as the "Tavistock method" began during his experiences at Northfield Barracks during World War II and was completed after the war at the Tavistock Clinic. As already noted, Bion, like Freud before him, observed that groups behave with a psychology that is characteristic of the group as a unit, above and beyond the psychologies of each of its members. A group convenes in order to focus on a common project; in the original case at Northfield Barracks, this was a return to the battlefront. In the course of the group's progression, resistance, not unlike resistances in individual analysis, develops toward the progress of the group's functioning. Members of the group seemed to cluster into resistance subgroups, which Bion designated as (1) fight or flight, (2) pairing, and (3) dependence. Bion analyzed the expectations of the individual and resistance subgroup members toward the leader as analogous to the transference expectations in individual analyses. The Tavistock method is largely known in the United States through the work of A. K. Rice (1965) and is used to study authority relationships in institutions. It has never found its way into formal group psychotherapy to any significant extent.

Experiences with Psychotics and the Origins of a Theory of Thinking

Overlapping and succeeding Bion's interest in the psychology of groups was his analytic work with psychotics and borderline patients. His first contribution stemming from this interest was "The Imaginary Twin" (1950). The patient discussed in this clinical paper was suffering from persecution by an imaginary twin, which seemed to be derived from an earlier conception of the breast as the first imaginary twin. In "Differentiation of the Psychotic from the Non-Psychotic Personalities" (1957a), Bion offered the thesis that every psychotic demonstrates a normal or neurotic as well as a psychotic personality, which long antedated Kernberg's similar formulations. His papers, "Notes on the Theory of Schizophrenia" (1954), "Development of Schizophrenic Thought" (1956), "On Arrogance" (1958a), "On Hallucinations" (1958b), and "Attacks on Linking" (1959) all examined the shizophrenic experience of attacking thoughts by attacking the links between objects and between object and self, the precursors of thoughts.

Ultimately, Bion saw the psychotic experience as the result of a failure by the mother to contain her infant's fear of dying. This is, again, the concept of the *container and the contained,* which was to have major significance not only for Kleinian metapsychology but also for psychoanalytic metapsychology generally. For Kleinian metapsychology it added the adaptive principle, the formal enfranchisement of the importance of external reality, a concept that previously was sadly lacking. It added the concepts of "thoughts without a thinker" and inchoate emotional sense impressions that need a thinker to think them – originally a mother-container whose ultimate internalization by the infant provides for this developing function. The concept of the container and the contained long anticipated Kohut's concept of the functions of selfobjects.

Another important contribution from Bion's work on psychoses is his conception of alpha function, alpha elements, and beta elements (Bion,

1962a, 1963). He used letters from the Greek alphabet in order to avoid terms that were in ordinary use and therefore already saturated with meaning. The second part of his terms, "functions" and "elements," he borrowed from mathematics for the same reason. Experience, according to Bion, begins as a *beta element*, which is a raw stimulus confronting the sense organs in order to be experienced. If the sense organ allows itself to experience the beta element stimulus, it does so through *alpha function* and therefore *transforms* the beta element into an *alpha element*. The latter is analogous to metabolized food—it is suitable for mental digestion, whereas the raw beta element is not. The alpha element comprises not just the impression of the senses, however, but also the inherent and/or acquired preconceptions of that experience, which the organism is prepared for beforehand; thus, the mating between preconception and beta element forms the alpha element, the necessary ingredient for mental digestion. The alpha element may then be transformed into dream or mythic elements for storage and/or may be processed by the mind for immediate experience, to be thought about and acted upon.

Bion stated that alpha elements are able to produce an alpha screen, something akin to a repressive barrier, which differentiates sleep from wakefulness. The psychotic, on the other hand, has so much fear of experiencing his or her feelings because of being overwhelmed that he or she projects out not only feelings and thoughts about these feelings, but also the mental apparatus that can accept, absorb, and process these feelings—the psychotic's very ego. As a consequence, the psychotic cannot "alpha-betize" sensory-emotional experiences—cannot allow them to be registered (cannot transform them through alpha function into alpha elements). These experiences do not become properly transformed for mental action; instead, they become pathologically transformed into altered beta elements or *bizarre objects*, which comprise delusions and hallucinations. The psychotic seems to develop a beta screen (rather than an alpha screen) of bizarre and persecuting objects which cluster around him or her and alienate him or her from the presence of and communication with others. The absence of an alpha screen forecloses on the psychotic's capacity to differentiate between waking and sleep and therefore between dreaming and reality or between the delusional and real worlds.

Bion began to realize that the sense organs of the psychotic "do not talk to one another to make common sense," and that the psychotic uses these sense organs to project sensations onto objects, which then become hallucinations because of their propensity for abnormal projective identification. The "arrogance" of psychotic thinking is the defensive smugness of the psychotic in believing that he or she can "think" by evacuating thoughts and the organ that thinks thoughts (the mind) into an object that is then subjected to the patient's curiosity – not for knowledge, but for control.

Bion formulated the notion of an infantile mental catastrophe as the basis for the development of a psychotic personality. This catastrophe is a result of the infant's hatred of experience in conjunction with a defective maternal container, which can not soothe or contain the infant's pain. Bion invoked the concept of catastrophe for normal thinking as well, and his ideas in this respect seem to have been misunderstood by many (see Hamilton, 1982). Catastrophe is a prerequisite for normal thinking, Bion believed, because thinking requires overcoming the steady state of homeostasis and therefore always involves pain. Thinking is in response to rents in the smooth surface of serenity; the adjustments and adaptations we have to make inaugurate the need for thinking. Thus, to Bion, catastrophe, in its theoretical sense, is a normal property of change, and thinking is our capacity to anticipate, adjust to, and regulate it. This conception of "normal" catastrophe does not obviate its counterpart, the child's normal epistemophilic tendency, with the attendant enthusiasm and joy in acquiring knowledge about the world.

During the years in which he worked on these concepts, Bion steadfastly endeavored to mathematize psychoanalytic concepts so as to give them "scientific precision." Bion's mathematical adventures occupy his first three major metapsychological works, *Learning from Experience* (1962a), *Elements of Psychoanalysis* (1963), and *Transformations* (1965). Bion's theory of transformations borrows from Melanie Klein's theory of the existence of the paranoid-schizoid and depressive positions, two basic sequential stages of development in early infantile mental life. The first stage is characterized by states of persecutory anxiety in the infant, the latter by states of depressive concern for the object, along with withdrawal of projections from the object back to the self. The depressive position is considered a state of integration, and the paranoid-schizoid position is considered a state of potential disintegration.

Bion proposed that all emotional states and thoughts begin in the paranoid-schizoid position as definitory hypotheses. In other words, the infant experiences as a definitory hypothesis a sense of certainty about its state of pain and feels persecuted by this pain. The infant thus experiences itself as the innocent victim of pain superimposed upon it by some outside source, the nurturing object. The infant who is able to tolerate this pain eventually may realize that the pain is like a hole or an absence where a breast belongs and that it developed in the first place because the breast was not there when it was needed. If the infant can tolerate the pain long enough, then the concept of an empty space develops (like

Kant's "empty thoughts"). The infant (and, by corollary, the patient) can use this space as an area of transformation in which a thought may alter from its original definitory hypothesis of persecutory pain to a depressive awareness of the need for the breast and of the pain of mother's absence. Thus, the "thought" or "feeling" undergoes a transformation from the paranoid-schizoid to the depressive position (P-S→D) on its way to integration and acceptance.

There are three major types of transformations: (1) rigid motion transformations, (2) projective transformations, and (3) transformations in hallucinosis (− K). A rigid motion transformation, a term borrowed from solid geometry, is one in which an experience from the past is experienced in the present virtually intact. It corresponds to the general classical notion of transference, that is, of a displacement of a past object experience to the analyst in the present. Projective transformations is Bion's term for Klein's conception of projective identification; it designates the projective translocation of aspects of the infant and/or patient in the present onto the image of the parent-analyst, who then is believed to be identified with the projection (transformed and controlled by it).

Transformations in hallucinosis designate a much more extensive and abnormal change. Bion believed that the psychotic cannot bear the experience of pain and therefore does not develop the space in which normal transformations can occur. Instead, he or she annihilates this space or never develops it in the first place. The psychotic also projects out not only the intolerable feelings and thoughts, but also the very mental apparatus, the ego, which feels the feelings and thinks the thoughts, along with them. Insofar as this is experienced by the "psychotic" infant as not being able to contain, feel, or think his or her thoughts, the infant correspondingly, thanks to projective identification, believes the object he or she is projecting the thoughts onto also cannot contain these thoughts and feelings or the infant's mind, which is also being projected into the object. The consequences, according to Bion, are as follows: The infant now is in a state of disorientation and is denuded of his or her mental capacity to experience his or her feelings and think his or her thoughts. The infant no longer has the alpha function to delay, sort out, and "alphabetize" feelings. He or she now lurks in the twilight of confusion between sleep and dreams, where neither is distinguishable from the other.

The object to which the infant's mind and feelings have meanwhile been projected has been *transformed* into a *bizarre object* (transformation of rejected beta elements), which is unstable and controlled by the psychotic projections within it. The latter seem to "swell up" and bizarrely distort the configuration of the object. They then fragment, disintegrate, and reorganize as a *beta screen* of psychotic impermeability, a pathological autistic shell "protectively" surrounding the denuded infant. This beta screen is experienced as delusions and hallucinations, which circumscribe the infant or patient as a "protectively menacing" envelope. It is protective in the sense that former painful relations with external objects no longer occur, thanks to the beta screen, but menacing insofar as the infant and/or patient is now in a veritible "concentration camp."

Eventually, the patient may seemingly recover from this psychotic catastrophe but, as in the example of the famous case of Schreber (see Freud, 1911), will reconstitute a private mental world of his or her own which is a bizarre mock-up of the abandoned external world, totally cut off from and impervious to it. This is the domain of $-K$, the final stage of a transformation in hallucinosis, otherwise known as a "fixed" delusional system.

A Brief Overview of Bion's Metapsychology

Bion's metapsychology is not only an elaboration of Freud's basic tenets amalgamated with the cartography of infantile mental life that Melanie Klein pioneered, but is also enriched with many unique contributions from general epistemology and some innovative speculations about mental life even beyond the caesura of birth. Bion believed that mental life may well begin when the sense organs first become operant, early in fetal life, and he postulated that there may be some dim "awareness" of the transition from the watery medium of the womb to the gaseous medium of postnatal life. These early "experiences" are "empty" in the Kantian sense and must await language in order to become filled as concepts. Before becoming "filled," they may be registered as *ideograms*. Psychoanalysis is an attempt to help the individual link up with his or her earliest preconceptions, giving language to those primordial experiences that are still beyond words and may date to a time before there were words.

Bion gradually became dissatisfied with the language of Freudian and Kleinian theory, because it dealt with objects that dwelled in the third dimension of external reality (the domain of senses). Bion's psychotic patients did *not* dwell in that third dimension but rather in dimensions alien to it. Because the dimensionality of the internal world normally and of the psychotic world abnormally is far different from that of the third dimension of external reality, it requires a language suitable to it. Today we might call this the domain of the nondominant hemisphere, which can be thought of as the zero dimension (see Grotstein, 1978).

Bion reminds us that Freud had postulated that the psyche's capacity for consciousness depends on mental processes that are "sensible" to the data of experience from external stimuli. Pleasure and unpleasure are the original "codes" of differentiation of these processes. Even though Freud hinted that the sense organ of consciousness was "sensible" to internal stimuli as well, there seems to be very little in the psychoanalytic literature to designate the exact nature of that internal sense organ system. Bion came to the rescue by reminding us that the sensual domain relates to the external world and that *intuition* is the sense organ that is responsive to the internal world. In order to be intuitively "sensitive" to this inner domain, one must blind oneself to the sensory capacities that are responsive to the external world of sense-dominated reality. Following a notion of Freud, Bion advocated abandoning memory and desire in order to allow oneself to be intuitively sensitive to this internal, dimensionless world. Ironically, we associate the pleasure principle with the id and therefore with the unconscious. Pleasure seems to be the designation by the sense organs that are responsive to external reality to code that form of information; therefore, paradoxically, we must eschew our tendency toward pleasure and desire (suspend them) to allow the "thoughts without a thinker" to emerge in the inner domain. These "thoughts without a thinker" do not have a language of their own and must borrow the language of external reality via free associations (day residue experiences) to become "visible" (sensible through intuition). Memory is the past tense of desire (of the senses), and desire designates the future (of the senses). Thus, the analytic procedure requires suspension of memory and desire so that there can be intuitive receptivity to the inner world. The ability to do this requires the "man of achievement," a designation Bion borrowed from Keats to connote the capacity for patience in a field of doubts, mysteries, and half-truths while awaiting the *selected fact*. The appearance of this selected fact rewards the "man of achievement" with intuitive security and clarification about inner meaning.

From another point of view, we can see this formulation as Bion's concern about the difference between Truth (O) and knowledge (K). Our sense organs are "sensible" to knowledge about Truth but are limited to the acquisition of knowledge about it. Words correspond to K; O is wordless and is the thing-in-itself, unknowable. Psychoanalysis attempts to be a transformation in O, not by our understanding of K, but rather via the experience of K. Thus, knowledge itself does not permit transformation in O, only experience does. K is important only in being able, once accepted, to be used to facilitate experience itself, the only route to O.

Genius and the "Messiah Thought"

In Bion's last metapsychological book, *Attention and Interpretation* (1970), he returned to his earlier work on group formations and integrated that work with his earlier conceptions of elements, experiences, and transformations. Once again, Bion drew the analogy between the individual mind and the group establishment and located within this group establishment the function of preserving and conserving the group's stability. The establishment resists change to defend against anticipated chaos. The protectors of the establishment need to anticipate rebellion or challenge to the stability of the group that may potentially endanger it. They therefore must locate the "enemies within," stigmatize them, and ultimately exile them from the group.

At the same time, the establishment must paradoxically anticipate the need for change so that the group unit does not decay or disintegrate of its own accord. It therefore must prepare the way for a *messiah* or *genius* (corresponding to the "messiah thought"), the new leader who is able to have a "memoir of the future" and to be able, as a "genius", to experience O directly without having to detour through K. The genius and the messiah thought correspond to the "thought without a thinker," the inherent preconception that has not yet been thought but that is needed to be known and thought so as to come to the rescue of the stalemated group establishment. The genius (and/or messiah thought) is then conceived of as the definitory hypothesis, the apodictic message to the group, which then attacks and challenges the veracity of this thought in an attempt to negate it.

When negation fails, the thought or feeling is accepted, notated, paid attention to, subjected to inquiry, and, finally, acted upon. These functions (definitory hypothesis, negation, notation, attention, inquiry, and action) occupy the horizontal axis of Bion's mathematical grid. The vertical axis develops in terms of the transformation from beta element → alpha element → dream thoughts or myths to preconception → conception → concept to scientific deductive system → algebraic calculus. Thus, whether in the group or the individual, the "thoughts without a thinker," when allowed a transformative space and time to be contained, thought about, and challenged, can then be accepted and allowed to undergo their matriculation into ever-ascending conceptual schemes. This is how individuals and cultures grow.

Bion meant this conceptualization of the messiah thought and its conflict with the very establishment that summoned not only to be a statement in general about the evolution and maturation of the individual and culture, but also, undoubtedly, to be a generalization about the difficulties he observed in the psychoanalytic establishment. The classical Freudian school, locked as it was in the oedipal paradigm, seemed unconsciously to evoke the need for the messianic thoughts that Melanie Klein brought to psychoanalysis about early infantile (preoedipal) mental life. The same battle fought by Freud, the erstwhile messiah of another age, occurred again, with Klein in opposition to Freud's descendants. As it has turned out, the "messianic" ideas of Klein have not safely

traversed the challenge imposed by the psychoanalytic establishment—
they have not cleared negation. Yet there are ingredients in her discoveries that are essential to the normal progression of psychoanalytic theory. It therefore seems as if a compromise formation has been instituted in classical analysis in which Kleinian ideas have been extracted from her matrix, alienated from her, and now regrafted to classical theory under a new name.

Transformations in which the genius and his or her messiah thoughts are accepted by the group establishment are termed by Bion *symbiotic*, as both the group and the genius benefit from the interchange. The fate of Kleinian ideas might correspond to what Bion calls a *parasitic* transformation, insofar as the establishment did not recognize that it was in fact dependent on her ideas for its future welfare and therefore "extracted" the ideas parasitically without full gratitude to their author. A third form of transformation, which Bion calls *commensal*, designates the simultaneous presence of two separate kinds of ideas or subgroups within a larger group that live in peace and harmony. They either have not yet come into conflict or are able to live in harmony without the necessity of interaction or conflict. In sociopolitical terms we might call this "pure democracy."

The other fate of the messiah idea, especially when it comes before its time, is to ignite the messianic idea in others via linear progression, much in the way that free associations transpire in a seemingly endless chain. Suddenly, the selected fact once again emerges as the messiah thought which is necessary for the survival of the person or group. The new messianic ideas may seem not to "remember" their ancestry. One can see this phenomenon today in the work of Kohut and self psychology with its emphasis on the empathic principle in psychoanalysis, which does not yet seem to know its ancestory in Sullivan, Fairbairn, Winnicott, Balint, Bowbly, and so many others, to say nothing of Klein.

The coming of the genius and the messianic thought he or she expresses is apparently a historical pattern with fortunate as well as revolutionary consequences. If the establishment cannot bear the strain imposed on it by the messiah thought, then there is catastrophic revolution with violent change (transformation in $-K$). If the thought is accepted by the establishment, it changes correspondingly, in which case there is a transformation in K on its way to experiencing O (the thing-in-itself, pure experience).

Bion's Conception of the Unconscious

When Freud first discovered the system unconscious, it comprised the domain of traumatically buried memories. Later, when he discovered the importance of fantasy, the unconscious became composed of the instinctual drives, those elements of experience that had become second-arily instinctualized and pulled into repression, the unconscious portion of the ego (especially the ego defense mechanisms), and the superego. Bion's invocation of inherent preconceptions modified this picture. First, he saw the psychic apparatus as being composed, as did Freud, by the ego, superego, and id. Unlike Freud, however, he saw them as three different *vertices* of experience of objects outside them. In other words, the phenomenon of pain can be understood from a moral or religious point of view (superego), from a rational or scientific point of view (ego), or from an esthetic or need-desire (id) point of view, and correlations be-tween these vertices of experience are required for integration.

Second, Bion's notion of inherent preconceptions modified the con-cept of the unconscious in yet another way by suggesting that what impelled its way into consciousness normally and abnormally was not so much the instinctual drives per se, but inherent preconceptions of dan-ger ("thoughts without a thinker") that traumatic experience has evoked. Thus, danger is not from the drives, but from the driving force of the most atavistic reminder of imminent danger. This is a vastly dif-ferent notion of psychic interaction, which can have enormous conse-quences in the treatment of patients, especially psychotic and border-line patients. It makes a great deal of difference if the therapist conceives of a patient's psychotic break as being due to id irruptions rather than to urgent warning signals of ancient preconceptions alarmed into readiness with an ego unable to listen or able to respond.

Bion the Philosopher

Bion was well versed in philosophy and was himself a philosopher as well. In terms of his formal philosophical background, I have already mentioned Plato and Kant. To this list must also be added Hume and many others, particularly the Intuitionistic mathematicians such as including Poincare. Bion the philosopher, however, was another matter. One always felt when talking with him that one was in the presence of a person who had thought profoundly and intimately about the nature of relationships.

Although he revered the highly special and unique relationship be-tween the patient and analyst, Bion correspondingly deprecated the su-pervisory relationship. He generally refused to take on supervisees for more than a few sessions. His rejection of the idea of supervision was based on his belief that the therapist seeing the patient, no matter how inexperienced and ill trained, has more authority about the experience that transpired than the "supervisor," who is removed from the experi-ence. All the "supervisor" can do is share his or her own feelings as a "second opinion," a favorite expression of Bion's.

A similar attitude was expressed in Bion's memorable reply to a member of a group that had been meeting with Bion who had presented some case material for his "second opinion." The case material referred to a patient's relationship to his sister. Bion (personal communication) stated:

> I don't know why your patient feels guilty about his feelings toward his sister. After all, she is a member of his father's family, not his. The father's family is a temporary family, a rehearsal family, if you will, which has been ordained, one must presume, to complete the rehearsal of childhood until such time as the human being is able to find his own family, the permanent one, the thing-in-itself. His sister is no concern of his. It is a concern of her father and mother, if they care to be concerned. On the other hand, if your patient does desire to be concerned, then that is his business, and he may be experiencing feelings from the time when he actually was a member of his father's family, along with his sister. Now that would be a different matter. Natural affection has no rules.

I hope the reader can follow the twists, turns, ellipses, and zig zags of this thinking. Bion was a magnificent tactitian and strategist not only in combat, but also behind the couch.

Another example of Bion's "philosophy of relationships" came out during one of my analytic hours with him. I was complaining to him about how disappointed I was in myself. His reply was instant and surprising:

> You are the most important person you are ever likely to meet, therefore it is very important that you be on good terms with this important person, you. You appear more than willing to bear testimony against yourself, yet are not supplying me with the evidence. Besides, whom am I to believe, the accusor or the defendant? You haven't yet presented evidence which either I or the defendant can respond to.

On yet another occasion, when Bion gave me a particularly powerful and cogent interpretation I (foolishly, in retrospect), said, "You know, you're right; that's a correct interpretation!" Bion sarcastically replied:

> "Oh yes, you would have me be right. How right I am! you state. I'm right only because I uttered a second opinion about your associations to me. I could just have easily have stated, 'you're right! By God, how right your free associations are!' "

What I came to realize from this encounter was that Bion was enjoining me to be myself, respect myself, reclaim my "power of attorney," and use the mind God gave me—that is, to accept the responsibility of my own importance and the importance of consulting my feelings and listening to my own responses to my experiences rather than trying to "understand" those who speak to me and whom I am in danger of making mentors rather than "partners" with second opinions.

Although also an astute logician, Bion was superbly "right brain" as well. He was not only an accomplished pianist and gifted artist in his on right, but he also had a high regard for the aesthetic vertex of human experience and this was his genius, he revered imagination, which he often designated as "image-ination." "All that can be imagined *is!*" he was fond of saying.

Bion in Perspective

Bion's public language, both in his speeches and writings, closely epitomize his metapsychological beliefs. He eschewed understanding because of his belief that understanding closed off the experience and therefore foreclosed the transformation in *O*. He often cautioned that one should not try to understand what he said or wrote but rather should be receptive to one's individual impressions and responses to what he said. "Do not listen to me, but listen to yourself listening to me," would be a succinct restatement of his view. He thereby clarified a theory of thinking whose rationalistic roots go back to Plato and have coursed through Kant. It embraces a philosophical conception of the human being as the innovator of imaginative conjecture, that intersects with the data of external experience (*K*) to emerge as thought. He arrived at these ideas about thinking from many years of psychoanalyzing psychotics who could not think. Psychoanalysis had previously concentrated on the treatment of neurotics who *could* think but would not in selected areas of inhibition. By clarifying that realm of psychotic transformation that is beyond repression and comprises the mutilation of thoughts and thinking, Bion added a whole new domain to our clinical knowledge as well.

The interested reader who wishes to become familiar with Bion for the first time, but who might be afraid of becoming lost in the progression of his works, might well begin by reading one of his last publications, *Bion in New York and Sao Paulo* (1980). No background is required, and the reader will be put quickly and effectively into Bion's way of thinking. For the more intrepid reader, I recommend all his works, especially his novel, *A Memoir of the Future* (1975, 1977, 1979), a trilogy that reflects his incredible virtuosity in fictional form and that constitutes a summary of his psychoanalytic thinking. For the reader who wishes to get to know Bion the man, I heartily recommend his autobiography, *The Long Week-End: 1897–1919*. This work is graphic, direct, uncharacteristically lucid, deeply personal, and moving.

REFERENCES

Bion, W. R. (1950). The Imaginary twin. In W. R. Bion, *Second Thoughts*, London: Heinemann, 1967, pp. 3–22.

Bion, W. R. (1954). Notes on the theory of schizophrenia. In W. R. Bion, *Second Thoughts*, London: Heinemann, pp. 23–35.

Bion, W. R. (1955). Language and the schizophrenic. *New Directions in Psychoanalysis*. (Eds.) Melanie Klein, Paula Heimann, and R. E. Miney-Kyrle. N.Y.: Basic Books, 1957, pp. 220–239.

Bion, W. R. (1956). Development of schizophrenic thought. In W. R. Bion, *Second Thoughts*, London: Heinemann, pp. 36–42.

Bion, W. R. (1957). Differentiation of the psychotic from the non-psychotic personality. In W. R. Bion, *Second Thoughts*, London: Heinemann, pp. 43–64.

Bion, W. R. (1958a). On arrogance. In W. R. Bion, *Second Thoughts* (pp. 86–92), London: Heinemann, 1967.

Bion, W. R. (1958b). On hallucination. In W. R. Bion, *Second Thoughts*, London: Heinemann, pp. 65–85.

Bion, W. R. (1959). Attacks on linking. In W. R. Bion, *Second Thoughts*, London: Heinemann, 93–109.

Bion, W. R. (1961). *Experiences in Groups*. London: Tavistock Publications.

Bion, W. R. (1962a). A theory of thinking. In W. R. Bion, *Second Thoughts*, London: Heinemann, pp. 110–119.

Bion, W. R. (1962b). *Learning from Experience*. London: Heinemann.

Bion, W. R. (1963). *Elements of Psycho-Analysis*. London: Heinemann.

Bion, W. R. (1965). *Transformations*. London: Heinemann.

Bion, W. R. (1970). *Attention and Interpretation*. London: Tavistock Publications.

Bion, W. R. (1975). *A Memoir of the Future: Book I: The Dream*. Brazil: Imago Editora.

Bion, W. R. (1977). *A Memoir of the Future: Book 2, The Past Presented*.

Bion, W. R. (1979). *A Memoir of the Future: Book 3, The Dawn of the Oblivion*. Perthsire: Clunie Press.

Bion, W. R. (1980). *Bion in New York and Sao Paulo*. Perthsire: Clunie Press.

Bion, W. R. (1982). *The Long Week-End: 1879–1919 – Part of a Life*. Abington: Fleetwood Press.

Freud, S. (1911). Psychoanalytic notes in an autobiographical account of a care of paranoia (dementia paranoides). *Standard Edition, 12*, 3–84.

Grostein, J. S. (1978). Inner space: Its dimensions and its coordinates. *International Journal of Psychoanalyis, 58*.

Hamilton, V. (1982). *Narcissus and Oedipus*. London: Routledge & Kegan Paul.

Rice, A. K. (1965). *Learning for Leadership: Interpersonal and Intergroup Relations*. London: Tavistock.

12 Paul Ricoeur: Reporting, Reading, and Interpreting

Robert S. Steele, Ph.D.

Hermeneutics is the reflective practice of interpretation. Although its primary concern is with textual exegesis, its domain extends throughout the humanities, from the social sciences to the arts. In his work, the eminent continental philosopher Paul Ricoeur has covered this territory. He has done close textual analyses and enlightening readings of what he called *The Symbolism of Evil* (Ricoeur, 1967), of religious faith and atheism, of the phenomenologies of Husserl and Jaspers, of psychoanalysis (1966, 1970, 1974), and of metaphor.

As a theory about the practice of interpretation, hermeneutic prescriptions can be made rather explicit (see, for example, Radnitzky, 1973 and Steele, 1979). However, these many guidelines about the text and reader relationship can be reduced to two conflicting demands that arise from the fact that books are both closed and open. A text, or any being or thing that is interpreted, is enclosed. It has its own boundaries, be they covers, the imaginary space inhabited by the "I," or the symbolic and real limits of our bodies. That closure or completeness must be respected, and a reading must be in part a reporting that presents the text on its own terms; one must be faithful to the letter. But, one must also help the spirit speak. When one opens a book, one enters a new place and, if the reading is engaging, the reader is changed by her or his immersion in the pages of another's thought. One owes it to the text and to the telos of modern consciousness to give back to the work the freedom it has given one. Interpretive readings open enclosures by bringing out what is latent, hidden, shy, or self-effacing in them.

Truth is opening. By reading Freud closely and sympathetically, Ricouer brings out of psychoanalysis new ways of seeing it that have been buried by the sediment of too many debates about the epistemological or, more specifically, scientific status of Freud's research. In my report on Ricoeur's work I will review these findings, discoveries that, when I first read Ricouer, revolutionized my thought about psychoanalysis.

In returning to Ricouer's *Freud and Philosophy* (1970) after nearly a decade, I have found not only that I have changed, but that the meaning of this book is also different. Of course, the words on the page are the same and my underlinings and marginal comments are still there to remind me of the joyous insights shared by author and reader, but what was once a manifestly brilliant work seems now to have a latent content, which casts a darker light on the surface text.

In my reading of Ricouer, the second part of this essay, I will bring to light what *Freud and Philosophy* does not say, and yet means. This reading will do violence to the text, because it breaks open its enclosed discourse by identifying the text's way of speaking as a symptomatic expression of androcentrism. I hope by naming this rather common textual constriction I will help others see it and thereby aid them in creating what Ricoeur many years ago helped me find: freedom.

The movement of the spirit is like a spiraling uroboros. In growing, consciousness continually consumes its previous insights. A book, a way of thinking, or a certain style of performance creates a new way of being in the world. Initially, perhaps, a book's message is resisted as unpalatable, but one comes to live its insights more and more, until one tires of the same fare day after day. Something new comes along, which is initially quite foreign, but in opening to it, in tasting it, one comes to like it and live it. The new way dates the old, in fact makes it old. One now has perspective on one's previous taste and can reflect upon it, criticize it, and perhaps preserve what is left of it by combining it in a new recipe for being.

Both the letter and the spirit of a work help us grow. The letter, the overt treatment of the issues, does this when we accommodate ourselves to it by letting it help us see in a different way; the spirit, what is manifestly unseen, does this by always promising new ways to be, even though within our present enclosure we feel complete.

THE REPORT

The son of Jules Ricoeur and Florentine Favre, Paul Ricoeur was born in Valence, France, in 1913. He married Simone Lejas in 1935, and they have five children.

Ricoeur's early work shows the influence of his mentor, Gabriel Marcel, but his intellectual scope has greatly expanded in the nearly half a century he has been writing philosophy. His many books and countless articles have made him a modern master. He holds appointments at the University of Paris and the University of Chicago.

Ricoeur's Place in the History of Psychoanalysis

Ricoeur's essays on Freud in *The Conflict of Interpretations* (1974) and *Freud and Philosophy* (1970) are part of the "return to Freud" movement which began in France in the late 1950s, flourished throughout the sixties, and was imported to America in the late seventies. Whereas Lacan was the charismatic, *enfant terrible*, psychoanalytic spokesriddler for "Freud's French Revolution" (Turkle, 1978), Ricoeur was the academic philosopher and scion of the rich phenomenological tradition.

"French Freud," as this genre has been called, stresses textual meditations on Freud's writings (Mehlman, 1976). These close, rich, and complex readings explore the ambiguities of psychoanalysis. The scope of these enquiries is broad ranging from Laplanche and Pontalis' (1973) marvelous essays on Freudian terms, to Derrida's (1976) at times baffling treatment of the meaning of inscription in Freud's writings, to Lacan's (1976) poetic and playful oedipal interpretation of Poe's "Purloined Letter," to the beautifully evocative prose of Irigaray (1980) on female sexuality.

For the French, American ego psychology is, if not anathema, at least in the dialectical position of antithesis to their synthesis. Where the Americans have stressed assimilation to the rigors of science, testing Freud's thought empirically, clarifying it by simplifying its ambiguities, and establishing sounder relations with biology, the French have abhorred the medical, scientific, and normative use of Freud by ego psychologists. If Hartmann's aspiration was to be a scientist, Lacan's was to be a poet.

As part of the French engagement with Freud, Ricoeur's work shares these prejudices. His reading reflects his tradition, which is phenomelogical and structural, but unlike Lacan's ricocheting potshots across the Atlantic, Ricoeur's treatment of Anglo-Saxon Freudian research is careful, concerned, and masterful. Like the Lacanian excavations of psychoanalysis, Ricoeur takes us into Freud. *Freud and Philosophy* is a textual, experiential exploration of the depths of psychoanalysis. Where the Americans point beyond Freud to a general psychology, the French, and Ricoeur in particular, return to Freud and teach us how to read him.

The Phenomenological Hermeneutic Tradition

Although, as noted, hermeneutics has traditionally been associated with textual exigesis, over the last century we have become conscious of ourselves as the ones who are interpreting. We have realized that humans are "hermeneutic animals" in that we read signs–be they tracks, traces, cries, auguries, data or texts. In our natural science we follow Newton in "reading the book of nature," and in our cultural sciences we find meaning in the artifacts of our being. Hermeneutics is interpretation; it is the practice of interpretation, the study of this practice, and reflection on such study. It is an articulation of the movement of consciousness from the inarticulate through to the well said.

Wilhelm Dilthey's vision of the province of hermeneutics was modest when, late in the nineteenth century, he declared that it was the methodological foundation of the *Geisteswissenschaften*. Trying to save the humanities from the progressive encroachment of the natural sciences, Dilthey asserted that the cultural interpreter had special access to his or her subject because, unlike the natural scientist who must observe nature objectively from the outside, the hermeneut is a participant within the historical field. Participant observation is at the heart of social analysis, because an understanding of the culture that constitutes us is only gained in and through our participation in civilization.

Unlike the scientist, who, through various cultural ritual, tries to separate him- or herself from phenomena classified as natural and is therefore necessarily removed from participation with the object of study, the interpreter is enmeshed in her or his humanity and thereby participates within the phenomenon being analyzed. Whereas the orthodox natural scientist must be freed from co-participation in nature and must block empathetic responses, the interpreter must begin with empathy and use it as the source from which to articulate her or his work.

Unlike natural science, which, in trying to universalizes its findings, resists attempts to relativize its objective results by submitting them to sociohistorical critiques, hermeneutics is firmly rooted in its history and constantly submits its seminal ideas and texts to reinterpretation. Whereas science orients itself in the replication and extension of observations, hermeneutics locates itself within language and our textual heritage.

Ricoeur's lineage goes back to Descartes, and his work traces the evolution and descent of the *cogito* and consciousness through the master works of phenomenology–the writings of Hegel, Nietzsche, Husserl, Heidegger, and Merleau-Ponty. His reading of Freud is a confrontation of his tradition–the hermeneutic phenomenology of consciousness– with the science of the unconscious–psychoanalysis. Ricoeur (1950) writes: "I should say at the start that reading works on psychoanalysis has convinced me of the existence of facts and processes which remain incomprehensible as long as I remain prisoner of a narrow conception of consciousness" (pp. 375–376). In exemplary hermeneutic fashion, Ricoeur is intent on submitting the prejudices of his training, which he recognizes as restricting, to the challenge of Freud's attacks on the narcissism of consciousness. All good readings are, however, dialectical: Not only was Ricoeur changed by reading Freud, but Freud, too, was altered. This is because the product of Ricoeur's years of Freudian study, *Freud and Philosophy: An Essay on Interpretation* (1970), is a book that has created a new understanding of psychoanalysis, not as some misfit science, but as a hermeneutic endeavor.

A Summary of Ricoeur's Reading of Freud

Freud and Philosophy is a master text. Its tone is one of reconciliation, restoration, and exploration. Its arguments are complex and demand an understanding of both the phenomenological and logico-empirical traditions. In reading it, it helps to have read Freud closely, because one then understands more deeply how Ricoeur's revisions are based both on the letter of Freud and the spirit of his project, which is to make the latent manifest.

This review will summarize four major interrelated themes that organize *Freud and Philosophy:* saving Freud from science, the place of consciousness after Freud, the semantics of desire, and Ricoeur's study of symbolism.

Saving Freud from Science. Although Freud located psychoanalysis within the domain of the natural sciences and insisted on its scientific status, his work has long been exiled from that land to which he was never granted a passport. His one prize, the Goethe, was in letters; he is studied in the humanities, not in biology or scientific psychology.

Ricoeur provides Freud a haven from his scientific critics by granting them their criticism. Ricoeur (1970) agrees that "psychoanalysis is not an observational science" (p. 358), but he uses this admission to counter behaviorist, experimental, and logico-empiricist attacks on psychoanalysis. Drawing the line clearly between psychology as a behavioral science and psychoanalysis, Ricoeur declares that the difference between them "comes at the beginning or never." He continues: "Psychology is an observational science dealing with the facts of behavior; psychoanalysis is an exegetical science dealing with the relationships of meaning between substitute objects and the primordial (and lost) instinctual objects" (p. 359). Whereas a fact in behaviorism is a datum that is verifiable by multiple independent observers, there are no facts, as science understands them, in psychoanalysis, "for the analyst does not observe, he interprets" (p. 365). Behaviors are significant in psychoanalysis because they are "signifiers for the history of desire" and not because they are "observables" (p. 364). For Freud, the focus of study is the meaning of symptoms, dreams, delusions, and faulty actions in a life story that is being unfolded. The analysand's speech and behaviors present these, and the analyst and analysand articulate their significance through interpretation.

If significant behaviors are operationally defined and recorded in settings that do not allow the ambivalence of human action to be shown or the ambiguities of speech to be expressed, then there is no need for psychoanalysis. This is because what is manifest in the observational situation is defined as the datum; it need not be read, but only recorded. Any such situation is neither entirely human nor psychoanalytic. Any capitulation on this point is to Ricoeur an abandonment of what he sees as Freud's central project: the explication of meaning through discourse. It is in the illusions and disillusionments of exchange between analyst and analysand, reader and text, ourselves and others as well as between us and our artifacts—paintings, music, machines, and dreams—that hermeneutics locates itself and in which Ricoeur places Freud's work.

The Place of Consciousness after Freud. Freeing epistemology from the dictates of scientific rationalism, liberating language from the demands of rational discourse, and saving the person from the rationalizations of false consciousness are three variations on one historical theme: "the dispossession of the ego" (Ricoeur, 1970, p. 55).

For Descartes the *cogito,* "I think, therefore I am," is a transparent certainty in a world of things and beings that are opaque and resistant to immediate understanding. However, if consciousness is not pellucid, if it "is not what it thinks it is, a new relation must be instituted between the patent and the latent" (Ricoeur, 1970, p. 33). Ricoeur continues: "After the [Cartesian] doubt about things, we have started to doubt consciousness" and those "masters of suspicion"—Marx, Nietzsche, and Freud—have fostered our distrust of the purity of consciousness, which is a given for empiricism and phenomenology. "All three [men] clear the horizon for a more authentic word, for a new reign of Truth, not only by means of a 'destructive' critique, but by the invention of an art of *interpreting*" (p. 33). To be suspicious means to doubt the given—be that the evidence of our senses, our instruments, our consciousness, or the text before us—and to create via interpretation from the latent, the unseen, the unconscious, and the unsaid a context that illuminates the ambiguities of the obvious.

Ricoeur began his reading of Freud in order to challenge the epistemologies of consciousness in which he was schooled, and so he is very careful in locating the position of consciousness in Freud's work. Freud displaces consciousness in two ways: He makes its position relative to other psychic processes in the mind, and he discounts the veracity of its testimony.

Freud not only removes consciousness from the center of mental being, he keeps changing its location and redefining its relations to the ego as he creates new representations of the psyche. Ricoeur painstakingly records and comments on these moves in Freud's texts, because with these models Freud is not only trying to locate consciousness, he is also redefining its relationship to knowing.

The first representation that Ricoeur considers (he does not examine Freud's psychic model in *Studies on Hysteria*), is the neuronal ego of *The Project for a Scientific Psychology* and the ω system with which Freud (1895) unsuccessfully tries to represent consciousness. Ricoeur calls Freud's neuropsychological model "a nonhermeneutic state of the system." This biophysics machine did not run, because within it Freud could not represent meaning; it did not explain consciousness. It was replaced by the mental apparatus of chapter 7 of *The Interpretation of Dreams* (1900), which is a topographical spatialization of the psyche with three regions—unconscious, preconscious, and conscious—and boundaries of censorship between them.

This topography improves on that of the Project because it not only pictures intrapsychic relations, it also helps to explain how we come to know. In it Freud combines the energetics of the Project with the hermeneutics of dream interpretation to describe the process of making the unconscious conscious. The dream work at the behest of the censorship between the unconscious and the preconscious distorts, by the mechanisms of condensation and displacement, unacceptable wishes in order to preserve the repose of the sleeping ego, which would be shocked by such desires. This dream work is undone by a countereffort of interpretation, as consciousness comes to know of these impulses retrospectively through interpreting their disguised expression in dreams. Freud has linked his energetics to his hermeneutics because the mechanisms of condensation and displacement not only signify transformations of energy, but they also provide interpretive concepts for understanding the distortion in dreams. Any picture or text will be garbled if its scenes are compacted and confused and its emphasis is misplaced. One brings out what is latent in it by unpacking and sorting out its images and relocating its emphasis. Knowing, within this model, means making evident to ego consciousness, through interpretation or undoing of the dream work, what it has been denied by its own censorship.

The next significant "dispossession of the ego" from its reign as all-knowing consciousness comes in Freud's papers on metapsychology. Working with the topography of the dream book, Freud (1914) further displaces the omnipotent ego by showing first that its esteem comes from its self-cathexis. Therefore the ego is, in part, narcissistic, self-absorbed, and infantile. He next explored the complexities of the relations between the conscious and the unconscious and linked these to concepts of instinctual representation and verbal inscription (Freud, 1915). He thereby cast more doubt on whether ego consciousness has unmediated access to its desires, its past, or the world, since what it knows directly is censored transcriptions of experience. Finally, in *Mourning and Melancholia* (1917), Freud forever violates the integrity of the ego by showing how it is structured by its identifications with significant others and altered by its incorporations of lost love objects.

In his papers on technique (circa 1911–15), Freud explored the implications for analysis of dealing with a consciousness that is an agent of the ego's defenses. No longer is the analysand's knowing simply dependent on an insightful interpretation that enlightens an anxious ego; insight now depends on working through in the analytic session all those traumas that have distorted one's relations with reality. Thus, the increasing complexity of Freud's representations of the energetics and topography of the psyche is mirrored by a corresponding complexity in what it means to make an interpretation that creates insight. Interpretation now comes to be imbedded in the transference relationship as the analysand relives via projection onto the analyst the scenes of a life which have worked to make consciousness resistant not only to the unconscious but to knowledge about itself (Freud, 1912).

These insights, along with Freud's work on the ontogeny and phylogeny of the Oedipus complex, are incorporated into Freud's last and most radical revisioning of the psyche in the structural model of *The Ego and the Id* (1923). In this work the solipsistic energy system of the Project is gone. The psyche is now a scene inhabited by near mythological personifications of nature (the "it"), culture (the superego), and identity (the "I"), which take their roles and masks from those that the "it" and the "I" have loved and lost. Consciousness in this model has been moved very far from center stage; it is now just a facet of the ego, which in itself incorporates nearly the entire psyche of the first topography. The "I" has its own unconscious, preconscious, and conscious regions.

The implications for epistemology of this last model are profound, because there is no grounding for positive knowledge in an ego consciousness free of the conflicts of life. The "I" has as its heritage, and built into its structure, an individual and cultural history of defense, censorship, and distortion. To undo this dream work of a lifetime, these oneiric deposits of civilization, becomes an interminable task of interpretation guided by the principles of psychoanalytic exegesis. The analytic setting still has its locus in the consulting room, but the analysand is now not only the individual patient with his or her fantasies and symptoms, but civilization with its religious delusions, sexual repression, and artifacts, which, like the ego, are the sediment of unfulfilled desire.

The Semantics of Desire.   The French psychoanalytic project is to articulate a semantics of desire, about which Ricoeur (1970) writes: "The semantics of desire . . . is bound up with [the] postponement of satisfaction, with the endless mediating of pleasure" (p. 322). In addition, it is tied to the never-ending postponement of meaning and the mediation of being through language. Freud's coupled discourses, the energics of pleasure and the hermeneutics of meaning, are dialectically interwoven in his attempts to represent the vicissitudes of longing. The energy metaphors – and they became metaphors when the psychic apparatus replaced the neuronal machine – are used to give an accounting of the disjunction between one meaning and another. The hermeneutics of desire involves the replacement of one meaning (the manifest) with another, more fundamental and authentic articulation of the wish (the latent). The energetics or economics of desire uses a system of interrelated concepts like cathexis, displacement, and condensation to account for the movement of forces from one place to another, movements that displace and disguise meaning. Force, place, and meaning, then, are the terms of Freud's thought, and every concept is determined by its coordinates in his topographical energic system of reading signs.

Desire arises from a lack, a void. In its generation it is already a substitute, which covers over with longing what cannot be said: the place of nothing, of mute death. Displacement and replacement are the two terms that are joined in the semantics of desire and in the homeopathic treatment of psychoanalysis. If neurosis arises from the displacement of psychic conflict into symptoms, and the symptoms replace the conflict with a symbiotic representation in the speech of the body or behavior, then analysis replaces the original conflict, restores the latent, by displacing the manifest symptoms via interpretation. This restoration, however, does not occur in the original context, the traumatic scene, but in its reproduction in the transference relationship. The analyst takes the place of significant others, as scenes of frustration are restaged in a situation where insight – intellectual pleasure – takes the place of desire. The desire to know, to have a life history without lacunae in its narration, is the substitute satisfaction offered by psychoanalytic interpretation for those carnal pleasures that can never be realized. The articulation of desire through interpretation is a sublimation of an unnameable longing.

The Study of Symbolism.   This longing is, perhaps, to become an "I," to be an identity that is not haunted by imagoes from long ago and is not a fabric of fantasies that serve as a gloss for the past. However, this very task remains the unnamed project in Freud's work, and "the empty concept of sublimation is the final symbol of this unspoken factor" (Ricoeur, 1970, p. 492). Freud could never give a satisfactory economic or energic account of sublimation, for it arises not from defense but from reflection. It is a transmutation of the natural into the cultural, of the carnal into the spiritual. Sublimation is a hermeneutic term which stands for a transcendental movement of the spirit toward the realization of consciousness. Freud, who did not speak of the self or things transcendental, could not, of course, say this. Ricoeur in his writing on symbolism, tries to name what is missing in Freud, to say what Freud cannot.

Symbols are products of desire; in fact, Ricoeur (1970) asserts, "If man could be satisfied . . . he would be deprived of symbolization" (p. 322). The symbol stands for desire, but unlike the symptom, which is but a disguised signifier for the repetitive insistence of desire to be signified, the symbol captures, contains, and transforms desire into a living sign in which signifier and signified are held together in a sublime icon.

Religion is a collective neurosis because its expression is a symptomatic repetition of the longing for the father. Its iconography requires belief, thereby blocking the process of individual participation and reflection essential to sublimation. Art does not repetitively recapitulate a man's or mens' past, because the work of art is not simply a projection of the artist's or the culture's conflicts; it is "the sketch of their solution." Dreams, symptoms, and religion "look backward toward infancy, the past; the work of art goes ahead of the artist; it is a prospective symbol of his personal synthesis and of man's future, rather than a regressive symbol of his unresolved conflicts" (Ricoeur, 1970, p. 175).

That "progression and regression are carried by the same symbols" is the Ricoeurian insight which mediates his hermeneutic phenomenology with Freud's psychoanalysis. The symbol arises from unfilled desire, and, therefore, points to the past; but it also takes one forward into the future, providing a guide for the movement of reflection. That Freud only reads symbols backward to their ontogenetic and phylogentic origins was pointed out long ago by Jung (1913) and has been elaborately critiqued by him (1916), by Ricoeur (1970), and by Steele (1982). The past Freud thereby creates, however, is itself symbolic, because Freud uses all his primal events and primary processes to delimit the boundaries of the imaginary and to provide narrative guidelines by which to organize his analyses of the present (Laplanche and Pontalis, 1968).

Ricoeur (1970) insists, as did Jung, that symbols must also be read progressively, because "the emergence of the self is inseparable from its production through a progressive synthesis." This is because "the truth of a given moment lies in the subsequent moment" (p. 464) and the significance of a symbol always lies in the future developments of its meanings, in the trajectory of interpretations and in the realization of the spirit. However, reflection on all of this always proceeds retrogressively. The past – the archaeology of the subject – and the future – the teleology of the spirit – meet in symbols whose interpretation engenders the development of self-consciousness, which arises by making the past present through retrospective analysis and the future imminent in the present through imagining the meanings of the symbols.

It is in this temporal duality of the symbol that Ricoeur finds hope not only for the synthesis of the self through the development of self-consciousness, but for a joining of the two styles of hermeneutics that have been at odds for years: the hermeneutics of suspicion and of restoration. The two come together in what serves as Ricoeur's epigram for *Freud and Philosophy* (1970): "Thus the idols must die – so that symbols may live" (p. 531).

Why psychoanalysis is necessary to phenomenology is that analytic suspicion is needed to break the thrall that makes us the slave of the idols of the past, be they parental imagoes, castration anxieties, or simple narcissistic egocentrism. Why psychoanalysis needs a hermeneutics of the spirit is to free it from its bondage to the past and to aid it in reconstructing a past, which serves as a ground for the present on which to build a future – a future that is not an illusion, because it comes from a less-distorted past.

THE READING

Consciousness grows by cannibalistic criticism of its grounds, its prejudices, and its embedded, unseen ways of being. For anyone with a history who grows, that which was once liberating becomes constricting, and that which was once a criticism of orthodoxies becomes an orthodoxy to be criticized. *Freud and Philosophy* helped free me from the prohibitions against thought that are fostered by an American scientific education and that make it hard to appreciate what is truly revolutionary in Freud's science: its pursuit of knowledge through dialogue, its concern with meanings over observables, and its devotion to the development of critical self-consciousness. However, in returning to Ricoeur after writing my own "conflicts of interpretation" (Steele, 1982), after teaching many brilliant and radical students, and after becoming a feminist, I feel that *Freud and Philosophy* promulgates many of the same oppressive values that are dear to both science and psychoanalysis. The common perspective of these becomes visible when one steps outside of it and sees that psychoanalysis, science, and hermeneutics share a masculinist world view, a weltanschauung, in which most of us were reared. One of the joys of feminist hermeneutics is standing apart from this very old tradition and showing how this embedded way of doing things is restrictive, antilibertarian, and often just plain wrong.

The masculine voice, which is shared by Ricoeur, Freud, and most scientists and academics, is rigorous, objective, concerned with authority, determined to debate the issues, mute or opinionated on the subject of women, and utterly positive about what is natural. In what follows I will show how Ricoeur's immersion in this way of speaking creates several interrelated problems in *Freud and Philosophy* and is responsible for various errors in it. None of the four topics I will consider are manifestly central to Ricoeur's text. Their position is latent, so their importance will only be established through an interpretive reading in which I shall show that Ricouer's dismissal of Jung, his overweening concern with authority, his disregard for women, and his reductive, demeaning conceptualization of nature are all aspects of the androcentric bias that dominates his book.

The Rejection of Jung

To anyone who has read Jung, Ricoeur's modifications of the psychoanalytic theory of symbolism will be repetitive, not innovative. Jung's *Symbols of Transformation* (1911–12), which helped speed the break with Freud, was about the regressive and progressive function of symbols and about their function of transforming carnal into spiritual fantasies. In his "On the Psychology of Unconscious" (1943), Jung does both analytic-reductive (Freudian) and synthetic-prospective (Jungian) interpretations of the same case; and his studies of the interrelations of transference, sublimation and symbolism (Jung, 1946) would have aided Ricoeur in his discussion of these.

There are no citations to Jung's works in *Freud and Philosophy*. Ricoeur dismisses Jung because he is confusing and not a rigorous thinker like Freud. Ricoeur (1970) says: "With Freud I know where I am going; with Jung everything risks being confused: the psychism, the soul, the arthetypes, the sacred" (p. 176). For Ricoeur, Freud is a strong, sure leader, whereas with Jung he fears being lost. This craving to always know where one is is typical of thinkers who are concerned with mastery and with following a master. It doesn't hurt to be lost or confused; one might just find something new. Jung explored the female symbolism of the unconscious and the importance of goddesses. This is something neither Ricoeur nor Freud, both of whom were unwilling to risk being lost in fantasy, in the "realm of the mothers," could find.

Although Jung's writing is associative, symbolic, suggestive, and often mythopoeic, it is usually only confusing to those who expect causal, argumentative prose and are uncomfortable with loose thinking. For the confused, however, Jung even provides a dictionary (1921).

I doubt if Ricouer ever really tried to read Jung. If he had, he would have soon discovered that his ideas on symbols were thoroughly Jungian. There has been, ever since Freud exiled Jung, a compulsive quality to psychoanalysis' dismissal of Jung's work. Ricoeur merely repeats Freud's actions, but he seems to have read even less Jung than did Freud.

This dividing into camps, schools, teams, and disciplines who worship a totemic founder is so obviously a primitive male bonding ritual that one would think that men of reason, like Ricoeur and Freud, would have renounced its practice. In modern times, however, the rite has merely been transformed through the cunning of reason into a proper and reasonable respect for authority.

Issues of Authority

Freud makes rules and leads. This makes him an authority to Ricoeur. Citing another great authority in order to justify his own feelings on what legitimates psychoanalysis, Ricoeur adopts Kant's view that a system is limited by what justifies it. Freud's determination to explain the most complex phenomena from the topographic-economic point of view is, according to Ricoeur (1970), a restriction "which gives psychoanalysis its rights" (p. 153). Such limits serve to facilitate Ricoeur's project, which is to conduct "a rigorous debate with the true founder of psychoanalysis" (p. xi).

If the boundary lines of knowledge claims are not clearly drawn, then debate about ideas, which are an intellectual's property, cannot be judiciously conducted, and the lineage of a thought cannot be unambiguously traced back to the father. In a short space it is difficult to critique the notion that ideas are discovered, owned, claimed, and adjudicated, except to suggest that if the outlines of such a critique are not obvious, then the reader is not aware of how much his or her thought is dominated by the tropes and practices of capitalism. That ideas come from a founder and are passed on to his followers is so obviously totemic, and so germane to both Freud's and Ricoeur's work, that I will take time to develop its connections with the biases of the masculinist perspective.

Much of *Freud and Philosophy* is about the significance of the Oedipus complex and the symbolism of the father. The father, for Ricoeur (1970), is "the name-giver and the lawgiver," with the institution of the father – patriarchy – serving the son by directing his education in the culture. Freud serves these purposes for Ricoeur: He named psychoanalysis and established the rules of its practice. More than this, however, psychoanalysis is an education in culture. Ricoeur (1970) says Freud's work is "a monument of our culture" and a place "in which our culture is expressed and understood" (p. xi).

To acquire culture then, one must be educated by Freud, and Ricoeur (1970) opens his work with the simple declaration that, "This work is a discussion or debate with Freud" (p. 3). This single line is a clear expression of the symbolism of the father in modern academic totemism. For "Freud," here, is a trope, the name "Freud" being a metonymy for the master's work. Debates with dead men are only possible in societies that revere their elders and have a set of cultural practices that preserve their deeds after their deaths. Our reverence for the immortal works of genius is just such a mechanism, and the idea that we can debate with these men is an obvious illusion. While Sigmund Freud was alive, few people held successful debates with him. Jung, with ideas very similar to Ricoeur's, tried and failed. But Ricoeur's metonymic Freud is much more the ideal or totemic father. He is not the primal tyrant that Wittels (1924) describes, but the embodiment of rigor, suspicion, and closely reasoned debate.

It is not some anomaly in Ricoeur's character that makes *Freud and Philosophy* an extended intellectual oedipal drama. It is that authority in our culture is paternal, and a man, to be a scholar, must make his place among the fathers. Ricoeur's scholarship is impeccable in this regard; he cites, critiques, modifies, and expands on the ideas of one master after another (Hegel, Kant, Marx, Nietzsche, Heidegger, etc.) in exemplary academic fashion, thereby displaying his expertise and ensuring that his work will be commented on by future generations. Indeed, *Freud and Philosophy* has become a master text upon which an ambitious son, displaying all his scholarly expertise, is commenting. This must stop, because identification with the masters means an acceptance of their discourse and their rules of debate.

The Omission of Women

There are almost no references to women in Ricoeur's work; in fact, the few places they are present in the text they are identified with the absent or the lost. Whereas the father is a strong presence throughout, and Ricoeur has much to say about him, he accepts Freud's portrait of the mother as an "archaic object . . . who bore us, nursed us and cared for us" (Ricoeur, 1970, p. 445). That is all he says, and he is speaking Freud's words.

The only other significant reference to women is in a discussion of Freud's (1910) analysis of Leonardo da Vinci's relationship with his mother. In this instance, Ricoeur's contact with females is mediated not by one man, but by two, and Ricoeur's theme is that symbols signify absence born of desire. The "unreal smile" of Mona Lisa is a symbol for "the smile of the *lost* mother" of Leonardo (Ricoeur, 1970, p. 177). If women are archaic, lost, and symbols of absence, this is not so much a description of them as it is a comment on their place in Ricoeur's discourse. They are simply absent from his text, and he seems to know about them only through their representation in the works of other men.

This omission of women, however, is no simple oversight; it is a near blindness born of masculine myopia. Ricoeur returns to Freud's analysis of Leonardo when he takes up the topics of religion and the Oedipus complex. Following Freud, Ricoeur (1970) writes,

If religious illusion stems from the father complex, the "dissolution" of the Oedipus complex is attained only with the notion of an order stripped of any paternal coefficient, an order that is anonymous and impersonal. Ananke is therefore the symbol of disillusion . . . Ananke is the name of a nameless reality, for those who have "renounced their father." It is chance, the absence of relationship between the laws of nature and our desires or illusions. . . . Ananke, it seems to me, is a symbol of a world view . . . in it is summed up a wisdom that dares to face the harshness of life [pp. 327–328].

In this passage the omission of women is oppressive. First, "an order of things stripped of any paternal coefficient" is not anonymous and impersonal. Women exist. As mothers they provide one of the most complex and personal relationships we will ever have. They lay down the law, and they are usually the person who gives us our first name and who we name first. As lesbians, feminist separtists, and as people whose identities come neither from their fathers nor husbands, women also exist.

Women are made invisible, anonymous, and impersonal by denying their existence or transforming them into things, into "its." Ananke is a female goddess, a she, not an it. But Ricoeur, twice calls her "it," thus ensuring her anonymity.

Denatured Nature

Ricoeur, like most other hermeneuts, has accepted science's grossly unnatural representation of nature. He speaks of "the laws of nature" and refers to "the conditions of objectivity of nature" (1970, p. 48). He characterizes Freud's energic tropes as nonhermeneutic, because such language describes the transformations of the natural order. Ricoeur nowhere sees that science interprets nature in some odd ways. Science has turned nature into a thing in order to investigate and exploit her (Griffin, 1978). There are no laws of nature, only laws of men, which are used to tame nature's unruly ways. Science uses nature as a stage on which to strut its prowess, but feminist critics have shown what is being done. A subset of existence has been set apart by us as an other, a mother, a "she" and an "it" and designated as natural (Dinnerstein, 1977). The "objectivity of nature" is pure projection onto this other, and science sees reflected back from this mirror its own projections onto her. Finally, nature is no more a system of energic transformations than it is God's creation or a giant turtle. The representation of the natural as energic is of recent origin and is the animism of a materialist, mechanistic culture (Merchant, 1980).

I think Ricoeur accepts the natural scientists' representation of nature because of the general acquiescence of authorities in one field to experts in another. The deal struck by Dilthey with science, "You take nature, we'll take culture," is still honored by his descendant, Ricoeur. Ricoeur follows other twentieth century covenants of rationality: He is respectful of genius and wary of mystics, and he believes what other men say about women.

REFERENCES

Derrida, J. (1976). Freud and the scene of writing. In J. Mehlman (Ed.), *French Freud: Structural studies in psychoanalyists* (pp. 73–117). Millwood, NY: Kraus Reprint Co.

Dinnerstein, D. (1977). *The mermaid and the minotaur: Sexual arrangements and human malaise.* New York: Harper.

Freud, S. (1895). Project for a scientific psychology. *Standard Edition, 1,* 295–397.

Freud, S. (1900). The interpretation of dreams. *Standard Edition, 4.*

Freud, S. (1910). Leonardo da Vinci and a memory of his childhood. *Standard Edition, 11,* 63–137.

Freud, S. (1912). The dynamics of transference. *Standard Edition, 12,* 99–108.

Freud, S. (1914). On narcissism: An introduction. *Standard Edition, 14,* 73–102.

Freud, S. (1915). The unconscious. *Standard Edition, 14,* 166–215.

Freud, S. (1917). Mourning and melancholia. *Standard Edition, 14,* 243–258.

Freud, S. (1923). The ego and the id. *Standard Edition, 19,* 12–66.

Griffin, S. (1978). *Woman and nature: The roaring inside her.* New York: Harper.

Irigaray, L. (1980). When our lips speak together (Carolyn Burke, Trans.). *Signs, 6,* 69–79.

Jung, C. G. (1911–12). Symbols of transformation. *Collected Works, 5,* 1956.

Jung, C. G. (1913). General aspects of psychoanalysis. *Collected Works, 4,* 229–242.

Jung, C. G. (1916). *The psychology of the unconscious* (B. Hinkle, Trans.). New York: Moffat, Yard & Co., 1916.

Jung, C. G. (1921). Psychological types. *Collected Works, 6,* 3–495.

Jung, C. G. (1943). On the psychology of the unconscious. *Collected Works, 7.*

Jung, C. G. (1946). The psychology of the transference. *Collected Works, 16,* 163–323.

Lacan, J. (1976). Seminar on "The Purloined Letter." In J. Mehlman (Ed.), *French Freud: Structural studies in psychoanalysis* (pp. 38–72). Millwood, N.Y.: Kraus Reprint Co.

Laplanche, J., & Pontalis, J.-B. (1968). Fantasy and the origins of sexuality. *International Journal of Psycho-Analysis, 49,* 1–18.

Laplanche, J., & Pontalis, J.-B. (1973). *The language of psychoanalysis* (D. Nicholson-Smith, Trans.). New York: Norton.

Mehlman, J. (Ed.). (1976). *French Freud: Structural studies in psychoanalysis.* Millwood, N.Y.: Kraus Reprint Co.

Merchant, C. (1980). *The death of nature: Women, ecology, and the scientific revolution.* New York: Harper.

Radnitzky, G. (1973). Contemporary schools of metascience. Chicago: Henry Regnery.

Ricoeur, P. (1950). *Freedom and nature: The voluntary and the involuntary* (E. Kohak, Trans.). Evanston, IL: Northwestern University Press, 1966.

Ricoeur, P. (1967). *The symbolism of evil* (E. Buchanan, Trans.). New York: Harper.

Ricoeur, P. (1970). *Freud and philosophy: An essay on interpretation* (D. Savage, Trans.). New Haven: Yale University Press.

Ricoeur, P. (1974). *The conflict of interpretations: Essays in hermeneutics* (D. Ihde, Ed.). Evanston, IL: Northwestern University Press.

Steele, P. (1979). Psychoanalysis and hermeneutics. *International Review of Psycho-Analysis, 6,* 389–411.

Steele, R. with S. Swinney (Consult. Ed.). (1982). *Freud and Jung: Conflicts of interpretation.* London: Routledge & Kegan Paul.

Turkle, S. (1978). *Psychoanalytic politics: Freud's French Revolution.* Cambridge, MA: MIT Press.

Wittels, F. (1924). *Sigmund Freud: His personality, his teaching, and his school.* New York: Dodd, Mead.

13 Jacques Lacan: Psychoanalyst, Surrealist, and Mystic

Jeanine Parisier Plottel, Ph.D.

Jacques Lacan's contribution to psychoanalytic theory and practice is and has been the subject of intense controversy. The quarrels between various factions of both enemies and disciples, the counterculture quality of his teaching, and the political implications of some of his positions have cast shadows on a correct appraisal of his work. The notoriety that came to Lacan in old age, his links with linguistics and structuralism, and his role as trend setter of the Paris intelligentsia have obscured his significant legacy to French psychoanalysis, psychiatry, and neurology. Although many facets of Lacan's approach to psychoanalysis may seem heretical, in fact, its archaeology, in the sense of Michel Foucault, leads to the nineteenth century French tradition of psychiatry and neurology – to Jean-Martin Charcot and other French masters of Freud. Indeed, when considering Lacan's evolution, it is important to remember that this very same tradition was one of the catalysts in Freud's development that led to the creation of psychoanalysis. A brief review of how the Viennese disciple viewed Charcot, his French teacher, will provide the first key to Lacan's texts.

It is common knowledge that Freud's studies with Charcot at the Salpétrière in Paris from October 1885 to the end of February 1886 marked a turning point in the direction of his interests. What may not be so well remembered is how much Freud admired Charcot's clinical presentations of patients. We cannot assert that Freud went so far as to give up the traditional German way in favor of French clinical technique, but this technique was surely integrated in his method. His description of how Charcot presented his patients (Freud, 1887–88) em-

333

phasizes the "concepts of the 'entité morbide', of the series, of the 'type' and of the 'formes frustes'" (p. 135). Such concepts are important in French clinical method and were quite foreign to the German perspective.

What especially struck Freud, however – and I am certain that the psychoanalytic infrastructures bear traces of this to this day – was Charcot's friendliness and openness, his responsiveness to students, whom he considered his peers. Freud (1893) ascribes "the intellectual significance" of this man

> to the magic that emanated from his looks and from his voice, to the kindly openness which characterized his manner as soon as his relations with someone had overcome the stage of initial strangeness, to the willingness with which he put everything at the disposal of his pupils, and to his life-long loyalty to them. The hours he spent in his wards were hours of companionship and of an exchange of ideas with the whole of his medical staff [p. 16]...

Freud went on to elaborate:

> As a teacher, Charcot was positively fascinating. Each of his lectures was a little work of art in construction and composition; it was perfect in form and made such an impression that for the rest of the day one could not get the sound of what he had said out of one's ears or the thought of what he had demonstrated out of one's mind [p. 17].

I am not going to delve into the substance of Charcot's science and art – a recent history of psychoanalysis in France, *La bataille de cent ans*, by Elisabeth Roudinesco (1982) has already done this – but I want to stress the oral aspect of his legacy. There is an analogy between knowledge transmitted in such a way and the transference that takes place in the course of an analysis. Spectacle and encounter captivated Freud, just as they had many other scientists and laymen. It can also be argued that the significance of Lacan's manner should be sought in the traditional mediums of Charcot and other French alienists that had struck Freud: oral presentation of clinical cases, lectures, and teaching in an asylum setting.

That Lacan wrote very little and published even less – in fact, only his thesis and a few articles – has been pointed out by several critics. In her recent book, *Vies et légendes de Jacques Lacan*, Catherine Clément (1981), a philosopher turned journalist, observes that most of the essays included in Lacan's *Ecrits* (1966) are papers and communications that were first read at meetings and congresses. The six volumes published to date in the *Séminaire* series (Lacan, 1953-54, 1954-55, 1955-56,

1964, 1972–73), transcripts of Lacan's so-called seminar ("lecture" is the American term), were edited not by Lacan himself but by Jacques-Alain Miller, his son-in-law. This *Séminaire* that is Lacan's major achievement, and we must always bear in mind that its essence is essentially oral. Although these lectures were very carefully prepared, ideas came to Lacan as he spoke before an audience, and some of the best parts were improvised. These improvisations were charismatic, even inspired, in the literal sense of the word. Their effect on the audience was comparable to the frenzy of an extraordinary bullfight, to the ecstasy of the mystics, and to the passion of absolute love. Then, little by little, as the year went by, the language miracle failed and the spell loosened. Inspiration ceased; the magician on the podium lost his power and turned into an old, hollow man.

In old age, Lacan became a Parisian celebrity, a household word in households where nobody had ready a single one of his paragraphs. With his friend Claude Lévi-Strauss, he was the representative of the new structuralism, the "ism" that had followed Jean-Paul Sartre's existentialism. For more than 20 years, attendance at Lacan's Séminaire was de rigueur for anyone who wanted to be in the mainstream of French thought – Barthes, Derrida, Leiris, Jakobson, Kristeva, and Sollers (Schneiderman, 1983), for example, and not merely out-of-town intellectuals. If Lacan happened to dine at Maxim's or some such place, his presence was noted. For instance, Stuart Schneiderman (1983) tells a story in which Lacan managed to upstage Roman Polanski, who was sharing his table. But I believe that Lacan's serious achievements belonged to the fortieth, fiftieth, and sixtieth decades of his life, before he actually attained notoriety and an international reputation.

It is obvious that the texts of Lacan's old age are as elusive as those of many certified psychotics. Are they poetry? Creations of a psychoanalytic Zen master? Do they signal a revolution in psychoanalytic form? Or have these texts been edited in such a way that they take on the stamp of the meanderings of the unconscious? The cliché, "Only time will tell," is in order here. However, although Lacan is indeed a difficult and precious writer, most of us find that, read in chronological order, he is quite accessible. Most of his writings are no more arcane than those of Melanie Klein or Heinz Hartmann. And most of Lacan's significant ideas were present at a time when he still wrote in an easily intelligible way. To my mind, the complicated mathematical knots, the abstruse formulas, the complex formal symbolism added little if anything to the substance of the most important psychoanalytical theorist since Freud.

What explanation can be offered? Clément (1981) puts it well when she states that for a long time, the author was Jacques-Marie Lacan, and when he was Jacques-Marie Lacan, he was comprehensible. We can apply to him his offhand remark about Napoleon (Lacan, 1950, p. 39; 1966, p. 171). "What is the difference between a madman who takes himself for Napoleon and Napoleon himself?" he asked. The obvious answer is that unlike the madman, Napoleon never believed he was Napoleon, but knew he was Bonaparte, and remembered very well what he had done in order to turn Bonaparte into Napoleon. So perhaps Jacques-Marie Lacan knew how he had become Lacan, the guru of French psychoanalysis. Perhaps only his disciples, those who call themselves Lacanians, take the legend seriously. It is likely that had the International Psycho-Analytical Association not cast him out, he would have remained an orthodox professional, but that is another story. I suspect that his exclusion from traditional psychoanalytic societies caused him enormous pain and anguish. His attempts to be reinstated by the IPA, his pleas with his former friends and colleagues – for example his letters to Loewenstein and Hartmann[1] – make this abundantly clear.

Jacques-Marie Lacan was born in Paris on April 13, 1901, and his career ran the usual obstacle course of a French doctor of medicine, psychiatrist, and psychoanalyst. His psychiatric curriculum vitae, printed in his thesis (1932), indicates that he had impeccable clinical credentials and the highest possible pedigree in the field. He worked with Henri Claude, an expert on schizophrenia and one of the foremost French psychiatrists of the early century, at the Clinique des Maladies Mentales et de l'Encéphale (Clinic for Mental Illnesses and Illnesses of the

---

[1]The letter to Loewenstein, dated July 14, 1953, contains the following:

I want you to feel how bitter this experience has been for us, and also how decisive.

I give you authority to communicate this [letter] – in spite of the tone of the confessional that is found and in spite of our special relationship – to Heinz Hartmann whose person I have always held in the highest esteem [p. 135].

The end of his letter to Hartmann on July 21, 1953, reads as follows:

Dear Heinz Hartmann, I regret that the chaotic events of past years, as well as the extreme isolation that is conditioned by our professional life prevented me from making myself better known to you.

But I count on your authority to make it possible for the authentic and deeply caring effort that is the foundation of my work in bringing Freud's teaching alive to be respected; to bring back the tone of reason to a fight that is as sterile in its forms as it is base in its motives, and to take the equitable measures necessary to preserve the audience that psychoanalysis is presently conquering in France and that this fight can only hinder. (p. 136)

Evidence that Marie Bonaparte might have been behind Lacan's exclusion from the IPA is apparent from excerpts of her own letters to Lowenstein published in the biography, *La dernière Bonaparte* (Bertin, 1982).

Encephalus) in 1927-28. In 1928-29, he was attached to the Infirmerie Spéciale Près de la Préfecture de Police (Special Police Headquarters Infirmary) and trained with Georges de Clérambault, whose theory of mental automatism was a decisive influence. "Our only master in psychiatry" is Lacan's appraisal of his role. From 1929 to 1931 he continued his training at the Henri Rousselle Hospital and spent the summers in Zurich at the Burgholzi, Eugen Bleuler's and Carl Jung's clinic. He obtained a diploma in forensic medicine, and in 1931-32, he returned to the Clinique des Maladies Mentales et de l'Encéphale.

Lacan co-authored his first articles with leading senior psychiatrists and neurologists, and he published in psychiatric journals, for example, *L'evolution psychiatrique*, whose contributors became early recruits of psychoanalysis. His doctoral thesis (Lacan, 1932), which we shall examine in more detail presently, was a traditional work, with meticulous references, careful research, and detailed clinical observations, written in a clear and straightforward style. The young doctor was well on his way to a successful psychiatric career. At this time there appear to be at least two developments in Lacan's professional vitae that must be taken into account to explain his deviations from the psychiatric and medical mainstream.[2] I am referring to his connections with surrealism and his contacts with psychoanalysis.

Further research is needed about actual relations between Lacan and surrealism. We do know that he published several fascinating articles (Lacan, 1933a,b) in *Le minotaure*, a surrealist journal, and that it was Lacan's ideas that prompted Salvador Dali's famous critical paranoia theory. He had contacts with René Crevel, the poet who shot himself playing Russian roulette with a loaded pistol (Lacan, 1966, p. 65) and he was a good friend of André Breton. His second wife, Sylvia Maklès, the star of Jean Renoir's film *Une partie de campagne*, attended the same school as the sisters Simone and Jeanine Kahn, who respectively married André Breton and Raymond Queneau. Sylvia's own first husband was Georges Bataille, a writer whose style Lacan imitated (Roudinesco, 1982).

The stamp of this movement is discernible in Lacan's own texts in several ways. First, many characteristics of automatic writing–for example, the use of puns, and arbitrary and striking comparisons and making verbal associations the organizing structure of an expository piece–are also characteristics of Lacan's own manner. A sentence such as *"A casser l'oeuf se fait l'Homme, mais aussi l'Hommelette"* (roughly trans-

---

[2]It is likely that more information will become available in the near future, particularly with the publication of the second volume of Roudinesco's history of psychoanalysis in France.

lated, "In breaking an egg *homme* (man) is made, but also an [h]omelet") and the allusion to "a large crepe moving about like an amoeba" in the sentence that follows (Lacan, 1966, p. 845) are pure surrealism.

Second, Lacan's contacts with poets led him to interpret the utterances of his psychotic patients just as he might interpret a surrealist poem, or for that matter any poem at all. For example, he analyzed (Lèvy-Valensi, Migault, & Lacan, 1931, p. 376) the following apparently senseless sentence from the writing of Marcelle C., a paranoiac patient: "*A londoyer sans meurs on fait de la bécasse*" ("Londoning without morals one makes woodcocks"). *Meurs* is a kind of portemanteau word composed of *moeurs* (customs, morals) and *meure* (from the verb mourir, to die). Lacan showed that underlying this ponderous formula is the rhythm of a famous line of poetry by the seventeenth century dramatist Pierre Corneille that is known by every French schoolchild: "*A vaincre sans pèril on triomphe sans gloire*" ("In conquering without peril one triumphs without glory"). What appears to be an original verse is in fact generated by a stereotypical automatic auditory mechanism. Familiarity with poets such as Robert Desnos, Philippe Soupault, and André Breton led Lacan to notice that patients gave different graphic renditions of the same phonic material in different places and poems: "*la mais l'as, l'ame est lasse, et la mélasse*" ("the but, the ace, the soul is tired, and molasses"). Or, "*le merle à fouine, la mère, la fouine*" ("The weaseled blackbird, the pitchforked mother"). We can give an English approximation of this mechanism by playing on the word molasses to produce "Moe's lassies, more losses, my asses." The result of Lacan's juxtapositions of such phrases is an awareness that psychotic productions may or may not have poetic value and that the substratum of a poem is often material that may be given the label "psychotic" in a clinical context and perspective. (For a fuller discussion, see Lacan, 1933a.)

Likewise, Lacan might have learned from surrealism and not necessarily from Freud how to interpret a literary work as though it were a living being. The seminar comes to mind that deals with Edgar Allen Poe's "The Purloined Letter" (Lacan, 1966), in which the letter stolen from the Queen by the minister is restored to her by Dupin, but many other instances can be given. For example, in his lecture of March 2, 1960, Lacan (1959–60) quoted a stanza by Arnaut Daniel, a great troubadour that Dante ranked with Virgil. His point was that this poem about courtly love embodied "the central void around which is organized and articulated whatever it is that sublimates desire" (p. 29). The same void and sense of nothingness is revealed in his appraisal of André Gide. When Gide's wife Madeleine took revenge on her husband by burning all the letters he had ever written to her, she knew what she was doing. The letters had been Gide's way of filling up his own sense of emptiness, the literal hole that he stuffed with all kinds of games, which allowed him to watch himself pretending to be himself. In *Et NUNC Manet in Te* (Lacan, 1966), written after the death of Madeleine, his wife, Gide confessed that after the letters' destruction, his relationship with her, *"n'offre plus, à la place ardente du coeur, qu'un trou"* ("left but a hole in the ardent part of his heart") (p. 762). The loss of this correspondence, of which Gide had no copy meant that whereas previously his mirror had been the substance of words, phrases, sentences, and paragraphs, it had turned into the vertigo of a ditch, a gap, nothing, and nothingness.

Lacan's sense of play and games would of course have delighted the surrealists. He liked using everyday imagery, slang, and ordinary words of our childhood and adolescence, anything from mustard pots to Picasso's ostrich cabbages, to illustrate philosophical and psychoanalytic concepts. He himself referred to "this seriousness that I always develop further and further to its punchline," (*"ce sérieux que je développe toujours plus en pointe"*). Elsewhere he says that he is the Gòngora of psychoanalysis. When he spells the French word *raison*, (reason) r-e-s-o-n, following the example of Francis Ponge, to show how the sound itself suggests something that resonates; when he puns on the French word *poubelle* (garbage can), referring to psychoanalytic publications—his own included—as *Poubellications;* when he dismisses the "Lacanians" by reminding them that he himself is a Freudian, Lacan is playing. But he is also playing when he ridicules his opponents and his disciples, when he applies linguistic and mathematical concepts to psychoanalysis. A surrealist is never more serious than when he is playing, of course, so in that sense Lacan remained a surrealist to the end.

Finally, Lacan is a surrealist because his own formulas are themselves short poems, or so they would have been defined by his friends Paul Eluard and André Breton. I am thinking of aphorisms such as *"Ton désir c'est le désir de l'Autre"* ("Your desire is the desire of the Other"); *"L'Inconscient est structuré comme un langage"* ("The Unconscious is structured like a language"); and *"Moi, la vérité je parle"* ("Me, I speak the truth").

To stress Lacan's surrealism is to remain true to French intellectual history. The so-called surrealist revolution coincided with the introduction of psychoanalysis. André Breton was one of the first French writers to read and write about *The Interpretation of Dreams*. Public opinion often attacked both surrealism and psychoanalysis for being foreign and hostile to "la clarté française,"—French clarity. Indeed, just as surrealists were drawn to the study of dreams and the exploration of the unconscious, so psychoanalysts were drawn to the surrealists. Lacan was not alone in being close to them. For example, Adrien Borel, one of the founders of the Société Psychanalytique de Paris (SPP) in 1926, analyzed Georges Bataille and Michel Leiris (Roudinesco, 1982, pp. 358–360). René Allendy, author of 200 articles on various occult subjects was one of Antonin Artaud's psychiatrists and was also Anaïs Nin's analyst. In a general way, many of the first- and second-generation French analysts were writers and had contacts with the world of arts and letters. Marie Bonaparte was a prolific author, and her book on Edgar Allen Poe was widely read. Eugénie Sokolnicka was André Gide's model for the character of Madame Sophroniska, the analyst who unsuccessfully treated Boris in *Les faux-monnayeurs* (*The Counterfeiters*). Edouard Pichon, the president of SPP, was co-author with his uncle, Jacques Damourette, of a monumental seven-volume study of French grammar, *De la langue à la pensée*, a book that Lacan often cites.

During Lacan's formative years, in the Paris of the 1920s and early 1930s, many young psychiatrists were drawn to the study of Freud and became psychoanalysts. These same psychoanalysts were interested in language, literature, and the arts; and artists and writers, in turn, took up psychoanalysis. The fact that Lacan had contacts with Breton, Crevel, Eluard, and Dali did not make him an isolated figure, but rather one who was very much in the mainstream of his avant-garde milieu. Psychoanalysis was itself a marginal discipline, but within it, Lacan was a member of the reigning establishment and a very classical, orthodox Freudian analyst. He was analyzed by Rudolph Loewenstein, and the analysis seems to have lasted a long time, from about 1932 to 1939. The two men remained on very cordial terms. As noted earlier, when Lacan left the Société Psychanalytique de Paris and began to have difficulties with the IPA, he wrote "Loew" a long letter justifying his position and asking him to intervene on his behalf with Hartmann, who was then president of the IPA.

An examination of Lacan's first book, *De la psychose paranoïaque dans ses rapports avec la personnalité* (1932), his doctoral thesis, completed before his own analysis, will show the synthesis of these various themes in a clinical case history, the case of Aimée.

Aimée

At eight o'clock one evening, a well-known Parisian actress arrived at the theater where she was scheduled to perform and was greeted by a nicely dressed woman whom she mistook for one of her many fans. This woman asked the actress whether she was Madame Z., and when the answer was yes, the woman pulled out a knife out of her handbag and turned the blade toward the star. Madame Z. managed to grab it, cutting two tendons in her fingers in the course of the scuffle. The woman, henceforth called Aimée A., was duly restrained and carted off to jail. Madame Z. did not press charges, and her assailant was moved to Ste. Anne Asylum, where Lacan observed her for a year and a half. At first, Aimée continued to have hallucinations, obsessions, and to heap abuse on her intended victim. But suddenly, 20 days after the incident, at seven o'clock in the evening, she began to weep as she realized that the actress was totally innocent of any wrongdoing. Her delirium dissipated completely and the vanity of her megalomanic intentions and the inaneness of her fears struck her all at once. She had recovered.

This 38-year-old woman was originally from Dordogne, born into a large peasant family, with three brothers and two sisters. She had a tenured job with a rail transport company; her record was outstanding, and her superiors were pleased with her performance and tolerated some of her idyosincrasies. She was married to another employee of the same company, but the couple lived in different towns. Her husband took care of their 8-year-old son, and she visited them more or less regularly. The patient herself had organized this life-style at the end of a previous voluntary commitment to a mental institution a year and a half earlier. At that time she had believed that a number of highly placed celebrities, including several writers, were going to have her son killed, and she had written a letter of resignation on behalf of her husband to their mutual employer. Then, forging his signature, she had applied for a passport to the United States.

The fixation on Madame Z. was not an isolated episode. Aimée had set her sights on celebrities before. For example, she had tried to establish contact with a well-known novelist, Mr. P. B., the initials of Paul Bourget, and with the Prince of Wales. She sent them letters and miscellaneous writings, including a weekly sonnet and a novel called *Le Dètracteur;* in turn, she collected newspaper and magazine clippings reporting their activities. Her initial infatuation for P. B. had turned to hatred, and she was now convinced that he was plotting to kill her son.

The changing of love into hate was another pattern of her relationships. Her first love, for example, was characteristic in this respect. She had become infatuated with the local Don Juan a month before she was transferred to another town. For three years she wrote him regularly and spent most of her leisure daydreaming about him, hiding her passion from everyone. She never saw him again, and one day her love changed to hatred and scorn: "I went from love to hate abruptly," she admitted spontaneously to Lacan (1932, p. 225). The same mechanism played in her friendship for Mademoiselle C. de la N., a fellow worker from an impoverished aristocratic family who influenced her deeply. It was this woman, in fact, who introduced Madame Z., a neighbor of one of her relatives, into Aimée's life. "You are not like the other girls,"

Mlle. C. de la N. is reported to have said. "I feel that I am masculine," was Aimée's response. "You are masculine," agreed her friend. Lacan characterized the manner in this book as *midire* (literally, to "midsay"–to speak in half tones). The suggestion that Aimée's attraction for her own sex may be a factor here would be readily accepted today, but in the early 1930s an observer might have neglected to note that at the time of her attempted crime Aimée had broken all contacts with her old friend. The circumstances of her change of heart went back ten years, when Aimée had given birth to a stillborn baby girl, strangled by the umbilical cord. Her friend had telephoned for news. The patient immediately felt that Mlle. C. de la N. was responsible for this calamity and that she had conspired to kill the little girl.

Throughout his account, Lacan took care to include long excerpts from Aimée's writing and to present her aspirations for the improvement of the social and human condition in such a way that his readers come to esteem rather than belittle this patient. He avoided the patronizing tone of the superior judge, the medical boss, or even the average Frenchman or Frenchwoman. The diagnosis was that she suffered from self-punitive paranoia (*paranoia auto-punitive*). Madame Z. represented an idealized version of herself, a mirror of her ideal ego. Like Aimée, Madame Z. had a career, and being a wife, mother, and homemaker was not the focus of her daily life. Her activites were covered by reporters, so that there was a connection between her life and print. Aimée herself aspired to literary renown, to a place in the newspaper. In many circles, the morality of actresses is questionable; and it seems likely that Aimée's own code of ethics would classify her in the category of fallen woman and sinner. That is just what Aimée felt herself to be; in her family's mythology she was the brightest child, the intellectual star, but also the one who was always late and kept everyone waiting, the one who could not pull her act together, the one who was disorganized and undependable. The feeling was that she should never have gotten married at all. Aimée incorporated Madame Z. into this image, and the stab wound that punished her was but a punishment inflicted upon herself. When Aimée came to realize the senselessness of her attempted aggression, she was in a sense cured. She had been punished, and now she had no more use for her delusions.

The root of this illness was found in her relationship with her older sister. Aimée recognized the virtues of this sister but nevertheless hated her and felt herself the victim of this woman, who had achieved her equilibrium at Aimée's expense. A childless widow, this sister now had an ersatz husband and child, that is to say, she lived with Aimée's husband and child. When Lacan interviewed the sister, she made it clear that her younger sibling's illness and incarceration suited her well, and she feared that a pardon would jeopardize her life. Aimée understood this, yet although her feelings could hardly have been more ambivalent, she rejected all criticism leveled against her rival. Lacan was especially struck by the sharp contrast between her words expressing hyperbolic praise and the icy tone in which she uttered them. Lacan (1932, pp. 232–233) characterized her attitude as a *Verneinung* (denial) reaction of the purest kind.

The interpretation here follows Freud's in *The case of Schreber*, quoted by Lacan. We can shape the famous paradigm of denial in paranoia so that it applies to females rather than males, and we can see how apt it is for Aimée: "I love her" may be denied to produce "I do not love her." This is equivalent to "I hate her" and leads to the projection, "She hates me," which is a leitmotif of the persecution theme here. A second type of denial, "I do not love her, but I love him," can be turned into "He loves me." We can thus interpret Aimée's infatuation with the male figments of her imagination – the Prince of Wales, the writer P. B., and her first love. In other words, she was able to mask her attachment to her own sex by denying it and substituting a "him" for a "her." The third denial structure, "It is not I who love the women – *he* loves them" (Freud (1911), p. 64 leads to the theme of jealousy, whether there is projection or not. "Delusions of jealousy, added Freud, contradict the subject, delusions of persecution, contradict the verb, and erotomania contradicts the object" (Freud (1911), p. 64–5. Recall that Aimée believed that the objects of her attention want to kill her son. Her unfounded fears were meant to hide the fact that it is not her child she loved, but the woman she connected with him. Finally, the fourth type of denial is an absolute denial: "I do not love her. I do not love anyone at all. I love only myself." This leads to megalomania and to a regressed narcissistic stage (Lacan, 1932, pp. 261–262).

The symptoms of Aimée's illness were but denials, displacements, and substitutes of a prototype, the sister persona. However, her actual choices of love-hate objects were determined by the conjunction of random coincidences and deep analogies of affect (Lacan, 1932, p. 234). The sister was the mirror that reflected an image that erased and displaced any other image of herself. Killing the sister meant wiping out the image that was but a reflection of her own self. The actress embodied Aimée's ideal ego insofar as she was a projection of her artistic endeavors, of her desire to better herself, to be in the public limelight, and to gain fame and glory. Madame Z. was only a shell, an image, an object. Aimée denied her otherness and perceived her only as an extension of Aimée's own imagination.

Lacan's (1937) looking-glass theory provides the tool for further elaboration of these mechanisms. At the heart of this theory is the observation that the human child goes through a mirror phase from 6 to 18 months. Unlike the chimpanzee, a human baby who sees himself or herself in a mirror is able to perceive that the baby in the mirror is indeed himself or herself, and the sight of his or her image fills the baby with joy. The baby will begin to laugh, to move with glee, and to express elation in every possible way. To describe this as jubilation is hardly an overstatement. What has happened is that the child has put himself or herself on: The child has fit himself or herself into the image in the mirror, and that structure becomes the identification—in the psychoanalytic sense—of the child's self. The "I" shapes itself before objectifying itself as an ego in the dialectic of identification with the imago of the double and before language assigns it the function of subject in the realm of the universal (Lacan, 1966, p. 94). In French, this fact becomes obvious when we consider the distinction grammar makes between *je* and *moi*, a distinction that roughly approximates the difference between "I" and "me" in English. When the baby recognizes his or her image in the mirror, the baby has a notion that he or she is an "I." The awareness of being an 'I' means that the image of a whole body, a body that is a totality replaces the image of a body in pieces in the Kleinian sense, in which the baby is part an organ of his or her own body and part an organ of another body. Indeed, when a patient's sense of self has utterly disintegrated, he or she will often dream that his or her body is cut up and its organs separated and disjointed with the wings and limbs like those represented in paintings by Hieronymous Bosch. When the "I" attempts to build itself up, however, dreams represent the id as fortified buildings, castles with elaborate walls, moats, towers, and other metaphors of inversion, isolation, duplication, annulment, and displacement characteristic of obsessional neurosis.

At the end of this mirror phase, another dialectical mechanism inaugurates the insertion of the "I" into the "me," and this takes place in situations that are elaborated by social relationships. Human knowledge is mediated through identification with the imago of the desire of the other. Perhaps the mirror also reflected another image; someone else may have been holding the infant—a mother and/or a father. The constructs that follow will be socially determined, and language will be the mediator.

The looking-glass phase provides an inkling of why Lacan rejected the positions of American ego psychology promoted by Rudolph Loewenstein, Ernst Kris, and Heinz Hartmann. It is doubtful that one of the reasons for his criticism of the "New York troika," as he often called it, was his sense of abandonment when Loewenstein set up residence in the United States during the war. In fact, Lacan's rejection of ego psychology lies at the very root of his thinking.

In America, Lacan claimed, psychoanalysis was a therapy whose goal was to make the citizen adjust to the environment. Put in a political perspective, members of society should behave and lead their lives according to the values of that society. But if we substitute the term "dominant ideology" for the term "values," then whether abiding by this ideology is a sign of equilibrium is highly debatable. Lacan held that this was not the goal of psychoanalysis. His position toward the use of psychoanalysis in the United States was similar to the position many Americans take about the use of psychiatry in the Soviet Union. It is possible that from a Soviet perspective, the mere fact of being a dissident is a sign that one is not "right in the head," that one is unhinged, and that treatment is needed. But it also seems quite clear that the purpose of psychiatry or of psychoanalysis is not to adjust these dissidents to the society in which they live. Today, it is difficult to argue with Lacan's position that the purpose of psychoanalysis is psychoanalysis – or, in other words, a quest for truth – rather than making patients adjust to the cultural mainstream.

Many of Lacan's most moving pages make this point over and over. In a sense, his most debatable technical innovation, the variable analytic hour, is a consequence of this quest for truth. He himself explained that closing off a session meant that an obsessional patient would not go on for months on end making small talk about Dostoevski's novels while his or her life wasted away. Forcing such a patient to pay more for less can be an effective truth serum! Be that as it may, the ultimate goals of analysis for Lacan is the moment of truth, an ineffable sense of unity and plenitude of one's being.

Lacan took great care to separate the various planes and relations that he expressed with the words "imaginary," "symbolic," and "real." These terms become intelligible when we examine the perception we have of ourselves. On a very literal level, since I have never seen myself, and since the only "me" I can actually "see" is an image of "me" in a mirror, this "me," this "ego" is an imaginary function. It is the discovery of an experience, and not an a priori category (Lacan, 1954-55, p. 50). Furthermore, this imaginary function will intervene in psychic life as if it were a symbol. "One uses the ME the way the Bororo uses a parrot. The Bororo says I AM A PARROT; we say, I AM ME" p. 52). (The Bororo are South American Indians found along the upper Paraguay River.)

The imaginary differs from the symbolic. Lacan's symbolic function is a transcendental function, beyond any image, and it is inscribed in memory. That is, one of its characteristics is that it is a presence in absence and an absence in presence. For example, when the baby takes a ball, hides, it, and takes it back again, all the while saying "here," "gone," "here," the baby is learning that the ball is present even though he or she cannot see it. When the baby does see it, when it is present, he or she knows that it may disappear and that its absence is a possibility. In Freud, of course, the disappearance of the object is linked to the disappearance of the mother. The paradox as Lacan sees it, is that the baby misses his or her mother when he or she notices she is not present. The mother's presence is acknowledged when she has gone. And when the mother is absent, the child learns that he or she can keep her image present in his or her mind symbolically. Making the ball appear and disappear is a symbolic expression of learning to cope with the mother as other.

In life, we cannot see the symbolic, of course, but it is present nevertheless. We build it and we learn how to build it just as, in order to play ball, we have to learn how to do so. For example, the baby boy sees himself in the mirror, and he also sees his father and mother. When he perceives his parents as images of his own projections, he functions in the realm of the imaginary. But his parents also exist as the other (*l'autre*) beyond their images in the mirror. They are parents, but they are also children and grandchildren of their parents and ancestors. In a sense, siring a child does not make a man a "father." A father becomes a "father" only when he takes on for himself the symbolic function of the "father" and is able to pass this Other on to his child. The child integrates the Other, (l'Autre), with an initial capital letter. His past, that is to say his history, is inserted into the present as well as the future – not only his own history, the history he knows, such as the childhood he remembers, but also the history he has forgotten and the history that his ancestores repressed but that he himself continues to perpetuate. When I claim that my cat Jeffrey is a devoted and caring father, I am guilty of anthropomorphism that attributes to the cat the feelings of a human father. My statement is articulated on Lacan's imaginary level in which my words reflect what I see in *my* mirror. When I write that the horse Prince William V may win the famous X derby because Prince William IV, an X derby winner – himself sired by Prince William III, also a winner – was his father, I am speaking on a level Lacan would call symbolic. My example may be imaginary – after all, I have made up the names of the racehorses – but because the racing world itself is a symbolic realm and because its customs and conventions make sense in a historical and human perspective, the racehorse as father is a symbolic entity.

Lacan's "real," the third element in the tryptich, is not reality. It is likely that Lacan uses this term in the same sense as Jeremy Bentham did when he meant that the "real" was the opposite of the "fictitious" (see Lacan, 1959-60, p. 60). The concept includes what is neither symbolic nor imaginary. It refers to very stuff that is structured by the symbolic. Applied to the concept of fatherhood, for example, the real would be the physiological act of procreating without any interpretation whatsoever. Anything at all that we say about the act, the very words I use to convey the information, immediately draw the reader and me onto the symbolic plane. The word "father" itself is a sublimation and a spiritual act. As Lacan (1959–60, p. 14), explained many times, the king is naked. The unconscious itself is structured around the symbolic function.

We are now in a position to understand why and how the unconscious is structured like a language. The real cannot be apprehended at all except through a symbolic operation. If there is no symbolic level, the real remains organic and dead, as it were. The initial perception is in a sign, and this sign is itself both a signifier and a signified, that is, an element of language.

A lot of ink has been spilled about Lacan's debt to Ferdinand de Saussure's (1915) *Cours de linguistique générale.* In fact, the ideas of the *Cours* are and were quite familiar to all French-speaking linguists and psychoanalysts of the early twentieth century. Ferdinand's own son, Raymond de Saussure, was a psychoanalyst, a member of the Soci:aceté Psychanalytique de Paris, and he knew Lacan well. It has been claimed (Roudinesco, 1982) that Raymond was totally ignorant of his father's contribution to linguistics, but I cannot believe this at all. When Lacan takes up Saussure's distinction between the "signifier" (*signifiant*)–the acoustic image, the sound of an utterance–and the "signified (*signifiè*)–the concept or concepts expressed by the utterance, he is using a linguistic shorthand that was widely used. Likewise, he is using appropriate modern terminology when he refers to the paradigmatic chain of thought – the principle of "clang" associations whereby "big" leads to "dig," and "dig" leads to "rig" or another such sound–and to syntagmatic associations, in which "big" may lead to "great," "Alexander," "Philip," and "Macedonia." In this perspective, the conclusion that the unconscious is structured like a language means simply that there are no innate ideas, and that the unconscious is a cultural rather than an organic entity.

The same point can be made about other applications of linguistics to psychoanalysis. Freud's analysis of dreams, his mechanisms of displacement, denial, and similarity, are themselves tropes. An attempt to determine whether a given symptom is expressed linguistically by, for example, a synecdoche (the trope that suggests a part for the whole, less for more, or more for less) or by a metalepsis (the phrase whereby an indirect expression is substituted for a direct expression[3]) may lead to an

---

[3]For example, in the French play *Phèdre*, by Jean Racine, the heroine in love with her stepson, Hippolytus, expresses her desire by pretending that she loves her husband Theseus, Hippolytus' father, not the way he is now, but the way he was when he was his son's age (Roudinesco, 1982, p. 158).

accurate descriptions of given speech pattern corresponding to given clinical configurations. Perhaps that is the significance of Lacan's coinage of the word *Lalangue*, a linking in one word of the article *la* and the noun *langue*, meaning tongue, in the sense of speech or language. The word also suggests André Lalande, the author of a famous French dictionary of philosophy, a book philosophy students refer to with the metonymy or synecdoche, *Lalande*. The reasoning goes something like this: I speak English just as you speak English, but my speech is different from yours, although it is also the same, so that my Lalangue is like your Lalangue, yet the two are not the same. Just like Humpty Dumpty, I make my words mean something different than you make your words mean, but we have to use the same words. Even when the unconscious coins new words – Lacan's Lalangue – it adapts signifiers of the linguistic and puts them to its own use. This new sign may remain a private term, or it may enter the linguistic mainstream. When it does, it modifies the Lalangue of everyone and in some way it changes the cultural unconscious, that is, the linguistic substratum of our culture.

Perhaps herein lies the explanation for Lacan's deliberate use of a language that bares his own linguistic associations. As a student of Saussure and a reader of Hegel and Heidegger, he knew that in a sense, each one of our utterances changes the total language of our linguistic community and that some utterances change it more than others. For example, his theory of the "Nom du Père" certainly modified the theoretical assumptions French psychiatrists and psychoanalysts have about psychosis. Here, in a sense, Lacan's Lalangue has begun to change not only clinical theory, but also its practice. Very simply put, the "Nom du Père" means not only the father's name, but also the father's "no," that is to say, the act whereby the father severs the symbiotic bond between mother and child. This "no" must take place if the child is to develop into an autonomous being. The name of the father cannot be transferred to the child unless the child receives it and accepts it on the symbolic level. In Lacan's terminology, the image in the mirror, my other, must have achieved a link with the Other, who is not myself, but who is constituted by my recognition of how my history can be integrated in the world in which I live – that is, the Name-of-the-Father. Why are the *N* in "Nom" and the *P* in Père capitalized? These capital letters suggest a symbolic level, and they are allusion to the Father in the Scriptures. The signifier goes beyond the actual daddy, and suggests that the Name-of-the-Father is sacred insofar as it gives a meaning to our lives and sustains the ideas and ideals of society, culture, and civilization.

"What makes a psychosis come about?" was the question Lacan asked himself. Years of clinical experience (it must always be kept in mind that

Lacan's theory and his reading of Freud took place in the context of his extensive clinical experience with psychotics) led him to perceive that in every case there was a *Verwerfung*. Lacan translates *Verwerfung* into French as *forclusion*, a term he borrowed from Damourette & Pichon's monumental grammar book, *Des mots à la pensèe*.[4] I would translate this into English as "shut out, forclosed, and excluded," suggesting something that might have opened, but remained closed. Pichon used *foreclusion* to describe characteristics of the second term in the French negative, for example, the words *pas* (not), *plus* (not), *rien* (nothing), *jamais* (never), *aucun* (none), and *personne* (nobody) in such phrases as *Je ne sais pas* (I don't know), *Je ne sais plus* (I no longer know), *Cela ne me dit rien* (That doesn't mean anything to me), *Elle ne sait rien* (She knows nothing), *Il ne va jamais au cinèma* (He never goes to the movies), *Il n'a aucun devoir* (He has no homework), and *Personne n'est venu* (Nobody came). In each of these sentences, and in this type of French sentence generally, the second negative casts out definitively something that might have been. Likewise, in psychosis, the 'Nom du Père" signifier is itself excluded.

In order for psychosis to manifest itself, the Name-of-the-Father, must be *verworfen*, excluded, foreclosed; it must have failed to reach the Other's place, and must now be called there in a symbolic opposition with the subject. The failure of the Name-of-the-Father at that place, by the hole that it opens in the signified, begins the cascade of signifiers whereby proceeds the growing disaster of the imaginary, until the level is reached where signifier and signified stabilize in a metaphor of delirium.

Lacan's theory, then, is that in psychosis the central signifier, that is, the Name-of-the-Father, has failed to inscribe itself in the subject's language register. At the place where it should have been incorporated, there is a gap, a hole, a void. When the occasion presents itself – for example, when an ersatz signifier happens to make its way into the appropriate chain – this vacuum will suck up any signifier at all that happens to come along, and an elaborate delusional system will come to occupy the place of the missing Name-of-the-Father. For example, in the case of Schreber, Geheimrat Professor Flechsig, remained for him the chief instigator during the entire course of his illness. Freud (1911) quotes Schreber: "Even now the voices that talk with me call out your name to me hundreds of times each day. They name you in certain constantly recurring connections, and especially as being the first author of the injuries I have suffered" (p. 38). God Almighty comes to play a part as

---

[4]Roudinesco (1982, pp. 392–395) points out that although Lacan is usually given credit for this term in psychoanaysis, in fact, he borrowed it from his colleague.

Flechsig's accessory, as does the soul of the chief attendant of Pierson's asylum, the clinic to which Schreber moves. They are but substitutes for the Name-of-the-Father; and the divine rays, the special birds, the nerves of God, and Schreber's own transformation into a woman are generated to fill the emptiness created by the absence of the transcendental signifier.

Lacan's theory of the unconscious is a materialistic theory: The unconscious is structured like a language—that is, a concept, a signified, is linked to a signifier, an acoustic image, and in turn this signifier suggests another signified, so that an idea is immediately turned into matter. It is paradoxical, therefore, that Lacan speaks like a a theologian. The psychotic—and Schreber is an an excellent example—makes God Almighty into the image of the father, but in fact, the correct stance and the condition of sanity is that the father be created in the image of God Almighty. The unconscious may be structured like a language, but if this language is to sustain interhuman relations, culture, and civilization, then it must itself rest on a transcendental signifier in the image of the Great Other (*le Grand Autre*), Lacan often said.

The dedication of Lacan's doctoral thesis to his brother, Reverend Father Marc-François Lacan, Benedictine monk of the Congregation of France, makes us wonder whether both brothers did not follow a similar path. Lacan was not a man of the church, but nevertheless he preached a gospel. In his gospel the tropes of psychoanalysis incorporated tropes of other disciplines—philosophy, theology, literature, art, linguistics, and anthropology—characteristic of the culture of a given time and place: the middle of the twentieth century in France, an anticlerical country with a strong Catholic tradition. Lacan's Christian Parisian cosmopolitanism may be the counterpart of Freud's Jewish middle European universalism.

ACKNOWLEDGMENT

The author gives grateful thanks to the Research Foundation of the City University of New York for a Faculty Research Fellowship.

REFERENCES

Bertin, C. (1982). *La dernière Bonaparte*. Paris: Librairie Académique Perrin.
Clèment, C. (1981). *Vie et légendes de Jacques Lacan*. Paris: Grasset.
Damourette, J., & Pichon, E. (1911–1950). *Des mots à la pensie. Essai de Grammaire de la langue francçaise*. 7 vol. Paris: d'Artrey.
Freud, S. (1887–88). Preface to Charcot. Standard Edition, 1.

Freud, S. (1893). Charcot. *Standard Edition, 3.*

Freud, S. (1911). Psycho-Analytic Notes on An Autobiographical Account of a Case of Paranoia. *Standard Edition, 12.*

Gide, A. (1925). *Les faux-monnayeurs.* Paris: Gallimard.

Lacan, J. (1932). De la psychose paranoïaque dans ses rapports avec la personnalité. Thèse pour le doctorat en médecine, diplôme d'état. In J. Lacan, *De la psychose paranoïaque dans ses rapports avec la personnalité, suivi de Premiers écrits sur la paranoïa.* Paris: Seuil, 1975.

Lacan, J. (1933a). Le problème du style et la conception psychiatrique des formes paranoïaques de l'expérience. In J. Lacan, *De la psychose paranoïaque dans ses rapports avec la personnalité, suivi de premiers écrits sur la paranoïa.* Paris: Seuil, 1975.

Lacan, J. (1933b). Motifs du crime paranoïque. In J. Lacan, *De la psychose paranoïaque dans ses rapports avec la personnalité, suivi de premiers écrits sur la paranoïa.* Paris: Seuil, 1975.

Lacan, J. (1936, July). The looking-glass phase. Paper presented at the 14th International Psychoanalytic Congress, July 31 Marienbad. (1947) 16th International Congress, July 17; Zurich . (1966) *Ecrits,* Paris: Seuil.

Lacan, J. (1950). Propos sur la causalité psychique. In L. Bonnafé, H. Ey, S. Follin, J. Lacan, J. Rouart Le Problème de la psychogenèse des névroses et des psychoses. Paris: Desclée de Brouver, (1966). *Ecrits.*

Lacan, J. (1953–54). *Le séminaire: Livre l. Les écrits techniques de Freud* (J.-A. Miller, Ed.). Paris: Editions du Seuil, 1975.

Lacan, J. (1954–55). *Le séminaire: Livre 2. Le moi dans la théorie de Freud et dans la technique de la psychanalyse* (J.-A. Miller, Ed.). Paris: Editions du Seuil, 1978.

Lacan, J. (1955–56). *Le séminaire: Livre 3.* Les psychoses (J.-A. Miller, Ed.). Paris: Seuil, 1981.

Lacan, J. (1957). Le séminaire sur "La lettre volée," April 26, 1955. In *Ecrits.* Paris: Seuil, 1966.

Lacan, J. (1958). Jeunesse de Gida ou la lettre et le désir. *Critique* (April, 1958), 131, pp. 291–315. (1966, *Ecrits*), Paris: Seuil.

Lacan, J. (1959–60). *L'éthique.* Paris: Editions du Piranha. Unauthorized transcript.

Lacan, J. (1964). *Le séminaire: Livre 11. Les quatre concepts fondamentaux de la psychanalysee* (J.-A. Miller, Ed.). Paris: Seuil, 1973.

Lacan, J. (1966). *Écrits.* Paris: Edition, du Seuil.

Lacan, J. (1966). Position de l'inconsicent au congrès de Bonneval repris de 1960 en 1964. In *Écrits.* Paris: Seuil.

Lacan, J. (1972–73). *Le séminaire; Livre 20. Encore* (J.-A. Miller, Ed.). Paris: Seuil, 1975.

Lacan, J. (1980). Le Séminaire de 1980: Dissolution. *Ornicar?* No. 20–21.

LaScisson de (1953, July 14). *Ornicar.* 1956, p. 136.

Levy-Valensi, J., Migault, P., & Lacan, J. (1931). Ecrits "inspirés: Schizographie. In J. Lacan, *De la psychose paranoïque dans ses rapports avec la personnalité, suivi de premiers écrits sur la paranoïa.* Paris: Editions du Seuil, 1975.

Miller, J.-A. (Ed.). (1976). La Scission de 1953 [Special supplement]. *Ornicar? 7.*

Roudinesco, E. (1982). *La Bataille de cent ans: Histoire de la psychanalyse en France.* Paris: Ramsay.

Saussure, F. de (1915). *Cours de linguistique générale.* Ed. Bally, C., Sechehaye, A. Geneva.

Schneiderman, S. (1983). *Jacques Lacan. The Death of an Intellectual Hero.* Cambridge, Mass. and London, England: Harvard University Press.

14 Adolf Grünbaum: Psychoanalytic Epistemology

Barbara Von Eckardt, Ph.D.

Adolf Grünbaum was born on May 15, 1923 in Cologne, Germany. He received his B.A. from Wesleyan University in 1943 with high distinction in mathematics and philosophy, his M.S. in physics from Yale University in 1948, and his Ph.D. in philosophy from Yale University in 1951. He began his teaching career at Lehigh University in 1950. Five years later he was appointed William Wilson Selfridge Professor of Philosophy. In 1960 he accepted a position at the University of Pittsburgh as Andrew Mellon Professor of Philosophy, where he has been ever since. In 1979 he was also appointed Research Professor of Psychiatry at the same university on the basis of his work on psychoanalytic epistemology.

Grünbaum is currently one of the leading figures in contemporary philosophy of science. He has been president of the Philosophy of Science Association for two terms, 1965–67 and 1968–70, and was elected president of the American Philosophical Association (Eastern Division) for 1982–83. In addition, he has received numerous honors and awards for his work, the most recent of which is a festschrift in his honor (Cohen & Laudan, 1983) containing essays by 14 of today's principal researchers in philosophy of science as well as two leading psychoanalysts.

Grünbaum's interest in psychoanalysis is relatively recent. His past work primarily concerned philosophical problems of space and time and the theory of scientific rationality (see Cohen & Laudan, 1983 for a complete bibliography). Since 1976, however, when his first paper on psychoanalytic epistemology appeared (Grünbaum, 1976), he has produced at least 10 papers as well as a book on the subject, which have succeeded

353

in completely changing the state of the art. The purpose of this essay, then, is to provide a summary and critique of this work.

The two fundamental questions that Grünbaum's work on psychoanalysis addresses are these:

1. What sort of standards of assessment ought we to invoke in evaluating psychoanalysis? That is, ought we to regard it as making knowledge claims, and, if so, what kind?

2. Given that we have chosen certain standards of assessment, how does psychoanalysis measure up to those standards?

With respect to the first question, Grünbaum has argued emphatically that (a) the most appropriate standards of assessment for psychoanalysis are those derived from empirical science, contrary to the claims of the hermeneuts, Jurgen Habermas, Paul Ricoeur, and George Klein (Grünbaum, 1983c, 1984); and (b) psychoanalysis meets the minimal conditions necessary for applying those standards, contrary to the claims of Karl Popper (1963) (who accepts Grünbaum's first statement but denies the second on the grounds that psychoanalysis is unfalsifiable) (Grünbaum, 1976, 1977, 1979). With respect to the second question, however, his stance has been severely critical. In his view, there are serious difficulties in the way of regarding psychoanalysis as good science. These stem not only from serious liabilities involved in the use of clinical data but also from the modes of reasoning that Freud used to provide evidential support for his theory (Grünbaum, 1983b, 1984).

It should be clear that any attempt to argue convincingly either for or against the scientific status of psychoanalysis ought to be informed by *both* a thorough understanding of the psychoanalytic literature and a sophisticated conception of the nature of science. The literature prior to Grünbaum's recent outpouring on the subject suffers, in my view, in both of these respects. That is, either it exhibits a very superficial understanding of psychoanalysis or it is naive about the nature of science. The importance of Grünbaum's contribution in the area of psychoanalytic epistemology rests on the fact that his work is unparalleled on both counts. Not only does he bring to bear a very great sophistication in the philosophy of science but, in addition, he has done his psychoanalytic homework.

In 1959, the philosopher John Hospers summed up the results of one of the first major conferences on philosophy and psychoanalysis as follows:

> As I try to get a composite picture of the results of the conference, the thing that stands out most in my mind is the lack of genuine communication between the psychoanalysts and the philosophers. Psychoanalysts are, quite understandably, too busy treating patients to have acquainted

themselves with the latest guns in the arsenal of epistemology and philosophy of science, and are therefore at a loss to reply to the charges leveled at them by the philosophers in the way the philosophers want. The philosophers, for their part, are – equally understandably – ignorant of the vast amount of empirical detail garnered by psychoanalysts in the last half-century as well as the complexity of many of the theoretical concepts employed in psychoanalysis. The inevitable result is that each party to the dispute only feels confirmed in his previous suspicion, namely that the other party's remarks are either incompetent or irrelevant, given to making either scandalously overblown claims or excessively demanding systematic requirements [p. 336].

I believe that Grünbaum has gone more than halfway toward closing this communication gap from the philosophical side. Not only is his work impressively learned with respect to the psychoanalytic literature, as already mentioned, but he has also worked very hard at establishing lines of communication with the psychoanalytic community. For all of this, however, his writing may not be easily accessible to psychoanalysts and students of psychoanalysis, for it does presuppose a considerable sophistication in the philosophy of science and the techniques of philosophical argumentation. It is chiefly this consideration that has dictated the style of the present essay. Grünbaum's work merits serious attention from anyone interested in the cognitive status of psychoanalysis. My principal concern, therefore, has been to make the most important of his ideas and arguments accessible to the reader. This approach has had several consequences. First, I have devoted a certain amount of space to providing background that seemed to me essential to understanding either the content of Grünbaum's writing or its importance. Second, I have had to strike a compromise between the demands of depth and breadth in the discussion of Grünbaum's work itself. Grünbaum's writing is exceedingly rich. In attempting to present clearly the central lines of argumentation, much of this richness has necessarily been lost. I thus urge the reader interested in his work to consult the original. In addition, certain topics have simply not been touched on at all. Where this is the case, I have tried to indicate what has been omitted in the appropriate place in my discussion.

SHOULD FREUDIAN PSYCHOANALYSIS BE ASSESSED AS SCIENCE?

Grünbaum's approach to this question has been twofold. First, he has repeatedly emphasized that Freud himself regarded psychoanalysis as scientific. In support of this claim, he cites passages such as the one in which Freud states that the explanatory gains from positing unconscious mental processes "enabled psychology to take its place as a natural science like any other" (Freud, 1940a, p. 158, see also 1925, p. 58; 1933, p. 159; 1940b, p. 282). Second, Grünbaum has devoted considerable effort to providing counterarguments to those who have suggested that, for one reason or another, Freudian theory ought not be regarded as scientific on the grounds that it fails to satisfy certain minimal requirements for scientific candidacy. These arguments have been directed, in particular, against Karl Popper, Jurgen Habermas, Paul Ricoeur, and George Klein.

Although it might appear that Grünbaum has simply adopted the strategy of shifting the burden of proof to those who wish to deny scientific status to Freudian theory, it is possible to view his discussion as part of an overall implicit positive argument as follows:

1. A body of work should be judged by the standards of adequacy subscribed to by the author or creator unless there is compelling reason not to.

2. Freud took himself to be doing science.

3. The reasons that have been offered in the literature against assessing psychoanalytic theory in terms of the standards of science are uniformly uncompelling.

4. Therefore, Freudian psychoanalytic theory ought to be assessed as science.

Since the second premise is not difficult to establish, the bulk of Grünbaum's discussion on this matter has been devoted to justifying the third premise. In the discussion that follows, we shall focus on his consideration of the arguments of Popper and Habermas. Readers interested in his discussion of Ricoeur and Klein should consult Grünbaum, 1984, pp. 43–93.

Psychoanalysis as Pseudo-Science

Popper's Challenge

In 1953, in a paper reviewing his philosophical work of the past 30 or more years, Karl Popper challenged the scientific status of psychoanalysis, claiming that it was nothing more than a pseudoscience. His reasoning was this: To be scientific, a theory must be falsifiable; however, psychoanalytic theory is not falsifiable. Therefore, psychoanalytic theory is not scientific. Interestingly enough, it was in part the case of psychoanalysis that led Popper to see the importance of falsifiability in the scientific process in the first place.

When the problematic nature of psychoanalysis first occurred to him, Popper's principal concern was the so-called "problem of demarcation." This is the problem of distinguishing theories that can *legitimately* be considered candidates for scientific evaluation from those that cannot, in particular, from those "pseudoscientific" theories such as astrology that share certan superficial characteristics with genuine scientific theories but that lack some essential feature. The accepted demarcation principle at the time was an inductivist one: A theory is scientific just in case it is inductively well confirmed on the basis of empirical evidence. It was in part the contrast between Freud's psychoanalytic theory and Einstein's theory of gravitation that led Popper to believe that this was an incorrect view. On intuitive grounds, something seemed to be wrong with psychoanalysis, but the problem could not be its lack of "verifications" because these seemed to be rampant. Popper began to suspect that the difficulty was precisely that psychoanalytic theory could always be verified *no matter what*. In contrast, a genuine scientific theory like Einstein's was distinguished by the fact that, *if* it were false, it could be *falsified* so easily, because potentially falsifying test outcomes were readily imagined. Popper (1963) wrote:

> I found that those of my friends who were admirers of Marx, Freud, and Adler, were impressed by a number of points common to these theories, and especially by their apparent *explanatory power*. These theories appeared to be able to explain practically everything that happpened within the fields to which they referred. The study of any of them seemed to have the effect of an intellectual conversion or revelation, opening your eyes to a new truth hidden from those not yet initiated. Once your eyes were thus opened you saw confirming instances everywhere: the world was full of *verifications* of the theory. Whatever happened always confirmed it. Thus its truth appeared manifest; and unbelievers were clearly people who did not want to see the manifest truth; who refused to see it, either because it was against their class interest, or because of their repressions which were still 'un-analyzed" and crying aloud for treatment.

> The most characteristic element in this situation seemed to me the incessant stream of confirmations, of observations which "verified" the theories in question. . . . It began to dawn on me that this apparent strength was in fact their weakness [p. 34].

In contrast, the situation with Einstein's theory was "strikingly different." On the basis of his theory of gravitation, Einstein had predicted that light from a distant star would be bent near the sun. What was impressive about this case, according to Popper (1963), was the *risk* involved in a prediction of this kind. For if observation shows that the predicted effect is definitely absent, then the theory is simply refuted. The theory is *incompatible with certain possible results of observation*—in fact with results which everybody before Einstein would have expected. This is quite different from the situation I have previously described, when it turned out that the theories in question were compatible with the most divergent human behaviour, so that it was practically impossible to describe any human behaviour that might not be claimed to be a verification of these theories [p. 36].

It was this purported insight that led Popper to his well-known principle of falsifiability. In addition, he proposed that *the* method of science is essentially one of bold conjectures and attempted refutations whose rationality lies in the facts that first, scientists are always seeking to falsify their theories and, second, they acccept their theories only (and always only tentatively) when they have successfully resisted numerous attempts at falsification.

The Response to Popper's Challenge

The philosophical response to Popper's challenge over the past 20 years has taken a variety of forms. In order to understand Grünbaum's contribution to this discussion, it will be useful to indicate briefly the major positions that have been taken.

It was noted quite early on that there is an important ambiguity in the claim that psychoanalysis is not falsifiable. Kennedy (1959), for example, pointed out that psychoanalysis can be considered unfalsifiable for two very different reasons: first, because of the attitude of its proponents in the face of allegedly unfavorable evidence; and, second, because of the logical structure of the theory. Martin (1964b) refined this distinction further by introducing four possible senses of the notion of refutability, two of which concerned the attitudes of proponents of the theory, and two of which concerned its logical structure. He wrote:

When we ask whether a theory T is a refutable theory, we may be asking any of the following questions:

(1) Are people who are advocates of theory T willing to specify what evidence could count against theory T?
(2) Are people who believe in theory T willing to accept some of the evidence brought forth to refute theory T instead of explaining it all away?
(3) Is the relation between the theoretical language and the observational language of theory T clear and unambiguous?
(4) Is it possible to give theory T, in which the relation between the theoretical and observational language is extremely vague and ambiguous, clear and unambiguous formulation [p. 81]?

Martin claimed, however, that the fourth question is not an interesting sense of 'refutable,' since *any* theory can be considered refutable in that sense, including those that we consider paradigm cases of unrefutable theories (such as that the absolute is perfect and developing in history).

If we subdivide Popper's challenge into two parts, one directed at the attitudes of its proponents and one at the logical structure of psychoanalytic theory, we find endorsements of both positions in the literature. For example, a number of people have argued that the proponents of psychoanalytic theory typically exhibit a very unscientific attitude with respect to putative disconfirming data. After proposing the four senses of 'refutability,' Martin (1964b) claimed that the answer to the first two questions is no. Typically, psychoanalysts are unwilling to specify what evidence will count against their theory. Furthermore, they tend to discount any allegedly disconfirming evidence. A similar view had been voiced earlier by Hook (1959a).

Cioffi (1970) took the charge much further. Psychoanalysis is a pseudoscience, he wrote, principally because it uses methodologically defective procedures:

> For an activity to be scientific it is not enough that there should be states of affairs which would constitute disconfirmation of the theses it purports to investigate; it must also be the case that its procedure should be such that it is calculated to discover whether such states of affairs exist. I use the word "calculated" advisedly. For to establish that an enterprise is pseudo-scientific it is not sufficient to show that the procedures it employs would *in fact* prevent or obstruct the discovery of disconfirmatory states of affairs but that it is their function to obstruct such discovery. To claim that an enterprise is pseudo-scientific is to claim that it involves the habitual and willful employment of methodologically defective procedures (in a sense of willful which encompasses refined self-deception) [p. 472].

Cioffi goes on to argue that Freudian psychoanalysis is pseudoscientific in precisely this sense. For it is characterized by a "host of peculiarities .. which are apparently gratuitous and unrelated, but which can be understood when once they are seen as manifestations of the same impulse: the need to avoid refutation" (p. 473). The principal devices that Freud uses to accomplish this end, according to Cioffi, are these: First, hypotheses presented prior to the discovery of apparently disconfirming evidence are, typically, formulated in a narrow and determinate sense; afterwards, however, they are construed in a "broader and hazier" way so as to avoid the disconfirmation. Second, prior to the discovery of apparently disconfirming evidence, Freud allows for the relevance of evidence from a number of intersubjective sources, including observation of the behavior of children, inquiry into the distinctive features of the current sexual lives or actual infantile sexual history of neurotics, or determination of the outcome of therapy based on his theory. In the face of apparently disconfirming evidence, however, he typically retreats to the claim that the only reliable source of evidence is material obtained during the psychoanalytic session and subjected to interpretation by a trained analyst. Third, his theory contains such a variety of mechanisms and interpretative principles that it is possible for him to interpret any phenomenon in a way consistent with his theory. Thus, "he typically proceeds by beginning with whatever content his theoretical preconceptions compel him to maintain underlies the symptoms, and then, by working back and forth between it and the explanandum, constructing persuasive but spurious links between them" (Cioffi, 1970, p. 497). Finally, his interpretations are not even constrained by considerations of logic; for it is not even necessary for the various meanings of a symptom to be compatible with one another.

The principal early supporter of Popper's position with respect to the nonfalsifiability of Freudian theory in the logical sense was Nagel. In a classic paper (Nagel, 1959) he offers us an analysis of precisely *why* psychoanalytic theory is problematic:

> The theory does not seem to me to satisfy two requirements which any theory must satisfy if it is to be capable of empirical validation. . . . In the first place, it must be possible to deduce determinate consequences from the assumptions of the theory, so that one can decide on the basis of logical considerations, and prior to the examination of any empirical data, whether or not an alleged consequence of the theory is indeed implied by the latter. For unless this requirement is fulfilled, the theory has no definite content, and questions as to what the theory asserts cannot be settled except by recourse to some privileged authority or arbitrary caprice. In the second place, even though the theoretical notions are not explicitly defined by way of overt empirical procedures and observable traits of things, nevertheless at least *some* theoretical notions must be *tied down to fairly definite and unambiguously specified* observable materials, by way of rules of procedure variously called "correspondence rules," "coordinating definitions," and "operational definitions." For if this condition is not satisfied, the theory can have no determinate consequences about *empirical* subject matter [p. 40].

Nagel argued that Freudian theory failed both of these conditions primarily because of its vagueness and metaphorical character.

> Freudian formulations seem to me to have so much "open texture," to be so loose in statement, that while they are unquestionably suggestive, it is well-nigh impossible to decide whether what is thus suggested is genuinely implied by the theory or whether it is related to the latter only by the

circumstance that someone *happens* to associate one with the other [p. 41].

Martin (1964b) provided further support for Nagel's view. As the quote from Nagel makes clear, the accepted view at the time was that the empirical import of a genuinely scientific theory (i.e., the link to its observation base) is mediated by so-called correspondence rules, consisting either of explicit or partial definitions of the theoretical vocabulary in terms of an observational vocabulary. Since the existence of such correspondence rules is a necessary condition of a theory being falsifiable, one way to ascertain the scientific status of psychoanalytic theory, according to Martin (1964b), is to try one's best "to separate the observational basis of the theory from the theoretical structure, and to extract rules of correspondence from the context of the uses of the two languages" (p. 85). When Madison (1961) used this strategy, he concluded that for some aspects of psychoanalysis, there was no associated observational language and rules of correspondence, whereas for others, there was. Martin, however, argues that Madison's allegedly positive results are incorrect. What Madison actually found, according to Martin (1964b), are "the rudiments of an observational language and rules of correspondence" (p. 86). Madison takes these rudiments and reformulates them into a clearer and more precise form, but he fails to distinguish his formulations from Freud's. Thus, he only shows that Freudian theory is falsifiable in Martin's fourth and, presumably, uninteresting sense.

There have been, however, a few dissenting voices. Salmon (1959) argued that psychoanalytic theory appears to be unfalsifiable only if one assumes that "a few restricted items of behavior can constitute evidence for or against the hypothesis" (p. 262). It is true, according to Salmon, that any single item of behavior may be compatible with a hypothesis, for example, that the patient suffers from unconscious hostility toward his father, for according to psychoanalytic theory, unconscious hostility can be expressed in a variety of ways and is served by a variety of mechanisms. This does not mean, however, "that every total behavior pattern is compatible with the hypothesis of unconscious hostility" (p. 262). A similar point was made by Hospers (1959). There are no "crucial experiments" for psychoanalysis, but neither do they exist for physics. What validates or invalidates psychoanalytic hypotheses are *patterns* of behavior. Correspondence rules do not take the form of "If *p*, then *q*"; rather they look like "If *p*, then *q* or *r* or *s* or . . . " followed by a finite disjunction of propositions. And since the disjunction is finite, Hospers (1959) argues, "it is emphatically *not* true that the Oedipus complex would be believed in no matter *what* the empirical facts are: if none of the items q, r, s . . . occurred, it would have to be concluded (and would be) that the individual in question had no Oedipus complex" (p. 343). More recently, Glymour (1974, 1980) has argued that there is a rational strategy for testing important parts of psychoanalysis and that this strategy was immanent in at least one of Freud's (1909) case studies, that of the Rat Man. In particular, the best available evidence concerning the actual life history of the Rat Man, Paul Lorenz, had refuted the hypothesis Freud held at the time concerning the sexual etiology of adult obsessional neurosis.

A number of philosophers came to Freud's defense in a quite different way. They agreed that if the falsifiability of a theory requires that the theory alone (mediated only be correspondence rules) entails a falsifiable observation statement, then Freudian psychoanalytic theory is, strictly speaking, unfalsifiable. However, this does not necessarily make it a pseudoscience. Why not? Farrell (1963, 1964) suggested that there was another option available. Psychoanalysis is, on his view, a *protoscience*. That is, it is an "empirical and speculative synthesis, which is premature in that it runs far ahead of the evidence that can upset or support it with reasonable certainty" (Farrell, 1963, p. 24). Nevertheless, there is reason, he claims, to take it seriously as a tentative basis for future research. The psychoanalytic method has produced an enormous amount of factual material, which the theory has to some degree succeeded in ordering, describing, and explaining. In addition, a lot of experimental work by psychologists attempting to test psychoanalytic theory seems to show that in places, at least, Freudian theory is "on to something."

Another, far more damaging reason for rejecting Popper's claim that psychoanalytic theory is pseudoscientific *because* it is unfalsifiable was offered by Lakatos (1970, 1971). He suggested that Popper's demarcation criterion can be assessed in terms of the following metacriterion: "If a demarcation criterion is inconsistent with the 'basic' appraisals of the scientific elite, it should be rejected" (Lakatos, 1971, p. 125). Given this metacriterion, Popper's demarcation principle is clearly problematic. For "exactly the most admired scientific theories simply fail to forbid any observable state of affairs" (Lakatos, 1970, p. 100). The principal reason for this is that most scientific theories are normally interpreted as containing a so-called *ceteris paribus* clause. That is, they *"forbid an event occurring in some specified finite spatio-temporal region . . . only on the condition that no other factor . . . has any influence on it"* (*p. 101*). But then if a prediction of the theory is not borne out, the theory is not automatically falsified because "by replacing the *ceteris paribus* clause by a different one the *specific* theory can always be retained whatever the tests say" (p. 101–102). In the philosophy of science literature of recent years, a more general version of this point has become commonplace. As we noted, in the early responses to Popper's challenge, it was generally assumed that theory and observation are mediated by correspondence rules. In recent years, however, it has been argued that the so-called "received view" of correspondence rules vastly oversimplifies the relationship between a theoretical hypothesis undergoing test and the observable evidence adduced in its behalf. Careful examination of scientific case studies has revealed that theory and data are often mediated by a complex array of auxiliary propositions: hypotheses from related theories, theories of measurement and theories of the data, assumptions about the experimenal situation, and assumptions about the ways in which the putative theoretical states causally influence the observable states of affairs (see Schaffner, 1969; Suppes, 1962, 1967; and more recently, Hempel, 1970, 1973).

That theories are connected with observable results only via a mediating link of auxiliary hypotheses has important implications for the testing of theories. For if theories confront data only in conjunction with other theories or hypotheses, then if a theory's prediction is not borne out, the most one can conclude is that *either* the theory *or* one of the auxiliary hypotheses is wrong. As the nineteenth century philosopher and physicist, Pierre Duhem (1906) wrote:

> The physicist can never subject an isolated hypothesis to experimental test but only a whole group of hypotheses; when the experiment is in disagreement with is predictions, what he learns is that at least one of the hypotheses constituting this group is unacceptable and ought to be modified; but the experiment does not designate which one should be changed [p. 187].

The point again is that if one takes Popperian falsifiability to require that the theory whose status is being determined can *in itself* make falsifiable predictions, then very few legitimate scientific theories, if any, will be falsifiable by themselves. Hence – so the argument goes – falsifiability ought to be rejected as a demarcation criterion.

Whether a revised version of falsifiability can be formulated that will be serviceable as a demarcation criterion is still a matter of controversy. Popper (1963, p. 112) himself briefly considers the matter (see Grünbaum, 1976 for a discussion of this passage). I have made some positive suggestions in this area (Von Eckardt, 1982) as has Lakatos (1970). In contrast, Laudan (1983) has recently argued that no satisfactory demarcation principle will be forthcoming, especially not one formulated along Popperian lines. However this issue is resolved, it is important to keep in mind that even if falsifiability cannot function as a *demarcation* principle (which requires it to be both necessary and sufficient for a theory's being scientifically entertainable), it may well constitute simply a necessary condition. In any case, it certainly behooves us to appraise Popper's rejection of psychoanalysis as pseudoscience on the alleged ground of unfalsifiability. Thus, if we are interested in the scientific status of Freudian psychoanalytic theory, it remains a worthwhile project to inquire into its falsifiability.

Grünbaum's Contribution

Grünbaum has had something to say on virtually every aspect of the issue of the falsifiability of Freudian theory. What makes his discussion so noteworthy is that it takes place against a background of serious consideration of the importance and relevance of the requirement of falsifiability in the scientific enterprise in general. Thus, before we turn to a discussion of his response to the pseudoscience challenge, I shall briefly summarize his work in philosophy of science that pertains to falsifiability.

As the previous discussion should have made clear, there are two extreme positions that someone can take on the importance of falsifiability in science. On the one hand, it can be argued, as Popper has done, that falsifiability is *the* "touchstone of scientific rationality." On the other hand, there is the view, inspired by Duhem, that falsifiability is completely unimportant in science because no scientific theory is ever, strictly speaking, falsifiable. In a series of important papers in the 1960s and 1970s, Grünbaum took on both of these extreme positions, advocating instead a more reasonable, middle-of-the-road view.

Grünbaum (1969) considered what he calls the "D-thesis," a view, that if not historically attributed to Duhem, represents the Duhemian philosophical legacy in contemporary philosophy of science. The D-thesis consists of the following two claims.

> D1. No constitutent hypothesis H of a wider theory can *ever* be sufficiently isolated from some set or other of auxiliary assumptions so as to be separately falsifiable observationally. H is here understood to be a constituent of a wider theory in the sense that no observational consequence can be deduced from H alone.

> It is a corollary of this subthesis that *no* such hypothesis H *ever* lends itself to a crucially falsifying experiment any more than it does to a crucially verifying one.

> D2. In order to state the second subthesis D2, we let T be a theory of *any* domain of empirical knowledge, and we let H be *any* of its component subhypotheses, while A is the collection of the remainder of its subhypotheses. Also, we assume that the observationally testable consequence O entailed by the conjunction H & A is taken to be empirically

false, because the observed findings are taken to have yielded a result O′ *incompatible* with O. Then D2 asserts the following: For all potential empirical findings O′ of this kind, there exists at least one suitably revised set of auxiliary assumptions A′ such that the conjunction of H with A′ *can be held to be true and explains O′*. Thus D2 claims that H can be held to be true *and* can be used to explain O′ no matter what O′ turns ought to be, i.e., *come what may* [p. 1070–1071].

Grünbaum (1966) argued the following three points with respect to the D-thesis: (1) There are quite trivial senses in which D1 and D2 are uninterestingly true and in which no one would wish to contest them (see pp. 276–280); (2) In its nontrivial form, D2 has not been demonstrated (see pp. 280–281); and (3) D1 is false, as shown by counterexamples from physical geometry (see pp. 283–295; Grünbaum, 1968, 1969). Grünbaum (1969) discusses this further and, in response to criticism, introduces a qualification with respect to the third point (3). Grünbam concedes to Hesse (1968) that if the falsification of H denied by D1 is construed as *irrevocable*, then his geometrical example does not succeed as a counterexample. However, he insists that it does succeed if falsification is construed in a scientifically realistic sense, that is, if one requires "only falsification to all intents and purposes of the scientific enterprise" (p. 1092). In sum, then, in Grünbaum's view, falsifiability is a meaningful notion in science.

Falsifiability is not, however, the only possible basis for a demarcation principle or the only possible ground for a theory of scientific rationality, as Popper has claimed. In Grünbaum's view, the alternative—inductivism—which Popper summarily dismisses, merits serious consideration as well. Grünbaum (1976, 1977, 1979) argues that Popper's rejection of inductivism rests on a serious misportrayal.

Inductivism offers the following demarcation principle: A theory is scientific ("I-scientific") if and only if it qualifies as empirically well supported by neo-Baconian standards of controlled inquiry. Note that this is quite different from a demarcation principle based on falsifiability, in that the focus is on the *credibility* of the theory rather than simply its *entertainability*. Thus, a speculative theory in physics, for example, for whom evidence has not yet been gathered, would not count as actually I-scientific, but only as *potentially* so, although the latter would qualify it as scientifically entertainable.

Grünbaum's dispute with Popper concerns what sorts of theories inductivism would count as being empirically well supported. According to Grünbaum (1977), Popper attributes the following to inductivism: "If a theory T can explain a sufficiently large *number* of observational results or has a suitably large number of so-called positive instance, then T *automatically* qualifies as *well-supported* by the evidence" (p. 224). The distinction between being a positive instance and being a supportive one is crucial here. According to Grünbaum (1976), "an instance is a 'positive' one with respect to a *non*-statistical theory T, if its occurrence or being the case can be deduced from T in conjunction with suitable initial conditions. But an instance is supportive of T, if it is positive *and* has the probative significance of conferring a stronger truth presumption on T than T has without that instance" (p. 217). Thus, Popper would claim that inductivism requires a positive instance to be *sufficient* for being a supportive one. This claim overlooks two important features of the inductivist position, in Grünbaum's view:

1. *The "declared consequence restriction."* Grünbaum (1979) states: "If, at a particular time, S is *declared* to be a logical consequence of T under the assumption of stated initial conditions, or is declared not to be such a consequence, then *neither* declaration is allowed to depend on *knowing* at the time whether S is true" (p. 133). The point is that what counts as a consequence of a theory T (and, hence, as a positive instance) is a function solely of the logical relations between T and this consequence; whether it is true or false is completely irrelevant. According to Grünbaum (1977) this requirement is "at least implicitly imposed by inductivists to preclude 'retroactive' tampering with the construal of T as follows: S is only *ex post facto* held to have followed from T after having been found to be true" (p. 227).

2. *The need for controls with respect to causal hypotheses.* According to Grünbaum, this need has been emphasized by inductivists ever since Francis Bacon wrote three centuries ago. Consider a causal hypothesis of the form, "Events of kind X are causally relevant to (either causally necessary for, causally sufficient for, or stochastically relevant to) events of kind Y." A merely *positive* instance for such a hypothesis will be an event of kind X coupled with an event of kind Y. For example, if the hypothesis (H) in question is "*Ceteris paribus*, daily consumption of at least one-fifth pound of coffee for two weeks [X] is causally sufficient as well as causally necessary for the remission of colds [Y]," then a positive instance of H would be one case of a person with a cold drinking at least one-fifth pound of coffee for two weeks *and* getting rid of his or her cold at the end of that period. Such a positive instance would *not*, however, count as *supportive*, in the inductivist view, *unless* it is conjoined with findings from an appropriate control group. For, as Grünbaum (1977) states "Even a large number of cases of X which are also cases of Y does not preclude that an equally large number of cases of non-X are also cases of Y. But being an X should make a difference with respect to being a Y," (p. 232) given the claim of causally sufficiency. In addition, "if there is to be inductive warrant for deeming coffee to be remedially nec-

essary, *every* known case of non-X would have to be a case of non-Y" (p. 232). In sum, Grünbaum concludes, "only the *combination* of positive instances with instances of non-X and non-Y could constitute inductively supportive instances of our strong causal hypothesis H" (p. 232).

Note that given this more accurate portrayal of inductivism, any theory containing causal hypotheses that is I-scientific will necessarily be falsifiable as well, although, of course, the converse will not be true. Thus, in Grünbaum's view, Popper was completely wrong in claiming that, in contrast to falsifiability, inductivism is powerless to impugn the scientific credentials of a theory like psychoanalysis. In fact, as we shall discuss later, one of Grünbam's principal theses is that the weakness of Freudian theory lies not in its unfalsifiability but in the fact that it fails to satisfy neo-Baconian standards of inductive credibility.

Let us turn now to Grünbaum's response to the challenge of unfalsifiability. His principal points are the following: First, the *arguments* that have been offered by Popper and others to show that psychoanalytic theory is unfalsifiable are inadequate. Second, although there is some merit to the charge that the majority of Freud's defenders, and even sometimes Freud himself, have exhibited a "tenacious unwillingness ... to accept adverse evidence" (Grünbaum, 1979, p. 138), Cioffi's *global* indictment of Freud's methodology as pseudoscientific cannot be sustained. And, third, given any reasonable scientific sense of falsifiable (that is, *modulo* revocable auxiliary assumptions and initial conditions), there are clear counterexamples to the thesis of unfalsifiability.

The thesis of unfalsifiability says that there does not exist even one way in which Freudian theory could, in principle, be falsified. As Grünbaum (1983b) points out, since a negative claim is here being made about an infinite class of consequences of the theory, it is not even clear what a good argument for this claim would look like. Certainly, what Popper offers us is not satisfactory. For instead of providing a *general* argument to support his general claim, he simply gives us a single alleged example of how Freudian theory could explain the facts no matter how they turn out. Popper (1963) describes two cases: that of a man who pushes a child into the water with the intention of drowning it; and that of a man who sacrifices his life in an attempt to save the child. He writes: "Each of these two cases can be explained with equal ease in Freudian ... terms. According to Freud the first man suffered from repression (say, of some component of his Oedipus complex), while the second man had achieved sublimation" (p. 35).

As an argument for the unfalsifiability thesis, this example fails miserably, according to Grünbaum (1979). First, "why would it necessarily be a liability of psychoanalysis, if it *actually* could *explain* the two cases of behavior with equal ease? Presumably there actually are such instances of self-sacrificing child-*rescuing* behavior no less than such cases of *infanticidal* conduct. And a *fruitful* psychological theory might well succeed in *actually* explaining each of them" (pp. 134–135). Second, even if this case were cogent, it is certainly not clear how it is supposed to *generalize* to cover the infinite class of cases which fall under the thesis. Popper seems to be relying on the method of "induction by enumeration," which he himself has rejected as inadequate. Third, the example is totally contrived. Popper should, at least, have chosen an example based on the Freudian text. Finally, Popper claims that Freudian theory could *explain* both of these cases. However, such explanations are forthcoming only if the psychoanalytic theorist is at liberty to posit initial conditions *at will*. But, asks Grünbaum (1979): "Is it clear that the postulation of initial conditions *ad libitum* without any *independent* evidence of their fulfillment is quite generally countenanced by that theory to a far greater extent than in, say, physics, which Popper deems to be a bona fide science?" (p. 135). Certainly, Popper gives us no argument to that effect. Eysenck (Eysenck & Wilson, 1973) puts forth another similar argument, which Grünbaum (1979, pp. 138–139) discusses and dismisses as inadequate.

Grünbaum considers Cioffi's (1970) claim that Freud's methodology was prompted chiefly by the need to avoid refutation. After carefully reexamining the textual passages on which Cioffi builds his case, Grünbaum (1980b) concludes that Cioffi "mishandled" his examination of Freud's reasoning and "was thereby driven to the gratuitous or mistaken conclusion that concern with pertinent evidence had played no essential role in Freud's rationale for espousing psychoanalysis" (p. 84). Freud was willing to acknowledge both the possibility and, on several occasions, the fact of falsification, according to Grünbaum. In support of this contention, he cites the following cases:

1. In his "Reply to Criticisms of My Paper on Anxiety Neurosis" Freud (1895) stated explicitly what sort of finding he would acknowledge to be a *refuting* instance for his hypothesis concerning the etiology of anxiety neurosis.

2. In 1897 Freud abandoned his hypothesis that actual episodes of traumatic seduction in childhood were responsible for the occurrence of hysteria in adulthood. Among the reasons that he explicitly cites (see Freud, 1954, pp. 215–216) is the fact that the hypothesis had extremely implausible consequences; in particular, the required incidence of perverted acts against children would have had to have been preposterously high (Grünbaum, 1979, p. 135).

3. In 1909 Freud recognized that the best available evidence concerning the actual life history of his "Rat Man," Paul Lorenz, refuted his prior hypothesis concerning the etiology of adult obsessional neurosis (Grünbaum, 1979, p. 137).

4. In "A Case of Paranoia Running Counter to the Psychoanalytic Theory of the Disease" Freud (1915) considered the case of a young woman who appeared to be paranoid but who initially failed to give any indication of the underlying homosexual attachment that Freud had hypothesized to be causally necessary for paranoia. At this point, he reasoned: "Either the theory must be given up or else, in view of this departure from our [theoretical] expectations, we must side with the lawyer and assume that this was no paranoic combination but an actual experience which had been correctly interpreted" (p. 266; Grünbaum, 1983b, p. 155).

5. Freud's (1933) "Revision of the Theory of Dreams" presents an acknowledged falsification on the basis of the recurrent dreams of war neurotics.

These cases not only suffice to undermine Cioffi's pseudoscience charge, they also function as counterexamples to the claim that, from a logical point of view, Freudian theory is unfalsifiable. To further emphasize the incorrectness of the logical unfalsifiability thesis, Grünbaum mentions a number of additional cases of either possible or actual (revocable) falsification:

1. In Freud's theory of personality types, both personality traits and a specific childhood etiology are associated with each character type. Thus, for example, Freud claims that the "oral" character is associated with dependency, submissiveness, need for approval, and pessimism and originates in such unfavorable childhood experiences as premature weaning. Grünbaum (1979, p. 137) suggests that this coupling of certain personality traits with certain childhood experiences is at least *prima facie* falsifiable.

2. Grünbaum (1979, p. 137) notes that experimental work has provided evidence counter to both Freud's doctrine of repression (see Holmes, 1974) and his theory of dreams (see Fisher & Greenberg, 1977).

3. Certain of Freud's hypotheses entail "statistical" predictions that might be tested. For example, Grünbaum (1983b) writes, Freud's hypothesis that repressed homosexuality is the specific etiologic factor for paranoia entails that

the decline of the taboo on homosexuality in our society should be accompanied by a decreased incidence of male paranoia. And by the same token, there ought to have been relatively less paranoia in those ancient societies in which male homosexuality was condoned or even sanctioned, for the reduction of massive anxiety and repression with respect to homosexual feelings would contribute to the removal of Freud's *conditio sine qua non* for this syndrome [p. 157].

Psychoanalysis as Critical Theory

Habermas's Reading of Freud

Like Popper, Habermas wants to hold that psychoanalysis cannot appropriately be regarded as natural science. However, his attitude toward psychoanalysis is quite different. Contrary to Popper who, as we have seen, wants to relegate Freudian theory to the epistemological dustbin of pseudoscience, Habermas seeks to make it an object of profound study. He believes that Freudian theory and practice represent a prototype (along with Marxian theory and practice) of a completely new form of knowledge—one he has chosen to designate "critical theory."

Habermas' interest in Freud is part of a much larger concern with the nature of knowledge in general. Although I cannot here do justice to his views, it will be useful for our purposes to attempt a rough characterization of some of his basic doctrines. First, Habermas assumes there to be three fundamentally different kinds of knowledge (*Wissenschaft*): (1) *empirical-analytic sciences*, of which the natural sciences are the paradigm; (2) *historical-hermeneutic sciences*, including the humanities (*Geisteswissenschaften*) and the historical and social sciences insofar as they aim at interpretive understanding of their subject matter; and (3) *critically oriented sciences*, in which he includes psychoanalysis as well as the critique of ideology (critical social theory).[1] Each kind of knowledge is distinguished, in his view, by both the cognitive structure of its theories and the mode of "testing" appropriate to it. Note that in taking this position, Habermas is consciously going counter to one of the principal theses of the logical positivist unity of science movement, namely, that the logic of inquiry of *any* science (*Wissenschaft*) is the same.

Second, Habermas has emphasized the importance of locating knowledge in the course of human life. According to McCarthy (1978),

---

[1] We are confronted, unfortunately, with a terminological difficulty concerning the word "science." English renditions of Habermas use the word 'science' as the translation of the German 'Wissenschaft.' Hence, it is used in the more inclusive sense, which encompasses not only the natural sciences but also the hermeneutic and critical sciences. In contrast, when we ask Grünbaum whether psychoanalysis is a science, we are using the term to refer paradigmatically to what physicists, chemists, and biologists do, and it becomes an open question whether the so-called cultural and critical "sciences" in fact count as science. I alert the reader to this fact so as to minimize possible confusion. I will try to make it clear in context which sense is intended.

Habermas' central thesis is that "the specific view points from which we apprehend reality," the "general cognitive strategies" that guide systematic inquiry, have their "basis in the natural history of the human species" (p. 55). In particular, Habermas believes that any search for knowledge is guided by certain cognitive interests and that distinct forms of knowledge are associated with distinct cognitive interests. Thus, Habermas (1971) assumes that each of the three kinds of knowledge he distinguishes is associated with its own kind of cognitive interest: "The approach of the empirical-analytic sciences incorporates a *technical* cognitive interest; that of the historical-hermeneutic sciences incorporates a *practical* one; and the approach of critically oriented sciences incorporates the *emancipatory* cognitive interest" (p. 308). Roughly speaking, the technical interest is an interest in making use of causal knowledge of nature for the purposes of prediction and control; the practical interest is an interest in establishing reliable intersubjective understanding in ordinary language communication; and the emancipatory interest is an interest in freeing oneself from ideological delusion and establishing social or intrapsychic relations "organized on the basis of communication free from domination" (McCarthy, 1978, p. 93). Furthermore, Habermas says that the specific kind of cognitive interest associated with a specific kind of theory shapes the cognitive structure of that theory to a large extent.

Much of Habermas' intellectual effort over the past 15 years has been devoted to elucidating and arguing for the existence of the third category of knowledge, critical theory. His first attempt to articulate the logic, methodology, and structure of a critical theory were published in 1967 and 1971. His more recent views on the topic are to be found in *Communication and the Evolution of Society* (1979). But it is the ealier *Knowledge and Human Interests* (1971) which is of most concern to us, for it is here that Habermas' most extended treatment of Freud is to be found.

Habermas' (1971) two principal claims about Freudian psychoanalysis are stated in the opening passage of his discussion of Freud:

> The end of the 19th century saw a discipline emerge, primarily as the work of a single man, that from the beginning moved in the element of self-reflection and at the same time could credibly claim legitimation as a scientific procedure in a rigorous sense. . . . Psychoanalysis is relevant to us as the only tangible example of a science incorporating methodological self-reflection. The birth of psychoanalysis opens up the possibility of arriving at the dimension that positivism closed off. . . . This possibility has remained unrealized. For the scientific self-misunderstanding of psychoanalysis inaugurated by Freud himself, as the physiologist that he originally was, sealed off this possibility [p. 214].

Habermas' claim that psychoanalysis involves self-reflection is, as we shall see shortly, essential to his construing it as a critical theory. "The dimension that positivism closed off" I take to be a reference to the possibility of a science existing (*Wissenschaft*) that differs in important ways from the natural sciences. Thus, Habermas is making two claims: (1) psychoanalysis is a "tangible example" of a critical theory; and (2) this fact has not been recognized because Freud himself was guilty of perpetuating a misunderstanding of his own enterprise, namely, the mistaken view that what he was doing was empirical-analytic science rather than critical theory and practice.

Habermas attempts to argue for his first claim by providing us with a description of Freudian doctrine that makes salient its "critical" features. To understand his reading of Freud, we need to say a bit more about the aims of a critical theory. We have already noted that, for Habermas, a critical theory is essentially tied to the emancipatory interest. More specifically, it has as its aim the emancipation of the agents that make use of it by means of their self-enlightenment. We can gain a clearer picture of what this emancipation and enlightenment is supposed to come to by viewing it as a transition from an initial to a final state. Geuss (1981) characterizes these states as follows:

> (a) The initial state is one *both* of false consciousness and error, *and* of 'unfree existence.' . . .
> (b) In the initial state false consciousness and unfree existence are inherently connected so that agents can be liberated from one only if they are also at the same time freed from the other. . . .
> (c) The 'unfree existence' from which the agents in the initial state suffer is a form of *self-imposed* coercion; their false consciousness is a kind of *self-delusion*. . . .
> (d) The coercion from which the agents suffer in the initial state is one whose 'power' . . . or 'objectivity' . . . derives *only* from the fact that the agents do not realize it is self-imposed.
> (e) The final state is one in which the agents are free of false consciousness—they have been enlightened—and free of self-imposed coercion—they have been emancipated [p. 58].

A critical theory is supposed to achieve such enlightenment and emancipation by inducing what Habermas calls "self-reflection." It is by reflecting, Geuss (1981) says, that the agents in question "come to realize that their form of consciousness is ideologically false and that the coercion from which they suffer is self-imposed. But, by (d) above, once they have realized this, the coercion loses its 'power' or 'objectivity' and the agents are emancipated" (p. 61).

It is not difficult to see how Freudian psychoanalysis can fit in with Geuss' schema. The first four statements constitute a quite straightforward (if abstract) description of certain of the central features of psychoanalytic *therapy*. Thus, we find Habermas arguing his thesis "that psychoanalytic knowledge belongs to the category of self-reflection" by reference to Freud's papers on analytic technique (see Habermas, 1971, pp. 228–236). The important point, however, is this: Because of his doctrine of cognitive interests, Habermas' view of psychoanalytic therapy as emancipatory self-reflection has certain consequences for his reading of the psychoanalytic theory of personality. That is, because he, in effect, subordinates the theory to the therapy, he ends up representing Freud's theortical claims in a certain idiosyncratic way. It is not only this idiosyncratic reading of Freudian theory but also his fundamentally mistaken views about the nature of (natural) science that become the target of Grünbaum's criticisms.

The Habermas-Grünbaum Dispute

Like most interpreters of Freud, Habermas divides Freud's theoretical claims into two parts: the metapsychology and the clinical theory. As I read him (which is not always a straightforward matter), in arguing that Freud was guilty of misunderstanding his own enterprise, Habermas provides us with two sets of arguments to the effect that Freudian psychoanalysis cannot correctly be regarded as an empirical-analytic science. The first of these considers the relationship of the clinical theory to the metapsychology; the second considers the scientific characters of the clinical theory itself.

Habermas begins by arguing that Freud took psychoanalysis to be scientific because psychoanalytic assumptions could be "reformulate[d] . . . in the categorical framework of a strictly empirical science" (p. 252), namely, the energy model of the metapsychology. That is, he attributes to Freud two beliefs: first, that the clinical theory could be "reduced" to the metapsychology, and, second, that the metapsychology was a "strictly empirical science." With respect to the second point, Habermas (1971) writes: "Freud surely assumed tacitly that his metapsychology, which severs the structural model from the basis of communication between doctor and patient and instead attaches it to the energy-distribution model by means of definitions, represented an empirically rigorous scientific formulation of this sort" (p. 253). However, in Habermas' view, Freud "erred" in adopting this reductionistic approach, because "psychology, insofar as it understands itself as a strict empirical science, cannot content itself with a model that keeps to a

physicalistic use of language without seriously leading to opera-
tionalizable assumptions" (p. 253). That is, the metapsychology is not
genuinely scientific *unless* its underlying energy model is opera-
tionalizable. But, Habermas continues, this is not the case:

> The energy-distribution model only creates the semblance that psychoan-
> alytic statements are about measurable transformations of energy. Not a
> single statement about quantitative relations derived from the conception
> of instinctual economics has ever been tested experimentally. The model
> of the psychic apparatus is so constructed that metapsychological state-
> ments imply the observability of the events they are about. But these
> events are never observed—*nor can they be observed* [p. 253; italics
> added].

Grünbaum's first point against Habermas effectively undercuts this
whole line of argumentation. For, according to Grünbaum (1984), careful examination of the Freudian text (Freud, 1914, p. 77; 1915a, p. 117,
1925, p. 32) reveals clearly

> that when Freud unswervingly claimed natural science status for his theo-
> retical constructions throughout his life, he did so first and foremost for
> his evolving clinical theory of personality and therapy, rather than for the
> metapsychology. For he had been chastened in his early reductionistic ex-
> uberance by the speedy demise of his Project. And, once he had repudi-
> ated his ephermeral neurobiological model of the psyche after 1896, he
> perenially saw himself entitled to proclaim the scientificity of his clinical
> theory *entirely on the strength of a secure and direct epistemic warrant
> from the observations he made on his patients and on himself.* In brief,
> during all but the first few years of his career Freud's criterion of
> scientificity was *methodological* and *not* ontologically reductive. (p. 6)

The consequence of Grünbaum's exegetical position here is that he
simply passes over Habermas' first set of arguments, presumably on the
grounds that they are simply irrelevant to the issue at hand. Implicitly,
Grünbaum's reasoning seems to be something like this: When Freud
claimed that psychoanalysis was scientific, what he chiefly had in
mind was that the clinical theory was scientific. And since the status of
the clinical theory does not depend in any essential way on the status of
the metapsychology, any argument that assumes that the scientificity
of the clinical theory *depends* on that of the metapsychology is irrelevant to the question of whether the theory in general is scientific.
Grünbaum therefore turns his attention to Habermas' second set of
arguments.

To be in a position to understand this second set of arguments and to
appreciate Grünbaum's replies, we must briefly consider Habermas'

conception of the clinical theory. The standard reading of Freud is that the clinical theory consists of a large number of universal generalizations about the human psyche. Habermas' view is somewhat different. Rather than viewing the theory of psychosexual development, say as a set of universal *claims* about the ontogenesis of human personality, Habermas (1971) takes it to consist of a set of *narrative schemata*. He writes:

> A *general* interpretation . . . has the form of a narrative, because it is to aid subjects in reconstructing their own life history in narrative form. But it can serve as the background of *many* such narrations only because it does not hold merely for an individual case. It is a *systematically generalized history*, because it provides a scheme for many histories with foreseeable alternative courses [p. 263].

Furthermore, in keeping with his (misplaced) emphasis on the centrality of the therapy to the psychoanalytic enterprise as a whole, Habermas takes the primary function of Freud's general interpretations to be their role in self-reflection. For it is by the application of such general interpretations to the individual case that patient and physician together create the interpretative *constructions*, by means of which the self-reflective process takes place. Habermas (1971) states:

> Only the . . . *systematically generalized history* of infantile development with its typical developmental variants puts the physician in the position of so combining the fragmentary information obtained in analytic dialogue that he can reconstruct the gaps of memory and hypothetically anticipate the experience of reflection of which the patient is at first incapable [p. 260].

On the basis of this rather one-sided conception of Freud's clinical theory, Habermas offers us a number of arguments that the clinical theory ought not to be regarded as science of the empirical-analytic sort. I label these "the argument from therapeutic application," "the argument from explanation," and "the argument from validation."

1. The Argument from Therapeutic Application. I pointed out earlier that, in Habermas' view, empirical-analytic theories are always associated with a technical interest in manipulating nature. The argument from therapeutic application relies heavily on the further assumption that such manipulation always occurs by means of the exploitation of causal laws. We can reconstruct the argument as follows:

1. If psychoanalytic theory were scientific (empirical-analytic), its application would consist in the manipulation of its domain by the exploitation of causal laws.

2. The application of psychoanalytic theory consists in the doing of psychoanalytic therapy.

3. However, psychoanalytic therapy does not work by the exploitation of causal laws; rather "it owes its efficacy to overcoming causal connections themselves" (Habermas, 1971, p. 271).

4. Thus, psychoanalytic theory cannot be scientific.

Habermas (1971) defends the key third premise as follows:

> Psychoanalysis does not grant us a power of technical control over the sick psyche comparable to that of biochemistry over a sick organism. And yet it achieves more than a mere treatment of symptoms, because it certainly does grasp causal connections, although not at the level of physical events – at a point "which has been made accessible to us by some very remarkable circumstances" [Freud, 1971, p. 436]. This is precisely the point where language and behavior are pathologically deformed by the causality of split-off symbols and repressed motives. Following Hegel we can call this the causality of fate, in contrast to the causality of nature. For the causal connection between the original scene, defense, and symptom is not anchored in the invariance of nature according to natural laws but only in the spontaneously generated invariance of life history, represented by the repetition compulsion, which can nevertheless be dissolved by the power of reflection [p. 271].

Habermas' point seems to be that the power of reflection can "overcome" the causal connections responsible for the patient's neurosis, because these causal connections are of a different sort than those posited by the empirical-analytic sciences. They constitute the "causality of fate" rather than the "causality of nature." What Habermas has in mind by this term is far from clear, although I suspect that it is, in some way, a consequence of his reading of the clinical theory as consisting of narrative schemata. Whatever it is, however, it is irrelevant. For, as Grünbaum argues, the kind of causality avowed by psychoanalytic etiologic and therapeutic theory does not permit this kind of "dissolution." In addition, careful examination of the causal assertions made by the theory exhibits the complete folly of this sort of talk of dissolution. In other words, Habermas has a case only by blatantly misconceptualizing psychoanalytic theory.

To be more precise, Habermas' account, in Grünbaum's view, *"flatly repudiates* the psychoanalytic *explanation* for the patient's therapeutic transition from unconsciously driven behavior to more consciously governed conduct" (Grünbaum, 1984, p. 10). This psychoanalytic explanation, first articulated in Breuer and Freud's (1893, pp. 6–7) "Preliminary Communication," rests on the etiological principle that repression is *causally necessary* not only for the initial development of a neurotic disorder, but also for its maintenance. The explanation of why therapy is efficacious then is as follows:

1. Repression of type R is the causal sine qua non of a neurosis of kind N.
2. Therapy largely consists of ridding the patient of R.
3. Therefore, therapy has the effect of obliterating N.

Grünbaum points out that, in this explanation, *therapy involves the instantiation or exemplification* of the etiologic causal relationship rather than its dissolution. For it is precisely because after the fulfillment of the second condition the patient no longer satisfies the sine qua non state that the symptoms are claimed (predicted) to disappear. Paradoxically, Habermas appears to accept both the etiological principle and the explanation; thus, he is guilty not only of contradicting the foundational postulate of Freudian theory but also of confusing the dissolution of the neurosis with the dissolution of its causal link to its original pathogen.

To further bring home his objection, Grünbaum (1984, p. 14) offers us a *reductio ad absurdum* argument to show that if Habermas' reasoning were legitimate, then thermal elongation in physics could also be shown to rest on the dissolution rather than the instantiation of a causal law:

> For consider a metal bar that is isolated against all but thermal influences. It is subject to the law $\Delta L = \alpha\Delta T \cdot L_0$, where L_0 is its length at the fixed standard temperature, ΔT the length increase or decrease due to this temperature change, and α the coefficient of linear thermal expansion characteristic of the particular material composing the metal bar. Now suppose that the bar, initially at the standard temperature, is subjected to a "pathogenic" temperature increase ΔT, which produces the elongation ΔT as its "pathological" effect. In addition to supplying this "aetiology," the law of linear thermal elongation also provides a basis for a corresponding "therapy": It tells us that if the bar's temperature is reduced to its "healthy" standard value, the "pathological" effect DL will be wiped out. Thus, we can correlate the "therapeutic intervention" of temperature reduction with the patient's remedial lifting of his own repressions. Similarly, we correlate the bar's "neurotic symptom" ΔL with the patient's repetition compulsion.

> By parity with Habermas' reasoning, we could then draw the following ludicrous conclusion: When the temperature reduction "therapeutically" wiped out the endurance of the "pathological" effect ΔL generated by the "pathogenic" temperature increase, this thermal termination also "dissolved" the stated law of thermal elongation.

What is overcome here is clearly the "pathological" effect, *not* the causal connection itself. And the same is true, according to Grünbaum, in the psychoanalytic case (that is, assuming the Freudian story is correct, as Habermas does). In sum, Habermas' claim that psychoanalytic therapy owes its efficacy to "overcoming causal connections" rather than "making use" of them is totally unsubstantiated.

2. The Argument from Explanation.   Habermas' (1971) second argument concerns the kind of explanation that results from the application of Freud's clinical theory to a specific case:

> In its logical form . . . explanatory understanding differs in one decisive way from explanation rigorously formulated in terms of the empirical sciences. Both of them have recourse to causal statements that can be derived from universal propositions by means of supplementary conditions: that is, from derivative interpretations (conditional variants) or lawlike hypotheses. Now the content of theoretical propositions remains unaffected by operational application to reality. In this case we can base explanations on context-free laws. In the case of hermeneutic application, however, theoretical propositions are translated into the narrative presentation of an individual history in such a way that a causal statement does not come into being without this context. . . . Narrative explanations differ from strictly deductive ones in that the events or states of which they assert a causal relation is [sic] further defined by their application. Therefore general interpretations do not make possible context-free explanations [pp. 272–273].

The passage is somewhat confusing because Habermas uses the term 'theoretical propositions' in both a narrow and broad sense. I assume that the first reference to such theoretical propositions is meant to refer to the theoretical propositions of empirical-analytic science, whereas the second reference includes also those that can have a "hermeneutic application." Given this reading, the basic structure of the argument seems to be the following:

1. The explanation of a particular phenomenon by means of the causal laws of an empirical-analytic science always results in a "context-free" explanation.
2. However, this is not the case for the application of the general interpretations of psychoanalytic theory; "general interpretations do not make possible context-free explanations."
3. Therefore, these general interpretations cannot be part of an empirical-analytic science.

Recall that, in responding to Habermas' first argument, Grünbaum took issue with Habermas' grasp of Freudian theory, in particular, his failure to see that the therapeutic conquest of a neurosis *instantiates* rather than dissolves its etiologic linkage to its pathogen. In this case, he objects that Habermas relies on a false view of natural science. In particular, Grünbaum offers an array of counterexamples from physics to the first premise of our reconstruction of Habermas' argument. In Grünbaum's view, Habermas is simply wrong that explanations in the natural science are never context dependent; thus, this cannot be used as a reason for distinguishing the Freudian enterprise from that of natural science. In arguing his point, Grünbaum (1984) again draws on his knowledge of physics, specifically, the physical theory of classical electrodynamics. He writes: "For that major physical theory features laws that embody a far more fundamental dependence on the history and/or context of the object of knowledge than was ever contemplated in even the most exhaustive of psychoanalytic explanatory narratives . . ." (p. 17; for a briefer version of this argument, see Grünbaum, 1983c). Grünbaum's (1984) specific counterexample is the following:

> Consider an electically charged particle having an arbitrary velocity and acceleration. We are concerned with the laws governing the electric and magnetic fields produced by this point charge throughout space at any one fixed time t. In this theory, the influence of the charge on any other test charge in space is postulated to be propagated with the finite velocity of light rather than instantaneously, as in Newton's action-at-a-distance theory of gravitation. But this *non*-instantaneous feature of the propagation of the electrodynamic influence contributes to an important consequence as follows: At any space point P, the electric and magnetic fields at a given time t depend on the position, velocity and acceleration that the charge had at an earlier time t_0. That earlier time has the value $t - r/c$, where r is the distance traversed by the influence arriving at P at time t after having traveled from the charge to P with the velocity c of light.

> Clearly, the greater the distance r that was traversed by the influence by the time t of its arrival at point P, the earlier its origination time t_0. Thus, for space points at ever larger such distances r in infinite space, the origination time $t_0 = t - r/c$ will be ever more remotely past. In short, as the distance r becomes infinitely large, the origination time goes to past infinity.

> It folows that at ANY ONE INSTANT t the electric and magnetic fields produced throughout infinite space by a charge moving with arbitrary acceleration depend on its own PARTICULAR ENTIRE INFINITE PAST KINEMATIC HISTORY! (p. 17).

This is not at all a unique case, according to Grünbaum. There are other cases that exhibit "hysteresis" in the sense that "a property of a physical system induced by a given present influence upon it depends not only on that present influence, but also on the *past history* of variation of that influence" (Grünbaum, 1984, p. 18; see also 1983c for a briefer discussion). These cases include the hysteresis behavior of highly magnetizable metals (e.g., iron, cobalt, nickel, etc.), the *elastic* hysteresis of certain solids, the electric hysteresis exhibited by dielectric substances in electric fields, and the hysteresis of a radiation counter tube. Even rubber bands exhibit like behavior, and metal fatigue in airplanes is a similar phenomenon. These cases clearly show, in Grünbaum's view, that some of the important laws of nature, and, hence, any explanation that makes use of them, exhibit context dependence. On the basis of these considerations, Grünbaum's (1983c) summary judgment of Habermas' second argument is a harsh one: Habermas (as well as Gadamer (1975) who echoes Habermas' view) have simply succeeded in "parlay[ing] the severe limitations of their own personal scientific horizons into a *pseudo*-contrast between the humanistic disciplines and the natural sciences" (p. 11).

3. The Argument from Validation. What I call "the argument from validation" consists of two subarguments – one concerning supposed differences between how psychoanalytic theory and empirical-analytic theories are confirmed; the other concerning how they are disconfirmed. The first subargument rests on the fact that, according to Habermas, there is the following "specific difference" between empirical-analytic theories and the general interpretations of psychoanalysis (that is, Freud's clinical theory):

> In the case of testing theories through observation . . . the application of assumptions to reality is a matter for the inquiring subject. In the case of testing general interpretations through self-reflection . . . this application becomes *self-application* by the object of inquiry, who participates in the process of inquiry. The process of inquiry can lead to valid information only via a transformation in the patient's self-inquiry. When valid, general interpretations hold for the inquiring subject and all who can adopt its position only to the degree that those who are made the object of individual interpretations *know and recognize themselves* in these interpretations. The subject cannot obtain knowledge of the object unless it becomes knowledge for the object – and unless the latter thereby emancipates itself by becoming a subject [pp. 261–262].

I take it that Habermas is here assuming that the general interpretative schemata of the clinical theory are confirmed only to the extent that they are inductively supported by valid individual constructions. The claim, then, is that the latter are confirmed, in turn, *only if* they become a part of the self-reflection of the analysand. That is, the analysand has, as Grünbaum puts it, complete "epistemic privilege" with respect to these constructions, even as against the analyst him- or herself. In contrast, according to Habermas, the objects of standard empirical-analytic inquiry do not have this kind of epistemic privilege. Here confirmation occurs on the basis of observations *of* the object *by* the scientist (the so-called subject of inquiry). We can reconstruct the argument thus:

1. Statements relevant to the confirmation of clinical psychoanalytic theory (for example, individual constructions) can be accepted by the researcher only if they have first been accepted as valid by the subject.

2. No such requirement holds for statements relevant to the confirmation of empirical-analytic theories, which are typically accepted on the basis of observation by the researcher.

3. Therefore, clinical psychoanalytic theory is not an empirical-analytic theory.

In replying to this argument, Grünbaum again attacks Habermas' conception of psychoanalysis, this time on the grounds that the thesis of privileged epistemic access expressed in Habermas' first premise is ill-founded. His first point is that the only argument Habermas supplies for his first premise is a question-begging one. For in the above quote, Habermas construes the "otherwise innocuous phrase 'testing through self-reflection' so as to *stipulate* that only the patient's own appraisal can carry out the application of general interpretations to his particular life situation." (Grünbaum, 1984, p. 23) Second, the epistemic privilege that Habermas assigns to the analysand does not accord with Freud's own views concerning when an individual construction ought to be regarded as true. In particular, Freud (1937) explicitly rejects recollection by the patient as essential.

> Quite often we do not succeed in bringing the patient to recollect what has been repressed. Instead of that if the analysis is carried out correctly, we produce in [the patient] an assured conviction of the truth of the construction which achieves the same therapeutic result as a recaptured memory [pp. 265–266].

Habermas might reply at this point that perhaps he was wrong about the need for recollection; however, this quote from Freud shows that the patient's *conviction* is necessary, which is enough to maintain some form of an epistemic privilege doctrine. This reply is inadequate, however. For, as Grünbaum also points out, in Freud's paper on "Constructions in Analysis" (1937), he argues (from the confluence of clinical induction) that the analyst could justify an individual construction on the basis of the totality of the patient's productions, even in the face of the patient's denial. (See also Freud, 1920, on the treatment of a young lesbian as a case in point.) Finally, Grünbaum points out that Habermas' attribution of epistemic privilege to the analysand has also been impugned by the contemporary psychoanalysts Thomä and Kächele (1973, pp. 315–316) and Eagle (1973) as being untrue to the psychoanalytic situation (treatment setting).

One might expect the subargument from disconfirmation to run exactly parallel to that from confirmation. That is, one might expect Habermas to argue that the difference between the disconfirmation of psychoanalytic theory and empirical-analytic theory is that the former relies on the failure of self-reflection whereas the latter relies on the failure of observable prediction. But this is not the case for the following reason: Although Habermas regards the acceptance of a construction C by the analysand during self-reflection to be sufficient for the correctness of C, the *absence* of self-reflection in the face of C does not falsify it. The patient's resistances might simply be too strong. Thus, Habermas focuses instead on the logic of disconfirmation in the two cases and claims that there is a fundamental contrast between them on the purported grounds that an unsuccessful prediction in the natural sciences automatically refutes the hypothesis used to make it. In fact, Habermas (1971) takes the existence of an alternative to disconfirmation in the face of apparently disconfirming evidence to be the distinguishing feature of the psychoanalytic case. He argues as follows:

> General interpretations do not obey the same criteria of refutation as general theories. If a conditional prediction deduced from a lawlike hypothesis and initial conditions is falsified, then the hypothesis may be considered refuted. A general interpretation can be tested analogously if we derive a construction from one of its implications and the communications of the patient. We can give this construction the form of a conditional prediction. If it is correct, the patient will be moved to produce certain memories, reflect on a specific portion of forgotten life history, and overcome disturbances of both communication and behavior. But here the method of falsification is not the same as for general theories. For if the patient rejects a construction, the interpretation from which it has been derived cannot yet be considered refuted at all. . . . [T]here is still an alternative: either the interpretation is false (that is, the theory or its application to a given case) or, to the contrary, the resistances, which have been correctly diagnosed, are too strong [p. 266].

But, as Grünbaum points out, it has become a commonplace of the philosophy of science, ever since Pierre Duhem's work before World War I, that precisely the same ambiguity of refutation holds for science in general. By and large, it is not theories alone that are at issue in prediction but theories in conjunction with a statement of initial conditions *and* various collateral hypotheses. This means that if a prediction is not borne out, the blame cannot be pinned on the theory with certainty. Thus, again, the alleged difference between psychoanalysis and empirical-analytic science rests on a false view of the latter.

IS FREUDIAN PSYCHOANALYSIS GOOD SCIENCE?

In considering the merits of psychoanalytic theory as a scientific theory, Grünbaum has been concerned with the extent to which Freud's theoretical claims are supported by the available evidence. He has focused, in particular, on the sort of evidence that Freud invoked, namely, evidence obtained "from the couch." In making his assessment, Grünbaum has relied both on logical considerations and on various canons of inductive support that have become standard since the time of Bacon. He makes three basic claims:

1. The therapeutic effectiveness of the characteristic constituent factors of Freudian psychoanalytic therapy is in serious question.
2. Clinical data are subject to so many epistemological liabilities as to render them virtually useless in supporting the cardinal hypotheses as Freudian theory.
3. Even if clinical data were not epistemologically contaminated and could be taken at face value, they would fail to sustain any of the central postulates of Freud's clinical theory as well as the investigative utility of the method of free association.

Let us consider each of these claims in turn.

The Question of Therapeutic Effectiveness

The effectiveness of Freudian therapy has been under attack at least since Eysenck (1952, 1966) published his classic challenge. Contending that available evidence does not adequately support the claim that psychoanalysis is therapeutically effective, Eysenck claimed to have telling evidence that psychoanalysis did no better than simply having people go on about their lives without therapy. Erwin (1980) has reconstructed Eysenck's argument as follows:

1. If there is no adequate study of psychoanalytic therapy showing an improvement rate of better than two thirds or better than that of a suitable no-treatment control group, then there is no firm evidence that the therapy is therapeutically effective.

2. There is no adequate study showing either rate of improvement.

3. Therefore, there is no firm evidence that the therapy is therapeutically effective.

Originally, Eysenck made use of an overall spontaneous remission rate across all varieties of neurotic disorder. In response to criticism, however, Eysenck (1977) has recently emphasized that different types of neurotic disorder have different incidences and/or time courses of spontaneous remission. He now claims that any comparative evaluation must focus on a particular diagnostic grouping and a diagnostically matched untreated control group.

In the light of much subsequent literature, Grünbaum proceeds on the assumption that the superiority of the outcome of analytic treatment over that of rival treatment modalities has not been demonstrated. However, in his essay, "How Scientific is Psychoanalysis?" (Grünbaum, 1977), he stresses the following additional fact which is frequently overlooked: *If psychoanalytic treatment outcomes do exceed the spontaneous remission rate, this alone does not suffice to establish that psychoanalytic treatment gains are due to mediation of analytic insight. It would not rule out an important rival hypothesis, namely, that such treatment gains are due to an *inadvertent placebo effect.* In defining this term, Grünbaum (1981, 1983a) notes that of the various constituent factors that make up a treatment process, we can distinguish those that are characteristic, that is, claimed by the theory to be remedial, from others it regards as incidental. Grünbaum (1980) continues:

> A treatment process t characterized by having constituents F, will be said to be an *inadvertant placebo* with respect to target disorder D and dispensing physician P just in case each of the following conditions is satisfied: (a) none of the characteristic treatment factors F are remedial for D, but (b) P credits these very factors F with being therapeutic for D and indeed he deems at least some of them to be causally *essential to the remedial efficacy of t*, and (c) the patient believes that t derives remedial efficacy for D from constituents belonging to t's *characteristic* factors [p. 330].

The point is that in assessing the effectiveness of psychoanalytic therapy or of any of its rivals, "one must try to disentangle from one another (i) the effects, if any, indeed due to those factors that the relevant therapeutic theory postulates as being genuinely remedial, and (ii) purportedly lesser changes due to the expectations aroused in both patients and physicians by their belief in the therapeuticity of the treatment" (Grünbaum, 1977, p. 238). As Grünbaum reads the relevant literature on treatment effectiveness (in particular, Fisher & Greenberg, 1977; Luborsky, Singer, & Luborsky, 1975; Meltzoff & Kornreich, 1970; Sloan et al., 1975), there is good reason to suspect that insofar as Freudian therapy is effective, it is, in fact, "placebogenic." The studies seem to point to two conclusions; (1) psychotherapy of a wide variety of types and for a broad range of disorders is better than nothing, but (2) there is either no difference between different treatment modalities or the behavioral treatment is better.

Epistemological Liabilities of Clinical Data

Eysenck (1963) not only impugned the effectiveness of Freudian therapy, he also raised serious questions about the epistemic validity of clinical data as had Wilhelm Fliess (see Freud, 1954) before him. In contrast, Freud himself, as well as most of his advocates (see Luborsky & Spence, 1978, for a recent statement) have regarded clinical evidence as *the* basis for the claims of psychoanalytic theory to truth.

In considering how clinical material is supposed to bear evidentially on Freudian theory, it is important to distinguish three levels of clinical material. At the lowest level, we have what we can call the patient's *productions*. These include their dream reports, slips of the tongue, memory reports, and free associations as well as assents or dissents to interpretations offered by the analyst. In addition, we have facts concerning the presence or absence of behaviors or bodily states that are regarded as symptoms. At the second level, we have the *interpretations* provided either by the analyst or by patients themselves of these productions and symptoms as expressions of unconscious wishes, resistance, and so forth. Finally, we have what Freud (1937) later called a *construction*, a whole psychoanalytic story about the patient's psyche from the patient's early infantile history to the present state, including, of course, an etiological account of the symptoms. Although it is possible to maintain that the patient's productions bear directly on Freud's universal theoretical claims, a more plausible epistemological reconstruction is roughly as follows: Most productions, such as dream reports, slips of the tongue, free associations, and expressions of feeling toward the analyst during transference are taken to be relevant insofar as they provide the raw material for interpretations, which, in turn, provide the building blocks for the ultimate construction. Some productions may also be taken to attest to therapeutic success. In constrast, others, such as the patient's assent to or protest against a proposed construction, are often taken as direct evidence for the truth of that construction. The constructions themselves, clearly, are supposed to bear on the theory in the way that a particular instantiation of a universal claim bears on the universal claim.

The principal epistemological liability to which clinical data are subject is that the analyst, who presumably is committed to the truth of Freudian theory, unwittingly influences both patients' productions and the course of the analysis. This point has been recognized for some time (by Fliess, as is clear from Freud, 1954; as well as Christiansen, 1964; Glover, 1952; Martin, 1964a; Nagel, 1959). What appears not to have been recognized, as Grünbaum (1983b) points out, is that Freud himself was aware of this problem and, in addition, had a very sophisticated, albeit unsuccessful, strategy for dealing with it. Freud (1917) acknowledges the so-called problem of suggestion in his *Introductory Lectures:*

> It must dawn on us that in our technique we have abandoned hypnosis only to rediscover suggestion in the shape of transference.
>
> But here I will pause, and let you have a word; for I see an objection boiling up in you so fiercely that it would make you incapable of listening if it were not put into words: "Ah! so you've admitted it at last! You work with the help of suggestion, just like the hypnotists! That is what we've thought for a long time. But, if so, why the roundabout road by way of memories of the past, discovering the unconscious, interpreting and translating back distortions—this immense expenditure of labour, time and money—when the one effective thing is after all only suggestion? Why do you not make direct suggestions against the symptoms, as the others do—the honest hypnotists? Moreover, if you try to excuse yourself for your long detour on the ground that you have made a number of important psychological discoveries which are hidden by direct suggestion—what about the certainty of these discoveries now? Are not they a result of suggestion too, of unintentional suggestion? Is it not possible that you are forcing on the patient what you want and what seems to you correct in this field as well?" [pp. 446–447].

By this time in his career, Freud had clearly recognized the importance of transference as a motive force in therapy. Thus, the challenge was that, as Freud (1917) so nicely put it, "what is advantageous to our therapy is damaging to our researches" for "the influencing of our patient may make the objective certainty of our findings doubtful" (p. 452). His reply was as follows:

> Anyone who has himself carried out psycho-analyses will have been able to convince himself on countless occasions that it is impossible to make

suggestions to a patient in that way. The doctor has no difficulty, of course, in making him a supporter of some particular theory and in thus making him share some possible error of his own. In this respect the patient is behaving like anyone else – like a pupil – but this only affects his intelligence, not his illness. *After all, his conflicts will only be successfully solved and his resistance overcome if the anticipatory ideas he is given tally with what is real in him* [italics added]. Whatever in the doctor's conjectures is inaccurate drops out in the course of the analysis; it has to be withdrawn and replaced by something more correct (p. 452).

Grünbaum has dubbed the underlined statement the "necessary condition thesis," NCT for short. (Elsewhere, Grünbaum, 1983c, calls it – more honorifically – "Freud's master proposition".) This assertion plays the key role in Freud's attempted solution to the problem of suggestion. What he is claiming, according to Grünbaum (1983c), is tantamount to the following: "(1) only the psychoanalytic method of interpretation and treatment can yield or mediate to the patient correct insight into the unconscious pathogens of his psychoneurosis, and (2) the analysand's correct insight into the etiology of his affliction and into the unconscious dynamics of his character is, in turn, *causally necessary* for the therapeutic conquest of this neurosis" (p. 184). NCT can then be used to vindicate the validity of the clinical data furnished by patients in analysis by means of what Grünbaum dubs the "tally argument" (referring to Freud's assumption that ideas given patients *tally* with what is real in them). The argument runs as follows:

1. The analysis of patient P was therapeutically successful.
2. NCT.
3. Therefore, the psychoanalytic interpretations of the hidden causes of P's behavior given to him by his analyst are indeed correct.

Freud's strategy was brilliant, according to Grünbaum. But was it successful? It should be clear from our discussion of the therapeutic efficacy question, that Grünbaum does not think so. For, although the tally argument is logically valid, there is a serious question concerning the truth of its premises, in particular, the crucial NCT. NCT claims that therapeutic success is mediated *only* by psychoanalytic insight. Insofar as there is either spontaneous remission of symptoms or there exist rival successful treatment modalities, NCT is false. As Grünbaum (1980a) argues – after extensive review of the relevant literature – there appears to be strong evidence for both. (Interestingly enough, Freud himself explicitly conceded the existence of spontaneous remission [Grünbaum, 1983c]). Grünbaum (1983b) concludes: "Since the Tally Argument is thus gravely undercut, any therapeutic successes scored by analysts, even if spectacular, have become *probatively* unavailing to the validation of psychoanalytic theory via that argument" (p. 208).

Grünbaum (1980a) considers one possible alternative to the use of the tally argument. This is to make use of a patient's introspections *once he or she has been successfully analyzed*. It might be thought that, if reliable, such introspections could provide the needed validation for two sorts of claims: (1) claims concerning the etiology of the patient's affliction, and (2) claims concerning the necessary role of the analyst's constructions in the therapeutic process. The validation of such claims could, in turn, provide direct evidence for Freud's psychogenetic theory as well as help to discredit the rival therapeutic hypothesis of placebogenesis. Unfortunately, however, these "hopeful speculations" are "fundamentally impugned" in Grünbaum's view by the findings reported by Nisbett and Wilson (1977) on the extent to which we have introspective access to the dynamics of our mental life. Nisbett and Wilson do not apply the results of their findings to the case of psychoanalysis. Grünbaum (1980a) believes, however, that they are directly relevant and that "they marshal telling empirical support" for the following conclusions:

> 1. Far from justifying the prevalent belief in privileged access to the dynamics of our psychic responses, the findings strongly indicate the following: Purportedly introspective self-perception of causal connections between one's own mental states is just as liable to *theory-induced* errors as is drawing causal inferences about connections between purely external events from apparent covariations among their properties. . . .
> 2. When asked how, if at all, a particular stimulus influenced a given response, the persons in the experimental studies, and ordinary people in their daily lives did not and do not even attempt to interrogate their memories of the mediating causal process. Although it may *feel* like introspection, what they actually do is draw on the causal *theories* provided by their culture or pertinent intellectual subculture for a verdict as to the effect, if any, of that kind of stimulus on that kind of response. . . .
> 3. As N & W remark: "Subjective reports about higher mental processes are sometimes correct, but even the instances of correct report are not due to direct introspective awareness. Instead, they are due to the incidentally correct employment of a priori causal theories" [Nisbett & Wilson, 1977, p. 233] [p. 363–364].

(See Rothstein, 1980, for some criticisms of Grünbaum's discussion of the epistemological liabilities of patient introspection and Grünbaum, 1981, for a reply.)

Grünbaum's point, then, is that neither the tally argument nor the use of patients' introspective judgments subsequent to successful analysis can be used to guard against the very real possibility that both patients' productions and therapeutic outcomes are due more to the suggestive influence of the analyst than to the causal mechanisms and states of affairs posited by Freudian theory. Grünbaum (1983b) considers the suggestion hypothesis to be more than a mere logical possibility. He discusses in detail three of the major kinds of clinical findings that Freud deemed either initially exempt from contamination or, at least, unmarred when gathered with proper precautions. These are the products of "free" association, the patient's assent to analytic interpretations that were initially resisted, and memories recovered from early life. Grünbaum finds "solid" evidence in the psychological literature that each of these instances is subject to "considerable epistemic contamination." Grünbaum (1983b) concludes:

> Thus, generally speaking, clinical findings—in and of themselves—forfeit the probative value that Freud claimed for them, although their potential heuristic merits may be quite substantial. To assert that the contamination of intraclinical data is *ineradicable* without extensive and essential recourse to *extra*clinical findings is *not*, of course, to declare the automatic falsity of any and every analytic interpretation that gained the patient's assent by means of prodding from the analyst. But it *is* to maintain—to the great detriment of intraclinical testability!—that, in general, the epistemic devices confined to the analytic setting cannot reliably *sift* or decontaminate the clinical data so as to *identify* those that qualify as probative [p. 270].

The Logical Foundations of the Theory of Repression

The problem of the contamination of clinical evidence is not the only epistemic problem to which Freudian theory is subject. In his most recent work, Grünbaum (1983b, 1984) has charted a number of further, even more serious, difficulties, the upshot of which is that *even if clinical data could be taken at face value, they would not support the basic tenets of Freud's theoretical structure.*

Grünbaum argues for this conclusion by considering the reasoning that Freud used at various stages of his career to support "the cornerstone" of his theoretical edifice. This is the hypothesis that it is *repressed material* that initially causes and continues to maintain psychoneurotic symptoms as well as other psychic phenomena such as dreams and parapraxes. Grünbaum begins by considering the reasoning used by Freud and Breuer to support the original version of this "repression hypothesis" for psychoneurosis. Although the evidence they adduced to support their theory was not completely unflawed, it did come up to a relatively high standard, according to Grünbaum. As it turned out,

Freud himself discovered that this evidence was spurious. Rather than abandoning the repression hypothesis at this point, however, Freud substituted a new version. The difficulty with this – and the basis of Grünbaum's complaint – is that Freud never succeeded in providing new evidence that was anywhere near as cogent as his original observations with Breuer. In addition, he proceeded to extrapolate from his repression hypothesis of the psychoneuroses to a more general repression hypothesis covering both parapraxes and dreams. But in neither case was there any new, compelling, evidence that would warrant the extrapolation.

The original Freud-Breuer hypothesis was that (1) the therapeutic conquest of hysterical symptoms is effected by the abreactive lifting of the repression of a traumatic memory, and (2) this posited therapeutic efficacy can be explained deductively by the etiologic hypothesis that the repression of the traumatic event was causally necessary for the formation and maintenance of the given hysterical symptom. Freud and Breuer's (1893) evidence for these claims was that "each individual hysterical symptom immediately and permanently disappeared when we had succeeded in bringing clearly to light the memory of the event by which it was provoked and in arousing its accompanying affect" (p. 6; emphasis in original). Grünbaum (1983b) reconstructs their reasoning as follows:

> First, they attributed their positive therapeutic results to the lifting of repressions. Having assumed such a *therapeutic connection*, they wished to *explain* it. Then they saw it would indeed be explained deductively by the following etiological hypothesis: the particular repression whose undoing removed a given symptom S is *causally necessary* for the initial formation *and* maintenance of S. Thus, the nub of their inductive argument for inferring a repression etiology can be formulated as follows: the *removal* of a hysterical symptom S *by means of lifting* a repression R is *cogent evidence* that the repression R was *causally necessary* for the formation of the symptom S [p. 218].

The beauty of their appeal to separate symptom removal was this. To support their hypothesis, Freud and Breuer had to show that removal of the repression was *sufficient* for the removal of the symptom. This would count as cogent inductive grounds for the claim that the repression was a causally *necessary condition* of the symptom. The difficulty was that given merely the conjunction of removal of the repression with removal of the symptom, there was a rival explanation – namely, that the therapeutic efficacy of the cathartic method was placebogenic. But, they argued, if the symptom removal were a placebo effect wrought by suggestion, one would expect all the symptoms to be removed at once.

Thus, in their view, the fact that they were removed one by one was evidence against the rival placebo hypothesis and in support of their own view.

Although Freud and Breuer deserve considerable credit for realizing the importance of the alternative rival placebo hypothesis and attempting to rule it out, their line of reasoning was not totally successful, in Grünbaum's (1983a) view. Precisely because of the analyst's evident focus on a specific memory for *each* symptom, the patient's conquest of the given symptom might be affected by suggestion. That is, on the basis of the analyst's behavior, the patient might come to *believe* that uncovering a memory associated with a given symptom would cause that symptom to disappear. Thus, *as a consequence of this belief,* rather than the state of affairs posited by the Freud-Breuer hypothesis, the symptom might then actually disappear.

As it turned out, the Freud-Breuer hypothesis had a far more serious problem to contend with – namely, that the crucial evidence concerning therapeutic success was spurious. As Freud (1925) put it:

> Even the most brilliant [therapeutic] results were liable to be suddenly wiped away if my personal relation with the patient became disturbed. It was true that they would be reestablished if a reconciliation could be effected; but such an occurrence proved that the personal emotional relation between doctor and patient was after all stronger than the whole cathartic process [p. 27].

Freud, however, continued to maintain a version of the repression hypothesis, substituting repression of infantile sexual wishes for the Freud-Breuer repression of a traumatic event in adulthood and calling on the full array of clinical material in support of his claims.

We have already seen that, according to Grünbaum, this clinical material is probatively hopeless because of the failure of the tally argument to protect against the ever-present problem of suggestion and because of the unavailability of any other vindication of the probity of clinical data. Let us suppose, however, that this is not the case. In the face of the demise of the *therapeutic* vindication of the tally argument, can clinical data nevertheless provide the support that Freudian theory so badly needs *without* relying on *therapeutic* success? According to Grünbaum, the answer is no; Freud's clinical data suffer from serious epistemic limitations as support for causal hypotheses, even if they are regarded as uncontaminated. Consider, for example, products of the method of free association. According to Grünbaum (1983b), the epistemic legitimation of free association as a reliable means of identifying and certifying pathogenic causes as such collapsed with the demise of the Breuer-Freud cathartic method. Thus, the most that the method of free association can come up with is the expression of a thought or wish that was previously repressed. But this is a far cry from the etiologic claim that the pertinent repression had been the *pathogen P* of the patient's neurosis *N* on the strength of its emergence as an association to the symptom. For, Grünbaum (1983b) argues:

> to support Freud's etiologic hypothesis that P is causally necessary for N, evidence must be produced to show that being a P *makes a difference* to being an N. But such causal relevance is *not* attested by *mere* instances of Ns that were Ps, i.e., by patients who are both Ps and Ns. For a large number of such cases does not preclude that just as many *non-Ps* would also become Ns, if followed in a horizontal study from childhood onward! Thus, instances of Ns that were Ps may just *happen* to have been Ps. Then being a P has no etiologic role at all in becoming an N. . . . Thus, to provide evidence for the causal relevance claimed by Freud, we need to *combine* instances of Ns that were Ps with instances of non-Ps who are *non-Ns*. Indeed, since he deemed P to be causally necessary for N – rather than just causally relevant – his etiology requires that the class of non-Ps should not contain *any* Ns whatever, and the class of Ps is to have a positive (though numerically unspecified) incidence of Ns [p. 277].

Furthermore, for the purpose of supporting *etiologic* (causal) hypotheses, the absence of such controls undermines the probative value of not only data collected by the method of free association, but also evidence based on memories such as those discussed by Glymour (1974) in Freud's Rat Man case.

Freud's causal explanations of dreams and parapraxes fare no better, as it turns out (see Grünbaum, 1983b, pp. 222–265). There are two basic difficulties. First, Freud's claim that dreams and parapraxes are like neurotic symptoms in the sense of being compromises between the demands of our unconscious and conscious life is simply an extrapolation from his theory of psychoneurosis. In fact, Grünbaum (1983b) argues that it is a *misextrapolation* because there is nothing akin to the therapeutic base of the latter. With respect to parapraxes, for example, "Freud did not adduce any evidence that the permanent lifting of a repression to which he had attributed a parapraxis will be 'therapeutic' in the sense of enabling the person himself to correct the parapraxis *and* to avoid its repetition in the future" (Grünbaum, 1983b, p. 225). Second, the method Freud used to identify the particular unconscious determinants of dreams and parapraxes is simply the method of free association. Hence, even assuming that it is free from epistemic contamination, the method is powerless to provide support for any *causal* hypothesis, including those pertinent to dreams and parapraxes.

Examination of a Radical Critique of Grünbaum's Views

Because most of Grünbaum's work on psychoanalysis is so recent, there has, as yet, been little time for critical reply. One exception is the strongly negative reaction of Flax (1981), who argues that "neither Popper nor Grünbaum offers an adequate philosophy of science by which psychoanalysis may be judged" (p. 561). Furthermore, she chastises Grünbaum for restricting his discussion to Freud, contending that "this is like confining a discussion of physics to Newton because contemporary physics is in such disarray and then throwing out physics because there are unresolved problems in Newton's theory" (p. 564). More specifically, she seems to believe that the more contemporary version of psychoanalysis embodied in object relations theory is immune from the epistemic difficulties Grünbaum attributes to Freud. In fact, she makes the astounding claim that "all the phenomena that Grünbaum counts as the clinical liabilities of psychoanalysis on empiricist grounds— epistemic contamination (i.e., intersubjectivity), suggestion, the placebo effect, etc. . . . are evidence that object-relations theory is correct" (p. 567). Since these points would, if correct, strike at the heart of Grünbaum's work, I will conclude my discussion of Grünbaum with a consideration of Flax's principal contentions.

Flax's strategy of attack involves isolating a number of assumptions "suppressed within this debate" that she takes to be problematic. To make her case, then, she must show both that these assumptions are problematic and that they are, in fact, *essential* to Grünbaum's arguments. I suggest that she does neither, with the failure on the second count the more serious. It is to this point that I will direct my remarks, for it suggests that she has seriously misunderstood the character of Grünbaum's arguments. Let me give a few examples.

"Empiricism," Flax (1981) claims, "is simply untenable as a methodology of philosophy of science. A datum is never observed as it is in itself. . . . Thus fact and theory cannot be totally distinct. Empirical experience loses its special status as the most privileged and unproblematic evidence. . . . All data are 'epistemically contaminated' " (p. 563). I take it that the assumption of concern here is that data gathered on the basis of observation are somehow epistemically privileged and independent of theory. Suppose, however, we take this to be false. Suppose we agree that observation is always "theory laden" in the sense that it always involves interpretation, and such interpretation is relative to a person's conceptual apparatus, beliefs, expectations, and so forth. Furthermore, we take it that observational claims, like any other, are subject to controversy and revision and must be supported if contested. Does it then follow that Grünbaum's epistemological liabilities arguments fail? Flax's reasoning seems to be that if all observation is theory laden, then all data are "epistemically contaminated," including the data of our most esteemed scientific theories. Hence, any argument based on the implicit assumption that a theory cannot be scientific if it is based on contaminated data will be an argument based on a totally unreasonable demarcation principle.

The difficulty with this line of reasoning is that it is perfectly possible to agree that all observation is theory laden and still maintain a distinction between data that are *biased* in a damagingly relevant sense and those that are not so biased. The ideal of objective data is possible at least to the extent that data relevant to a given theory T can be collected by someone whether he or she believes in T or even, in fact, whether he or she has knowledge of T. Scientists have become increasingly aware of the ways in which experimenters' bias toward their pet hypotheses can affect the outcome of experiments. With animal subjects, bias often operates in the recording of observations; with human subjects, it can be unintentionally conveyed in the communication of experimental instructions. But is it important to note that the result of this increasing knowledge about the potential pitfalls of experimenter bias has not been despair over the inevitable irrationality and arbitrariness of scientific theorizing. Rather, it has been the adoption of new and more stringent *controls* to minimize or eliminate such bias. For example, the use of socalled "double blind" experimental procedure has become standard for experimentation with human subjects in drug and other medical research.

Grünbaum's quarrel with the use of clinical evidence as support for psychoanalytic theory is precisely that it consists of data subject to the charge of investigator bias. Not only are the data being gathered in the clinical setting obtained by someone firmly committed to the truth of the theory, but they are gathered in such a way – during the course of a therapeutic process in which transference plays a major role – that even Freud (1917, pp. 446–447) worried about the charge of suggestion.

Furthermore, as Grünbaum (1983d) points out, Flax fails to distinguish between data that is merely theory-laden and data generated by the self-fulfilling *use* of the theory in their production. As Merton's (1949) studies of self-fulfilling and self-defeating predictions in the social sciences have shown, "*identifiable alterations* of the presumed initial conditions, rather than *mere* theory-ladenness, generate phenomena that furnish demonstrably spurious confirmations and disconfirmations" (p. 50). Again, it's not mere theory ladenness but the occurrence of precisely such alterations of the presumed initial conditions that is the object of Grünbaum's concern. In Grünbaum's (1983d) view, this occurrence "has been tellingly demonstrated *experimentally* in studies [reported in Marmor, 1970] of the purportedly "free" associations produced by patients in analysis" (p. 50). Grünbaum can perfectly well grant that all data are theory laden and still maintain that *certain* forms of theory-ladenness are epistemically unacceptable.

Another one of Flax's (1981) objections is that "a purely internal philosophical analysis of theories and theory shifts is not adequate . . . [to] explain why a theory is accepted as "credible" or when this acceptance occurs" (p. 563). The problematic assumption she has in mind is obviously that such a purely internal philosophical analysis of theories and theory shifts *is* adequate for such purposes. What Flax means by such a "purely internal philosophical analysis" can be gleaned from the sorts of considerations she thinks are left out of account. She writes: "At least equally important and under dispute is what counts as a fact, how data are to be interpreted and which data must be explained" (p. 563). I take it then that such a purely internal analysis, then, is one that focuses solely on the relationship of theory to evidence as the basis of theory choice. And the putatively problematic assumption would be that it is possible to give a complete account of why scientists in fact accept theories as credible at particular moments in the history of science solely in terms of the logical relations between theory and evidence. Now, I have grave doubts as to whether most normative philosophers of science, including Grünbaum, would accept this assumption. But the main point again is: What of it? Suppose we agree that the assumption is wrong. It seems to me that Grünbaum's discussion of the problems inherent in the use of clinical data rests on no assumptions whatsoever concerning the sorts of considerations that must be invoked to explain particular historical occurrences of accepting particular theories. Someone interested in the *assessment* of the evidential grounds claimed to provide support for a theory is simply interested in a different question than someone interested in explaining why those who have accepted the theory did so. The former is a question about epistemic merit, the second about human psychology. Comments by Flax (1981) such as "Neither Grünbaum's nor Popper's philosophy, can provide an adequate account of the scientific process" (p. 563) indicate that she has no real understanding of the normative project. Certainly one can argue that the facts of scientific practice bear on one's choice of normative principles. And given certain views about what down-to-earth normative philosophy of science should be like, one can fault a particular exercise in appraisal for using utopian standards. However, all this in no way affects the point that normative philosophy of science is not concerned with giving a psychological or political or sociological or historical explanation of why particular episodes in the history of science occurred as they did, and, therefore, ought not be criticized if it does not do so.

Perhaps Flax in some sense realizes this, for her last criticism concerning the putatively problematic nature of Grünbaum's grounds goes for the jugular. Flax (1981) writes:

> Some of the greatest weaknesses of both Popper's and Grünbaum's accounts of science stem from the attempt rationally and arbitrarily to reconstruct the nature of scientific practice. Integrally connected with rationalization is their claim to legitimately legislate what counts as science and to evaluate how well it is done. Neither Popper nor Grünbaum give a scientific or philosophic justification for this claim, and there are good philosophical grounds for questioning its validity [p. 564].

Flax does not tell us here what those grounds are but simply refers us to Rorty (1979).

Surely, one might think, I cannot charge Flax with irrelevance here. For certainly, Grünbaum's criticism of Freudian theory does at least presuppose that normative philosophy of science is a legitimate enterprise. My reply is, yes and no. Normative philosophy of science is not just one sort of thing, but many. I believe that what Flax is attacking is a far more ambitious form of the enterprise than the one Grünbaum undertakes in his recent writings. The ambitious form aims at a global rational reconstruction of at least those parts of scientific practice that seem to be governed by reason. This involves an attempt to find a set of principles that serve to *rationalize* the decisions, acts, and heuristic rules that belong to actual scientific practice.

This ambitious form of normative philosophy may well not be possible. But the enterprise can be made more modest in a number of ways. First, rational reconstruction can be done in a piecemeal rather than a global way. Second, the philosopher of science can engage in the appraisal of specific scientific contributions not as an external critic, invoking, as Scheffler (1967) puts it, norms based on "an abstract epistemological ideal" but rather as a *participant* whose norms are "an ideal which, regulating the characteristic activities of science, may enter into its very description" (p. 73). Flax fails to understand that in Grünbaum's various epistemological liabilities arguments, he is playing it very close to the ground. The normative principles he invokes do not stem from any philosophical rational reconstruction of scientific practice. They are part of that practice itself. This is particularly true of the inductivist principles he marshals in his criticism of Freud's attempts to establish his causal claims. Furthermore, Grünbaum mounts a persuasive case that these normative principles are ones Freud himself explicitly avowed. Thus, it seems quite true, as Grünbaum (1983c) himself says, that the verdict he reaches concerning the scientific merit of psychoanalysis "is hardly predicated on the imposition of some extraneous methodological purism" (p. 13). The point, then, is this. Even if Flax were to convince us that a global rational reconstruction of science were impossible, I do not see how this would undercut Grünbaum's critique in any way.

Grünbaum (1983d) himself has replied to Flax's other charges. He is particularly insistent that the critique he has offered of Freud's claims is equally applicable to more contemporary psychoanalytic theorists such as Heinz Kohut and the object relations school. These latter-day theorists

> all claim clinical sanction for the generic repression-aetiology of neuroses. And they hold that free association has the *epistemic capability of* identifying the unconscious *causes* of all kinds of thought and behavior, such as dream content and parapraxes. Moreover, qua being psychoanalytic, the post-Freudian versions also deem the successful lifting of repressions to be the decisive agency in the postulated insight dynamics of the therapy [p. 47].

Eagle, a psychoanalytically oriented clinical psychologist, has recently voiced full support for these claims of Grünbaum's. After examining recent formulations in psychoanalytic object relations theory and self psychology, Eagel (1983) concludes:

> Contrary claims notwithstanding, Grünbaum's criticisms of Freudian theory are neither vitiated nor undone by these recent developments. In no way do current formulations somehow manage to weaken or even constitute a response to these criticisms. The clinical data generated by an object relations theory or self psychology approach are as epistemologically contaminated as data generated by the more traditional approach. There is a little, or perhaps even less, evidence available on therapeutic process and therapeutic outcome. And finally, the etiological claims made in more current formulations are perhaps even more logically and empirically flawed than Freud's etiological formulations [pp. 49-50].

Thus, Flax's analogy to the case of physics completely misfires, Grünbaum (1983d) asserts, "if only because the much vaunted post-Freudian versions have not remedied a single one of the methodological defects" (p. 48) that Grünbaum charges against the psychoanalytic method of clinical investigation.

SUMMARY

In his recent work on psychoanalytic epistemology, Grünbaum has exhibited an extremely impressive command of both the psychoanalytic literature and the philosophy of science. His views thus ought to be taken very seriously by anyone interested in the epistemic status of psychoanalytic theory. I have attempted here to extract the principal points and arguments contained in that body of work.

Grünbaum addresses himself to two fundamental questions: (1) What sorts of standards of assessment ought we to invoke in evaluating psychoanalysis? and (2) How does psychoanalysis measure up relative to those standards? Because Freud himself insisted that psychoanalysis was a natural science, and because, in Grünbaum's view, there are no good arguments to the contrary, Grünbaum has insisted that psychoanalysis ought to be assessed as an empirical science. To support his position, he has engaged in debate with Popper, Habermas, Ricoeur, and George Klein, although we have restricted our attention here to his consideration of the views of Popper and Habermas.

Popper's famous contention that psychoanalysis is not scientific because it is unfalsifiable was historically important not only because it raised interesting questions about the epistemic status of psychoanalysis but also because it raised fundamental issues about what makes something scientific. In the context of replying to Popper's challenge, Grünbaum has argued that (1) falsifiability is a meaningful notion in science, although it is not the touchstone of scientific rationality as Popper maintains; (2) in particular, Popper is completely wrong in claiming that inductivism is powerless to impugn the scientific credentials of a theory like psychoanalysis; (3) Popper has no good arguments for his claim that psychoanalysis is unfalsifiable; and (4) in fact, psychoanalysis is falsifiable, if one applies a scientifically reasonable notion of falsifiability.

Habermas has argued that psychoanalysis ought to be regarded as a *critical* science rather than as an empirical-analytic one. Habermas rests his case on two sets of arguments. The first concerns the relationship of the clinical theory to the metapsychology. The second concerns the epistemic properties of the clinical theory itself. Grünbaum has addressed these arguments as follows: First, Freud rightly saw that the scientific status of the clinical theory is not dependent on that of the metapsychology; hence, any argument which assumes that there is such a dependence is irrelevant to the question of whether the clinical theory is scientific. Second, the *specific* arguments that Habermas advances to show that the clinical theory is not appropriately regarded as an empirical science fail, either because Habermas does not correctly understand psychoanalysis or because he is ignorant of certain features of the natural sciences.

In considering the *merits* of psychoanalysis as a scientific theory – that is, in reply to the second of the questions he sets himself – Grünbaum has argued for three points: (1) the therapeutic effectiveness of the characteristic constituent factors of psychoanalytic treatment is seriously in question; (2) all known attempts to save clinical data from the charge of contamination from suggestion fail, so that such data are virtually useless in providing support for the cardinal hypotheses of Freudian theory; and (3) even if clinical data were not epistemologically contaminated, they would not support the basic tenets of Freud's theoretical structure, *because Freud's major clinical arguments are basically flawed.*

The most explicit critique of Grünbaum's views to date is to be found in the work of Flax (1981). Flax argues that Grünbaum's discussion of psychoanalysis makes use of a number of implicit assumptions regarding the nature of science which, in her view, are seriously questionable. To make her case, she must show both that these assumptions are problematic and that they are essential to Grünbaum's arguments. I have argued that, in fact, she does neither. The second failing is the more serious because it indicates that Flax does not clearly understand the sort of normative philosophy of science in which Grünbaum is engaged.

REFERENCES

Breuer, J., & Freud, S. (1893). On the physical mechanism of hysterical phenomena: Preliminary communication. *Standard Edition, 2,* 1–18.

Christiansen, B. (1964). The scientific status of psychoanalytic clinical evidence: III. *Inquiry, 7,* 47–79.

Cioffi, F. (1970). Freud and the idea of a pseudo-science. In R. Borger & F. Cioffi (Eds.), *Explanation in the behavioural sciences* (pp. 471–499). Cambridge: The University Press.

Cohen, R. S., & Laudan, L. (Eds.). (1983). *Physics, philosophy and psychoanalysis: Essays in honor of Adolf Grünbaum.* Dordrecht, Holland: D. Reidel.

Duhem, P. (1906). *The aim and structure of physical theory* [La théorie physique son objet et sa structure]. Princeton, NJ: Princeton University Press, 1954.

Eagle, M. N. (1973). Validation of motivational explanation in psychoanalysis. *Psychoanalysis & Contemporary Thought, 2,* 265–275.

Eagle, M. N. (1983). The epistemological status of recent developments in psychoanalytic theory. In R. S. Cohen & L. Laudan (Eds.), *Physics, philosophy and psychoanalysis: Essays in honor of Adolf Grünbaum* (pp. 31–56). Dordrecht, Holland: D. Reidel.

Erwin, E. (1980). Psychoanalytic therapy: The Eysenck argument. *American Psychologist, 35,* 435–443.

Eysenck, H. J. (1952). The effects of psychotherapy: An evaluation. *Journal of Consulting Psychology, 16,* 319–324.

Eysenck, H. J. (1963). *Uses and abuses of psychology.* Baltimore, MD: Penguin.

Eysenck, H. J. (1966). *The effects of psychotherapy.* New York: International Science Press.

Eysenck, H. J. (1977). *You and neurosis.* London: Temple Smith.

Eysenck, H. J., & Wilson, G. D. (1973). *The experimental study of Freudian theories.* London: Meuthen & Co.

Farrell, B. A. (1963). Psychoanalytic theory. In S. G. M. Lee & M. Herbert (Eds.), *Freud and psychology* (pp. 19–28). Middlesex, England: Penguin, 1970.

Farrell, B. A. (1964). The status of psychoanalytic theory. *Inquiry, 7,* 104–123.

Fisher, S., & Greenberg, R. P. (1977). *The scientific credibility of Freud's theories and therapy.* New York: Basic Books.

Flax, J. (1981). Psychoanalysis and the philosophy of science: Critique or resistance? *Journal of Philosophy, 78,* 561–569.

Freud S. (1895). Reply to criticisms of my paper on anxiety neurosis. *Standard Edition, 3,* 123–129.

Freud, S. (1909). Notes upon a case of obsessional neurosis. *Standard Edition, 10,* 155–318.

Freud, S. (1914). On narcissism: an introduction. *Standard Edition 14,* 73–102.

Freud, S. (1915a). Instincts and their vicissitudes. *Standard Edition, 14,* 117–140.

Freud, S. (1915b). A case of paranoia running counter to the psychoanalytic theory of the disease. *Standard Edition, 14,* 263–272.

Freud, S. (1917). Introductory lectures on psychoanalysis. Part III: General theory of the neuroses. *Standard Edition, 16,* 243–463.

Freud, S. (1920). The psychogenesis of a case of homosexuality in a woman. *Standard Edition, 18,* 147–172.

Freud, S. (1925). An autobiographical study. *Standard Edition, 20,* 7–70.

Freud, S. (1933). New introductory lectures on psychoanalysis, xxix–xxxv. *Standard Edition, 22,* 5–182.

Freud, S. (1937). Constructions in analysis. *Standard Edition, 23,* 254–269.

Freud, S. (1940a). An outline of psychoanalysis. *Standard Edition, 23,* 141–208.

Freud, S. (1940b). Some elementary lessons in psychoanalysis. *Standard Edition, 23,* 281–286.

Freud, S. (1954). *The origins of psychoanalysis.* New York: Basic Books.

Gadamer, H. G. (1975). *Truth and method.* New York: Seabury.

Geuss, R. (1981). *The idea of a critical theory: Habermas and the Frankfurt School.* Cambridge: Cambridge University Press, 1981.

Glover, E. (1952). Research methods in psychoanalysis. *International Journal of Psychoanalysis, 33,* 403–409.

Glymour, C. (1974). Freud, Kepler, and the clinical evidence. In R. Wollheim (Ed.), *Freud* (pp. 285–304). Garden City, NY: Anchor.

Glymour, C. (1980). *Theory and evidence.* Princeton, NJ: Princeton University Press.

Grünbaum, A. (1966). The falsifiability of a component of a theoretical system. In P. K. Feyerabend & G. Maxwell (Eds.), *Mind, matter and method: Essays in philosophy and science in honor of Herbert Feigl* (pp. 273–305). Minneapolis: University of Minnesota Press.

Grünbaum, C. (1968). *Geometry and chronometry in philosophical perspective.* Minneapolis: University of Minnesota Press.

Grünbaum, A. (1969). Can we ascertain the falsity of a scientific hypothesis? In M. Mandelbaum (Ed.), *Observation and theory in science* (pp. 69–129). Baltimore: Johns Hopkins Press, 1971.

Grünbaum, A. (1976). Is falsifiability the touchstone of scientific rationality? Karl Popper versus inductivism. In R. S. Cohen, P. K. Feyerabend, & M. W. Wartofsky (Eds.), *Es-*

says in memory of Imre Lakatos (Boston Studies in the Philosophy of Science, Vol. 38 (pp. 213–252). Dordrecht; Holland: D. Reidel, 1976.

Grünbaum, A. (1977). How scientific is psychoanalysis? In R. Stern, L. Horowitz, & J. Lynes (Eds.), *Science and psychotherapy* (pp. 219–254). New York: Haven Press.

Grünbaum, A. (1979). Is Freudian psychoanalytic theory pseudoscientific by Karl Popper's criterion of demarcation? *American Philosophical Quarterly, 16,* 131–141.

Grünbaum, A. (1980a). Epistemological liabilities of the clinical appraisal of psychoanalytic theory. *Noûs, 14,* 307–385.

Grünbaum, A. (1980b). The role of psychological explanations of the rejection or acceptance of scientific theories. In *Transactions of the New York Academy of Sciences: Vol. 39 A Festschrift for Robert Merton,* (pp. 75–90).

Grünbaum, A. (1981, March 5). How valid is psychoanalysis? An exchange. *New York Review of Books, 28,* 40–41.

Grünbaum, A. (1983a). Logical foundations of psychoanalytic theory. Festschrift für Wolfgang Stegmuller, *Erkenntnis, 1983, 19,* 109–152. In J. Reppen (Ed.), *Future directions of psychoanalysis.* Hillsdale, NJ: Lawrence Erlbaum Associates. (Also reprinted in T. Millon, Ed., *Theories of psychopathology and personality,* 3rd edition. New York: Holt, Rinehart & Winston, 1983.)

Grünbaum, A. (1983b). The foundations of psychoanalysis. In L. Laudan (Ed.), *Mind and medicine* (Pittsburgh Series in the Philosophy and History of Science, Vol. 8, pp. 143–309). Berkeley: University of California Press.

Grünbaum, A. (1983c). Freud's theory: the perspective of a philosopher of science. Presidential Address to the American Philosophical Association, Eastern Division. In *Proceedings and Addresses of the American Philosophical Association, 57,* 5–31.

Grünbaum, A. (1983d). Is object relations theory better founded than orthodox psychoanalysis? A reply to Jane Flax. *Journal of Philosophy, 80,* 46–51.

Grünbaum, A. (1984). *The foundations of psychoanalysis: A philosophical critique.* Berkeley: University of California Press.

Grünbaum, A. (in press). Explication and implications of the placebo concept. In L. White, B. Tursky, & G. F. Schwartz (Eds.), *Placebo: clinical phenomena and new insights.* New York: Guilford Press.

Habermas, J. (1967). *Zur Logik der Sozialwissenschaften.* (Philosophische Rundschau, Belheft 5). Tübingen, West Germany: Siebeck & Mohr, 1967.

Habermas, J. (1971). *Knowledge and Human Interests.* (J. J. Shapiro, Trans.). London: Heinemann.

Habermas, J. (1979). *Communication and the evolution of society.* (Thomas McCarthy, Trans.). Boston: Beacon Press.

Hempel, C. G. (1970). On the standard conception of scientific theories. In M. Radner & S. Winokur (Eds.), *Minnesota Studies in the Philosophy of Science,* Vol. 4, (pp. 142–163). Minneapolis: University of Minnesota.

Hempel, C. G. (1973). The meaning of theoretical terms: A critique of the standard empiricist construal. In P. Suppes, L. Henkin, A. Joya, & G. C. Moisil, (Eds.), *Logic, methodology and philosophy of science,* Vol. 4 (pp. 351–378) Amsterdam: North Holland Publishers.

Hesse, M. (1968). Induction, confirmation and philosophical method. [A review of P. K. Feyerabend & G. Maxwell (Eds.), *Mind, matter, and method: Essays in philosophy and science in honor of Herbert Feigl].* The British Journal for the Philosophy of Science, 18,* 330–335.

Holmes, D. S. (1974). Investigations of repression: Differential recall of material experimentally or naturally associated with ego threat. *Psychological Bulletin, 81,* 632–653.

Hook, S. (Ed.) (1959). *Psychoanalysis, scientific method and philosophy.* New York: New

York University Press.

Hospers, J. (1959). Philosophy and psychoanalysis. In S. Hook (Ed.), *Psychoanalysis, scientific method and philosophy* (pp. 336–357). New York: New York University Press.

Kennedy, G. (1959). Psychoanalysis: protoscience and metapsychology. In S. Hook (Ed.), *Psychoanalysis, scientific method and philosophy* (pp. 267–281). New York: New York University Press.

Lakatos, I. (1970). Falsification and the methodology of scientific research programmes. In I. Lakatos & A. Musgrave (Eds.), *Criticism and the Growth of Knowledge.* Cambridge, England: Cambridge University Press, 1970.

Lakatos, I. (1971). History of science and its rational reconstruction. In R. Buck & R. Cohen (Eds.), *PSA 1970: In memory of Rudolf Carnap.* (Boston Studies in the Philosophy of Science, Vol. 8). Dordrecht, The Netherlands: D. Reidel, 1971.

Laudan, L. (1983). The demise of the demarcation problem. In R. S. Cohen & L. Laudan (Eds.), *Physics, philosophy and psychoanalysis: Essays in honor of Adolf Grünbaum.* Dordrecht, Holland: D. Reidel.

Luborsky, L., Singer, B., & Luborsky, L. (1975). Comparative studies of psychotherapies: Is it true that "Everyone has won and all must have prizes"? *Archives of General Psychiatry, 32,* 995–1008.

Luborsky, L., & Spence, D. P. (1978). Quantitative research on psychoanalytic therapy. In S. L. Garfield & A. E. Bergin (Eds.), *Handbook of psychotherapy and behavior change* (pp. 408–438). New York: Wiley.

Madison, P. (1961). *Freud's concept of repression and defense: Its theoretical and observational language.* Minneapolis: University of Minnesota Press.

Marmor, J. (1970). Limitations of free association. *Archives of General Psychiatry, 22,* 160–165.

Martin, M. (1964a). The scientific status of psychoanalytic clinical evidence. *Inquiry, 7,* 13–36.

Martin, M. (1964b). Mr. Farrell and the refutability of psychoanalysis. *Inquiry, 7,* 80–98.

McCarthy, T. A. (1978). *The critical theory of Jurgen Habermas.* Cambridge, MA: MIT Press.

Meltzoff, J., & Kornreich, M. (1970). *Research in psychotherapy.* New York: Atherton Press.

Merton, R. K. (1949). *Social theory and social structure.* Glencoe, IL: Free Press.

Nagel, E. (1959). Methodological issues in psychoanalytic theory. In S. Hook (Ed.), *Psychoanalysis, scientific method and psychoanalysis* (pp. 38–56). New York: New York University Press.

Nisbett, R. E., & Wilson, T. D. (1977). Telling more than we can know: Verbal reports on mental processes. *Psychological Review, 84,* 231–59.

Popper, K. (1963). *Conjectures and refutations: The growth of scientific knowledge.* New York: Harper & Row. (First presented as a paper, *Science: Conjectures and reflections,* 1953.)

Rorty, R. (1979). *Philosophy and the mirror of nature.* Princeton, NJ: Princeton University Press.

Rothstein, E. (1980, October 9). The scar of Sigmund Freud. *New York Review of Books, 27,* 14–20.

Salmon, W. C. (1959). Psychoanalytic theory and evidence. In S. Hook (Ed.), Psychoanalysis, scientific method and philosophy (pp. 252–267). New York: New York University Press.

Schaffner, K. (1969). Correspondence rules. *Philosophy of Science, 36,* 280–290.

Scheffler, I. (1967). *Science and subjectivity.* Indianapolis: Bobbs-Merrill.

Sloane, R. B., Staples, F. R., Gristol, A. H., Yorkston, N. J., & Whipple, K. (1975). *Psychotherapy vs. behavior therapy*. Cambridge, MA: Harvard University Press.

Suppes, P. (1962). Models of data. In E. Nagel, P. Suppes, & A. Tarski (Eds.), *Logic, methodology, and philosophy of science: Proceedings of the 1960 International Congress*. Stanford, CA: Stanford University Press, 1962.

Suppes, P. (1967). What is a scientific theory? In S. Morgenbesser (Ed.), *Philosophy of science today* (pp. 55–67). New York: Basic Books.

Thomä, H., & Kächele, H. (1973). Wissenschaftstheoretische and methodologische Probleme der klinisch-psychoanalytischen Forschung. *Psyche, 27*, 205–236, 309–355. [Translated as Problems of metascience and methodology in clinical psychoanalytic research. *The Annual of Psychoanalysis*, 1975, *3*, 49–119.]

Von Eckardt, B. (1982). The scientific status of psychoanalysis. In S. Gilman (Ed.), *Introducing Psychoanalysis* (pp. 139–180). New York: Brunner/Mazel.

Notes on Contributors

ANNI BERGMAN, Ph.D. is a research scientist for the Margaret S. Mahler Psychiatric Research Foundation and a faculty member of the Clinical Psychology Department of the City University of New York. She is co-author of *The Psychological Birth of the Human Infant* as well as two films and has written several papers on aspects of the separation-individuation process.

MONICA CARSKY, Ph.D., is Instructor of Psychology in Psychiatry, Cornell University Medical College, and Staff Psychologist at the New York Hospital–Cornell Medical Center, Westchester Division. A graduate of Swarthmore College, she received her Ph.D. in clinical psychology from the City University of New York. She completed an internship at Bronx Psychiatric Center, Albert Einstein College of Medicine, and a postdoctoral fellowship at the New York Hospital–Cornell Medical Center, Westchester Division, and is currently a student at the New York Center for Psychoanalytic Training.

MORRIS N. EAGLE, Ph.D., is Professor and Chairman of the Department of Psychology at York University, Toronto. He recently completed six months as Visiting Professor of Psychiatry at Western Psychiatric Institute and Clinic and Fellow at the Center for the History and Philosophy of Science. In private practice of psychotherapy and a consultant at the Clarice Institute of Psychiatry in Toronto, he is author of *Recent Developments in Psychoanalysis: A Critical Evaluation.* Dr. Eagle received his Ph.D. in 1958 at New York University with George Klein and worked at the New York University Research Center for Mental Health, followed by a directorship of the Clinical Program and chairmanship of the Psychology Department at Yeshiva University.

STEVEN ELLMAN, Ph.D., is Professor and Director, Clinical Psychology Doctoral Training Program of the City University of New York.

JAMES S. GROTSTEIN, M.D., is Associate Clinical Professor of Psychiatry at the University of California, Los Angeles; Attending Staff Physician at Cedars-Sinai Medical Center; and Director of the Interdisciplinary Group for Advanced Studies in Psychotic, Borderline, and Narcissistic Disorders.

VICTORIA HAMILTON was born in Aberdeenshire, Scotland in 1941, studied at Glasgow School of Art, and graduated in philosophy at University College, London. Her psychoanalytic training was undertaken at the Tavistock Clinic, London, during which time she attended John Bowlby's seminars on ethology, child development, and attachment. She has worked as a child psychotherapist for the National Health Service and the Child Guidance Service in London and in private practice in Los Angeles. She currently lives in London.

IRWIN Z. HOFFMAN, Ph.D., is Assistant Professor, Department of Psychiatry, University of Illinois College of Medicine, Chicago; Consultant, Illinois State Psychiatric Institute; faculty member at the Chicago School for Professional Psychology; and candidate at the Chicago Institute for Psychoanalysis. He is the author of several articles on adaptation to loss, psychotherapy, and the psychoanalytic process. He was awarded the Chicago Institute's Edwin Eisler Prize in 1980.

FREDERIC J. LEVINE, Ph.D., is Associate Professor and Coordinator of the Internship Training in Psychology in the Department of Mental Health Sciences at Hahnemann University. He is a Diplomate in Clinical Psychology (ABPP), an Associate Member of the American Psychoanalytic Association, and a member of the Division of Psychoanalysis of the American Psychological Association.

ZVI LOTHANE, M.D., is in private practice of psychoanalysis in New York; an Assistant Professor of Psychiatry at Mount Sinai School of Medicine, City University of New York; and Training Analyst at the Institute for Psychoanalytic Training and Research and the National Psychological Association for Psychoanalysis. He has written papers on psychoanalytic methodology, listening as an instrument in psychoanalysis, and hallucinations.

HYMAN L. MUSLIN, M.D., is a Professor of Psychiatry at the University of Illinois, College of Medicine at Chicago and a practicing psychoanalyst. His interests have become focused on the application of self psychology to the transformation of the self in patients with cancer; the application of self psychology in literature and history; and the learning and teaching of self psychology.

STANLEY R. PALOMBO, M.D., practices psychoanalysis in Chevy Chase, Maryland. He is Associate Clinical Professor of Psychiatry at George Washington University and a faculty member of the Washington School of Psychiatry. His book, *Dreaming and Memory: A New Information-Processing Model,* redefines the process of dream construction through the application of information theory.

JEANINE PARISIER PLOTTEL, Ph.D., is Professor at Hunter College and the Graduate Center, City University of New York, where she is director of the Twentieth Century Conference. She writes about literature and psychoanalysis, is on the editorial advisory boards of the *Review of Psychoanalytic Books* and *Dada/Surrealism,* and is publisher of *New York Literary Forum.*

JOSEPH W. SLAP, M.D., is Training and Supervising Analyst at the Institute of the Philadelphia Association for Psychoanalysis, and Clinical Professor in the Department of Mental Health Sciences at Hahnemann University where he participates in the training of psychiatric residents and doctoral candidates in clinical psychology. He is in private practice in Philadelphia.

DONALD P. SPENCE, Ph.D., is Professor of Psychiatry at Rutgers Medical School, University of Medicine and Dentistry of New Jersey, and Visiting Lecturer at Princeton University. He received his Ph.D. from Teachers College, Columbia University, was certified in psychoanalysis at the New York Psychoanalytic Institute, and was formerly a professor of psychology at New York University.

ROBERT S. STEELE, Ph.D., teaches at Wesleyan University, where he is co-coordinator of the Women's Studies Program and an Associate Professor of Psychology. He gardens, raises cats, and has written several pieces on psychoanalysis, including *Freud and Jung: Conflicts of Interpretation.* His recent work has been in feminist criticism.

BARBARA VON ECKARDT, Ph.D., is Assistant Professor in Philosophy at Yale University. She received her Ph.D. from Case Western Reserve University in 1974, and subsequently spent three years at the Massachusetts Institute of Technology as a postdoctoral fellow in the Department of Psychology. Her major research interests are in philosophy of psychology and philosophy of science.

Author Index

Subject Index